Labor Courts and Grievance
            Settlement in Western Europe

LABOR COURTS AND GRIEVANCE SETTLEMENT IN WESTERN EUROPE

Edited by Benjamin Aaron

Essays by
XAVIER BLANC-JOUVAN, *France*
GINO GIUGNI, *Italy*
THILO RAMM, *West Germany*
FOLKE SCHMIDT, *Sweden*

UNIVERSITY OF CALIFORNIA PRESS
BERKELEY LOS ANGELES LONDON 1971

University of California Press
Berkeley and Los Angeles, California

University of California Press, Ltd.
London, England

Copyright © 1971 by The Regents of the University of California
ISBN: 0-520-01757-9
Library of Congress Catalog Card Number: 72-123628

Printed in the United States of America

CONTENTS

FOREWORD vii
by Benjamin Aaron

I. THE SETTLEMENT OF LABOR DISPUTES IN FRANCE
by Xavier Blanc-Jouvan

1. Introduction — 3
2. The Labor Courts — 15
3. Jurisdiction of Other Courts in Individual Labor Disputes — 37
4. Procedures for the Settlement of Collective Labor Disputes — 41
5. Conclusion — 72

II. LABOR COURTS AND GRIEVANCE SETTLEMENT IN WEST GERMANY
by Thilo Ramm

1. Introduction — 83
2. The Labor Courts — 96
3. Pretrial Screening Procedures, Arbitration, and Works Courts — 128
4. Conclusions and Reflections — 145

III. THE SETTLEMENT OF EMPLOYMENT GRIEVANCES IN SWEDEN
by Folke Schmidt

1. Introduction — 161
2. Negotiations as a Means of Settling Grievances — 185
3. The Labor Court — 198
4. Various Arbitral Boards — 227
5. An Evaluation of the Swedish System — 239

CONTENTS

IV. THE SETTLEMENT OF LABOR DISPUTES IN ITALY
by Gino Giugni

1. Introduction	249
2. Labor Disputes in Civil Procedure	257
3. Voluntary Settlement of Labor Disputes by State Agencies	285
4. Contractual Settlement of Labor Disputes under Collective Agreements	301
5. Voluntary Settlement Procedures in Operation	318
6. Conclusions	329

INDEX 339

FOREWORD

This volume is the second in a series of comparative labor law studies by the Comparative Labor Law Group, which was initiated with the publication in 1969 of *Employment Grievances and Disputes Procedures in Britain,* by K. W. Wedderburn and P. L. Davies. A brief description of the project is included in the foreword to that volume.

The present study consists of national reports on dispute settlement procedures in France, West Germany (the Federal Republic), Sweden, and Italy. As was explained in the foreword to the British report, the first three of these countries were selected because each of them has a well-established labor court system with special features distinguishing it from the others. Italy was chosen because it has neither a labor court system nor a general private system for settling labor disputes, which are handled largely, at the present time, by the ordinary courts.

None of the reports in the present volume is encyclopedic, but each provides a substantial body of accurate information. Of even greater value are the insights and commentaries of these four gifted and authoritative scholars regarding the strengths and weaknesses of the policies and practices employed in the settlement of labor disputes in their respective countries.

In analyzing the effectiveness of the tripartite Swedish Labor Court *(Arbetsdomstolen),* Professor Folke Schmidt finds it impossible to estimate the extent to which the laymen on the bench have either influenced the decisions of the court or have helped to educate employers and unions in a number of basic principles of the law of labor relations. He prefers to stress the institutional role of the whole court, and credits it with important innovations. Of particular interest to readers brought up in an adversary system of administering justice—a system which has carried over to a considerable degree into the administration of labor law, at least in the United States—is Professor Schmidt's observation that the Swedish Labor Court's standards of interpretation of collective agreements "are based upon the idea that those who take part in negotiations are each responsible for their own contribution to

FOREWORD

the new agreement, and have a duty to disclose facts in order that no misunderstanding shall arise as to the true meaning of a new clause" (p. 240).

Despite broad consensus on basic labor relations policies and the relative sophistication of the bargaining parties, the decisions of the labor court have often produced dissents, particularly by the labor members. Professor Schmidt notes that the court, being a judicial body, lays down general principles and relies on precedent, a legalistic approach disliked by unions in most countries. He also observes that "the common law applied in the court was alien to the actual practices of the workshops," a fact similarly noted by the United States Supreme Court.[1] Perhaps as a consequence, the Swedish trade unions have evinced a preference for replacing judicial procedure with arbitration in dismissal cases and other specialized matters. Nevertheless, arbitration is resorted to only rarely, so there must be some other reason why the annual number of labor court decisions has dropped from an average of about 200 in the early 1930's to only about 30 to 40 in the mid-1960's. Professor Schmidt ascribes this phenomenon primarily to the system of central negotiations between the collective bargaining parties, especially those at the national level. In explaining what he calls the "maturity" of the national employer and trade union confederations in Sweden, whose representatives tend increasingly to resolve their differences through negotiation rather than in court, he points out that the officers on both sides remain in office until retirement. He concludes that they must, of necessity, find some *modus vivendi*.

American readers in particular will be interested to learn that in Sweden, as in the United States, the union or the employer association, as the case may be, "owns" the individual grievance of its members, and a member cannot bring suit in the labor court unless he can prove that his union or association has refused to take action.[2] On the other hand, neither the union nor the association is competent to waive a member's right.[3] Professor Schmidt confirms the conclusion of Professor Clyde W. Summers that, generally speaking, Swedish workers have confidence in their unions and accept the decisions of their organizations as fair,[4] but he notes that on occasion "union officers are

---

[1] E.g., United Steelworkers v. Warrior & Gulf Navigation Co., 363 U.S. 574 (1960).
[2] Cf. Republic Steel Corp. v. Maddox, 379 U.S. 650 (1965).
[3] Cf. Elgin, Joliet & Eastern Ry. v. Burley, 325 U.S. 711 (1945).
[4] Summers, "Collective Power and Individual Rights in the Collective Agreement —A Comparison of Swedish and American Law," 72 *Yale L. J.* (1963), pp. 421 ff.

FOREWORD

too tame in their defense of the interests of the individual employee when he is involved in a conflict with his fellows and they bring pressure on the employer" (p. 244).

In the opinion of Professor Xavier Blanc-Jouvan, the French system of specialized, bipartite labor courts *(conseils de prud'hommes)* has functioned rather well; indeed, there is a widespread demand for its extension. The popularity of the system is due in part to the success of the labor courts in resolving disputes either through conciliation—a process which by law must precede the judgment session—or in the judgment session itself, without the intervention of a judge of the regular court. The latter participates only in the relatively infrequent event that the bipartite board deadlocks. France has no appellate labor courts, however; appeals must be brought to the ordinary courts of appeals *(cours d'appel)*, which are not bound by the findings of the labor courts. "Final" decisions of both the labor courts and the courts of appeals can be appealed to the Supreme Court *(Cour de Cassation)* on the ground that the lower court exceeded its powers or violated the law. The Supreme Court has no power to revise lower court decisions; it may only affirm or invalidate in whole or in part. Professor Blanc-Jouvan reports noticeable sentiment, particularly among trade unions and the labor courts themselves, for modifications in the present law that would provide specialized appellate labor courts.

One of the principal problems in the French system of labor dispute settlement arises out of the long-established distinction between individual and collective disputes. The former, which are based on rights exclusively, are heard by the labor courts; the latter, which may involve rights as well as interests, are either submitted to the regular courts for adjudication or are resolved through conciliation, mediation, or arbitration. Professor Blanc-Jouvan states that the distinction between individual and collective disputes is blurred and ambiguous and has resulted in conflicting decisions by the courts. With other commentators, however, he thinks this distinction is gradually breaking down, and is likely to become less important with the passage of time.[5] The reason is that "the attribution of individual or collective character to a labor dispute depends very largely on the way the parties look at the conflict" (p. 11); thus, the distinction has a continuing utility because it permits parties to select the procedure in any given case which holds forth the best prospects for a satisfactory settlement. It is pos-

---

[5] See, e.g., Lyon-Caen, "Le procès de travail en droit français," 5 *Rivista di diritto internazionale e comparato del lavoro* (1965), pp. 138 ff.; William H. McPherson and Frederic Meyers, *The French Labor Courts: Judgment by Peers* (Urbana, Ill.: University of Illinois Press, 1966), pp. 24-27.

sible, for example, for the parties to treat the same dispute as both individual and collective, and to make use of both types of procedures simultaneously or successively.

The French procedures for conciliation, mediation, and arbitration should be of special interest to British and American readers. French law provides for both contractual and statutory conciliation, the latter form being used in the absence of the former, but sometimes also in addition to it. Theoretically, resort to conciliation is compulsory; but the law does not require that it precede the strike or the lockout. The conciliation procedure is thus rendered largely ineffective in strike or lockout situations. There are, in fact, numerous examples in French case law of strikes that were held lawful, even though they were not preceded by attempts at conciliation or were initiated during a conciliation procedure. The reason for these decisions is that the French constitution guarantees the right to strike. No similar guarantee is provided for the right to lock out; so lockouts are usually held by the courts to be unlawful unless all attempts to reach a peaceful settlement have been previously exhausted. Preemptive lockouts, such as those occasionally permitted in the United States for compelling business reasons,[6] are thus not sanctioned under French law.

Mediation of collective labor disputes in France is a process that combines elements of compulsion and voluntarism. Voluntary invocation of mediation by one party to the dispute sets in train prescribed procedures which are compulsory as to the other. The role of the mediator depends upon the nature of the dispute: if it is a conflict over rights, the mediator may not make specific recommendations for settlement; if it is a conflict over interests, he may propose any solution he thinks appropriate to terminate the dispute. Professor Blanc-Jouvan observes, however, that this sharp theoretical line between disputes over rights and disputes over interests is not maintained in practice. He reports that the mediator has greater powers than those provided by law "because the problems may be intertwined and he may play at least an advisory and persuasive role in *all* types of disputes" (p. 57). The French mediator thus performs a function somewhat similar to that of a British arbitrator, as described by Wedderburn and Davies.

Labor arbitration in France is now limited to collective disputes. During the period 1936–1950, all collective disputes were subject to compulsory arbitration after conciliation had failed. But since 1950, resort to arbitration is voluntary and must, unlike mediation, be agreed to by both parties to the dispute. Moreover, as in early American

---

[6] E.g., American Ship Building Co. v. NLRB, 380 U.S. 300 (1965).

FOREWORD

common law, agreements to arbitrate future disputes are unenforceable; the only effective arbitration agreement is one executed after the dispute has arisen. Resort to voluntary arbitration of collective disputes, even those involving conflicts over rights, is very infrequent, however, and is a negligible factor in the total system of dispute settlement.

Professor Blanc-Jouvan's conclusions about the defects in the French system of labor-dispute settlement are in marked contrast to those of Wedderburn and Davies about the British system. Whereas the latter argue strongly for the retention of voluntarism and against any attempt to draw sharp distinctions between conflicts over rights and conflicts over interests, Blanc-Jouvan believes that the defects in the French system are caused by too much voluntarism and the absence of a clear-cut distinction between rights and interests. He believes in compulsory procedures for the settlement of collective disputes over rights. On the other hand, his attitude toward collective disputes over interests seems to accord with the opinion which, up to now at least, has prevailed in both Britain and the United States, namely, that these conflicts, if not resolved through mediation, should be determined in a test of economic strength between the parties themselves.

The West German labor court system, in contrast to that of Sweden and France, consists of three levels: the regular labor courts *(Arbeitsgerichte)*, which are regarded simply as special civil courts; the appellate labor courts *(Landesarbeitsgerichte)*, which hear appeals on points of fact and of law; and the Federal Labor Court *(Bundesarbeitsgericht)*, which hears appeals on points of law only. All courts are tripartite in composition.

Professor Thilo Ramm, who is sharply critical of the labor courts, concedes, nevertheless, that at the present time they are firmly entrenched and could not possibly be abolished. "The courts are a part of the social establishment," he observes; "they decide all individual and most of the collective labor disputes, except those over new terms of collective bargaining agreements" (p. 83), a subject not covered in his essay.

Most collective bargaining agreements in West Germany are between unions and employer associations. The "normative" terms of a collective agreement, consisting of the provisions relating to working conditions, are not only binding upon employers and employees who are members of the contracting organizations, but also become part of individual contracts of employment. As a consequence, an employee may sue in the labor court for alleged violation of his individual contract of employment, as amended by the normative provisions of the collective agreement. Unlike their counterparts in Sweden, France, and the United States, German unions cannot bring suit in their own names.

Although German law, like that of France, recognizes a distinction between individual and collective labor disputes, the German labor courts, in contrast to the *conseils de prud'hommes*, have jurisdiction over both types. Indeed, virtually all labor problems are subject to the jurisdiction of the labor courts; only criminal and political matters, such as political strikes, are excluded.

In general, the Labor Courts Act of 1953 reflects a hostile attitude toward arbitration. There are only two types of cases in which the jurisdiction of labor courts may be excluded. The first consists of disputes over the implementation and interpretation of a collective agreement between the parties thereto; these are always collective disputes. The second consists of individual disputes over the implementation or interpretation of collective agreements relating to a small number of specialized occupations. Arbitration agreements within these permissible areas are binding only on the members of the union and the employers' association which entered into the particular agreement. Under certain conditions, however, they can be extended to other parties whose working relations are regulated by the collective agreement.

Unlike the situation in France, about 80 percent of the arbitration clauses in German collective agreements provide for exclusive arbitration in all future disputes, while *ad hoc* arbitration is rare. In contrast to the practice in the United States and Britain, the individual arbitrator is unknown in German law. In some instances the arbitration board is tripartite from its inception; in others the board, following the pattern of the French *conseils de prud'hommes*, is bipartite, and an impartial chairman is called in only if the board deadlocks. Professor Ramm reports that impartial chairmen are usually judges of the regular courts; he adds that the parties apparently "do not want labor lawyers or persons familiar with labor matters to serve on their boards, preferring neutral individuals . . ." (p. 136).

Arbitration procedures are left to the discretion of the arbitration boards except for a few basic regulations laid down in the Labor Courts Act. Significantly, these procedures usually involve conciliation sessions similar to those which play so important a role in the labor court systems of Germany and France. Moreover, as in Britain and to a lesser degree in the United States, the impartial chairman of the German arbitration board, though lacking specific authority to do so, "functions as a mediator," and "negotiates separately with the parties and the wingmen if the case is in deadlock" (p. 137).

FOREWORD

Under the German Labor Courts Act, suits may be brought in the labor court to vacate an arbitration award, and can be appealed all the way to the federal level. An award may be vacated not only if it violates statutory law, but also if it violates a "legal norm," that is, any provision in the "normative section" of the collective agreement. Professor Ramm disapproves of this arrangement, pointing out that very often (as in Britain) "interpretation consists of establishing terms not covered in the existing agreement, thus creating a new, supplementary agreement in questions of minor importance" (p. 138). By this process the sharp distinction between disputes over rights and disputes over interests is substantially removed, with the willing consent of the parties. The vacation of such an award by the labor court thus frustrates the desires of the parties.

Professor Ramm believes that "the distinction between individual and collective disputes obviously cannot be observed in practice and must lead to an overlapping jurisdiction of labor courts and arbitration board" (p. 139). For example, a dispute over the interpretation of an individual contract of employment is a matter for the labor court. The disputed provision, however, may have been added to the individual employment contract by a collective agreement which provides that disputes over interpretation shall be decided by arbitration. Thus, the same issue may be decided in its separate aspects by different agencies.

In summing up his analysis of the strengths and weaknesses of the German system, Professor Ramm makes an interesting observation that is of particular importance in comparative law: "The concept of efficiency includes more than the mere working of the system—all systems will more or less work" (p. 155). He faults the German labor court apparatus because of its failure to protect individual employees who take cases to court from acts of retaliation by their employers, noting that, in consequence, employees generally do not bring suits until their individual contracts of employment have expired. In this respect German law is similar to French law, which expressly denies the courts the power of reinstatement.

Professor Ramm believes, however, that it is not the labor court system alone which is to blame, but the entire German labor law. He terms it "an unfortunate combination of state intervention, collective bargaining practices, and the system of works councils." He finds that "none of these components is strong enough to provide a foundation of labor law, but each of them prevents the other from developing a perfect system" (p. 155).

The tripartite structure of the labor courts is also attacked by Professor Ramm as a device favored by "German academic labor lawyers"

FOREWORD

to enhance the dominant position of the state. By participating as members of these courts, employer and union representatives become agents of the state. And the labor courts themselves, he adds, play an essentially undemocratic role, because they compete with Parliament and do not adhere strictly in their judgments to the constitution, statutes, collective bargaining agreements, and employer-works council agreements. He questions the value, particularly to unions, of continuing to participate in the labor court system, and concludes: "Today, an increase in arbitration with the aid of lawyers trained in observance of the law, even a return to the practice of bringing suit in private courts, would certainly be more to their advantage" (p. 157).

Italy represents a unique case. For a time it too had a system of labor courts. An early statute (1893) established specialized, tripartite bodies, the *Collegi dei Probiviri,* modeled after the French and Belgian *conseils de prud'hommes,* to deal with all types of labor disputes on a local basis for each industry. With the coming of the Fascist regime, however, the *Collegi* were abolished in 1928, and their jurisdiction was transferred to the regular civil courts, where it still remains. One consequence of this change was that labor disputes were no longer decided according to principles of equity, but were thenceforth determined on the basis of the strict rule of law.

Proceedings in the Italian civil courts are governed by the 1942 Code of Civil Procedure. Although this Code was promulgated under the Fascist regime, it was, according to Professor Gino Giugni, "a piece of legislation with a sound technical basis and very few concessions to Fascist ideology" (p. 254). Its main purpose was to establish a quicker and more informal procedure than had formerly prevailed in the civil courts; however, Professor Giugni remarks, "it did not work" (p. 254). As a consequence, what was intended as a reform resulted, in his opinion, in a "counterreform" (p. 329).

Italian law, like that of France and West Germany, distinguishes between individual and collective disputes. Only individual disputes come within the jurisdiction of the civil courts. These disputes are processed through a multilevel system of courts, none of which, however, has a jurisdiction limited solely to labor matters. On the other hand, special procedures for labor disputes are prescribed. Professor Giugni notes that although the law does not specify compulsory conciliation, attempts at conciliation emerge naturally in the course of informal conferences between the judge and the parties. A court order certifying that conciliation has taken place, once signed by the parties or by their attorneys, is enforceable against the defendant, usually the employer. But it is also true that conciliation before the court is im-

FOREWORD

mune to an attack, based on the general principle that the worker cannot waive his rights. Apparently, the possibility that a worker may be compelled to accept an unfavorable settlement is much greater in Italy than, for example, in Sweden. Professor Giugni is critical of the conciliation procedure, both in and out of court, because of the tendency on the part of judges and of even the complaining worker's own counsel to compel him to settle for less than what the law allows.

The worker's reasons for acquiescing in this kind of pressure are explained by the chronic problem of the law's delay. The court dockets are heavily overcrowded and the number of judges and clerks is insufficient. Of even greater consequence, however, in the opinion of Professor Giugni, are the opportunities available to the parties under existing procedures to delay a decision. American litigants, in particular, will appreciate his comment that "Attorneys fight bitterly over the briefs, but they get along very well when requesting the examining judge to postpone the hearings" (p. 271).

Nevertheless, when it comes to the quality of their labor decisions, Professor Giugni gives the Italian civil courts, especially those at the lower levels, rather high marks. He believes that in the last twenty years labor law in Italy has advanced considerably because of court decisions. Even the Supreme Court *(Corte di Cassazione)*, which has demonstrated strong conservatism in criminal cases, is characterized by Giugni as only "more cautious than the lower courts" (p. 279). He concludes that the Italian courts "may be characterized in terms of the German labor courts of the Weimar Republic, namely, they tend to favor the individual worker rather than to enlarge the legal framework of collective action" (p. 279).

This latter observation points up a clear contrast between the law in Italy and that in Sweden and the United States. Professor Giugni notes that the court "almost never considers the need for stability in collective bargaining and will upset an agreement in order to uphold the interests of the individual worker" (p. 280). Similarly, settlements of workers' complaints through union channels, unlike those reached before a court, are subject to attack if they involved a waiver or compromise of a worker's rights. But, as Giugni also points out, the courts are not entirely to blame; for by limiting their jurisdiction to individual disputes, the law necessarily deemphasizes the importance of collective interests.

It appears, however, that in Italy, as in France, the sharp distinction between individual and collective disputes is more apparent than real in actual practice. Disputes involving large numbers of workers are brought to court in two ways: as a "pilot" action consisting of a single claim which, if successful, may induce an employer to change a practice or to accept a reasonable compromise, or as a "mass" action, quite similar to the American class action. Professor Giugni remarks that mass actions, which are accomplished by joining a large number of identical claims in one suit, are often actually "invented" by the lawyers, who then induce a sufficient number of workers to sign a complaint. He concludes that pilot and mass actions have met the practical need of solving the dilemma of collective disputes, but that a more economical solution would be to permit the filing of collective disputes.

Regional and provincial labor offices were established in Italy after the second world war, and included in the miscellaneous responsibilities assigned to them was the task of attempting to settle labor disputes. Their jurisdiction is not exclusive; collective disputes are sometimes handled by the *Prefetto,* the highest ranking provincial representative of the government, or, in the case of national disputes, by the Minister of Labor. Conciliation is first attempted, and if it fails, the parties are subjected to "strong" mediation by the Ministry of Labor. Arbitration in such cases is almost unknown.

Collective disputes obviously may involve both rights and interests, but Professor Giugni reports that (as in France) both types are handled in the same manner. "A dispute over rights taken to a labor office becomes a dispute over interests because it is settled by negotiation rather than by adjudication" (p. 287). Thus, a conflict over rights will be processed and recorded only as a collective dispute.

Italian voluntary procedures for dispute settlement include conciliation, fact-finding, and tripartite arbitration. All of these contractual procedures are available only to union members or, sometimes, to workers who assign specific powers to a union. The Italian labor force, like the French, is pluralistic, however, and an unorganized worker who is refused assistance by one union can simply appeal to its rival.

The Italian law of arbitration is also unique. Under the 1942 Code of Civil Procedure, any agreement of submission to arbitration, even though negotiated directly by the parties to a contract of employment, was declared void. Yet, Professor Giugni notes, the practice of arbitration has received considerable support from the courts themselves. Thus, formal arbitration awards are enforced as a court's judgment after they have been filed with a judge, who checks their compliance with formal regulations. But parties desiring to avoid legal complications and court costs may resort to informal arbitration. This is, in effect, a "blank" compromise agreement between two parties, who appoint a third to supply the terms. The award is in such a case upheld as an agreement, not as a judgment. This means that in the event of subsequent noncompliance, the aggrieved party would have to bring suit in court to obtain a judgment.

Summing up, Professor Giugni concludes that two basic concepts obstruct the extensive changes in the Italian system of dispute settlement that he believes to be necessary. The first is the incorrect identification of labor disputes with civil disputes generally, which has resulted in the submission of labor disputes to the civil courts with very little variation in procedure. He believes that there are two distinctive features peculiar to labor disputes. One is the "irreversibility" of the situation; the other is the inequality of bargaining power between the parties. By "irreversibility" he means the almost uniform tendency of the present system to provide mere palliatives instead of real remedies to the complaining workers, and he notes that this tendency is greatly enhanced by the practice of Italian workers, like those in France and Germany, not to file suit until their employment contract has expired.

The second concept which he sees as impeding necessary changes is the individualistic approach that prevails in Italian labor law. Even voluntary systems for dispute settlement, he observes, are based on the principle that the individual "owns" the grievance. Yet, as previously noted, in spite of this emphasis on individual rights, group interests do prevail, as in the cases of "pilot" and "mass" actions. Giugni believes this trend should be encouraged, although not at the expense of the basic interests of individuals.

Professor Giugni's final word reflects his own view of a balanced system for settling labor disputes:

Justice cannot be achieved without a real balance of power between the parties to a dispute. A radically revised system operated by the government would, therefore, be most welcome, but it would never eliminate the necessity of voluntary machineries (p. 337).

A reading of these four essays will provide further evidence, if more is needed, that the dispute settlement machinery in any country grows out of and is conditioned by a wide variety of factors—historical, economic, and social. Of the four countries, Sweden appears to have enjoyed the greatest success in shaping a system that meets the needs of its people, but it has certain advantages over the three other countries. Among these are its small, homogeneous population and a notable absence of wide disparities in economic and social status. But the Swedes have made the most of their opportunities. On fundamental issues of labor relations policy—the right to organize, union security, and exclusive management functions, for example—they have achieved a broad consensus. Union membership is high, embracing more than

95 percent of manual workers and about 80 percent of all salaried workers below the managerial level, and this is matched by an equal degree of organization among employers.

The three other countries not only lack Sweden's natural advantages, but have also failed to establish the kind of consensus on basic issues that makes the Swedish system function so well. There are many reasons for this; in the case of Germany and Italy none is more obvious than the cataclysmic impact of oppressive Fascist regimes, the Second World War, or both. In France, on the other hand, the lack of consensus antedated the war and has not yet been achieved.

Foreign observers will note, however, that despite the many differences between the dispute settlement procedures in these four countries, there are a number of significant similarities. France, West Germany, and Sweden all provide for the participation of lay representatives of labor and management on the labor courts. Those three countries, and Italy as well, have introduced the process of conciliation into the judicial process, with notable success. (In Sweden, however, disputes are so carefully screened by the major collective bargaining parties that only those between unions and unorganized employers are likely to be amenable to conciliation once they reach the labor court.) The time consumed by appeals to higher courts in France, Germany, and Sweden is relatively short, at least when compared to the situation in the United States. Only Italy appears to suffer from serious delays. And the relative costs of litigating labor disputes in all four countries are substantially less than those in the United States.

Another feature that all four countries have in common that should be of particular interest to foreign observers is the multiplicity of mechanisms, both public and private, for settling labor disputes. It is significant that in the three countries with highly developed labor court systems, the parties resort, no less than in Italy, to conciliation, mediation, and voluntary arbitration, as well as to litigation. In part this is because of the limited jurisdictions of the courts; but it may also be true, as Professor Giugni has suggested, that a real balance in the bargaining power of the parties cannot be achieved without the establishment of private machinery for the adjustment of labor disputes through collective bargaining. That, certainly, has been the American experience.

One also notes a curious paradox in the handling of the rights–interests dichotomy in the six countries covered by the investigations of the Comparative Labor Law Group. Britain alone rejects this distinction; the remaining five countries adhere to it. In France, West

FOREWORD

Germany, and Italy, all operating under labor laws greatly influenced by jurisprudential theory, the practice belies the theory to the extent, as we have seen, of either ignoring or substantially blurring the distinctions between rights and interests in some classes of cases. By contrast, in the United States, where the law is claimed to be pragmatic rather than theoretical, the rights–interests distinction is observed perhaps more rigidly than in the other countries. Only in some private arbitration systems is it sometimes ignored.

American readers of these essays will be impressed once again by the enormous consequences that flow from our system, almost unique among the industrialized nations of the world (Canada also has it), of granting exclusive bargaining rights to a union representing a mere majority of workers in an appropriate bargaining unit. What appears, in retrospect at least, as the most obvious and inevitable result is the judicially created doctrine of the union's duty of fair representation to all members of the bargaining unit, union and nonunion alike. This combination of union rights and obligations, together with the ascendancy of the collective agreement and the virtual disappearance of individual contracts of employment, has made it almost impossible for the individual worker in an organized plant to keep control of his grievance. The union "owns" it and has broad latitude in deciding whether or not to process it. Even if he quits or is fired, the worker cannot sue his employer unless he first is able to prove that the union has violated its obligation to represent him in good faith.[7] Yet, one of the countervailing advantages of this system is seen with greater clarity when we compare it with the Italian system, in which the worker "owns" the grievance and in which a judicial settlement of his claim may undermine an entire collective agreement.

Another area of comparison, in which the American worker appears to have a distinct advantage, is reinstatement of workers dismissed without just cause. This remedy, so common in the United States, is virtually unknown in France and Italy, and is available only on limited grounds in Sweden. (Reinstatement in Britain is common, but is a consequence of the union's economic power, rather than a statutory or contractual right, as in the United States. The right also exists in Germany, but in recent years, because of prevailing full employment, workers prefer to get another job and to accept compensation in lieu of reinstatement from the former employment.) Moreover, American workers seem to have far greater security against employer retaliation than do those in France, Germany, and Italy, who typically wait until

---

[7] *See* Vaca v. Sipes, 386 U.S. 171 (1967).

FOREWORD

their individual contracts of employment have expired before bringing suit for redress of grievances. As several of the authors of this volume have pointed out, these delays often substantially limit or prevent the possibility of an adequate remedy.

Finally, these essays serve to enhance one's feeling that no matter how attractive some features of the labor law of another country may be, they cannot be imported and incorporated into another system. Rejection of these transplants is almost sure to follow, because they cannot flourish in a society which is bound to be alien in so many ways to the one that gave them life.

This volume, like the one by Wedderburn and Davies, was financed largely by the UCLA Committee on International and Comparative Studies, out of a Ford Foundation grant to the University of California, Los Angeles. Supplementary support for my own research in this country, to be published subsequently, was provided by the Walter E. Meyer Research Institute of Law. The UCLA Institute of Industrial Relations provided space, secretarial assistance, and some financial support for the project. The Institute's editor, Felicitas Hinman, assisted in editing the manuscripts and prepared them for publication. My colleagues in the Comparative Labor Law Group join me in expressing our thanks for this cooperation and assistance.

BENJAMIN AARON
Professor of Law and Director,
Institute of Industrial Relations, UCLA

I

THE SETTLEMENT OF LABOR DISPUTES IN FRANCE

by Xavier Blanc-Jouvan

Professor of Law
University of Paris, France

1.
INTRODUCTION

The problem of establishing machinery for the settlement of labor disputes depends in great part on the context of industrial relations in a given country at a given time. Labor disputes affect all aspects of the employment relationship, and their settlement involves all institutions of labor law. This study is limited to workers employed in private industry and excludes all civil servants and public employees, whose employment relationship is based on very particular rules.

The rules governing the status of workers derive from three different sources, which developed successively in the history of French labor law: free negotiations between employer and employee, legislation, and collective agreements.

Until the mid-nineteenth century, labor relations consisted of strictly individual relationships between an employer and each of his employees. Individually bargained wages and working conditions were included in a written document, the individual contract of employment, the only source of rights and obligations for both parties. Called characteristically a contract of lease of services *(locatio operarum)*, it was governed by the Civil Code and subject to the ordinary law of contract. State intervention in labor relations occurred only in disputes arising out of this individual contract of employment. Such disputes were resolved by special labor courts, created as early as 1806 and composed of lay judges who were selected from among employers and employees.[1]

In the latter part of the nineteenth century, the applicability of the ordinary law of contract was challenged when it became apparent that

---

[1] Employers and employees could not be organized at that time because the law was proscriptive with respect to collective labor relations. SECTIONS 414 and 415 of the Penal Code contained criminal sanctions against membership in coalitions and concerted strike action, and SECTION 291 prohibited all forms of association of more than 20 persons established without government authorization.

the lease of services involving human relations could not be adapted to the concept of the lease of objects. The employment relationship became increasingly regulated by legislation, which, in turn, led to the emergence and growth of state intervention. It became increasingly widely accepted that labor relations concerned not only the two parties immediately affected—employer and employee—but also the state, which thus had the right to act in order to protect the working class and maintain industrial peace.[2]

More recently, the legislation encouraged the negotiation of collective agreements as a new source of law in labor relations. This was the result of the development of collective action, which passed through three main phases. The worker's right to form temporary coalitions for concerted economic actions, such as strikes, was first recognized by law in 1864. The right to strike, first protected against criminal sanctions and later against civil sanctions as well, is now guaranteed by the constitution of 1958. Strikes do not constitute breach of contract and cannot be the basis for disciplinary dismissals.

In 1884, workers and employers gained the right to form or join unions, that is, groups specifically devoted to defend collective interests. In France union membership is always voluntary so far as the individual is concerned; it cannot be made compulsory under any circumstances. Union pluralism is particularly important to the extent that several unions compete for members in each craft or industry. At the company level, different groups of workers belong to various unions while some may not belong to any union. It is a fundamental principle in French law that no union can represent all the workers of an enterprise. The concept of exclusive representation in the American sense does not exist in France, and terms such as "organized enterprise" or "recognized union" are meaningless. However, the unions have important and diverse representation functions (by the Law of December 27, 1968, representatives of locals gained official status within the enterprise): they collaborate with various state agencies in adminis-

---

[2] A large number of statutes were then enacted, which contained optional *(facultatives)* and compulsory *(obligatoires)* provisions regulating the terms and conditions of employment. The most significant statutes were enacted after 1890, some of which have been incorporated into the Labor Code since 1910; these statutes are still an important source of labor law. On the other hand, intervention by administrative authorities is guaranteed by statutes that do not directly regulate the employment relationship but confer powers on administrative agencies: the *Préfets* who head each *Départment,* central agencies under the Ministry of Labor, various consultative bodies, and the *Inspection du Travail et de la Main d'Oeuvre,* which was created by a Law of November 2, 1892 and has frequently been reorganized, each time with increased powers. Labor inspectors of the latter agency now often serve as informal mediators or arbitrators.

tering social security programs, they bring actions in court in behalf of their members, and they negotiate collective agreements. Although there are some autonomous unions, most unions are affiliated with a confederation.[3]

Collective agreements, first recognized by the Law of March 23, 1919, are now governed by the Law of February 11, 1950. Terms and conditions of employment departing from statutory law to the extent that they are more favorable to the worker are automatically applicable to the individual employment relationship in the same manner as are statutory provisions. A collective agreement is binding on all workers whose union was a party to it, and on all employees whose employer is bound because he has personally signed it or he is a member of an employers' association which was a signatory to the agreement. Thus, the employer's status determines the status of his employees, whether they are union members or not, and as a result all employees in a given enterprise are subject to similar rules and regulations.

Collective agreements, though negotiated at different levels, can have simultaneous and cumulative application. Each agreement negotiated on a broad territorial basis (for example, at the national or regional level) provides minimum rights that cannot be reduced by agreements negotiated on a smaller territorial basis (for example, at the local level or at the level of the enterprise); the latter can only add terms more favorable to the worker. In addition, when an agree-

---

[3] There are four large confederations; three are rivals and are divided on ideological grounds, and one, the *Confédération Générale des Cadres* (C.G.C.), is ideologically neutral and organizes a special category of employees, the *cadres*, which include most of the managerial, supervisory, and technical employees. The largest and oldest union is the *Confédération Générale du Travail* (C.G.T.), which is more or less closely linked with the Communist Party. After the second world war, the *Confédération Générale du Travail-Force Ouvrière* (C.G.T.-F.O.) split off from the C.G.T.; it is less combative and more oriented to the French tradition of socialism. A third group is represented by the *Confédération Française Démocratique du Travail* (C.F.D.T.), which, under a new name and in laicized form, succeeded in 1964 the *Confédération Française des Travailleurs Chrétiens* (C.F.T.C.) created in 1919 by the Christian element in the labor movement. It should be noted, however, that an appreciable minority in the C.F.T.C. has opposed this change into the C.F.D.T. and has remained organized under the former name; it comprises many unions that have a stronghold in a number of specific industries.

It is difficult to evaluate the relative significance of these confederations on the basis of their membership, which is low and not formalized by regular payment of dues. A better indication of their actual influence may be found in results of elections, notably for the designation of employee representatives at the company level: the C.G.T. takes approximately 45 percent of the vote, the C.F.D.T. 20 percent, the C.G.T.-F.O. 15 percent, and the C.G.C. 5 percent; the remaining votes go to miscellaneous organizations.

ment has been signed by the so-called most representative unions, the Minister of Labor may order the extension of terms that relate directly to conditions of employment to all enterprises in a geographical area, even though these were not covered by the agreement because the employer was not a party to its negotiation. In sum, the overwhelming majority of French workers, especially in the industrial sector, are covered today by one or another form of collective agreement.

Grievances of workers may be presented to management by the *délégués du personnel* (roughly comparable to shop stewards), who must be present in all enterprises with more than ten workers. The *comité d'entreprise* (works committee), which acts in an advisory and consultative capacity, is composed of employer and employee members and must be established in all enterprises of more than fifty workers. The *délégués* and the employee members of the works committee are elected by all workers in the enterprise, irrespective of union membership.

These are the main developments in collective labor relations in France. State intervention has not been abolished, and the individual contract of employment remains, at least formally, the foundation of the employment relationship, in which all provisions derived from statutory law and from collective agreements are implicitly contained. Thus, it can be said that all regulations concerning the terms and conditions of employment acquire a contractual nature between the parties; they are enforceable as contractual provisions and their violation is considered a breach of contract. In fact, the supremacy of the individual contract of employment becomes most significant in dealing with problems of violations of the law and with labor disputes.

THE CONCEPT OF LABOR DISPUTES

In discussing the concept of labor disputes, only those situations are considered here in which (1) the dispute relates to labor matters; (2) the dispute arises between the actual parties to labor relations, that is, between employer and employee (or groups of them); and (3) the dispute has reached a certain stage of development, that is, the parties have completed all preliminary screening procedures.

The category *labor disputes* includes all conflicts relating to the terms of employment or to any aspect of the employment relationship. Excluded are all conflicts relating to other matters, for example, when a union is engaged in a dispute over its own rights and interests as a corporate body (relations with its members, protection of its property, etc.), or when the rights or interests of an entire craft or industry (for which the union serves as a kind of agent) are concerned if labor matters are not directly or principally at issue.

The dispute must arise directly and exclusively between an employer or group of employers on one side and an employee or group of employees on the other. Excluded are disputes in which one of the parties is a third party to the employment relationship, notably the state. This is the case, for example, when the dispute arises out of the interpretation of constitutional provisions affecting labor relations. This refers especially to SECTIONS 34 and 37 of the constitution of October 4, 1958, which divide the power to enact rules governing labor law and union law between the Parliament and the government. When there is doubt or conflict over the meaning of these provisions, the case is brought before a special jurisdiction: the Constitutional Council. Disputes involving the legality of administrative decisions in labor matters are also brought before special jurisdictions. A large number of labor disputes come under the jurisdiction of administrative courts because they have given rise to an administrative decision that is being challenged; the dispute between the two parties to the employment relationship then has given way to a dispute between one of the parties and the administration. Although both types may involve exactly the same subject, they are different in kind and the latter cannot properly be considered labor disputes. The administrative courts have developed an important body of case law in matters involving industrial relations. Although many of their cases are quite similar to those brought before other courts under different circumstances, the decisions are not always alike and a comparison is often instructive. Likewise, disputes in which an employer or employee is charged with a criminal offense are not regarded as labor disputes; they are brought before the criminal courts.

Excluded also are all disputes not involving the opposing interests of an employee or group of employees and an employer or group of employers, that is, disputes between employees, between unions, between employers, or between associations of employers. Although such disputes occasionally have been submitted by statutory law or case law to the procedures normally provided for the settlement of labor disputes,[4] this must be explained in terms of special circumstances that

---

[4] For instance, statutory law extends the jurisdiction of labor courts to "disputes arising between employees in connection with their work"; but this is only a subsidiary and, in fact, almost negligible function of the court. Occasionally, some judicial decisions treat disputes among several unions over the problem of their representativeness and prerogatives attached thereto as collective disputes (Superior Court of Arbitration, May 13, 1950, *Droit Social*, 1950, 229). But these decisions are dependent on peculiar facts and do not constitute general precedents.

do not affect the nature of the conflict; it is by no means a labor dispute.

Preliminary screening procedures for grievances have been established by statute, by collective agreements, or by the unilateral decision of an employer in written shop rules (*règlement intérieur*) that must be provided in every enterprise of more than twenty workers. Their use is compulsory or optional, and they are distinguished according to the type of machinery employed: (a) procedures within the enterprise; (b) procedures before agents of the Labor Administration; and (c) procedures conducted with union participation.

Screening procedures within the enterprise may be conducted with the help of the *délégués du personnel* or the works committee, who enjoy special privileges to perform this function. Grievances, which may be individual or collective, may include all problems relating to wages and conditions of employment, health and safety matters, disciplinary actions, and layoffs and dismissals. In procedures before officials of the Labor Administration, the officials are empowered by law to settle grievances that could give rise to a labor dispute, for example, layoffs or dismissals of particular categories of workers. They also act as informal mediators in settling labor disputes at an early stage, that is, they effect a compromise between employer and workers in grievances resulting from alleged violations of statutory law or provisions of collective agreements. The union's role in screening procedures is narrowly defined by legislation, but it is sometimes augmented by collective agreement when there is such an agreement at the company level. A kind of grievance procedure is then established in which representatives of the local union are invited to participate. There may also be informal discussions between the employer and the representatives, but there is such variety of practice that it cannot properly be called part of a "procedure."

VARIOUS TYPES OF LABOR DISPUTES

The differences between the various types of labor disputes are extremely important because they affect the procedures provided for their settlement. Most countries make a distinction between disputes over rights and those over interests. Disputes over rights, often called in France juridical conflicts, turn on the existence or the content of a right claimed by a party, that is, on the application or interpretation of existing law, whether it has its source in legislation, in a collective agreement, or in the individual contract of employment. Disputes over interests, often called economic conflicts, turn on amendments and improvements in existing law or even on the development of new law through the channels normally open to the parties, that is, the negotiation of collective agreements.

The distinction between these two types of disputes is of fundamental theoretical importance because of different requirements involving the procedures established for their settlement. Procedures in disputes over rights must lean closer to settlement procedures established for ordinary kinds of conflicts, and they must have the same judicial character because the problem involves the correct application of the law. Procedures in disputes over interests are necessarily more specialized because they lead to the creation of new law, a function that normally exceeds the powers of any jurisdiction. They are not meant to be included in this study because they are actually closer to the process of collective bargaining than to the judicial process. However, such a distinction between the two types of disputes is not really made in France, either in statutory law or in most collective agreements. Settlement procedures for disputes over rights and those over interests have the same general features and are handled by the same authorities; differences concern the details of settlement machinery only.

On the other hand, a fundamental distinction is drawn in France between individual and collective disputes. This distinction has grown with the development of labor law. Its exact nature is difficult to define because the case law, which established the distinction, does not originate from a single hierarchical court system but from several authorities, each determining the scope of its jurisdiction. Labor and ordinary courts under the authority of the *Cour de Cassation* have provided the definition of individual disputes, and ordinary courts and arbitrators (the latter being controlled by the Superior Court of Arbitration, which has a specialized and limited jurisdiction) have elaborated the concept of collective disputes. As a result, it is theoretically possible that some disputes are not covered by either definition. Each definition is based upon two criteria: the subject of the dispute and the nature of the parties involved.

A labor conflict is individual if its object concerns only one employer and one employee, without affecting a group or collectivity on either side. Consequently it always concerns a question of rights because the inequality of power between employer and individual worker rules out disputes over interests. There are definite rights to which the workers are entitled by law, but which are counterbalanced by rights granted the employer, and the individual conflict turns precisely on the existence or the contents of these rights. Such individual conflicts are usually initiated by the worker because of his subordinate position, which puts him in greater need of legal remedies. In any case, whatever right may be invoked by the employer or employee, all have their source in the individual employment relationship. An individual dispute is often defined as a conflict arising out of the application or interpretation of the individual contract of employment; it may involve wages and other benefits, the termination of a contract of employment by layoff or dismissal, conditions and hours of work, and so forth.

However, a conflict can be considered individual only if it actually arises between a single employer and a single employee, without any intervention by a group or collectivity acting as party to the dispute. If there are several individuals who have similar claims to present, this merely results in a juxtaposition of individual disputes, not in their transformation into a collective one.[5] And herein lies the real difference between individual and collective labor disputes.

A labor conflict is collective when it turns on the rights or interests of a group of workers, and when its solution is likely to affect the situation or the terms of employment of all the members of that group. The conflict may be over rights or over interests; the two parties are here believed to be equally or at least comparably powerful and they may use their power to support any allegation, that is, they may enter into a dispute on the basis of an existing right as well as an interest. However, to render the conflict collective it is also necessary that a group of workers, not merely an individual employee, be effectively a party to the dispute. The group may be organized (in most cases it will be a union) or unorganized; it may vary in size (all workers in a plant or company, workers of several enterprises or of an entire industry at the local, regional, or national level); and it is irrelevant that a single employer or a number of them, whether or not organized in associations, opposes it.

In theory it seems simple to determine the nature of the disputes: both elements described—the subject of the dispute and the nature of the parties involved—must be used together to make a distinction between individual and collective disputes. But in reality the distinction is not so clear-cut, especially insofar as conflicts over rights—the only conflicts investigated here—are concerned. It may be difficult to draw a precise line between the violation of an individual right and the interference with a collective interest. Or a dispute may have both an individual and a collective subject because there was a simultaneous

---

[5] *Cour de Cassation, Chambre Sociale* (hereafter referred to as C. Cass., Ch. Soc.), June 21, 1951, *Gazette du Palais* 1951, II, 261.

violation of an individual right and a collective interest, for example, when the conflict turns on the application of a general rule that is directly applicable to the individual workers through their contracts of employment.

In sum, it is clear that the criterion of distinction derived from the subject of a dispute is ambiguous. At most it can be said that a conflict, based on that criterion alone, *may be considered* individual or collective, but not that it *is* individual or collective or that it will be so treated by the competent authorities. Therefore, the nature of the parties involved, whether it is a single, isolated worker or a group of workers, must also be used to distinguish between individual and collective conflicts.

But this criterion, again, may be difficult to apply; it is not related to the true nature of the dispute but rather to the manner of instituting proceedings. Moreover, it may be unclear for two different reasons. On the one hand, a union can admittedly intervene in an individual dispute on behalf of an employee, either to assist in the proceedings or to act in his place. On the other hand, several employees can act simultaneously to defend their own individual rights when these are alike, allegedly having been violated by the same event or at least by similar events. Proceedings then are initiated simultaneously and may even be consolidated into one single action from a procedural point of view. But such an action cannot be regarded as collective as long as the individuals concerned are considered separately, not as members of a collectivity. There is then a cluster of several individual disputes, but not a collective dispute. Thus, the attribution of individual or collective character to a labor dispute depends very largely on the way the parties look at the conflict, and this results, at least in fact if not in law, in the application of a criterion that is more subjective still: the intention of the parties or their goals.[6]

The ambiguity and vagueness of the distinction between individual and collective disputes have led to contradictory decisions in this area of labor relations that have caused serious concern. But a certain margin of judgment in determining the true nature of a conflict and assigning settlement procedures that appear to be best suited and most adequate may be welcome indeed.

In its practical application the distinction has undergone a long and significant evolution, linked to the existence and relative success of the procedures provided for the settlement of each type of conflict. Until

---

[6] These terms are expressly used by the courts. See, e.g., C. Cass., Ch. Soc., June 23, 1960, *Droit Social* 1961, 48.

1936 the concept of collective disputes had not been closely defined, and this can be explained by the fact that an effective procedure for the settlement of conflicts involving groups of employees was not available. Consequently, broad content was given to the notion of individual disputes, and the courts established to deal with them did not hesitate to extent their jurisdiction. The reverse situation prevailed between 1936 and 1939, when new procedures (and particularly arbitration procedures) were established in order to settle collective conflicts. The arbitrators and the newly created Superior Court of Arbitration had to determine the limits of their jurisdiction, and this resulted in a considerable extension of the concept of collective disputes. This development was accompanied by a restriction of the concept of individual disputes, as both notions were considered to be mutually exclusive at the time. Since the end of the Second World War, however, the situation has changed again because the procedures for the settlement of collective disputes have lost much of their efficiency. There are misgivings today about classifying a dispute as exclusively "collective," because it would compel the parties to resort to machinery which is, in most cases, doomed to failure, and there is a preference to classify the dispute as "individual" whenever possible in order to permit the recourse to satisfactory settlement procedures. A still better solution, more often employed, is the admission of the twofold nature of the dispute—individual and collective—thereby allowing the parties to choose the settlement procedure they consider best suited, even to resort to both procedures, simultaneously or successively, if they so desire. Therefore, it is not unusual to see a dispute originating as individual and developing as collective. Conversely, even though a dispute may arise as a collective conflict, failure of the proper settlement procedures may encourage the parties to transform it into an individual dispute or, more commonly, into a group of individual disputes in order to gain access to settlement procedures provided for such conflicts.[7]

Ambiguous and blurred as it is, the distinction between the two types of disputes remains important in French labor law. Despite the fact that they may be used together, the procedures provided for the settlement of each type remain distinct and must be studied separately. The choice between them may be imposed by the nature of the conflict involved, but the parties themselves may freely select the machinery

---

[7] The courts have permitted such a procedure after failure of a procedure of conciliation (C. Cass., Ch. Soc., May 29, 1962, *Informateur du chef d'entreprise* 1962, 859) or of a procedure of mediation (C. Cass., Ch. Soc., March 2, 1960, *Bulletin* IV, n. 224).

SETTLEMENT OF LABOR DISPUTES IN FRANCE

they wish to use. This proves erroneous the widely accepted notion that the only procedure established for the settlement of labor disputes in French law takes place before the labor court. In fact, a great diversity of procedures has been created over time. Today all of them play an important role and their combination represents a complex system.

COMMON FEATURES OF SETTLEMENT PROCEDURES

Although diverse, the existing procedures for the settlement of labor disputes have some features in common: they are designed to accommodate the uniqueness of labor disputes as much as possible, and many alternatives are open to the parties. When cases are submitted to a judge or to an arbitrator, he is usually a specialist in labor matters and proceedings are conducted according to special rules. The labor courts, likewise, are not organized like the ordinary courts, and labor court judges are subject to special regulations concerning their recruitment and status. More generally, all of these authorities tend to avoid too narrowly defined legal methods of reasoning in dealing with labor problems in order to improve and enlarge their evaluation of the factual background of the dispute and of social reality.

However, because each of the procedures established by law applies to a certain kind of conflict, some labor disputes are not covered by them, at least theoretically. Moreover, the jurisdiction of special agencies may be restricted geographically and does not cover all of France. Thus, when special procedures are not available for a given dispute or when their use is voluntary, the parties have recourse to the ordinary judicial procedures pursuant to the rule that there must always be a forum for any dispute.

In contrast to other countries, labor disputes in France are never settled within the enterprise. Internal organizations representing workers have only limited powers; they may promote voluntary settlement of a grievance or act as a screening agency, but they have no decision-making powers and cannot really take part in the final settlement of a dispute. Such a settlement, in fact, always implies the intervention of an authority external to the enterprise—judge, state official, or private person. Labor unions, likewise, play a minor role in the settlement of labor disputes, at least at the company level. Union participation is more or less insignificant because of the principles that govern union activities in France—union pluralism and the rule that unions can represent their members only—and because settlement procedures are usually prescribed by statutory law rather than by collective agreement. It is a traditional concept in French labor law that all employees are entitled to the same minimum protection, which must be furnished by the legislature. Thus, existing procedures tend to accommodate state agencies, such as judges and government officials, rather than unions or private individuals, and the French system may be characterized as one of public order in which the state is almost omnipresent.

2.
THE LABOR COURTS

HISTORICAL DEVELOPMENT

The French system of labor courts is the oldest in the world and has served as a model for similar courts in several other countries. The *conseils de prud'hommes*, or councils of wise men, as they are called, are the only courts really specialized in the settlement of individual labor disputes. Although they do not have exclusive jurisdiction in this field, their role is nevertheless important and constitutes a distinctive feature of the French system of labor law.[1] The courts were established in 1806 during the reign of Napoleon. Initially restricted to the manufacturing industry, the system developed rapidly from 20 courts in 1810 to 69 in 1847, all located in the main industrial cities with the exception of Paris, which did not have a labor court until 1844. The general rules for the structure and operation of the courts were laid down in 1809; they have since been amended mainly to strengthen the principle of equality between the employer and employee members of the courts. In 1907 the jurisdiction of the labor courts was extended to industries besides manufacturing, especially to mining and transportation and to all commercial occupations including white-collar workers. The legislation of 1907, which was incorporated into the Labor Code in 1924, remained for half a century the basic text for the operation of the labor courts. Although new statutes and regulations were enacted during that time, the fundamental features of the labor

---

[1] William H. McPherson and Frederic Meyers have written an excellent study of the *conseils de prud'hommes*, "The French Labor Courts: Judgment by Peers" (University of Illinois, 1966). We are much indebted to these authors for the information provided in their book.

courts were not significantly changed. It must be noted, however, that the development of the system was somewhat uneven. Until 1914 new courts were established by government decrees and the jurisdiction of existing ones was extended. But that trend slowed down after World War I; few new courts were created after 1945, though the jurisdiction of existing ones continued to be extended by numerous decrees,[2] and though some reforms were also initiated to make the jurisdiction of the courts more exclusive, thus reflecting the success of that institution.

By and large, the entire legislative movement was favorable to the labor courts, but more recently it has been felt that a new, comprehensive statute should be enacted to restructure existing legislation and add minor amendments. In late 1958 the judiciary was reorganized; an Ordinance of December 22, 1958, and a Decree of the same date are now the basic laws concerning the labor courts. One of the purposes of this new legislation was to extend the jurisdiction of labor courts in order to include all occupations.

It can be stated that the existence and fundamental characteristics of the labor courts are almost universally accepted in France today.[3] Although the evolution of the system certainly has not reached its end, it probably will not lead, at least in the foreseeable future, to any revolutionary changes. The balance reached between opposing interest groups and agreed upon by the majority of the parties concerned is likely to be maintained for a long time to come.

ORGANIZATION OF THE LABOR COURTS

The geographical distribution of the labor courts does not cover all of France. There are many areas where there is no labor court or where the existing court has no jurisdiction over disputes involving particular occupations. Historically the *conseils de prud'hommes* were not created simultaneously according to a general plan, but sporadically whenever a particular need arose in a given area. The same system prevails today. Each labor court must be created by government de-

---

[2] From 1945 to 1967, only 14 new courts, including 32 sections, were created, and only 13 new sections were established within already existing courts.

[3] There are, of course, some jurists who adopt, as a matter of principle, a hostile attitude towards all specialized courts, including the labor courts, and who advocate their suppression to the benefit of the ordinary courts. But this is a rather theoretical view that has no chance of adoption by the majority, especially with respect to the labor courts.

cree, after certain rules and formalities have been observed.[4] There are presently 242 labor courts in metropolitan France and another 5 in the overseas *Départements,* but the 14 courts located in Alsace-Lorraine operating under separate local legislation are not included in this study.

The decree under which a labor court is created or reorganized also determines its internal structure and its territorial and occupational jurisdiction. Each court has its seat in a town of some size and importance, and its jurisdiction covers a specified area around that town. However, there cannot be more than one court in any town, and many areas, especially agricultural regions, are outside of the territorial jurisdiction of a labor court.

The occupational jurisdiction of the labor courts, although it could theoretically include all occupations, even employees of public enterprises,[5] is defined by the decree under which the court is organized. It determines the number of sections into which the court can be divided and the number of categories into which the occupations in its jurisdiction can be distributed. According to the law there may be as many as four different sections, each distinct and autonomous and corresponding to a certain type of activity. But many courts have only one section, and no court has all four sections that are theoretically permissible. The basic Industrial Section that exists in every labor court handles all cases arising in industry or commerce and involving manual workers *(ouvriers)* or foremen who actually do production work. It also has jurisdiction over domestic workers if the court does not have a Commercial Section. A labor court may have several specialized Industrial Sections, as, for example, the court in Paris, which has four such sections. In addition, the court may have a Commercial Section for disputes involving white-collar workers *(employés)* and supervisory personnel, an Agricultural Section having jurisdiction over manual and

---

[4] ARTICLE 2, Book IV of the Labor Code provides that each labor court must be created upon proposal by the Ministry of Justice, the Ministry of Labor, and the Ministry of Agriculture, after the municipal councils of the towns to be included in the jurisdiction of the court have been consulted, and after all professional organizations, public and private, and all persons interested in the issue have been given one month in which to express their opinions. The same formalities must be observed for modifications of structure or dissolution of existing labor courts. These rules also apply to extending the jurisdiction of an existing court.

[5] Employees of public enterprises are subject to the jurisdiction of the labor courts when these enterprises meet the following requirements: they must have a legal personality distinct from the state, they must be industrial or commercial enterprises, they must operate according to the rules of commercial law patterned on private enterprise. (C. Cass., Ch. Soc. July 12, 1950, *Dalloz* 1950, 665; February 17, 1956, *Dalloz* 1956, 415.) This ruling does not apply to civil servants.

white-collar workers in agriculture, and a Miscellaneous Section covering all other occupations; but the latter section, although feasible under legislation of 1958, has never been established at any court.

The specialization of the labor courts is a handicap insofar as it prevents many employees from bringing their individual disputes before the courts. It is noteworthy that, excepting manual workers of industry and commerce and domestic workers, the existence of a labor court does not in itself guarantee the existence of a section with jurisdiction over a specific dispute, and it is regrettable that the government does not fully implement existing law; nowhere in France, not even in Paris, is there a labor court with all four sections as authorized by statute. There are no doubt practical considerations, such as finding competent judges and the expenditure of their salaries, but these obstacles could be overcome by extending the occupational jurisdiction of existing sections. The opponents to such a solution contend that it would affect the principle of specialization among the sections with respect to the appointment of judges and the distribution of caseloads, or that it might even lead to the abandonment of the section system, upsetting the whole structure of the labor courts and the notion of judgment by peers. But the collaboration of persons engaged in different types of activities could surely be obtained, as proven by the fact that no distinction is now made between industry and commerce in the Industrial and Commercial Sections, and that manual and white-collar workers are lumped together in the Agricultural Section.[6]

Another problem relates to the jurisdiction of the labor courts: it derives from the existence of various categories into which are grouped the occupations covered by each court. These categories represent a further degree of specialization. Although they affect neither the structure of the courts nor the distribution of the cases, they play a role in the determination of the court's jurisdiction and in the designation of the judges. The law does not prescribe a minimum or maximum number of occupational categories, nor does it stipulate the occupations covered. Both are set forth in the decree under which the court is organized, and occupations not specified are excluded from the jurisdiction of the court even if it has a section for the type of activity under which the occupation normally would fall. In practice, however,

---

[6] It is sometimes suggested that, if this specialization between sections disappeared and the labor courts had general coverage over all employers and employees without distinction between types of activities, such coverage should be voluntary rather than compulsory. In other words, the parties could bring their disputes either to the labor courts or to some other courts, as is now the case for the *cadres*.

this limitation is not much of a handicap; categories usually are defined in very broad terms, and the courts do not hesitate to extend the content of some categories to include occupations that are not expressly covered by the decree. It will be shown later that the division into categories is more important for the election and appointment of judges than it is for the determination of the jurisdiction of the court.

In sum, there is no doubt that the present system has serious shortcomings. There are not enough courts and the jurisdiction of the existing ones is too limited. Thus, a large number of employers and employees cannot bring their cases before a labor court; according to some estimates, more than one third of all individual labor disputes arising in France fall in that category. Nevertheless, the existing courts handle an impressive number of disputes, on the average between 55,000 and 60,000 per year.

A major shortcoming of the present labor court system is the absence of an appellate jurisdiction. Although decisions of the *conseils de prud'hommes* can be appealed under certain conditions, the appeals are brought before courts not specialized in labor matters. Two main kinds of appeals are possible under French law: appeals based on points of law *or* on points of fact *(appel)* are filed with the ordinary courts of appeals, whose social chamber *(chambre sociale)* handles social matters including labor disputes. There may be a special section for appeals from labor courts in the larger courts of appeals.[7] Appeals based exclusively on points of law *(pourvoi en cassation)* are brought before the *Cour de Cassation,* which sits in Paris and forms the top of the hierarchy of the ordinary court structure. Its *chambre sociale* also handles social matters including labor conflicts.

The absence of a specialized labor court at the second and third level of the court structure tends substantially to offset the advantages and guarantees offered by the *conseils de prud'hommes* in the first instance. Either party to a dispute may appeal the decision of a labor court in order to escape judgment by peers and reenter the jurisdiction of an ordinary court. Such maneuvering usually works to the advantage of the employer, who may carry his case to the court of appeals or the *Cour de Cassation* with the express intention of having it decided by

---

[7] This is the case in the Paris court of appeals. The court has three social chambers, each divided into two sections composed of 3 judges. Two chambers, composed of a total of 12 judges, exclusively decide appeals from the decisions of the labor courts or of the ordinary courts when these serve as substitutes for the labor courts.

an ordinary court.[8] But an employee may also have good reasons for filing an appeal, and he will then reluctantly take his case to an ordinary court.

The creation of specialized appellate labor courts, endorsed by unions as well as labor court judges, would help to strengthen the concept of judgment by peers. But members of the legal profession are opposed to any further development of specialized jurisdictions, and most employers and their associations do not favor an extension of the labor court system. A compromise could be reached by creating appellate labor courts at the second level and preserving the right of ultimate appeal to the *Cour de Cassation*. However, this would probably lead to a change in the pattern of labor courts at the appellate level, that is, the bipartite system of the *conseils de prud'hommes* would have to be replaced by a tripartite one in which professional judges would sit with lay judges. Such a system of *échevinage* would have the advantage of combining the qualities of both kinds of judges, providing a transitional stage between the courts of the first instance, entirely staffed by lay judges, and the supreme court, composed exclusively of professional judges. But this solution contains dangers as well: there is fear that the principle of tripartitism, once admitted at the appellate level, may gradually extend downward to the level of the first instance and lead finally to the establishment of a completely tripartite system. A transformation of this kind would upset the whole structure of the labor courts and would undoubtedly work to the disadvantage of the employees, who are most attached to the principle of bipartitism. Therefore, although there are numerous proposals for establishing labor courts above the first level, none really has a likely chance of being adopted in the near future.

COMPOSITION OF THE LABOR COURTS

The rules governing the composition of the labor courts are essentially designed to commit the settlement of labor disputes to judges who are specialized in labor matters and true representatives of the different interests involved. Therefore, these courts are composed of lay judges, who are not trained jurists but are members of the social groups primarily involved in labor disputes. They must be familiar with the industrial relations environment, with labor–management relations practices, and with the customs of industry (even though the

---

[8] It is easy to verify historically that all the laws which facilitated appeal against the decisions of the labor courts have been promulgated in favor of the employers.

relative importance of these customs has declined in recent years because of the development of a body of labor law that is somewhat more accessible to professional judges than to laymen). This has led to the conviction that labor court judges should come from the same industrial sectors that are subject to their jurisdiction. They must be chosen from among persons who are actually (or, at least, have been at one time) employers and employees, in other words, who can provide "judgment by peers."

Although this system has been criticized because it contains the danger of judicial incompetence in legal matters, experience shows that it has worked rather satisfactorily. Unions and employer associations try to nominate candidates who have some understanding of legal problems, and the judges, once elected, strive to improve their knowledge and abilities. Another unjustified criticism concerns the lack of time that confronts the judge who pursues his normal occupation while serving on the bench,[9] but this is an unavoidable consequence of the requirement that members of the court must be employers and employees, actively engaged in industrial life. However, several suggestions have been made to alleviate this problem, for example, reduction of the term of office, reduction of caseloads, and higher salaries.[10]

The principle of specialization of the labor courts requires that the judges composing these courts must have the same background of activity or occupation that is covered by the jurisdiction of the court, as determined by the decree creating the court. While this is fully accomplished at the section level of the court, each section being comparable

---

[9] There is no problem, of course, if the judges are selected from among retired persons. This practice is not uncommon, especially on the employers' side, but it also raises some very serious and obvious problems for the parties. Thus, employers and employees usually are very reluctant to appoint such judges, who are likely to be less partisan in defending the interests of management or of labor; but this, after all, may be considered an advantage if it increases the impartiality of the judges.

[10] The law provides, since the Decree of June 6, 1956, that all judges receive some remuneration that does not, however, constitute a salary. It is designed simply to compensate employees for loss of wages during hours off from work that are spent on the bench, because the employer is not expected to compensate the employee for these hours. Furthermore, the remuneration must also compensate for work done at the court during other than normal working hours (night sessions are frequent), and cover all expenses (e.g., travel expenses) connected with the discharge of judicial functions. The minimum amount is set forth by the decree under which the court was created, but it can be raised by a decision of the *Préfet* after consultation with the councils of the towns covered by the territorial jurisdiction of the court and to which the payments will be charged. In general, remuneration varies from $30 to $40 per month—sufficient compensation in view of the small number of sessions that the judges have to attend.

in some respects to an independent court, it is not always realized at the category level. The categories are not separate and distinct units, and although each judge comes himself from a particular occupational category, he may extend his jurisdiction beyond its limits. Thus, parties belonging to a particular occupational category have no assurance whatsoever that their case will be heard by judges having the same occupational background, but efforts are often made in practice to call judges who share the parties' occupational category to the bench for conciliation hearings as well as for judgment sessions. The French system of labor courts, as a whole, tries to give real meaning to the concept of "judgment by peers."

That concept implies yet another kind of specialization that is essential to the system: specialization of employer and employee judges who represent opposing interest groups.[11] There is no doubt that lack of judicial impartiality or objectivity could compromise the entire system, but again experience shows that these problems do not really arise. In 95 percent of the disputes, a majority usually emerges among judges who traditionally have been divided on ideological and sociological grounds (even in courts in which the majority of employee judges are members of unions affiliated with the militant C.G.T.). These results are very important in practice as well as in theory because they are the primary condition for a successful operation of the labor courts. The long tradition in France of judicial impartiality[12] and the collegial composition of the courts help to generate mutual control among the judges,[13] and the parties themselves, being accustomed to judicial objectivity, do not expect justice based on class division.

---

[11] Although this was not always admitted in the past (until 1848 the judges were selected from among employers and some privileged classes of employees, such as foremen and licensed employees), it seems quite natural today. It is for that very purpose that the law defines employer and employee with great precision in order to avoid all difficulties concerning possible intermediate classes. For example, "employees" include all foremen and supervisors, and "employers" include owner-operators, partners, general managers, and chairmen of executive committees as well as various types of upper-level administrators, department heads, highly skilled technicians, etc. (ART. 21 of the Decree of December 22, 1958).

[12] The labor unions, however, had insisted at the end of the nineteenth century that the employee judges should have, by virtue of a *mandat impératif*, the obligation always to vote in favor of the employees appearing before the court. This proposition met with such resistance that it produced the opposite effect; it actually strengthened the attitude of impartiality among the judges. The *mandat impératif* today is expressly outlawed by ART. 46 of the Decree of December 22, 1958.

[13] In addition to guarantees that are part of their position (especially with respect to security of tenure and disciplinary matters), other guarantees are created by the procedural rules followed when decisions are rendered. For example, the presence of two members of each side (employers and employees) and the secrecy

SETTLEMENT OF LABOR DISPUTES IN FRANCE

The law contains other provisions to assure that the judges truly represent the diverse interests involved in labor disputes. They are elected from among members of their occupational categories through procedures contained in the Decree of December 22, 1958.[14] At least two employer and two employee judges have to be elected in each of the categories set forth by the decree establishing the court, but that figure may be doubled because of heavy caseloads. Lists of candidates are prepared at the level of the category, separately for employers and employees. At each election only half of the current vacancies on the courts are filled, because the panel of judges must then change half of its membership and some continuity is desirable. Elections take place every three years, and the term of office is six years. There may be two ballots if needed, the first ballot being decisive only if the candidate receives 50 percent of the votes cast by at least 25 percent of the electorate. The judges, of course, can be reelected.

The present controversy in France involving the labor courts is mainly directed at this system of electing the judges. It is alleged that it increases the dangers of judicial incompetence and partiality, that it contains too many practical difficulties involving preparations and finding suitable candidates, and that the vote itself usually generates little interest among employers and even less among employees. As a result, the judges actually are elected by the most active employers and workers, backed by their employers' associations and labor unions. But because the elections are based on majority vote and the division of the electorate results in a very small number of judges being elected in each category (one or two), it is often impossible to achieve a distribution of judgeships among several unions according to their respective importance; the strongest union, the C.G.T., often has a kind

---

of the vote prevent open knowledge of each judge's individual decision. Even if unanimity is achieved in favor of a particular decision (and it is highly probable that this is often the case), it will not be known to anybody; and this prevents any person from attributing a certain vote to a particular judge. It is precisely because these guarantees are not given to the judges who act as conciliators or as reporting judges that accusations of partiality can sometimes be made at these two stages.

[14] The electorate includes all persons who can vote in political elections and who have practiced for at least 3 years one of the occupations enumerated in the decree creating the court, at least 1 year in the territory covered by the jurisdiction of the court. There is, however, an important exception. Domestic workers and their employers are not eligible to vote and, therefore, may not serve as judges although they fall under the jurisdiction of the courts. This is because their employment relationship does not exist within an enterprise. Under the law, manual and white-collar workers are placed in different categories; in addition, each category contains two distinct electorates consisting of employers and employees, and each of these selects a certain number of judges from among its members.

of monopoly. This practice, of course, is contrary to the French tradition of union pluralism, and it is regrettable though few complaints of discrimination based on union membership have been raised. The adoption of another system of selecting judges is now often advocated, for example, appointments by the government to ensure fair representation of the various unions as well as judicial competence. But the Parliament and the government so far have not intervened, and even some of the unions are opposed to any change because they fear the loss of their quasi-monopoly. Finally, a change might have adverse psychological effects on the workers if they were to lose their right to select their own judges.

Another feature to ensure fair representation is the equality of employer and employee judges at the labor courts with respect to their number of votes.[15] Thus, in its normal and permanent form the labor court does not seat any member other than the employer and employee representatives, either as president, as regular judge, or as counselor with a consulting voice. The principle of fair representation does not permit the mixing of lay judges with professional judges (the system of *échevinage,* practiced in many other countries), government intervention, or, more generally, any intervention on the part of jurists or experts in labor relations. The strict application of bipartitism is considered necessary to free employer and employee representatives from any kind of pressure by a third party, who could become the real arbiter in labor disputes when employer and employee judges cannot reach agreement.

However, while the introduction of a third party may deprive the lay judges of their decision-making power, the inclusion of professional judges would also compensate for the lack of legal training of the lay members and help prevent too prejudiced or partisan points of view. This is now largely accomplished by the presence of a secretary in each court, who is a permanent, full-time civil servant appointed by the *Préfet* and knowledgeable in the administration of justice. In addition, labor court decisions can be appealed to the ordinary courts composed

---

[15] Under the law an equal number of employer and employee representatives (at least 2 of them) are to be elected for each occupational category to ensure perfect parity within a given section of the court (at least 6 employers and 6 employees). Employer and employee judges on the bench must also sit in equal number for each dispute, 1 member of each group must be present on the conciliation board, and 2 of each on the judgment board. The only exception to this rule provides that the court, section, or board shall act without equality of representation in the event of collective abstention of a part of the electorate or withdrawal of some judges from the court.

of professional judges, who then act as neutral, third parties, correcting *a posteriori* errors made in the first instance.

A more serious shortcoming of the bipartite system of the labor courts is the difficulty or even the impossibility of reaching a majority opinion among the judges, but several measures have been designed to permit the normal operation of the courts. The problem arises, first, in all internal or administrative matters that have to be settled at the level of the whole court or at that of the section. While the most important decisions in that field have to be made by the entire court or by the individual sections, routine problems are solved in each section by the president and the vice-president, who must be elected by the judges from among themselves and alternately from among employers and employees. If the court has several sections, all the presidents and vice-presidents form an assembly to select from among themselves a president and vice-president of the court. But the problem also arises to prevent deadlock in cases before the judgment board. The law provides that in case of a tie vote a second hearing will take place, at which a third, external and neutral person will be seated in addition to employer and employee judges—a professional judge.[16] However, there have been few cases of deadlock, and it can be argued that the threat of intervention of a professional judge motivates the lay judges to impartiality and objectivity. In other words, it is the fear of tripartitism that makes bipartitism successful or that permits it to operate.

On the whole, the French system of labor courts operates rather satisfactorily. Although there is no dearth of criticism—members of the legal profession would like to seat professional judges and the labor unions favor an extension of the system to the appellate level—most proposals for a complete change have had little success. Only minor reform, no revolutionizing transformation, can therefore be expected in the near future.

OPERATION OF THE LABOR COURTS

The operation of the labor courts will be discussed here only insofar as it concerns the settlement of individual labor disputes.[17] In order to justify their existence as specialized courts, the labor courts must offer

---

[16] Since 1950, cases in which lay judges cannot reach agreement are reheard by the same judges under the chairmanship of the *juge d'instance*. That judge normally sits as the *tribunal d'instance*, the civil court having jurisdiction over small claims in the geographical area in which the labor court is located.

[17] It must not be forgotten that the labor courts also have other functions. More particularly, they are entrusted with the custody of a certain number of legal documents that have to be deposited, according to the law, in their secretariat and

the parties involved in litigation significant advantages as compared with the ordinary courts. These concern the situation of the parties before the court and the procedures in conciliation and judgment sessions.

SITUATION OF THE PARTIES BEFORE THE LABOR COURT

Under the law, access to the labor courts must be available to all persons engaged in individual labor disputes, without any preconditions; access should in no way be obstructed as soon as it is clear that an individual labor dispute exists. Although preliminary procedures established in collective agreements or in written shop rules may be used by the parties, such use is optional and serves neither as a substitute for action before a labor court nor as a precondition. Of course, attempts at conciliation prior to submitting a dispute to adjudication are highly desirable; they would lighten the caseloads of the courts and give the judges more time to devote to more complex cases. But such attempts are also dangerous to the extent that they imply the active intervention of the unions; there is then the risk of discrimination against nonunion workers. Therefore, the present system adheres more closely to the principle of complete equality of all workers, making the labor courts accessible at all times to all persons, without preconditions of any kind. In other words, employees cannot be forced to discuss their grievance with management before they have access to the judge.

In keeping with that principle, proceedings before the labor court are designed to be as simple, informal, and inexpensive as possible. For example, venue is determined by the defendant's place of work rather than by his residence, proceedings are initiated by filing a form at the office of the secretary of the court, summons and writs may be served by registered mail, the procedure is largely oral, and the parties need not be represented by counsel. Court costs are very low, and the plaintiff is responsible for such charges only if he loses his case; if he wins, he will be reimbursed by the defendant for all of his expenses connected with the proceedings. In addition, financial help is available through a system of legal assistance.

As a result of these advantages a large number of cases are brought

---

that concern collective labor relations: written plant rules, collective bargaining agreements, conciliation agreements, agreements following mediation or arbitration procedures, etc. They also have consultative powers on questions submitted to them by public or administrative authorities.

before the labor courts, most of them involving claims of employees. They show great variety,[18] including, for example, unjustified dismissal, the rights and duties of the *délégués du personnel,* members of the works council or union representatives, and so forth. Because the court cannot order reinstatement, most actions are brought after the termination of the contract of employment, and they involve monetary matters (notably damages in sums of money).

The role of unions and employers' associations before the labor courts is limited by law. They may assist the parties financially or by providing legal counsel to advise a party or plead before the judge on his behalf. In addition, they may provide persons who act as representatives of employers or employees in judgment sessions, appearing in their place (Decree of December 22, 1958, ARTICLE 69).

The presence of lawyers (*avocats* or *avoués*) before the labor court is not required, but it is always permitted. It is usually of greater help in judgment than in conciliation. Unions and employers' associations may delegate one of their own representatives to assist the parties or appear on their behalf before the court, and it is no longer required that the latter are members of the respective organization.[19] Employers and employees may also hire their own lawyers, and they may be assisted by colleagues who come from the same occupational background as they do (excluding *délégués du personnel* and members of the works councils, when acting in these capacities).

In addition to representing members or assisting parties, unions and employers' associations may also appear before the labor courts in their own name. They may appear to exercise their members' rights of action in their place in all individual actions based on the interpretation or the application of a term of a collective agreement, and (at least if they are constituted as *syndicats*) in all individual actions on behalf of home workers relating to their wages. In these two types of cases the organization acts in its own name, not as an agent for its member; it suffices that the member is notified of the organization's intent to act on his behalf. The organization is not required to name those on

---

[18] Some interesting figures on the approximate distribution of these various types of claims are given in McPherson and Meyers, *op. cit.,* pp. 34-35.

[19] The *Cour de Cassation* in a number of landmark decisions prior to 1958 ruled that these representatives must themselves be members of their respective organizations. See, e.g., C. Cass., Ch. Soc., June 17, 1954, *Bulletin* 1954, 420, p. 316. Although recent case law on this point is not available and the question has not been completely resolved, there seems to be little doubt that unions and associations may delegate one of their own officials to appear before the labor courts, even though he is not an employer or an employee; however, he must be a member of his organization under the conditions provided by the law.

whose behalf it acts, nor does it have to state their number, but the individual or individuals involved in the action may personally intervene in the proceedings at any time.

Although not much use is made of this possibility it has definite advantages, particularly for the employee who is relieved of the burden of court proceedings and is provided with anonymity and thus protection against possible retaliation by his employer. Moreover, in grievances affecting a number of employees, action initiated by an organization has the advantage of simplicity and expeditiousness: there is only one dispute and one final decision having a general effect.

An action exercised by the organization in the place of the individual workers is very interesting from a theoretical point of view because it has collective as well as individual aspects. Of course, the individual character remains predominant and the action falls under the jurisdiction of the labor court.[20] But the final decision will affect more than one person, more even than those on whose behalf it was initiated; it will affect all persons subject to the statutory or contractual rules interpreted by that decision.

In addition to the type of action just described, unions and employers' associations can also intervene in proceedings initiated by an individual employer and employee. The organizations then act in their own name and on their own behalf, becoming a party to the litigation in support of an individual claim or defending a collective interest involved in the same action.[21]

THE CONCILIATION SESSION

The first part of the procedure before the labor court is a compulsory conciliation session reflecting the desire to conciliate rather than adjudicate the dispute, a desire that has been a basic feature of the labor court system since its inception. It is based on the belief that the parties to a dispute must have a chance to reconcile their points of view, that the unfortunate consequences of a judgment that always

---

[20] See C. Cass., Ch. Soc., June 23, 1960, G.P. 1960, II, 162.

[21] According to ART. 31, t, Book I of the Labor Code, all organizations whose members are bound by a collective agreement have the right to intervene in individual disputes turning on the application or the interpretation of a term of that agreement, on the basis of the collective interest involved in the conflict. Moreover, all organizations constituted as *syndicats* have the right to intervene when a collective interest is involved in an individual dispute.

leaves one party dissatisfied may be avoided, and that the labor courts, rather than outside screening procedures, supply the proper climate for conciliation.

Conciliation takes place before judges of the labor court, who sit on conciliation boards (sometimes called Special Bureaus, as in the Paris court) within each section of the court in panels of two, one employer and one employee; each session is chaired alternately by the employer or the employee judge. In addition, the secretary of the court or his assistant is always present, acting as liaison between parties and judges from conciliation board to judgment board if the case is not settled. Under the law, the parties must appear in person and they cannot be represented by proxy. Although they can be assisted as described above, they must be present at these sessions *in corpore*. However, the courts admit representation by proxy if that person has been given express powers to agree to settlement by conciliation. Absence of the plaintiff is considered as withdrawal of his claim, and absence of the defendant as renunciation of conciliation. The case is then referred immediately to the judgment board. In order to make the conciliation session as effective as possible, it is closed to the public to prevent external pressures, witnesses cannot be called, and cases usually are heard within fifteen days from the date of filing. Sessions are scheduled at least once a week in each section of each court. The judges participate actively, hearing and questioning the parties, and often acting as mediators rather than as conciliators.

Successful conciliation results in the unilateral withdrawal by one of the parties of his claim, or in a real compromise between the parties involving mutual renunciation of their claims or mutual concessions. If conciliation is partly or completely successful, the results are officially recorded in the *procès-verbal de conciliation,* a document prepared by the judges, signed by the parties, and containing all the terms agreed upon by them. It is just as enforceable as a judgment. If conciliation fails in whole or in part, the case is referred to the judgment board, the points on which the parties could not reach agreement being set forth in the *procès-verbal de non-conciliation.* The judges on the conciliation panel then advise the parties as to the proper presentation of their case, thus helping to save time when it is called for adjudication. It must be noted, however, that informal conciliation always remains a possibility, even after termination—and failure—of the conciliation session. Bargaining may continue and agreement reached until the case is actually brought before the judgment board.

Although available statistics show variations according to the courts involved (there are significant differences between Paris and the provinces), the branches of activity, the types of cases, the ability of the court personnel, etc., it seems that more than one-third of the cases filed in the labor courts are settled by conciliation before reaching the judgment board. This figure includes formal and informal conciliations.

The following conclusions can be drawn from these data: conciliation is more successful in the provinces (45–55 percent) than in Paris (30 percent). The rate is higher in industries that traditionally have good labor–management relations, for example, in the printing industry, and in the industrial sections of the courts than in the commercial ones. The latter conclusion shows that white-collar workers are more aware of their rights and offer more resistance to outside pressures. In addition, the rate of successful conciliations is also higher in courts in which the secretary plays an active role, an argument that can be cited in favor of tripartitism, even at the conciliation stage. Finally, there seems to be a decline in the number of cases actually settled by conciliation: in 1946, of 53,331 cases filed, 25,874 (48 percent) were settled by conciliation, 20,850 (40 percent) during the conciliation session; in 1958, of 53,932 cases filed, 20,830 (39 percent) were settled by conciliation, 15,690 (29 percent) during the conciliation session. In 1964, the respective figures were 58,770 cases filed, 20,739 (35 percent) settled by conciliation, 14,889 (26 percent) during the conciliation session. For 1967, the figures were 61,671 cases filed, 20,375 (33 percent) settled by conciliation, 14,698 (24 percent) during the conciliation session.[22]

Although the existence of a conciliation procedure before the labor courts compensates to a large extent for the absence of preliminary screening procedures, it could be further improved by increasing the number of judges or scheduling more sessions and by encouraging the parties to explore all opportunities for conciliation. This would help to eliminate the variations in settlements accomplished among the courts and increase the overall rate of settlements before the cases are referred to judgment.

THE JUDGMENT SESSION

When a labor dispute is referred to judgment, a second phase begins in the proceedings before the labor court. Three main principles govern the procedure during the judgment session: (1) the usual procedural imperatives that apply to proceedings before any court, (2) encourage-

---

[22] *Compte général de l'administration de la justice civile et commerciale et de la justice criminelle,* 1946, p. 146; 1958, pp. 98 and 99; 1964, pp. 421 and 422; 1967, p. 493.

ment of conciliation at all stages, and (3) quick settlement of the dispute.

The parties must appear before a judgment board (sometimes called a General Bureau, as in the Paris court) composed of at least four judges—two employers and two employees. The president or vice-president of the respective section alternates as chairman and must be present at each session.[23] The number of judgment sessions actually held varies in each court or section, depending on the caseload. The session normally is open to the public but may be held *in camera* if ordered by the judge; the judgment itself is always rendered in public. The parties need not appear in person, and they may be assisted as well as represented. If either party fails to appear, the hearing does not take place and the court hands down a judgment by default. In complicated cases the court may organize a procedure of investigation, which includes the hearing of witnesses, an investigation at the place of work, the opinion of experts, and the appointment of a reporting judge.

The reporting judge is chosen from among the judges of the court because of his particular ability, judicial competence, and time he may have available. After a thorough study of all aspects of the dispute, he submits a report and recommendations to the court. The growing resort to reporting judges has often been criticized because it is not provided in the law, it tends to complicate proceedings, and it contains the danger of transferring the power of decision form a bipartite jurisdiction to a single judge. In recognition of that danger, the Chemical Section of the Paris Labor Court now appoints two reporting judges, one employer and one employee; but if they cannot reach agreement between themselves, they submit two reports with contradictory recommendations. This difficulty could be solved by eliminating the need of a final recommendation or calling on a third, neutral party for that task. In any case, appointing a reporting judge or any kind of expert always interrupts the normal course of proceedings, and another judgment board must be called that may be composed of different judges.

In the final part of the proceedings before the judgment board, a decision is reached by majority vote in secret ballot. In cases of dead-

---

[23] Although the judges are appointed on a rotating basis, one or two of them already may have heard the case in conciliation. In some courts special efforts are made to have these judges on the judgment board because of their familiarity with the dispute. To guard against any conflict of interest (kinship, employment relationship, etc.), the law provides for objection procedures that guarantee the impartiality of the judges.

lock, rehearings are scheduled within the shortest possible time before another judgment board composed of the same four judges who were present at the first hearing, but chaired by the *juge d'instance* who has jurisdiction in the geographical area. Final decisions are obtained in 35 to 40 percent of the cases, which makes more than 20,000 judgments per year.[24]

The parties have several possibilities to appeal the decisions of the labor court. In cases of judgment by default, the defendant may use the special procedure of *opposition* under which the case will be reopened before the same labor court,[25] or the party may file an appeal with the court of appeals on any ground.[26] Another possibility is the *pourvoi en cassation*, an appeal exclusively based on an alleged violation of the law. The case is then taken to the *Cour de Cassation*, either directly from the labor court or from the court of appeals.

Conciliation is permitted and encouraged at all stages of the proceedings before the judgment board. If it is accomplished prior to the hearing, the plaintiff may withdraw his case or it results in a judgment

---

[24] In 1946, out of a total of 53,331 cases submitted to the labor courts, there were 13,940 judgments (24 percent); in 1958, out of 53,932 cases, 19,891 judgments; in 1964, out of 58,770 cases, 23,641 judgments; in 1967, out of 61,671 cases, 24,735 judgments (40 percent). The total number of judgments thus appears to be increasing, as does its ratio to the total number of cases. (Sources cited in n. 22 *supra*.)

[25] However, this procedure of opposition can be used only once in each case. If the defendant again is found in default at the second hearing, he cannot reinstate the case a second time. This rule is necessary to prevent the delays that are so important to avoid in this field.

New legislation was passed in 1958 and 1960, restricting access to this procedure. As a general rule, recourse to opposition will not be granted if the defendant was personally served with the summons for the hearing, or if a normal appeal (*appel*) can be filed against the decision of the court. This last restriction has sometimes been criticized on the ground that it permits the defendant, by refusing to appear before the labor court and afterwards filing an appeal, to deprive the other party of a normal hearing before the labor court. This could make possible fraudulent tactics, especially on the part of the employers.

[26] Some proposals are regularly made to raise the minimum interest involved for filing an appeal (currently F.2,500) in order to limit the number of appeals. The number of reversals—and consequently the number of appeals, too—probably could be reduced if the judges of the labor courts were in a better position to adapt their judicial practice to the practice of the courts of appeals. This implies that they would be informed of the reasons that lead to the reversal of their decisions. Until recently nothing had been done in that direction. A certain custom seems to develop today, upon the repeated request of the labor courts, by which the court of appeals not only notifies the labor court of the fact that it has confirmed or reversed its decision, but the reasons for it; the best solution would be sending a copy of the judgment of the court of appeals to the labor court. Such a development is important because it may lead to a better adjustment of the practice of the labor courts to that of the courts of appeals.

by default. The parties may reach a compromise at any time, either on their own motion or on the initiative of the judges. In fact, some courts have conciliation teams composed of judges from both sides who continue to attempt conciliation during the entire course of the judgment session. Conciliation can take place in the last minute, that is, just before the members of the board decide the case.

All rules governing the judgment session are also determined by the principle of quick settlement of the dispute. Special legislative efforts have been made to avoid delaying tactics on the part of the disputants as well as the judges. Although the length of proceedings varies according to the kind of case and from one court to another,[27] it is usually not excessive.[28] Of course, some attempts have been made further to reduce the time involved, but it is impossible to go too far in that direction for procedural reasons. As has already been discussed, the use of a reporting judge or other neutral expert extends the proceedings to a second and even a third judgement session. Final settlement may also be delayed if the parties challenge the decision of the labor court. The dispute then is not fully resolved until a new decision is handed down, either by the same court or by a higher one. An appeal causes considerable delay, often four to five months; it may be filed deliberately, especially by employers who wish to put off a final decision.

Although a considerable number of rules concerning proceedings before the labor court depart from the ordinary law, there are also basic similarities between the labor courts and other civil or commercial courts in all matters relating to the adjudication of labor disputes and to the types of decisions that finally will be reached. In spite of all its special features, the labor court essentially is a court designed to settle disputes over rights, which affects its methods of reasoning as well as its remedies. Labor court judges use strictly legal methods of reasoning, that is, they apply the law and resolve a dispute in compliance with existing statutory provisions or contractual clauses. Like any other judge, they do not ignore legal provisions to meet the alleged

---

[27] A very close and well-informed study of this problem may be found in McPherson and Meyers, *op. cit.*, pp. 74-81. The figures quoted there concern essentially the four Industrial Sections of the Paris court.

[28] A claim usually reaches a conciliation board within two weeks from the date of filing; if conciliation fails, it must be sent to the earliest possible judgment session, which may be one currently empanneled. In general, the waiting period may be from 3 weeks to 2 or 3 months. Depending, of course, on the nature of the case, quick settlement seems to be obtained in about 40 percent of the cases reaching the judgment board.

requirements of natural justice or of the public interest. In practice, of course, this principle is tempered by the fact that labor court judges are not trained jurists, by the greater emphasis placed by the parties on the facts rather than on the law (especially if they are not assisted or represented by counsel), and by the general context of labor-management relations. Labor court judges may be inclined to apply the law less strictly than professional judges; but these are only tendencies that should not be reflected in the final decision, which could then be reversed by the court of appeals or, more certainly, be quashed by the *Cour de Cassation* because it does not conform to the law.

The remedies available to the labor courts, again, are those available to any court in France. For example, if a party does not execute a contract the court may only grant damages to that party; it cannot demand any kind of specific performance from the other party. ARTICLE 1142 of the French Civil Code, stating that "any obligation to act or refrain from acting can be remedied only by damages," must be observed by all courts, including the labor courts. French law is firm on this point, and the result is that the labor court is not allowed to order the reinstatement of a discharged worker. It makes no practical difference whether the dismissal of a worker proves to be unlawful because it was malicious or arbitrary and, consequently, not based on just cause, or whether it is null and void because it involved a union representative, a shop steward, or a member of the works committee and violates the statutory provisions that grant special protection to these categories of employees.[29] In all of these cases the labor court cannot order reinstatement, but can only award damages measured by the loss actually

---

[29] Of course, the solution is theoretically different in these two cases. If the dismissal is considered to be without just cause, as it can be for any ordinary employee, it cannot be set aside for that reason only. It must produce its normal effect and the employment relationship is consequently broken. But because it is in itself a breach of contract, the employee has the right to redress. It is on this basis that the judges would have ordered reinstatement if it had been possible under French law, and it is on this basis that they actually award damages to compensate for the prejudice suffered. However, there are cases in which a dismissal is held to be void, especially when it concerns an employee who has a representative function in the enterprise and when that employee is discharged without consent of the works council or the labor inspector. A different situation then results, at least in theory, because the law provides that such a dismissal is ineffective; consequently actual reinstatement ordered by the judge is unnecessary because the contract is still in force and the employment relationship still in existence. Nevertheless, it is impossible to order the specific performance of the contract. If the employer does not, in fact, want to allow the worker to continue to work, he cannot be forced to do so. Thus, the only remedy available to the worker is damages unless he prefers to keep his status, that is, to receive his wages and to retain his representative functions without working for the employer. He cannot

incurred according to the usual standards. While it may be argued that compulsory reinstatement of a worker would be contrary to the personal character inherent in the employment relationship and would interfere with the authority of management in the plant, the lack of this remedy is also one of the main shortcomings of the entire labor court system. There is no doubt that many individual disputes arise out of the termination of a contract of employment by unilateral action of the employer, that is, layoff or dismissal. But the awarding of damages in such situations does not satisfy the worker whose main objective, and the only form of complete redress, is reinstatement.[30] It does not satisfy either the whole collectivity of workers because the threat of damages may not deter an employer from taking similar unlawful actions in the future towards other employees. (However, the law provides criminal sanctions against employers when the unlawful discharge concerns persons with representative functions in the enterprise, for example, union representatives, *délégués du personnel,* etc.)

The result is very clear: employees are often reluctant to take a case to the labor court prior to the termination of their contract of employment. Statistics show that the great majority of cases taken to the labor courts are presented by employees who already have lost their job or who are about to lose it. In addition, fellow employees are often reluctant to appear in court as witnesses.

Thus, the present system does not protect the worker against possible retaliation by his employer if he brings suit or testifies before the labor courts. One means of alleviating this situation would be more actions brought by unions in their own name, but on behalf of their members, in which the workers involved can remain anonymous. Or a worker engaged in litigation could be granted some kind of immunity from dismissal for a certain period of time after he was a plaintiff or witness in an action against his employer. But even that is no effective protection against unlawful discharge—always because the judge cannot order reinstatement.

In sum, the impossibility of reinstatement is the most fundamental gap in the French system of labor law. But while real reform is urgently needed, it would imply a complete transformation of the substan-

---

insist on the right to continue working; he can demand only that the employer discharge his obligations, to the extent that they do not include a personal action or an abstention from action. Such a situation, however, is practically unworkable, and it simply confirms that there is almost no actual difference between dismissal without just cause and void dismissal.

[30] Although the judge has wide discretion with respect to the amount of damages, this may be difficult to evaluate depending on the situation of the labor market and possibilities of reemployment.

tive law, affecting areas of law other than labor law. As long as the *conseils de prud'hommes* are courts, they are bound to apply a body of law—the labor law. And as long as labor law is law, it must conform to the general principles of the legal system of which it is a part and in which it develops. Therefore, it becomes clear that the present system of labor courts cannot give sufficient protection to the workers; it can only protect them in an imperfect and, from a certain point of view, illusory way.

3.

JURISDICTION OF OTHER COURTS IN INDIVIDUAL LABOR DISPUTES

The labor courts do not have sole jurisdiction over individual labor disputes. Such disputes also may be brought before courts more specialized than the labor courts (with jurisdiction limited to a certain kind of labor conflict), or before those less specialized (with jurisdiction primarily over civil or commercial matters). The cases in which other courts have jurisdiction can be arranged according to four fundamental principles affecting the dispute: (1) the substantive jurisdiction of the labor courts does not extend to all kinds of individual labor disputes; (2) it is optional in certain cases; (3) the dispute does not come under the territorial or occupational coverage of an existing labor court; and (4) there are no labor courts at the appellate level.

Individual labor disputes involving seamen, that is, disputes arising from a contract of employment concluded between shipowners and seamen, or between shipmasters and fishermen *(contrat d'engagement maritime)*, are regulated by the Maritime Labor Code and must be brought before the local *juge d'instance*. That judge must follow a special procedure in which a high official of the Maritime Administration acts as conciliator. In addition, a special jurisdiction, the *Conseil des prud'hommes pêcheurs de la Méditerranée* has jurisdiction over individual disputes between shipmasters and fishermen in the provinces of Provence and Languedoc.[1] Individual labor disputes arising under

---

[1] There are several such courts in the south of France. The *conseils* are a vestige of the *Ancien Régime,* and they have no counterpart in the Atlantic provinces. They are similar to ordinary courts in their composition, structure, and operation, but their decisions can be appealed only to the *Directeur de l'Inscription Maritime,* an administrative agency whose decision can be attacked only before the *Conseil d'Etat.*

the provisions of the Penal and Disciplinary Code of the Merchant Marine are brought before the ordinary criminal court *(tribunal correctionnel)* or a special jurisdiction, the Commercial Maritime Court.

Special agencies also have been established for the settlement of labor disputes involving journalists: the *Commission arbitrale des journalistes,* an agency unique to France that determines only the amount of severance pay that must be paid to journalists at the time of dismissal if that amount, normally fixed by statute, must be modified because of special circumstances; and the *Commissions de la carte d'identité des journalistes professionnels,* which verify that journalists meet the requirements to receive professional identity cards. These courts and agencies operate in very limited areas, outside of which the jurisdiction over individual labor disputes belongs to the labor courts.

Although the jurisdiction of the labor courts is compulsory in most cases, it is optional in disputes involving the *cadres.* Under the law a *cadre* may choose between the labor court and another court, at least when he is the plaintiff and irrespective of the amount in dispute.[2] This right of choice is an exception of the general rule that the jurisdiction of the labor courts is exclusive and compulsory in all individual disputes arising out of the application of the individual contract of employment, as soon as that jurisdiction has been extended to a certain area and to specific occupations.[3] Experience shows that most *cadres* actually avoid bringing their cases before the *conseils de prud'hommes.*

---

[2] Although the labor courts are divided into different sections for manual and white-collar workers, the *cadres*—upper level supervisory, technical, or managerial employees — are not assigned a special place. As an occupational group the *cadres* are not satisfactorily represented in the composition of the *conseils de prud'hommes;* therefore, they enjoy special status. Although they are put into the same class as the ordinary white-collar workers and are subject to the jurisdiction of the Commercial Sections of the labor courts, they are not obliged to bring their disputes before these jurisdictions if they feel that their interests will not receive proper consideration.

For the same reasons, special treatment might also be granted to the foremen and all kinds of supervisory personnel, even to those at the lower levels. They too may be afraid of improper representation by manual or white-collar workers with whom they are thrown together in the Industrial or Commercial Section of the labor court. However, their particular situation is not recognized from that point of view and the possibility of an option, which is given to the *cadres,* is not available to them.

[3] Today this is the only case in which an option is given to one of the parties. Until 1956 an option of the same type was given to all white-collar employees in all cases in which the amount in dispute exceeded a specified minimum. But this option was a vestige of the time before 1907, when there was no Commercial Section in the labor courts. Disputes involving white-collar workers were then brought before other jurisdictions (civil or commercial courts). After the establishment of Commercial Sections from 1907 on, the plaintiff (whether employer or

According to the law, they must then take their disputes to the court that normally would have jurisdiction in the absence of a labor court, the commercial court or the *tribunal d'instance*. The latter, a civil court composed of a single professional judge, then follows the same rules of procedure that normally apply to the labor court.[4] With respect to the *cadres'* right of option, the law expressly provides that it must be exercised after the dispute already has arisen, not in advance. It cannot be renounced by accepting the compulsory jurisdiction of any of the courts open to their choice.

Another important restriction of the authority of the *conseils de prud'hommes* occurs when a dispute does not come under the territorial or occupational coverage of an existing labor court. It must then be brought before a *tribunal d'instance* or, if the employer-defendant has a commercial profession, the plaintiff may go before a commercial court.

All these gaps in the present system of labor courts in France are further aggravated by the absence of appellate labor courts and by the fact that all appeals must be brought before ordinary civil courts (courts of appeals and *Cour de Cassation*). According to credible estimates, an average of between 8 and 10 percent of all disputes first brought before a labor court are ultimately decided by civil courts composed of professional judges. This is significant because the cases decided by these higher courts are the more important ones with respect to the amount in dispute, and the decisions have more weight as precedents than those rendered by the lower courts. It is therefore the *Cour de Cassation* that plays the decisive role in the formation of case law for labor matters.

---

employee) could choose between the labor court and the civil or commercial court in all cases concerning white-collar workers and involving more than a specified minimum amount. This option was naturally a great advantage for the employers, who were tempted to bring their cases before the commercial courts exclusively composed of other employers and therefore very sympathetic to the employer's point of view. The commercial court was thus a kind of substitute for the labor court in all cases concerning salaried employees. It is precisely this possibility of abuse that led to the indispensable reform; the Law of December 18, 1956 has restricted the option to cases involving the *cadres,* and when the *cadre* himself is the plaintiff, but without any restriction as to the amount of the claim.

[4] The question of whether jurisdiction should be given to the *tribunal de grande instance,* the ordinary civil court in cases involving the right of option, has not been finally settled. Before 1956, when problems arose involving the right of option which was then available to all white-collar workers, the question usually was answered in the negative. But the opposite result was achieved by a decision of the *Cour de Cassation,* which ruled in 1956 that the *tribunal d'instance* (then called justice of the peace) cannot have exclusive jurisdiction if the amount in dispute is higher than the maximum amount in the cases usually assigned to the tribunal (now F.5,000). (C. Cass., Ch. Soc., May 4, 1956, J.C.P. 1956, 9478.)

In sum, though the labor court may characterize the French system of settling labor disputes, the system cannot be reduced to it because the *conseil de prud'hommes* is not the only forum for these disputes. Furthermore, special and exclusive machinery has been established for collective labor disputes, which will be discussed in chapter 4 of this study.

4.

PROCEDURES FOR THE SETTLEMENT OF COLLECTIVE LABOR DISPUTES

Labor disputes became collective in nature when labor relations began to involve groups of employers and employees. Several legislative reforms have contributed to the growth of collective labor relations and, as a result, of collective labor disputes.[1] Because such disputes may lawfully give rise to economic actions, e.g., strikes and lockouts, the legislature has attempted to provide special machinery for their peaceful settlement.

THE CONCEPT OF COLLECTIVE LABOR DISPUTES

The concept of collective labor disputes is not as broadly defined in France as it is in other countries, in which most of the rights established under collective agreements and exercised through labor unions have a collective nature. The continuing importance of the individual contract of employment accounts for the large number of individual disputes in the French legal system; however, there are many collective disputes that fall into various categories.

Some of these disputes are exclusively collective because they involve the rights of a collectivity rather than those of one or several individuals. In this category fall disputes over the interpretation or application of a statutory provision or clause of a collective agreement that covers a group of workers and is not subject to individual application. Examples are disputes involving rules of labor–management relations or

---

[1] For example, recognition of the right to form coalitions (1864), the right to form and constitute unions (1884), and the right to enter into collective agreements (1919 and 1936).

regulations concerning the status of labor unions, and disputes involving the so-called contractual clauses of collective agreements, that is, clauses relating to the conclusion, revision, or renewal of these agreements. In the same category also fall disputes over the validity or abstract interpretation only of general rules that affect a collectivity and hence a collective interest, even if these rules otherwise are individually applicable, for example, terms of collective agreements determining wages and other conditions of work.

However, some collective disputes concerning the interpretation of a general rule may simultaneously have an individual aspect to the extent that they arise out of the alleged violation of one or several individual rights. The real object of the dispute then is not the abstract interpretation of the rule, but its application to a concrete situation by a specific measure. This category includes the large majority of labor disputes, for example, disputes arising out of individual measures taken against employees who perform official representation functions, enjoying special protection provided by statute and possibly extended under collective agreements. They obviously affect simultaneously the individuals directly concerned and the collectivity represented by these persons, and they are therefore the most typical two-sided conflicts having an individual as well as a collective aspect.

In such cases the parties have a kind of option between settlement procedures, that is, the individual worker who has personally suffered a violation of his rights may bring action in a labor court while the collectivity may choose other types of settlement procedures. In fact, the nature of the conflict eventually depends on the party who brings action, the worker or the group, and only in the latter case will the conflict definitely be considered collective.[2] But even the active intervention of a group does not necessarily render the conflict collective, because several actions brought simultaneously though grouped together by several employees may be treated as individual actions. Therefore, the group really must intend to handle the dispute as a collective one, and it must try to obtain satisfaction for a collective interest. In the final analysis, then, it is the intention of the parties that is decisive in this matter.[3]

---

[2] The group may be structured and organized; for example, a union may act without a mandate from the work force of an enterprise and in the absence of a specific claim presented by them. Or several unions together may bring an action. Or the group may be unorganized consisting, for example, of employees of a shop or of a certain occupational category, such as the *cadres*.

[3] It should be remembered that all of these criteria are, in fact, cumulative; each would be insufficient in itself to characterize a conflict as collective. For example,

SETTLEMENT OF LABOR DISPUTES IN FRANCE

In spite of their different aspects, however, all of these collective labor disputes—at least those covered in this study— have some basic features in common that affect the procedures established for their settlement: they are conflicts over rights, and they are collective in nature.

Jurisdiction over these disputes cannot be conferred upon the *conseils de prud'hommes* because all rules concerning the organization and operation of the *conseils* are designed to settle individual disputes. If a court were to be specialized in resolving collective labor disputes, it would have to include among its members union representatives; but there is no such court in France.[4] Therefore, the ordinary civil courts normally have jurisdiction according to the principle that they are competent in all cases for which special jurisdictions have not been established by statute.[5] The disputes are brought before the *tribunal de grande instance,* a court composed of three professional judges, and appeals are lodged in the court of appeal and the *Cour de Cassation.* The jurisdiction of the ordinary civil courts is compulsory; it is imposed by public policy and cannot be ignored by special contractual clauses. Only in exceptional situations and for very special problems may another court have jurisdiction.[6]

---

that the collectivity is a party to the dispute does not render this dispute collective if the object of the conflict has no collective aspect, e.g., if an employee has been dismissed for purely personal reasons (such as a technical fault in the performance of his job); the conflict then remains individual. This is true even if the union decides to support the claim of the employee by calling a strike, for even then there is no collective interest involved. See e.g., Superior Court of Arbitration, June 15, 1938, *Dalloz* 1938, *Somm.* 20. There is, however, some doubt on this last point in case law. Some court decisions have admitted that as soon as there is a strike or a threat of strike, that is, a collective action, the dispute becomes collective because the final objective of all the machinery established for the settlement of collective labor disputes is precisely to serve as a substitute for the strike. The question, in fact, has not been definitely resolved.

[4] However, labor unions sometimes demand that the *conseils de prud'hommes* be given jurisdiction on collective as well as individual labor disputes. The demand was made as early as 1906 and has been repeated several times more recently, but the legislature has never acceded to it. It is even admitted that the exclusion of collective disputes from the jurisdiction of the labor courts is imposed by public policy; all terms to the contrary that could be included in a collective agreement, for example, would be unlawful and void.

[5] See *Tribunal civil de Nantes,* September 27, 1955, I.C.E. *(Informateur du chef d'entreprise),* 1955, p. 1020.

[6] This is the case, for example, for all disputes which may concern the regularity of elections of personnel representatives in the enterprise. Some special statutory provisions then give jurisdiction to the *tribunal d'instance,* even though it is a collective conflict involving the internal organization of the enterprise and the rules governing these elections have been laid down by a collective agreement. On the other hand, it is admitted that the *tribunal de grande instance,* which is the ordinary civil court, retains its normal and exclusive jurisdiction to decide on the

XAVIER BLANC-JOUVAN

A group bringing action in court, whether acting as plaintiff or defendant, must qualify as a legal person to be able to appear in its own name; that is, it must be an association of employers or a labor union. Second, it must be entitled to defend the collective interest involved in the dispute. The law provides that any employers' association or labor union can defend its own rights as granted by the legislature (for example, the union can act in order to prevent the employer from taking antiunion discriminatory action or from hampering the normal activity of the labor union within the enterprise) or bring all judicial actions involving the validity, interpretation, or execution of collective agreements. It also provides that the employers' association or the labor union can defend the interest of a broader collectivity, including all those having the same occupation, provided it is constituted as a *syndicat*.[7] This type of action, *action syndicale*, is very important from a theoretical as well as a practical point of view: in addition to its members, the *syndicat* may represent in judicial proceedings all employers or all workers of a certain industry whenever their collective interest has been violated at the local, regional, or national level.[8] The case law contains many examples of such actions seeking damages, brought by unions for violations of statutory provisions or terms of collective agreements involving working conditions, the operation of the works committee, holiday and vacation pay, health and safety measures, etc.[9]

Thus many collective labor disputes can be brought before the ordinary civil courts whose jurisdiction cannot be waived in advance by

---

validity of, or to interpret, a collective agreement, even if that agreement has been extended to the whole industry by a decree of the Minister of Labor, that is, by an administrative regulation; such extension by decree is not enough to give jurisdiction to the administrative courts in lieu of the ordinary courts.

[7] All *syndicats*, employers' associations and labor unions, have the express right, granted by case law in 1913 (C. Cass., Chambres Réunies, April 5, 1913, *Sirey* 1920, I, 49), and by statute in 1920, to bring actions in court to defend the interest of the collectivity from which they recruit their members.

[8] *Action syndicale* is normally brought before the ordinary civil courts unless it is accessory to another action that must be brought before a special court, for example, a criminal or an administrative court. Also, if a union intervenes in the individual action of a person whose individual rights have been violated directly by a measure taken by an employer, it will do so before the court that has jurisdiction over the main action, that is, one of the courts having jurisdiction over individual labor disputes: the labor court, *tribunal d'instance*, commercial court, etc.

[9] There is also a very particular case in which the union is given the right to defend before the courts the interests of a certain category of workers: under ART. 33 p, Book I, of the Labor Code, the union may institute judicial proceedings in order to enforce the statutory rules concerning the wages of the homeworkers belonging to the same branch of activity as the union, even if none of them is a member of the union.

the parties to a collective agreement. But there are also cases that cannot be brought before a court, or the parties to the dispute may prefer to use other procedures of settlement that have been especially created for collective conflicts.[10]

Because the disputes considered here are *collective* conflicts, settlement procedures must be available that can really prevent recourse to economic actions.[11] No fundamental distinction is made in that respect between disputes over rights and those over interests, which largely accounts for the absence of a true criterion of demarcation. It is often said that a careful distinction cannot be made because, first, problems of rights and of interests are often intertwined and, second, they give rise to similar questions. Of course, there may be some minor differences in the settlement procedures established for the two types of conflicts, but they are not very significant. It is considered more important to accommodate the *collective* aspect of the disputes, which requires (1) that they do not take place before the courts[12] but before agencies that do not employ the ordinary rules of judicial procedure, and (2) that the groups that normally are parties to collective labor relations, especially the unions, play an important role in the proceedings. The procedures are established by statute but may be amended by terms of collective agreements; they usually imply the intervention of public authorities; they must always safeguard the principle of voluntary compliance of the parties with the terms of settlement, but they must also contain an element of compulsion and of external pressure in order to have a chance of ending the dispute.[13]

The present system is closely linked to the growth of collective labor relations and the development of collective agreements, because effective settlement procedures obviously are a necessary precondition for

---

[10] It should be noted that these two types of machinery are not mutually exclusive, and the parties often decide to bring their dispute to the court after they have unsuccessfully tried to settle it through the special machineries of conciliation or mediation.

[11] Such economic actions are, however, lawful. The right to strike is especially well protected. For example, the inclusion of no-strike provisions in collective agreements can be considered void, even for a limited period of time, and only minor restrictions to the right to strike can be admitted.

[12] We may, of course, reserve the possibility of ultimate control over the conformity of the decisions finally reached with the law—control that is normally committed to a court. See *infra* the role played in that respect by the Superior Court of Arbitration.

[13] The third party, who is usually present in the proceedings, either may confine himself to assist the parties in negotiations or work out the terms of settlement with their consent.

the efficient execution of these agreements.[14] Three different procedures are now available that may be used successively or independently, but none of them is really satisfactory.[15] They may be used in all types of collective labor disputes over rights, irrespective of the size of the conflict (involving, for example, a section of an enterprise or a whole branch of activity). In addition, they are available for industry, commerce, and agriculture,[16] as well as for certain public enterprises such as banks, insurance companies, etc., whose personnel is subject to the ordinary labor law. In the following analysis of the procedures of conciliation, mediation, and arbitration, the problem of voluntary compliance of the parties will be approached from three points of view: compulsory use of the procedures, role of the parties in working out the terms of a settlement, and the binding force of such settlement. Finally, to appreciate the effectiveness of the entire machinery, the procedures must be evaluated together because each in some way acts upon the others and its effectiveness can only be examined in the light of their existence and effectiveness. Therefore, a more general view of this area of labor law will be possible only at the end of this study.

---

[14] The first statutory procedures for conciliation and arbitration were established in 1892. After World War I, a trend developed to create voluntary procedures, but it declined in the early 1920s. A new and important step was taken in 1936, following a wave of sit-down strikes in all industries, political gains of left-wing parties, and the formation of the *Front Populaire* in which the most radical political parties were united with the labor unions. Several important statutes were then enacted to promote collective agreements and procedures for the peaceful settlement of collective labor disputes. The Law of December 31, 1936, amended by the Law of March 4, 1938, provided for a completely new system of settlement procedures, under which collective disputes were distinguished from individual ones, labor unions were given a more active role, and more emphasis was placed on the non-judicial aspects of settlement. This development was interrupted by World War II, when all legislation concerning collective labor disputes and collective agreements was suspended by a Decree of September 1, 1939. The Law of February 11, 1950, which is still in force, marked the return to normalcy. It contains new regulations for collective agreements and for the peaceful settlement of collective disputes. The two procedures of conciliation and arbitration were restored, but without the compulsory elements contained in the Law of 1936. A new procedure, patterned after the American system of mediation, was introduced by the Decree of May 5, 1955, as amended in 1957, but after initial success it practically fell into disuse.

[15] Full regulations are contained in the second title of the Law of February 11, 1950, as amended by the Law of July 26, 1957 and completed by a Decree of July 18, 1958; they have not been incorporated into the Labor Code because the legislature feels that the procedures need further improvements.

[16] There is, however, a certain particularism in the regulation concerning two branches of activity—agriculture and the merchant marine. We shall briefly mention in this study the special features concerning agricultural enterprises.

SETTLEMENT OF LABOR DISPUTES IN FRANCE

CONCILIATION

Conciliation is the simplest and easiest procedure that may be conceived for the settlement of labor disputes. Its significance for individual disputes already has been noted, but it is no less important for the settlement of collective conflicts for which it also exists in various forms. This study is confined to official conciliation, which implies that a procedure was created and organized in advance according to certain formalities.[17]

Present legislation provides for "contractual" and for "statutory" conciliation procedures, depending on whether the details of the machinery are determined by private contract or by the statute itself. Contractual procedures may be established by employers and labor unions through collective bargaining, becoming part of their collective agreement, in agreements concluded at all levels, particularly at the company level *(accords d'entreprise),* or by parties to a collective dispute in *ad hoc* agreements after a conflict already has arisen.[18] The law even expressly provides that all collective agreements must establish such a procedure for collective disputes arising out of their application or

---

[17] An optional conciliation procedure in which the local judge *(juge de paix)* acted as conciliator was first established by the Law of December 27, 1892. By the Law of December 31, 1936, that procedure of conciliation was considerably improved; it was made compulsory and had to precede any strike or lockout. It was suspended in 1939 because of the war, but was reestablished in 1950 and amended by legislation in 1957 and 1958.

[18] The Law of July 26, 1957 also provides that such contractual procedures of conciliation can be established in public enterprises not covered by the Law of February 11, 1950, whose work forces are subject to a status enacted by the legislature or by the government. No statutory procedure is available in these enterprises, and the Law of 1950 had not even provided for the establishment of a contractual procedure. But the Law of 1957 has officially stipulated that possibility in an attempt progressively to introduce in these enterprises a conciliation system adapted to their particular situation. The procedure must be determined by agreement between the management, the labor unions most representative of the work force, and the Minister who has jurisdiction over the enterprise; the conciliation board to be established will also have this tripartite composition, while being necessarily placed under the chairmanship of the Minister. This is particularly important because the final agreement resulting from the procedure must be formally accepted, not only by those who are directly parties to the dispute, but by the members of the conciliation board, including the Minister, as well. This obviously changes the nature of the conciliation process because it removes its bipartite character. In fact, few agreements of this kind have actually been signed and there have been still fewer successful conciliations, especially in conflicts over rights (successful conciliation is more frequent in conflicts over interests, notably those turning on problems of wages). Therefore, the problem of peaceful settlement of such conflicts in public enterprises remains unresolved. It is sometimes suggested that conciliation could be more effective in this area if it were made compulsory by law, in which case the conciliation board would be established by the legislature itself.

interpretation (conflicts over rights), or out of their revision of renewal (conflicts over interests).[19] Details of the procedure are determined in the agreement by which it is established, and there is no statutory limitation on the freedom of the parties. Thus, there are great variations in the composition of conciliation boards, their powers, steps in the proceedings, sanctions, and so forth, but the majority of workers are covered by agreements that contain a conciliation clause.

A statutory procedure was established by law and must be used in all cases in which a contractual procedure is not available, or when there is "any reason" why an existing contractual procedure has not been used.[20] It is sometimes used in addition to the contractual procedure, for example, after conciliation commissions provided for by contract have failed to resolve a dispute. The parties may then submit their dispute to commissions established by statute, which serve in an appellate capacity providing a second step of conciliation.

1. Recourse to conciliation is compulsory to the extent that the parties are required by law to meet and discuss their grievances when a conflict first arises. The law provides that all collective conflicts, particularly those over rights, must "obligatorily and immediately" be submitted to a conciliation procedure.[21] However, the real effect of this obligation depends on its sanctions, and these are different in the two procedures.

The contractual procedure can be made compulsory under a collective agreement, which can provide sanctions in case of noncompliance. Although the parties cannot be prohibited from bringing their dispute immediately before a court, the agreement can provide sanctions against economic action by making unlawful all strikes and lockouts before initiation of the procedure, during its course, or during a certain period after it was begun. The courts usually enforce such agreements, at least when they do not constitute an excessive restriction of the constitutional right to strike, but they are careful in their interpretation of them. The conditions under which the procedure must be initiated are also determined by the agreement. Once the conciliation commission is convened, refusal to appear by any person or group bound by

---

[19] This obligation is largely theoretical, however, because it is accompanied by sanctions only when collective agreements are subject to extension by a decree of the Minister of Labor (ART. 31 g, Book I of the Labor Code).

[20] ART. 7, ¶1 of the Law of February 11, 1950.

[21] This obligation is removed only if the parties agree to resort immediately to one of the other procedures of peaceful settlement—procedures that are supposed to be more effective than conciliation because the parties leave it to a third party to propose (mediation) or to impose (arbitration) a solution to their dispute. But this happens only in exceptional cases.

the agreement constitutes breach of contract, involving not only the possibility of damages but also the fact that any strike or lockout initiated by that party may become unlawful from that moment on. If both parties agree not to use the contractual procedure, they must use the statutory procedure.

The statutory conciliation procedure is compulsory under the law itself. A dispute must be brought "within one month" before a conciliation commission, but the law does not set forth how this period is to be determined and it does not provide sanctions in case of noncompliance. Here again, the parties cannot be prohibited from bringing their dispute immediately before a court, nor are strikes or lockouts necessarily unlawful if the procedure was not used. As a result, it is unrealistic to call the statutory conciliation procedure compulsory.[22] The case law contains many examples of strikes that were considered lawful, even though they were not preceded by attempts at conciliation[23] or were initiated during a conciliation procedure. The courts are more strict in cases of lockouts; these usually are considered unlawful if all attempts at peaceful settlement of the conflict have not been exhausted.[24]

The change in the law and in the practice of compulsory conciliation in recent years has been significant. Between 1936 and 1939, conciliation was practiced as a matter of habit, and the fear of compulsory arbitration encouraged the parties to seek agreement through conciliation. Since 1950, however, arbitration is only optional in any case; therefore, successful conciliation is no longer required to avoid it. The parties know that, in any case, they will retain complete freedom of action, and there is no incentive for them to attempt conciliation prior to a show of force through strikes or other forms of economic action. Under these circumstances, conciliation is no longer a means to stop a strike but becomes part of a kind of collective bargaining under the influence of the relative power of the parties during the strike, without any consideration for the application of the law. Obviously, then, such a procedure is better adapted to resolving conflicts over interests than

---

[22] In 1936 the law expressly provided that conciliation should be "preliminary to any strike or lockout," but strikes or lockouts initiated before conciliation were not always declared unlawful. In 1950 and in 1957, the legislature refused to provide that conciliation should be preliminary to an economic action. It even refused to admit that the conciliation procedure, once initiated, could effectively suspend a strike already begun, for the reason that the right to strike has been officially recognized under the constitution of October 27, 1946 (to which the present constitution of October 4, 1958, expressly refers).

[23] C. Cass., Ch. Soc., May 24, 1955, D. 1955, 567; Oct. 23, 1963, D. 1964, 286.
[24] C. Cass., Ch. Soc., Oct. 30, 1952, D. 1953, 132.

conflicts over rights, though it remains available for both kinds because of the confusion in French law between them.

Public authorities, which are naturally interested in the settlement of collective labor disputes, can play a significant role in the recourse to statutory conciliation. This is why the parties are under the obligation to notify the *Préfet* of the Department that a dispute exists, and the *Préfet* himself can initiate informal preconciliation sessions with the labor inspector.[25] If preconciliation fails, the *Préfet*, the Minister of Labor, the labor inspector, or the parties themselves can bring the dispute before a conciliation commission. Refusal to appear before the commission is considered refusal to reach agreement and failure of the procedure is recorded in a *procès-verbal de non-conciliation,* but since 1957 criminal sanctions may also be pronounced against a party refusing to appear after having been served successively with two summonses.

The statutory conciliation procedure is rarely used in practice today—according to some estimates in only 5 percent of the cases in which it is theoretically available. Between December 2, 1950 and June 15, 1967, only 1,804 collective labor disputes (those over rights and those over interests, because the statistics do not distinguish between them) were brought before official conciliation commissions, an average of slightly more than 105 disputes per year that is still declining.[26] Thus it may be concluded that compulsory recourse to conciliation, the only aspect of the procedure that contains an element of obligation, exists more in theory than it does in reality; this is all the more important as there is no coercion in subsequent steps of the procedure.

2. When conciliation leads to a settlement, the terms of the settlement are worked out by the parties themselves. The conciliation procedure rests on the fundamental principle that the parties themselves decide to settle their dispute; they are free to propose any solution and they are never bound to accept suggestions from a third party. In that sense conciliation really is organized negotiation, and a settlement by conciliation undoubtedly resembles a contract more than a judgment.

In the statutory procedure the parties must appear in person at the conciliation session, whereas in the contractual procedure that matter is settled by the agreement. They may be represented by an agent only if personal appearance is not possible because of a serious event and

---

[25] ART. 8, Law of July 26, 1957.
[26] Figures supplied by the *Ministère des Affaires Sociales* and quoted in "Liaisons sociales," Supplement No. 3244, p. 86.

if that agent has full powers to negotiate and conclude an agreement in his name, or if a party is a corporate body, that is, a company, an employers' association, or a union. The courts are strict concerning the powers of such agents, insisting that instructions must be clear and complete and must define all points that may be discussed, as well as commitments that may be made in the name of the respective organization.[27]

The organization of the procedure is also different, depending on its definition by contract or by statute. Contractual procedures usually are organized in advance in collective agreements, which may provide for one or several permanent conciliation commissions at various levels—enterprise, local, regional, or national. Thus, a dispute may be considered at the level at which it has arisen, and a kind of appeals procedure is provided through the hierarchy of conciliation commissions.[28] As a general rule, the composition of the conciliation commissions is bipartite rather than tripartite, but a neutral third party may be called to serve as expert on an *ad hoc* basis or as president of the commission if so specified in the collective agreement. Members are representatives of the employers or employers' associations and of the labor unions that were parties to the agreement. At the company level, employee representatives *(délégués du personnel* or members of the works committee) and union representatives (chosen from among the various unions having members in the enterprise) may also be members of the commissions. Thus, these members are often the parties to the dispute or at least their representatives; they then have to settle a dispute that has arisen between themselves and act as negotiators rather than as conciliators.

---

[27] Under the Decree of July 18, 1958, ART. 10, the agent must be a member of the same organization as the party that he represents, or he must hold a permanent position in the enterprise in which the conflict arose. Parties who appear in person before the commission may also be assisted by a member of the union or association to which they belong.

[28] If conciliation fails at a certain level, the parties may have an obligation to bring their dispute before the commission at a higher level, or the commission itself must refer the case to a higher commission under the terms of the collective agreement. The possibility of appeal may also be available if several commissions were established at various levels under different collective agreements that are simultaneously applicable. The entire system thus provides several steps of conciliation, thereby increasing the chances of a peaceful settlement of the dispute. It was already noted that the same result can also be obtained if the parties, after failure of conciliation before the contractual commissions, bring their case before one of the statutory commissions. This is usually done at the initiative of the parties themselves, who may decide by an *ad hoc* agreement on this additional opportunity (this is not uncommon in practice), but it could conceivably also be imposed by the collective agreement itself.

Contractual procedures may also be organized by an *ad hoc* agreement, that is, by a contract concluded when a particular dispute already has arisen. Temporary commissions established at the level at which the dispute has arisen may include the parties to the dispute or other persons on a bipartite or tripartite basis.

The procedure itself is primarily concerned with a quick settlement of the dispute; parties often meet within three or five days after it was initiated, and they may be heard separately before appearing together before the commission.

Although contractual conciliation commissions are usually available for all types of collective conflicts, a different commission and a distinct procedure may be prescribed in collective agreements for disputes arising out of the interpretation of terms of the agreements. There are then two commissions: a conciliation commission, and an interpretation commission that exists at the level at which the collective agreement was concluded. Members of the latter commission are usually chosen from among persons who took part in the negotiation of the agreement, making conciliation a kind of continued collective negotiation during the life of the agreement. The disputes are considered in the abstract and the parties involved are not summoned to the sessions. Interpretation commissions play an important role in conciliation of collective labor disputes over rights, and sometimes even in individual disputes before the plaintiff decides to bring action in a labor court. However, their role is not as important as it could be because the parties often prefer other means of settlement.[29] There are also job classification commissions, which attempt to resolve disputes arising from the classification of jobs that have not been determined in the agreement.

As mentioned before, the statutory conciliation procedure becomes applicable when contractual procedures were not established in collective agreements or on an *ad hoc* basis or when such procedures were not used. The conciliation commissions before which the statutory procedure takes place exist at the national and regional level, but there may also be departmental sections within the regional commissions. The national commission sits in Paris and has a kind of general jurisdiction over all types of collective labor disputes.[30] The commissions are

---

[29] If action is brought in court, the court is then required to decide the dispute. But it often postpones adjudication if it finds it necessary or even useful to obtain the opinion of the commission concerning the interpretation of the collective agreement. However, there is no way to force the court to do so.

[30] Commissions at the various levels are needed only because there should be a commission corresponding to the size of each dispute; they do not provide an appeals procedure, as is the case under contractual conciliation.

tripartite, including employer and employee representatives and officials of administrative authorities.[31] The presence of these officials has been criticized as too much predominance of the government, but it has definite advantages; it renders the commissions more competent and authoritative, and experience shows that it is often the government representative who plays the decisive role in conciliation.

3. The parties to a conciliation procedure are under no obligation to settle their dispute, a fact that considerably limits the chances of a peaceful resolution of the conflict; they merely have to go through all the steps of the procedure. If they settle their dispute, it will be recorded in a *procès-verbal de conciliation*,[32] which is enforceable like a collective agreement. If it turns on the interpretation of the terms of a preexisting collective agreement or on problems of wages and other conditions of work, the law expressly provides (ARTICLE 29 of the Law of 1950) that it has the same coverage as such collective agreement and, if violated, gives rise to the same sanctions. It also can be extended by decision of the Minister of Labor, such extension being mandatory if the dispute involves a branch of activity or a geographical area in which a preexisting collective agreement was so extended and if it is requested by all organizations that were parties to that collective agreement. When the conciliation agreement is con-

---

[31] The chairman of the commission is always one of these officials. The national commission is chaired by the Minister of Labor or his representative, and the regional commission by the regional labor inspector. Each chairman is assisted by representatives of other public agencies, but the number of government representatives cannot be more than three, that is, not more than the number of representatives of each party, employer and employee. Special regulations apply to the composition of the commissions established for the conciliation of collective labor disputes in agriculture. The national commission is then chaired by the Minister of Agriculture or his representative and includes as members the Minister of Labor or his deputy and a representative of the Minister of National Economy; the regional commission is chaired by the regional inspector of social legislation in agriculture and includes as members the regional labor inspector and a high official of the Administration of Agriculture. The composition of the departmental section is patterned after the regional commission of which it is a part.

[32] This document must be submitted to the Minister of Labor and to the *Préfet* of the *Département*. It becomes effective from the date shown or from the date of initiation of the conciliation procedure, provided that one copy is deposited within 24 hours with the secretariat of the labor court (or with the *tribunal d'instance* if there is no such court in the area with jurisdiction over the type of activity involved in the dispute). It is, however, admitted that even when it is not deposited at the secretariat of the court, the agreement is enforceable between the parties when it itself establishes the day on which it will become effective (C. Cass., Ch. Soc., Oct. 3, 1962, D. 1962, 630).

It must be noted that some contractual procedures expressly provide that the agreement becomes enforceable after it was accepted by referendum by the majority of the workers involved. But this is a rather exceptional situation.

cluded by members of the interpretation commission and involves the interpretation of a preexisting collective agreement, their decision, if unanimous, immediately becomes a part of the collective agreement, actually forming a supplement that is binding on all parties involved in the dispute as well as on all groups and individuals who will be covered by the collective agreement in the future.

However, if a dispute is only partially settled the points of disagreement are recorded in the *procès-verbal*, and if conciliation fails a *procès-verbal de non-conciliation* is drawn up that must be sent to the Minister of Labor and to the *Préfet* of the Department.

Failure of conciliation occurs frequently, partly because the law does not contain incentives to reach agreement (e.g., the threat of compulsory arbitration that existed from 1936 to 1939), and partly because the parties have too much freedom to use conciliation or, for that matter, any other procedure to settle their dispute. While statistics on contractual conciliation procedures are not available, those on statutory commissions indicate the limited success of the conciliation procedures established by law. The data in table 1 cover the period of December 2, 1950 to June 15, 1967.

TABLE 1

Statutory Conciliation Commissions	Number of Conflicts Examined	Conciliations			Lack of Jurisdiction of the Commission
		Totally Successful	Partly Successful	Unsuccessful	
National Commission	47	20	3	22	2
Regional Commissions	531	125	32	372	2
Departmental Sections	1226	282	85	858	1
Total	1804	427	120	1252	5

SOURCE: Figures supplied by the *Ministère des Affaires Sociales* and quoted in "Liaisons sociales," Supplement No. 3244, p. 86.

It can be concluded from these figures that although the rate of successful conciliations is higher at the national level than it is at the regional or departmental level, it remains on the whole rather low. Not more than 25 percent of all cases submitted were resolved—not more than 30 percent if partly successful conciliations are included.

MEDIATION

Mediation as a procedure for the settlement of collective labor disputes was adopted much later than conciliation.[33] It was created in

1955 as a kind of experiment with uncertain outcome — there is no similar legislation in the history of France—but first results of its practical application were encouraging and the procedure was often successful, at least in large conflicts. The system was improved in 1957 through extensive legislative reform, but the procedure lost much of its effectiveness shortly thereafter and is now rarely used for the solution of labor conflicts, especially of disputes over rights. However, the laws affecting mediation have not been repealed and a resurgence may occur at any time, especially in view of the wide application that was provided by the legislature in 1957. Notably, the procedure is now available for all types of collective labor disputes, and it can be used for such disputes irrespective of the level at which they have arisen (before 1957, conflicts involving a single enterprise could not be brought to mediation unless the Minister of Labor himself instituted the procedure on the ground that the dispute involved a public interest).

Like all other settlement procedures in France, mediation contains both elements of voluntary compliance and of external pressure. The voluntary element is present at all steps of the procedure because successful mediation eventually depends on the good will of the parties themselves, but external pressure is also necessary in order to make mediation really work.

1. The voluntary element is certainly predominant at the first step of the procedure, although there is, even then, an element of compulsion.

---

[33] The idea of mediation developed after World War II and was applied in practice in 1950, when a procedure of recommendation very similar to mediation was introduced in the former French colonies by the *Code du travail des territoires d'outre-mer*. However, it was never applied and was replaced in 1955 by a procedure of expertise largely based on the same principles. In France itself a mediation system was actually used, despite the absence of legislation, beginning in May 1948 in connection with a conflict involving some nationalized enterprises, and continuing later on in other industries, especially in the merchant marine. A strong movement developed for the official establishment of a mediation system by legislation, which was considerably influenced by the American experience: the mediation procedure of the federal and state conciliation services, and particularly the fact-finding boards appointed to settle important labor conflicts. Between 1951 and 1955, several bills were introduced but received no serious consideration in Parliament. Finally an official mediation procedure was created by the Decree of May 5, 1955 as amended by the Decree of June 11, 1955, which had, however, limited application with respect to the type of conflict (as to the industries covered, its range was similar to that of other conciliation and arbitration procedures as defined by the Law of February 11, 1950). The procedure was further improved by the Law of July 26, 1957 and the Decree of July 18, 1958, modifying previous legislation on mediation and integrating it into the Law of February 11, 1950, as amended—the basic statute for procedures for the peaceful settlement of collective labor disputes.

There is no problem when the parties agree to bring their dispute before a mediator; they can even do so without first going through the conciliation procedure. But it is more frequent that only one of the two parties wants to go to mediation after conciliation has failed to resolve the dispute. The law provides that that party can submit a written petition of the unresolved points to the president of the conciliation commission (the Minister of Labor if the conflict arose at the national level, or an official of the labor administration if it arose at the regional, local or company level), who then initiates the procedure. In such cases mediation remains voluntary for the petitioning party, but it is mandatory for its opponent. In addition, the Minister of Labor[34] or the president of the conciliation commission is empowered under the law to initiate mediation, even though neither party petitioned to use the procedure.[35] It is then compulsory for both parties, not by law but by virtue of an administrative decision. The parties can object to the procedure only if they must immediately go to arbitration because an arbitration provision is contained in a collective agreement or an arbitration agreement was concluded *ad hoc* in consideration of the dispute at hand.[36] This role given the labor administration authorities proves the importance of public intervention as early as at the first step of the procedure. In fact, public intervention here can be regarded as one of the main features of the French system of mediation, appearing not only at the first but in all steps of the procedure.

2. In mediation the settlement of the conflict is proposed by a third party, the mediator. He may be appointed by the parties to the dispute or by a public official (the Minister of Labor or the president of the conciliation commission, who selects a candidate from lists prepared in advance and published in the *Journal Officiel*).[37] The office of mediator is limited to one person in each dispute who conducts an investigation and prepares a recommendation; there are no panels or commissions of mediators. The mediator can summon the parties as well as witnesses as often as needed. They must appear in person, refusal being subject to fines, and they must furnish the mediator and the

---

[34] In conflicts involving agriculture, the role of the Minister of Labor is naturally assumed by the Minister of Agriculture at all stages of the mediation procedure, even for the designation of the mediator. (See *infra*.)

[35] In 1955 the Minister of Labor even had the exclusive power to initiate mediation when the conflict concerned a single enterprise, in all cases in which he ruled that a public interest was involved. Even the parties could not at that time exercise that same power.

[36] There is no doubt that, on the other hand, the parties will be allowed to conclude an arbitration agreement and to resort to arbitration after failure of mediation.

opposing party with briefs of their respective positions. In fact, a party's refusal to surrender relevant documents is subject to the same sanctions as refusal to appear.[38]

The mediator can suggest a resolution to the dispute informally during the procedure, but he must make a final recommendation when the parties cannot reach agreement. In the latter case, the law makes a fundamental distinction between conflicts over rights and those over interests. In disputes turning on the interpretation or alleged violation of a statutory provision or term of a collective agreement, he may not himself make positive recommendations for a settlement. He can only, and indeed he must, recommend that the parties bring their case either before the court that normally would have jurisdiction or before an arbitrator (ARTICLE 15 of the Law of 1957). In conflicts over interests, on the other hand, the mediator has every power to recommend any solution that he thinks appropriate to end the dispute. Thus, the distinction between the two types of disputes here is clearly drawn. No doubt, the mediator is not denied the power to handle disputes over rights; but he is obliged to disqualify himself from making recommendations for their settlement, and he must to some extent do the same in disputes containing both problems over rights and over interests, in which case he can only recommend a resolution for the latter.

This is, of course, the theory. In practice he has more powers than those provided by the law because the problems may be intertwined and he may play at least an advisory and persuasive role in *all* types of disputes.[39]

---

[37] If the conflict arises at the regional, departmental, or local level, the Minister of Labor can also delegate his power to appoint a mediator to the president of the regional conciliation commission. It may be difficult to find persons qualified to serve as mediators in addition to their regular employment. Remunerations are paid by the Ministry of Labor, ranging approximately from F.250 to F.750 according to the importance of the conflict, which merely cover expenses that are actually incurred. The office is considered to be honorary and mediators usually are chosen from among engineers or economists of the industry, with a few judges of the civil or administrative courts (about 20 percent) and professors of law (20 percent) serving as well.

[38] It is remarkable to what extent criminal law is used here to increase the effectiveness of the mediation procedure.

[39] Although he may realize that a dispute is one over rights, there is nothing that can prevent him from investigating it and making recommendations; there is no possibility of appeal and there are no sanctions. But, as will be discussed, his recommendations are not enforceable in themselves; they are binding only after they were freely accepted by the parties. The mediator may be subject to informal criticism for his confusion of the issue, particularly if his recommendations are to be published, but he can avoid that by drafting them carefully.

3. In any event, mediation does not necessarily lead to a resolution of the dispute because the mediator's recommendations, unlike an arbitration award, are not binding unless they are freely accepted by the parties. His recommendations cannot be appealed and are not subject to any kind of judicial control. And this is the main idea on which the entire system is founded: it is designed merely to propose a resolution of the dispute, not to impose one. In the final analysis, it is the voluntary compliance of the parties that is the essential and decisive factor in the settlement of the conflict.[40]

In sum, it appears that mediation is a compromise between voluntary compliance and external pressure so far as the parties to the dispute are concerned. Compared with conciliation and arbitration, it is more coercive than the former but less so than the latter because of the effect of the mediator's recommendations. With respect to use of the procedure, however, mediation is more voluntary than conciliation and less so than arbitration: even if there is no general or statutory obligation, a certain element of coercion nevertheless exists at all steps.

Statistics show that after the enactment of the Decree of 1955, mediation was very popular and successful. Between August 1, 1955 and the end of that year, as many as 37 disputes were submitted to mediation, mostly because of social unrest during that period and the large number of strikes. Out of 37 disputes, 20 were submitted by employers,[41] 4 by labor unions, 10 by agreement between both parties, and 3 by the Administration on its own initiative (but in none of these 3 cases did the Minister of Labor act against the will of either of the two parties).[42] In 1956, 45 cases were brought to mediation, and from

---

[40] The procedure is the following: the mediator submits his recommendations to the parties in writing; if accepted they are treated like an agreement reached at the conclusion of the conciliation procedure, that is, like a collective agreement. But points of disagreement may remain because, first, the recommendations may not cover all questions of the dispute and, second, not all parties to the dispute may accept the recommendations. Or the parties may reject the recommendations in their entirety. The conflict then is considered unsettled and mediation is considered to have failed. At that point public authorities may intervene (the Minister of Labor under ART. 16 of the Law of 1957) to enlist public opinion by publishing the recommendations in the *Journal Officiel* or by announcing them over the news media.

[41] The fact that in 1955 most procedures were initiated by employers must be attributed to particular circumstances of the time. Some important conflicts involving many strikes had arisen, and many employers were inclined to use mediation in order to end this strike movement.

[42] The figures are quoted for the year 1955 in an article by A. Barjot, "L'expérience de cinq mois de médiation," *Droit social*, 1956, pp. 72 ff.; for the following years, in "Liaisons sociales," Supplement No. 3244, p. 86 (figures supplied by the *Ministère des Affaires Sociales*).

January 1 to August 1, 1957, there were 16 cases. The figures for the first half of 1957 already show a decline that gained considerable momentum after enactment of the new statute in 1957: from August 1, 1957 until December 31, 1966, only 77 cases were submitted to mediation.[43] Thus, a total of only 175 disputes were brought to mediation since the procedure was introduced by legislation. The rate of successful mediation is not appreciably higher than that of conciliation, as is shown in table 2.

TABLE 2

	August 1, 1955 – August 1, 1957	August 1, 1957 – December 31, 1966
Disputes submitted to mediation	98	77
Disputes completely resolved	48	31
Disputes partially resolved	11	10
Agreement reached between the parties under special circumstances	3	4
Failure of mediation	35	20
Special situations or results unknown	1	12

SOURCE: Figures supplied by the *Ministère des Affaires Sociales* and quoted in "Liaisons sociales," Supplement No. 3244, p. 86.

It is clear that voluntary compliance is inherent in the very nature of mediation, distinguishing it from conciliation at the beginning of the procedure and from arbitration at the end. But it also renders the procedure unfit for resolving *all* kinds of labor disputes, particularly conflicts over rights. Therefore, it should be used in conflicts over interests only, and more specifically in disputes that justify the intervention of high-placed and prestigious persons as mediators. And this seems to be the trend in France today.

ARBITRATION

Although arbitration can be used in France in all fields of the law as a kind of substitute for the judicial procedure, it is generally discouraged by the legislature because it tends to deprive the judiciary of its normal role. Arbitration in civil and commercial disputes is subject to many preconditions, the procedure is strictly regulated, and arbitral awards can be enforced only by court decision. Arbitration in

---

[43] Disputes submitted to mediation between 1957 and 1966 are as follows: 1957, 17; 1958, 13; 1959, 4; 1960, 8; 1961, 6; 1962, 9; 1963, 8; 1964, 5; 1965, 5; 1966, 2. Figures supplied by the *Ministère des Affaires Sociales* and quoted in "Liaisons sociales," Supplement No. 3244, p. 86.

individual disputes seems to be no longer available since the Decree of December 22, 1958 extended the jurisdiction of the labor courts,[44] but it is openly encouraged by the legislature in collective disputes.

The idea of using arbitration for the settlement of collective labor disputes developed at the end of the nineteenth century, when arbitration provisions were first included in some collective agreements. A voluntary procedure was officially established by statute in 1892, but its lack of success soon led to proposals for compulsory arbitration.[45] During World War I a form of arbitration was indeed compulsory for resolving collective labor disputes in a number of war industries (Decree of January 17, 1917), but these were temporary measures to be abolished after the war because they were linked to a prohibition of all strikes and lockouts. There were no significant changes in the postwar period, but the idea of compulsory arbitration gained support and finally led to legislation in 1936, providing that all collective labor disputes must be submitted to arbitration after conciliation had failed and prior to any strike or lockout. The arbitrator was empowered to deal with the issues submitted by the parties or by public authorities, and with all problems related to the conflict in arbitration. A large number of labor disputes were then taken to arbitration and successfully resolved, and as a result most strikes and lockouts were avoided.[46] However, voluntary arbitration was restored by the Law of February 11, 1950, and there have not been any changes in the system since then.

"Social arbitration," as arbitration in collective labor disputes became to be known, is in many ways an improved version of ordinary arbitration, a quasi-judicial procedure which is clearly distinct in that respect from the other two procedures provided for the peaceful settlement of collective labor disputes—conciliation and mediation.

The difference between all of these procedures lies essentially in the degree of voluntarism or coercion or, more precisely, in the point at which the necessary balance between these two requirements is achieved. It is inherent in the nature of arbitration that the resolution

---

[44] This question has not definitely been resolved by the courts because it has never arisen in practice and there is no case law on that point. But the aim of the legislature, namely to discourage the parties from bringing cases before a private arbitrator instead of a labor court, nevertheless has been achieved.

[45] The best-known proposals were presented by Waldeck-Rousseau and Millerand in 1900, and by Briand in 1910 for the railway industry, but they did not gain support and were later abandoned.

[46] The number of strikes decreased considerably, from 16,907 in 1936 to 2,616 in 1937 and 1,220 in 1939. Figures quoted in *Traité de Droit du Travail*, Vol. VI, H. Sinay, "La Grève," p. 438.

to the dispute is worked out by a third party, the arbitrator, and the main problem lies therefore in compensating for that external pressure at the two main steps of arbitration: initiation of the procedure and enforcement of the award.[47]

1. So far as the initiation of the procedure is concerned, the voluntary element is stronger in arbitration than it is in the other two procedures. Recourse is not compulsory by law (as it is in conciliation), it cannot be imposed upon the parties by public authorities, nor can one party force the other to go to arbitration (as is the case in mediation).

The situation was, of course, very different under the legislation of 1936 and 1938, when arbitration was compulsory. The law provided that a contractual procedure had to be included in all collective agreements, but it also established a statutory procedure that was available in the absence of such an agreement. Even in that case, however, a certain contractual element was retained to the extent that the power was given the parties to conclude a submission agreement (to select an arbitrator and determine the subject of the dispute) after the conflict actually had arisen. And if the parties were unable to agree to a submission agreement, an arbitrator could be appointed by public authorities. At that time, there were important differences between the so-called "statutory" and "contractual" procedures.

Everything has been changed, however, since the legislature repealed compulsory arbitration. On the one hand, arbitration is not compulsory by law; the procedure cannot be initiated without agreement between the parties to the dispute (this is why it can be said that there is no purely statutory procedure). On the other, that agreement must be concluded subsequent to the rise of the dispute itself. Arbitration cannot be made compulsory by a previous arbitration clause contained in a collective agreement governing all undetermined and future disputes. Not only is such a clause any longer required by law, but it has also lost most of its usefulness because, according to the prevailing opinion, it cannot create an obligation to go to arbitration. Clauses providing for compulsory arbitration can occasionally be found in some collective agreements (notably in agreements concern-

---

[47] French law has taken various positions on that point. As stated above, arbitration began as a purely voluntary procedure (Law of December 27, 1892), but it was made compulsory in 1936 (Law of December 31, 1936, amended by the Law of March 4, 1938). A compromise was established under new legislation (Law of February 11, 1950, as amended by the Law of July 26, 1957), providing that use of the procedure is voluntary but that the award is binding. As a result, social arbitration has moved somewhat closer to ordinary arbitration and has lost almost all of its effectiveness.

ing agricultural workers),[48] but the courts would probably refuse to enforce them if they were asked to do so, under the pretext that this would lead to a considerable restriction of the right to strike.[49] In fact, it is admitted that the voluntary nature of arbitration is a matter of public policy that must be protected even against the will of the parties themselves. The result is that most collective agreements explicitly state that recourse to arbitration is not compulsory and that it is subject, in each case, to the consent of the parties involved in the dispute. When arbitration provisions are contained in collective agreements (which is increasingly less frequent today), they serve only to appoint an arbitrator and to organize in advance the various steps of the procedure. This is the only effect of the so-called "contractual" procedure.[50] But in any case, a special agreement is required after the conflict actually has arisen.

Thus, it seems that everything depends on the submission agreement *(compromis d'arbitrage)* by which the parties consent to arbitration for a particular dispute, and this explains why there is no fundamental difference between the contractual and the statutory procedure. A submission agreement is necessary in any case, and that agreement really is the heart of the arbitration procedure. The law provides that it can be included in the *procès-verbal de non-conciliation* (it is often signed at the end of the conciliation procedure when the parties cannot settle their dispute, or after failure of mediation), defining the points of disagreement and determining the jurisdiction of the arbitrator. It must be signed by both parties or by their representatives, whose powers are subject to certain limitations. (These problems were discussed in connection with the conciliation procedure.)

2. A third party, the arbitrator, plays the decisive role in arbitration. He is appointed by the parties to the dispute, who also determine his jurisdiction subject to certain legislative requirements. For example, it

---

[48] Recently such agreements have been concluded in agriculture for the resolution of disputes arising from the application or interpretation of their own terms.

[49] This opinion is challenged by some who claim that it is contradictory with the letter of the statute, which expressly authorizes the inclusion of an arbitration provision in collective agreements while prohibiting it in other civil or commercial contracts. But it is supported by others who maintain that the opposite interpretation would lead to a restoration of compulsory arbitration. The fact that there is no case law on this point proves that the question has more theoretical than practical significance.

[50] Paradoxically, an arbitration clause of a collective agreement can also serve to limit recourse to arbitration by imposing preconditions to initiation of the procedure or by restricting arbitration to certain kinds of conflicts, e.g., after failure of conciliation, to conflicts arising from the interpretation of the collective agreement, etc.

cannot be extended to problems that have not been expressly submitted to arbitration, even though they may concern the same labor dispute for which he was appointed. Indeed, defining the arbitrator's range of jurisdiction often causes great difficulty in practice.

The parties also determine procedural details. It is even the main objective of the arbitration provision contained in a collective agreement to establish in advance the details of the procedure; if a conflict arises, the submission agreement concluded at that moment merely sets the procedure in motion. In the absence of contractual provisions, however, the submission agreement not only establishes the principle of recourse to arbitration but procedural details as well. And herein lies the important difference between the two situations. In the first case, the conditions under which arbitration will take place are determined in the abstract; they apply to all conflicts that arise during the life of the agreement and they are necessarily determined by the negotiators of the collective agreement, that is, by persons who may not be the parties to the dispute. On the other hand, when the conditions of arbitration are determined in the submission agreement, they are always determined *ad hoc* and in consideration of a particular dispute between the parties to that dispute.

Each method, of course, has advantages and disadvantages. The procedure established in advance helps to avoid difficulties and saves time when a conflict already has arisen, while a special submission agreement serves to set up machinery that may be more adapted to the particular type of conflict involved. A combination of the advantages of both procedures is often used, in which the collective agreement defines the general framework of the procedure and the submission agreement provides for its details.

The arbitrator may be a single person (government officials, mayors, or *Préfets* often serve in that capacity), or panels of arbitrators may be organized (several officials or members of the conciliation commission). Or each party may appoint one or more arbitrators in equal number, but if they cannot reach agreement, a *surarbitre* must be appointed either by mutual consent among the arbitrators themselves or by a third party; the *surarbitre* will then cast the decisive vote.[51] It

---

[51] This system was compulsory by law in 1936 and 1938. The arbitrators were to be appointed by each of the parties; failing agreement they were to be selected by the Minister of Labor from a list prepared by both employers and labor unions. When such a list did not exist, they were appointed by the Minister himself. A similar procedure existed for the designation of the *surarbitre* whenever that was necessary; as a last resort the *surarbitre* was to be chosen by the *President du Conseil* (President of the Council of Ministers) from among the highest officials

is important to note that the government cannot appoint an arbitrator for the parties without their express consent. Public authorities do not prepare lists of candidates, from which one could be proposed or imposed upon the parties as is the case in mediation. Indeed, the absence of public intervention at this point of the procedure once more stresses the voluntary nature of arbitration.[52]

The law is silent with respect to procedural details; it merely stipulates that the arbitrator cannot exceed his jurisdiction as defined by the parties, in violation of which he would decide *ultra petita*. But his methods of reasoning are regulated by the statute, which applies in this matter whatever the terms of the submission agreement.

Under the Law of December 31, 1936, the arbitrator could decide *en équité*, that is, in conformance with the requirements of natural justice; while he could not rule against existing law, he could interpret it more freely than a judge and he could even "create" law whenever there was a gap in the legislative order.[53] But his powers were considerably restricted by new regulations (Law of March 4, 1938, and ARTICLE 23 of the Law of February 11, 1950), which were essentially passed because of the need to distinguish between conflicts over rights and those over interests. In the former (also called juridical conflicts, which explains the name *juridical arbitration*) the arbitrator must decide *en droit*, that is, he must apply and interpret the law according to the methods commonly employed by judges. But arbitrators usually are more flexible than professional judges, and their decisions often reflect a more liberal attitude towards the workers than those of most judges of the regular courts. In conflicts over interests (also called

---

of the state. However, this system finally proved to be unsatisfactory because the arbitrators appointed by each of the parties were inclined to consider themselves representatives of those parties, bound to defend their interests and lacking the necessary impartiality. As a result, the two arbitrators were often unable to reach agreement and had to call a *surarbitre*, who was then in most cases the real arbitrator of the dispute, but much time and energy had been wasted before he was called. The experience clearly showed that the plurality of arbitrators merely resulted in making the procedure longer and more complex. The alleged advantage facilitating the designation of the arbitrators proved to be an illusion because it merely postponed the problem until the time when the *surarbitre* had to be appointed. Under present legislation the parties may still use a system of this kind, but they are no longer compelled to do so; they usually prefer to use a single arbitrator.

[52] This certainly is an advantage. But while it is felt that arbitration under the legislation of 1936 and 1938 allowed for too much administrative intervention, the present arrangement may account for the great practical difficulties involved in appointing an arbitrator, which are among the main reasons for the decline of the institution.

[53] The arbitrators often used this opportunity to include in their awards informal recommendations and advice for the parties.

economic conflicts, which explains the name *economic arbitration* that is sometimes used), the arbitrator can still decide *en équité*. He has quasi-discretionary powers in such cases, applying his own standards and creating new law, in other words, performing the task that is normally delegated to the parties through negotiation.[54]

3. The arbitration award is binding and enforceable in itself; if the arbitrator has not exceeded his powers as defined in the submission agreement, formal acceptance by the parties is not required. The law merely provides that the arbitrator must notify the parties of his award by registered mail within 24 hours, and that he must send a copy to the office of the secretary of the local labor court (if there is no labor court, to the *tribunal d'instance*).[55] But even these requirements do not have much weight in practice; the *Cour de Cassation* is reluctant to set aside the few awards that are actually delivered because of noncompliance with a mere formality.

An award can be compared to a court decision insofar as it is subject to judicial control. Like any judge, the arbitrator must state the reasons for his decision, but the regular courts do not control "social arbitration" (as distinct from other forms of civil or commercial arbitration) through *exequatur*.[56] The awards cannot be appealed in the courts of appeals or the *Cour de Cassation;* rather, appeals must be lodged before a special and autonomous jurisdiction, the *Cour supérieure d'arbitrage* (Superior Court of Arbitration), which was created in 1938 and reorganized in 1950.[57] The court is now bipartite, composed of four members of the Council of State (the highest administrative court) and four judges of the courts of appeals or the *Cour de Cassation,* all of them appointed to this position by the government. The president of the court is chosen from among presidents of the sections of the Council of State, or the vice-president of that Council serves himself. That regulation is important because it assures that judges of the ad-

---

[54] But even here there is danger that the arbitrator may abuse his power of creating law and try to substitute regulations unilaterally worked out by himself for the agreement between the parties with respect to wages and other conditions of work. It is dangerous because the arbitral award is binding on the parties and just as enforceable as a collective agreement, and it explains the complete decline of arbitration in conflicts over interests; in fact, the question never arises in practice today.

[55] Art. 28 of the Law of 1950.

[56] Law of March 4, 1938. Except in social arbitration an arbitral award can be enforced only by a decision of *exequatur,* which must be delivered by the president of the *tribunal de grande instance* (Art. 1021 of the Code of Civil Procedure).

[57] Law of February 11, 1950, supplemented by a Decree of March 15, 1950.

ministrative order are in the majority. Judicial review turns on points of law only[58] and extends to all arbitral awards, provided that an appeal is based on an alleged *excès de pouvoir* (excess of power by the arbitrator) or a violation of the statute law. On the first appeal the court may set aside the award and remand the case to the parties if it finds that a violation of the law has occurred.[59] The parties then can initiate new proceedings and designate another arbitrator. But if that award is also appealed and again set aside, the court can designate one of its members to make an additional investigation, and it can deliver its own award that is not subject to any kind of appeal. This is the only case in which the court can deal with points of fact.

Although the Superior Court of Arbitration now is more or less inactive, it was very important in 1938 and 1939 when recourse to arbitration was compulsory and most labor disputes were settled by arbitration. A considerable number of awards were then appealed to the court, which handed down as many as 1,350 decisions in seventeen months. It could thus control the practice of the arbitrators and contribute to its uniformity, thereby creating a body of case law that has had a significant impact on the development of labor law in France. Because of its autonomous position, the court created case law distinct from the ordinary case law, not only of the regular courts but of the labor courts as well. It was generally less dominated by tradition and legal orthodoxy, giving arbitrators more freedom in their awards that clearly led to innovations and new concepts. For example, between 1936 and 1939, the arbitrators and the Superior Court of Arbitration ruled that strikes should not lead to termination but to suspension of the individual contract of employment; that the burden of proving unlawful termination did not lie with the worker but with the employer; and above all, that a worker unlawfully dismissed should be reinstated in his job. This last point was particularly important: while the courts granted damages in money because they had to do so under ARTICLE 1142 of the Civil Code, the arbitrators could order the only effective sanction—reinstatement.[60] Although many of these innovations were

---

[58] In 1938, the Minister of Labor had special powers to file an appeal against an arbitral award in the Superior Court of Arbitration for mere reasons of fact. However, this type of appeal was not restored by the legislation of 1950.

[59] The appeals procedure is defined by the Law of February 11, 1950, as supplemented by the Decree of March 15, 1950, and as amended by the Law of July 26, 1957.

[60] However, some difficulties arose in connection with the execution of such an order of reinstatement. When the employer refused compliance, it did not seem advisable to use police force to bring about enforcement and the dispute was finally settled by awarding damages. But, as we shall see, there had been few cases of such refusals during the short period from 1936 to 1939.

not retained by the courts after the arbitration procedure was suspended in 1939, many others have been incorporated into the ordinary case law and some have led to progressive legislation (for example, in relation to the doctrine of suspending the contract of employment, which was at least implicitly incorporated in ARTICLE 4 of the Law of February 11, 1950).

The similarity between an arbitration award and a collective agreement is obvious:[61] both have the same function and the same goal; both derive directly or indirectly from the mutual consent of the parties; and both normally produce the same effects. This is especially true of awards involving the interpretation of a preexisting collective agreement or relating to wages and other conditions of work. These are automatically included in individual contracts of employment concluded between all employers and all employees covered, just like provisions of a collective agreement. Thus, an award affects more persons than does an ordinary court decision, and its provisions are not necessarily limited to groups or persons who were directly parties to, or at least represented at, the arbitration proceedings (the members of the various organizations). As is the case in collective agreements, it is the situation of the employer with respect to the award that determines the situation of his employees.

An award, again like a collective agreement, may also be extended by decree of the Minister of Labor to all employers and employees of the same industry or branch of activity in the same territorial area. In fact, the Minister must decree such extension when there is a preexisting collective agreement that has been extended and if it is requested by all groups or persons who were party to that agreement. The award then has the same coverage as the collective agreement and becomes a part of it.

The similarity between arbitral awards and collective agreements is also evident with respect to sanctions that can be applied in case of noncompliance. Like violations of provisions of a collective agreement, violations of terms of an award may give rise to a new labor conflict, individual or collective according to the criteria described above, which must be resolved by the courts (regular or labor courts) or by the procedures already mentioned. However, the only remedy available is an award of damages; its effectiveness naturally is difficult to evalu-

---

[61] This fact is now emphasized by the law (ART. 28 of the Law of February 11, 1950). The situation was different in the past. The arbitration award was not binding on the parties in 1892, when the procedure was first introduced; it became binding and enforceable by legislation, implicitly in 1936 and expressly in 1938 and 1950.

ate because of the few awards that are now delivered and the even smaller number in which an enforcement problem actually arises.[62]

But this is only one weakness of the present law of arbitration. There are other shortcomings, all of them stemming from the great emphasis that is put on the voluntary aspect of the procedure. It is a fact that use of arbitration has considerably declined since voluntary recourse was restored by the legislature; although precise statistics are not available, it seems to be used in only two or three cases a year. Even though most of these disputes involve conflicts over rights for which arbitration certainly is better suited than for conflicts over interests, this is an almost negligible rate. Therefore, the principle of voluntarism itself comes into question, but an investigation of that problem cannot be restricted to arbitration. Rather, it must include all procedures for the peaceful settlement of collective labor conflicts because all are closely related, forming parts of what must be seen as a single machinery. A quick evaluation of that system may shed some light on its effectiveness.

The procedures for the settlement of collective labor disputes are profoundly divergent in theory and in practice. In theory French legislation provides for a great variety in order to avoid strikes or other forms of economic action. While the parties to a dispute can always take their case before an ordinary court, it was felt that bodies had to be established that were not part of the judiciary, not being bound to strict legalism from either a procedural or a substantive point of view. Specialized settlement procedures are not only better suited to resolving collective labor disputes than are procedures before the ordinary courts, they are also designed to obtain the cooperation of the parties. Finally, each of the existing procedures is especially adapted to resolve

---

[62] Before World War II, the legislature attempted to improve that situation by providing other possible sanctions (Decree of November 12, 1938): *astreinte*, punitive or threatening damages consisting of sums much higher than the injury actually suffered; sanctions against the employer's profession, e.g., forbidding him to conclude contracts with the state or other public collectivities or declaring him ineligible to hold certain offices (e.g., judge of a labor court or commercial court, member of a *Chambre de Commerce* or *Chambre des Métiers*); and most important, the option given to employers to terminate individual contracts of employment, without risking damages, of workers refusing to comply with an award and especially of those who decided to go or remain on strike. Statistics show that this system was very effective. Between 1936 and 1938, only 53 awards were not complied with, 10 because of workers' actions and 43 because of employers' actions, notably when the award ordered reinstatement of the worker. (Figures quoted from the book by P. Laroque, *Les rapports entre patrons et ouvriers*, p. 400.) The government attempted to restore these sanctions in 1950, but Parliament refused to go along. Thus, the only sanctions available today are damages in terms of money.

a certain kind of collective dispute, for example, mediation to conflicts over interests, arbitration to those over rights, and conciliation to either. Therefore, the present system could be expected to work rather well, but the record for the past nineteen years tells another story.

The experience shows that the procedures are used in an almost negligible number of conflicts, and that they often fail to bring about a settlement. It seems that the legislature has been unable to strike the proper balance between the opposite requirements of voluntarism and coercion; while it has attempted to retain an element of voluntarism in each procedure at one stage or another, either in recourse to the procedure, in working out a resolution of the conflict, or in achieving a real settlement, it may have gone too far in that direction by not sufficiently stressing the need for coercion. Lacking that element, the parties may be tempted to resort to their economic weapons, especially when they are embroiled in conflict. The conclusion is clear: while the parties must retain enough freedom to make the settlement machinery successful, too much voluntarism inevitably deprives it of its effectiveness. Thus, the whole system could be improved by strengthening the element of obligation in the procedures.

This problem is particularly acute in the final steps of the proceedings, because there the various procedures react upon one another. In other words, the parties to the dispute must eventually be obliged to use a procedure that leads to a binding decision, because only this final obligation can determine the success of the whole machinery. And among existing procedures arbitration is best suited to bring about a final settlement of labor conflicts, at least of conflicts over rights; it is a quasi-judicial procedure in which the arbitrator decides in conformance with the law albeit with more flexibility than a judge.

An argument for the reestablishment of compulsory arbitration, which worked so successfully from 1936 to 1939, can certainly be made.[63] While there could be objections that arbitration leaves the final resolution to a third person rather than to the parties to the dispute, in

---

[63] The experience of three years of compulsory arbitration—1936 to 1939—clearly shows its effectiveness: from March 5, 1938 to August 1, 1939, the *surarbitres* delivered 4,250 awards, and the Superior Court of Arbitration decided 1,350 cases. During that time, conciliation as well was more successful: of 9,810 disputes brought before the departmental conciliation commissions, 3,583 were settled as early as at the first step of the procedure. The statistics show that during the years 1937 and 1938, of 12,939 disputes submitted to the *Préfets*, 12,477 were definitely settled either by conciliation or by arbitration. As was pointed out above (*supra*, n. 46), the number of strikes during that period was considerably reduced. (Figures quoted from A. Brun and H. Galland, *Droit du Travail*, III, No. 191, pp. 932 and 933.)

a way abandoning the principle of voluntarism, the threat of compulsory arbitration would also be conducive to reaching compromise, especially if the parties could work it out themselves, say, through conciliation. Indeed, it is often argued that compulsory arbitration is the missing link that is needed in the present system to make it really effective. Failing an element of obligation, this system is bound to remain weak, incomplete, and almost useless. Compulsion should come as late as possible—but come it must.

All these reasons, however, do not seem entirely conclusive. It is clear that compulsory arbitration cannot be imposed by the legislature against the wishes of those directly involved in labor relations—the employers, the workers, and their respective organizations—and that it can work only in a favorable social climate.[64] To the extent that such climate does not now exist, there is little chance that the machinery established in 1936 will be restored in the near future.

The employers are reluctant to permit the intrusion of a third party, the arbitrator, into their affairs, who could make decisions that normally are within their authority. The workers and the labor unions maintain that the obligation to resort to arbitration is incompatible with their constitutional right to strike.[65] Finally, the state itself may have reason to fear that an excessive development of arbitration, even in labor relations, is incompatible with the normal operation of the courts; moreover, it has increasingly become an employer and may share the attitude of other employers with respect to arbitration. While it is

---

[64] The acceptance in the industrial world of compulsory arbitration in 1936 can be cited here, but it was brought about by special circumstances: a socialist government allied with the labor unions, the rash of sit-down strikes in 1936, and relatively unorganized employers facing strong labor unions. When the problem of establishing new settlement procedures arose in 1950, the political and social context was far different and the principle of compulsory arbitration had become unacceptable. A bill introduced by the government was opposed by all sides, employers' organizations and labor unions as well as all political factions. As a result, the Law of February 11, 1950 merely established a system of voluntary arbitration.

[65] This aspect of compulsory arbitration is important to note, because it refers to the main characteristic that renders the system simultaneously so valuable and so difficult to impose upon the labor unions. And this point is all the more critical as the strike obviously plays an essential role in the settlement of labor disputes under the present regulation. When a conflict first erupts, a threat of strike may induce the employer to accept recourse to a peaceful settlement procedure; during the procedure, it is an element of the bargaining power of the union; and at the end, if the procedure fails, it is the ultimate weapon to which the union may resort in order to obtain direct satisfaction of its claims. The strike is therefore important at all stages of the settlement procedure, even before it is begun and after it is terminated. Thus, the unions are eager to keep the strike as a weapon, and there is little chance that they will ever agree to renounce it—except under special circumstances such as those that prevailed in 1936.

admitted that all these oppositions to the principle of compulsory arbitration are not equally strong, it appears that the most serious obstacle to restoring the previous system is the resistance of the labor unions—an obstacle that is practically impossible to overcome because of the futility of sanctions that could be pronounced against the noncomplying organizations. This proves that the real problem lies in the alleged incompatibility of compulsory arbitration with the right to strike, and with the rule that that right may be limited but cannot be completely suppressed.

In view of the present situation, there is no doubt that the failure of the arbitration system is responsible for the failure of the entire machinery established for the peaceful settlement of collective labor disputes. By making conciliation compulsory and arbitration optional, the Law of 1950 established a compromise between the opposite requirements of voluntarism and coercion, but only in appearance. Voluntary arbitration has resulted in making the whole system—even conciliation—purely voluntary in fact. As a first consequence, arbitration has fallen into almost complete disuse, followed by a decline in conciliation. A new mediation procedure was introduced in 1955, but it, too, proved to be ineffective and has practically disappeared from the scene. Nothing has been done since to fill this gap in the law created by the absence of compulsory arbitration, and the problem of the peaceful settlement of collective labor disputes remains unresolved.

5.
CONCLUSION

There is today general consensus in France that labor conflicts are unique, and that they cannot be settled by ordinary procedures. Special procedures have now been in operation for a long time, and it is out of the question to revert to a system in which labor conflicts are treated like other conflicts before the ordinary courts. It seems quite normal that the special statutory law created for labor relations be applied by special bodies, according to special methods of interpretation and serving as a basis for the development of special case law. But these bodies are necessarily diverse, and several settlement procedures are needed because labor conflicts themselves vary in nature.

In some countries conflicts over rights are distinguished from those over interests, and in others individual disputes are distinguished from collective ones. In France the main line of demarcation has traditionally been drawn between individual conflicts, which always turn on rights, and collective conflicts, which may turn on rights as well as on interests. This can be explained by historical reasons, and by the fact that all labor law has developed from a system that was characterized by the supremacy of the individual contract of employment into one in which collective forms of action play an important role and collective agreements are an essential source of law. These two kinds of labor relations have developed successively, but the latter have not replaced the former. Even today French labor law is concerned with two different but equally important areas: the individual employment relationship between employer and employee and collective labor–management relations.

A special system for the settlement of individual conflicts could have been created within the enterprise, for example, a grievance procedure in which the *délégués du personnel* would have played an essential role; but it would have raised too many problems leading perhaps to competition between these *délégués* and the labor unions, and it would have been impossible to establish more than a simple screening procedure with limited effectiveness. Or settlement procedures could have been created in which the labor unions themselves would have participated at the level of the enterprise or at a higher level; but this did not seem feasible either because the unions are not directly parties to the conflict and their participation at the side or in place of the individual worker must necessarily be limited to ensure that all workers are equally protected. Union membership is voluntary in France and each union is entitled to represent its members only. Also, the fact that an individual conflict is always one over rights makes recourse to the economic power of the union unnecessary; it will be resolved by application of the law, not by virtue of the balance of power between the parties. In view of all these factors, the legislature created a procedure that is similar to ordinary legal procedure in its judicial nature but unique in its application to labor disputes. And the *conseils de prud' hommes* reflect this twofold concern: they are courts, but courts of a special nature.

It is unanimously admitted that in general the labor courts function rather well. Nevertheless, suggestions for reform are regularly presented by employers' associations, labor unions, members of the *Conseil Economique et Social* and of the legal profession, and by the judges of the labor courts themselves. Most of the current proposals are directed at specific points in an attempt to correct some of the shortcomings of the present system that were discussed earlier in this study. There are few critics of the principle of specialized labor courts composed of lay judges representing employers and employees.[1] In fact, there is widespread demand for an extension of the present system, either by creating new labor courts (which involves serious financial problems) or by extending the coverage of existing ones both from a territorial and occupational point of view. In the extreme this would

---

[1] Some opposition to this principle comes essentially from two sides. Especially among the most conservative jurists, there is a certain feeling against the very existence of specialized jurisdictions and in favor of a reunification of the judiciary. But if this feeling can be enlisted against the creation of new specialized courts, it does not appear to be strong enough to promote the discontinuation of those that already exist, mainly the labor courts that have successfully operated now for more than 150 years. There are also some proposals to replace the lay judges composing the labor courts with professional judges specialized in labor matters, under the pretext that the presence of professional judges in these courts is necessary in any case and that it is preferable not to have both professional and lay judges. (See *infra*, n. 7.) But this seems to be only a theoretical point of view, at least under the present circumstances.

lead to a division of all of France into a number of districts, each having a labor court with jurisdiction over all occupations irrespective of the number of its specialized sections.

This movement for extension is proof that most parties to a dispute prefer to bring their case before a labor court rather than before an ordinary court. While the unions and the *prud'hommes* themselves are particularly anxious to accomplish this reform, they also support other modifications that would increase the autonomy of the labor courts, especially measures improving the appeals procedure. Appeals now must be lodged with the ordinary courts of appeals or the *Cour de Cassation*, the latter being a symbol of conservatism so far as labor law is concerned. It has been suggested that appellate labor courts be established, either bipartite as requested by the unions as early as 1907 or tripartite, being chaired by a professional judge, and that a supreme labor court complete the hierarchy of the system of labor courts. In addition, more autonomy could be obtained by granting the labor courts more freedom in their methods of reasoning or in choosing remedies.[2] Other groups have asked for changes in the structure of the labor courts affecting the election system of the judges[3] and the bipartite composition of the courts.[4]

These are the major current trends in the development of labor courts. There is little chance that any of the proposals for reform will be adopted in the near future, except perhaps an extension of the labor court system on the territorial and occupational level. There is no doubt that the labor unions and the public in general hold the present system in high esteem—it is considered to be a victory of the working class and a system that is one of the most favorable to workers that could possibly have been established. And this in a way guarantees the status quo.

---

[2] For example, laying the burden of proof in normal or unlawful discharges on the employer rather than on the worker himself, or ordering reinstatement of an employee who was unlawfully dismissed. Decisions in these two senses currently would be in contradiction to the rules of the Civil Code.

[3] See *Advice* given by the *Conseil Economique et Social* on May 13, 1964.

[4] See an article by M. Hamiaut, "Vers un Tribunal social," in *Droit Social*, 1966, pp. 18-28. The author recommends the creation of a social chamber, in each *tribunal de grande instance* (the ordinary civil court), composed of one professional judge and two lay judges representing employers and employees. This chamber would be specialized in the settlement of individual disputes relating to the individual employment relationship as well as to other social matters; it would be the equivalent, at the level of the first instance, of the social chambers already existing within the courts of appeals and the *Cour de Cassation*. Such a reform naturally would bring the settlement system for individual labor disputes closer to that for ordinary disputes, marking a return to more legalism.

See also *Advice* given by the *Conseil Economique et Social* on May 13, 1964.

However, the situation is quite different with respect to collective labor disputes, even when they turn on rights. Although settlement procedures established for such disputes are also external to the enterprise, they do not involve specialized courts. The parties to such disputes can choose between two kinds of procedures representing two extremes: they may go before an ordinary court and the dispute then will be treated like any civil matter, or they may use a series of procedures (conciliation, mediation, arbitration) that do not take place before the courts and are indeed most unlike court proceedings because of their large emphasis on voluntary compliance. Although these procedures are in a way well-suited to resolving collective labor disputes—the unions retain a major role and there is a possibility of deviating from strictly legal methods of reasoning—the overemphasis on voluntarism has diminished their effectiveness. In addition, though they are available for all collective conflicts without distinction between those over rights and those over interests, it appears that they are better suited to resolving the latter.

The experience shows that all of these procedures have proved to be a complete failure, and there is clearly need for change. It is not enough that some collective conflicts can be considered under their individual aspects and treated as individual disputes, falling under the jurisdiction of the labor courts.[5] It is also necessary to set up procedures that are particular to collective conflicts and take into consideration their collective character. Numerous proposals for reform in that direction have already been presented. For example, procedures within the enterprise with union participation (under the Law of December 27, 1968, the unions are officially recognized and have legal status within the enterprise) or joint commissions could be established, but these would probably be little more than screening procedures because compliance, again, would largely be voluntary. Indeed, the only effective reform would consist of new procedures in which more emphasis must be put on coercion at the expense of voluntarism. And if such procedures again could not be used for all collective disputes but only for disputes over rights, it would finally prove that nothing can be ac-

---

[5] In most cases this can easily be accomplished because of the ambiguous distinction between collective and individual disputes and the fact that most conflicts are actually mixed. It is interesting to note that the success of procedures created for the settlement of collective conflicts between 1936 and 1939 led to an extension of the very concept of collective disputes, at that time and especially on the part of the Superior Court of Arbitration, while the present failure of the procedures now leads to a restriction of that concept and to an extension of the concept of individual disputes, in practice and especially on the part of the labor courts and the *Cour de Cassation*.

complished without the introduction in French law, in one way or another, of a fundamental distinction between collective labor disputes over rights and those over interests.

Any careful study of the present situation and any attempt at reform always brings us back to that essential problem. Until 1938, the need for the distinction was more or less ignored because it then appeared sufficient to place individual disputes opposite to collective ones. Although the distinction was introduced in 1938 and has been constantly extended since then, it is still of limited significance. But it is nevertheless fundamental, and the chances of achieving the effective settlement of labor disputes no doubt would be much greater if different procedures, based on different principles, were at the disposal of the parties.

With respect to conflicts over interests, the most desirable procedures would also be the most flexible, focusing on the agreement between the parties which is here indispensable; even arbitration in these conflicts seems to be too coercive. Indeed, some kind of mediation procedure would be preferable and, as was already noted, there is a trend to establish at least in larger conflicts *ad hoc* procedures of inquiry and recommendation that closely resemble traditional mediation. These procedures would assist the parties in bargaining, and the government would play an important role to safeguard the public interest involved in such conflicts. If the procedures fail and the parties cannot reach agreement, their ultimate solution will be recourse to economic actions such as strikes or lockouts.

But just the opposite solution must prevail in conflicts over rights. Obviously there must be some compromise between the simple application of ordinary judicial procedures before the ordinary courts and the special procedures that are devoid of any judicial aspects. Because collective labor conflicts over rights basically turn on points of law, they imply resort to a judicial or quasi-judicial procedure for their resolution, that is, a procedure in which the emphasis is on compulsion rather than on voluntarism and in which one or several judges decide the case in conformance with the law. It cannot properly be expected that these conflicts can be resolved by voluntary and flexible procedures such as conciliation, mediation, and even noncompulsory arbitration, the ineffectiveness of which can indeed be ascertained today. We do not think that developing procedures of this type would be useful, even with more active participation of the state through so-called mediation or conciliation services or through public officials specialized in this function, as has been proposed.[6] A possible solution may be

---

[6] See the proposal made by Francois Block-Lané in his book *Pour une réforme*

recourse to a system of compulsory arbitration similar to the one that had been established in the prewar period, but it must be acknowledged that the principle of private arbitration is not really in conformance with the French tradition, which leans to recourse to the courts, administering justice in the name of the state. Indeed, the courts seem to be the best protection against arbitrariness and a better guarantee of good, equal, and impartial justice. Moreover, it may be feasible to arrange conciliation sessions before these courts because the roles of conciliator and judge are not incompatible in the tradition of civil law, and it is perfectly admissible that they are simultaneously performed by the same person. Perhaps a solution to the present dilemma lies in that direction and new procedures to be created for the settlement of collective conflicts over rights should take place before the courts, just like procedures provided for the settlement of any dispute involving an issue of rights. Meant here, of course, are not the ordinary courts since the conflicts with which we are concerned are special conflicts —first because they concern labor relations, and second because they have a collective character. The fact that they are related to social and economic problems and that they involve relations of force determines that they cannot be resolved by a mere application of the law, but that other circumstances also have to be taken into consideration. Thus, new courts would have to be created that would be specialized in the settlement of collective labor conflicts over rights, just as the *conseils de prud'hommes* were set up for the settlement of individual labor conflicts.

But at this point a problem arises: is it possible or even advisable to unify the procedures established for these two kinds of labor conflicts over rights—individual and collective—and, consequently, should there be one kind of labor court before which all labor conflicts could be brought? There have been several proposals in that direction. The labor unions requested an extension of the jurisdiction of the *conseils de prud'hommes* to collective labor conflicts as early as 1906, but this

---

de l'entreprise, published in 1963, which generated great interest in France. The author proposes the establishment of independent agencies at the regional and national level, composed of public officials specialized in this function who would be called to play a role in the settlement of a certain number of collective conflicts, including at least all conflicts over rights and especially those over the application or interpretation of collective agreements. This role would essentially consist of conciliation, mediation, and arbitration. The procedure would remain voluntary to a very large extent and would not replace the usual recourse to the ordinary courts; it would replace only the procedures created by the Law of 1950. In fact, it would merely amount to a kind of remodeling of the present system, with even more intervention by the public authorities.

would have entailed significant modifications in the structure and operation of the courts, especially in seating, in addition to employer and employee members, representatives of employers' associations and labor unions who are most often parties to the collective conflicts. Even today the C.G.T. sometimes advocates a reform of this kind because of its belief in a court system organized on a purely bipartite and elective basis. But many other proposals, including more recent ones,[7] favor the establishment of a new type of labor court, which would partly replace the existing *conseils de prud'hommes* but would have a larger jurisdiction because it would handle individual and collective labor conflicts as long as they turn on points of law. Two basic ideas are behind these proposals.

First, it is felt that the distinction between individual and collective conflicts is obsolete and does not fit present circumstances. For example, there is growing difficulty clearly to distinguish between the two kinds of conflicts, and more and more disputes are given a mixed character permitting the parties to exercise a kind of option. There is also a growing tendency to extend either one of the two categories at the expense of the other (from 1936 to 1939 collective conflicts, and since 1950 individual conflicts) in order to enlarge or restrict the range of application of this or that procedure. Likewise, the power of the *délégués du personnel* to submit workers' grievances to management was restricted to individual grievances in 1936, but since 1946 it covers all grievances without distinction as to their individual or collective nature. Moreover, it seems that a growing number of collective agreements that establish a conciliation procedure for disputes arising from the interpretation of their terms do not distinguish between the so-called individual and collective conflicts. Therefore, it seems that the time has come for the distinction between individual and collective disputes to give way to one between conflicts over rights and those over interests.

---

[7] See, for example, Pierre Laroque, "Contentieux social et juridiction sociale," in *Droit Social*, 1954, p. 271. He proposes the creation of a hierarchy of "social courts," which would be characterized by three main features. They would be competent to decide all kinds of labor conflicts, individual as well as collective, includin some kinds of conflicts involving social matters that now fall under the jurisdiction of very specialized courts considered to be administrative courts. They would be special courts composed exclusively of professional judges specialized in labor matters, without any participation of lay judges. They would be autonomous from other courts, forming a complete hierarchy consisting of courts at the lower and regional level and a Supreme Court. This hierarchy would accommodate an appeals procedure and provide a forum for each conflict corresponding to its size and the level at which it arose. It is understandable that such a project meets with very strong opposition from the labor unions.

Second, the establishment of a single hierarchy of labor courts with jurisdiction over all labor conflicts over rights would certainly have many advantages of procedural unification and simplification. It would avoid the excessive fragmentation of the French judicial system, which is often and rightly criticized, and it would reflect the current movement of reaction (especially since 1958) against the existence of too many specialized courts. This hierarchy could also be more autonomous from the regular court system than are the *conseils de prud' hommes*, because the new courts could be created at the various possible levels—the lower, the appellate, and even at that of the Supreme Court. The courts probably would be established on a tripartite basis, composed of professional judges specializing in labor problems and of laymen representing employers and employees.

However, such a reform of the labor court system would also raise many problems and present obstacles that may outweigh its advantages. For the reasons already mentioned, it is hardly conceivable today that the labor unions and public opinion would accept the abolition of the *conseils de prud'hommes*, in their present form, for the settlement of individual labor disputes. Rather, it seems much more likely that future developments will proceed in another direction—one that seems preferable indeed—despite the obvious danger that yet another specialized jurisdiction will be created in addition to those that already exist in the various branches of the law. The *conseils de prud' hommes* would remain intact and retain jurisdiction over individual disputes, but new courts would be created to handle collective labor disputes over rights. In fact, a project sponsored by the government for establishing such a system is currently under way as part of a major reform effort to increase within the enterprise the collective rights of the workers (policy of "participation") and to improve the legal status of their representatives. The new courts would have to enforce most of the legal provisions concerning the *délégués du personnel*, the employee members of the works committees, and the *délégués syndicaux* (union representatives within the enterprise). The courts would exist only at the level of the first instance and each would be constituted as a special chamber—called social chamber—of the ordinary court at that level, the *tribunal de grande instance*. But this social chamber would be largely independent of the other chambers of the *tribunal;* its composition, organization, and operation would be quite unique. Its president would be a professional judge, and there would be four wingmen, two representing the employers and two representing the employees; these wingmen would be appointed for terms of three years after their names were drawn by lots from lists of candidates prepared by the most representative employers' associations and labor unions. Appeals against decisions of the social chamber could be lodged before the social chamber of the corresponding court of appeals, just like appeals filed against decisions of the *conseil de prud'hommes,* but it should be mentioned that such social chambers at the appellate level would not constitute new and independent jurisdictions because they already exist, with a composition and organization similar to those of the other chambers of the court of appeals.

There is still much debate about points such as the exact composition of these *Chambres Sociales,* their jurisdiction and their powers, and many details still have to be worked out. A first draft prepared by the government in the spring of 1970 already has been abandoned because of the strong opposition of the labor unions, but it is very likely that a new draft will be presented in the near future. There now is a good chance that legislation of this kind will finally be passed and that new courts or sections of courts designed to deal with this particular type of collective conflicts over rights will finally come into existence. It can even be expected that, in the long run, the role of such newly created bodies will be increased, and there is a possibility that they will be asked to safeguard the exercise of all collective rights belonging to the workers; their jurisdiction would then extend to all collective conflicts over rights.

It is clear that such a reform of the French labor court system would result in combining under the law the two distinctions now made between labor disputes: disputes over interests and disputes over rights —and, among the latter, individual and collective conflicts. While there would have to be two distinct hierarchies of courts for the various types of conflicts, entailing no doubt inconveniences and additional complexity of the system, it is only at this price that a network of procedures can be established to accommodate in the best possible way the growing variety of labor disputes.

II

LABOR COURTS AND GRIEVANCE SETTLEMENT IN WEST GERMANY

by Thilo Ramm

Professor of Law
University of Giessen, West Germany

1.
INTRODUCTION

1. "One cannot imagine any more the legal life of our state without the labor courts. This proves again the fact that they cope fully and satisfactorily with their task of adjusting, appeasing and balancing in the interest of social peace." With these words, a young German labor jurist concluded his historical survey of German labor courts, and his remark truly reflects the general attitude towards labor courts in the Federal Republic of Germany.[1] Today nobody could demand the removal of the labor courts with the slightest hope of success. The courts are a part of the social establishment; they decide all individual and most of the collective labor disputes, except those over new terms of collective bargaining agreements. This strong position of the West German labor courts can be explained only by their historical development.

2. Germany has had labor courts since 1926. They survived the era of National Socialism and, after being closed for a short time in 1945, were reestablished in the German states. Their legal status is now regulated by the *federal* Labor Courts Act of 1953,* a revised and improved version of the Labor Courts Act of 1926 of the Weimar Republic.

The history of the labor courts begins long before 1926. We may go back to 1815, when Prussia acquired the Rhine Province from France and with it some newly established *conseils de prud'hommes*. Or it is

---

[1] This study concerns West Germany (the Federal Republic) only. In East Germany (German Democratic Republic) law has been developed in a different way since 1951, especially since 1953 when the so-called *Konfliktskommissionen* (conflicts boards) were established. At first East Germany followed the pattern of the Soviet Union, but since 1963 it has developed its own system.

* *Arbeitsgerichtsgesetz*, hereafter referred to as LCA.

even possible to consider the Berlin factory court *(Fabrikengericht)* of 1792 a precursor of the labor courts. Decisive, however, was the establishment of the industrial courts *(Gewerbegerichte)* in 1890 and of the commercial courts *(Kaufmannsgerichte)* in 1904. These were tripartite labor courts composed of two laymen, one from the employee's and the other from the employer's side (wingmen), and an impartial chairman who had to be a professional judge or, at the commercial courts, a higher civil servant. But, and herein lies the difference from the present situation, they were only competent to settle disputes of factory workers and commercial clerks and apprentices. Agricultural workers were not covered by this new jurisdiction; for them the feudal law *(Gesinderecht)* remained in force until the end of the first world war.

The history of the industrial and commercial courts has yet to be written;[2] therefore, their decisive influence on the development of German labor law is not as well-known as it should be. They began their activities after the persecution of the socialists under the Anti-Socialist Act of 1878 to 1890 had come to an end, and demonstrated politically the desire of the state to help the proletarians as the economically weaker segment of the population in their struggle against employers for better working conditions. This support by the state was necessary. The trade unions, to some extent certainly because of their Marxist hostility towards private property, failed in concluding collective bargaining agreements in important branches of industry and trade. They were not even recognized by the textile and metal industries as representatives of the workers. The employers claimed to be the "master in the house"; they dictated the working conditions. Therefore, the establishment of the new courts exercised a strong psychological influence upon the workers: for the first time they were recognized by the state as equal partners in the employment relationship. The workers, who were influenced by the political ideas of Marx' famous rival, Ferdinand Lassalle, expected help from the state, and it was in these state courts that employees and employers learned to cooperate.

The right of the state to assign the power of decision in labor disputes to courts was never in doubt. The individual contract of employment was considered to be like all other contracts under common

---

[2] A short survey is given by Wenzel in "75 Jahre deutsche Arbeitsgerichtsbarkeit. Rückblick auf die Geschichte eines Gerichtszweigs," *Juristenzeitung* (1965), 696 ff. at 749; see also the excellent articles by Stieda on "Gewerbegerichte," *Handwörterbuch der Staatswissenschaft*, 2d ed. (1900), vol. 4, p. 393, and 3d ed. (1909), p. 880.

law and, after 1900, under the German Civil Code; therefore, it could be covered by the jurisdiction of the courts. The statutes on industrial and commercial courts merely created new courts for labor matters, replacing to that extent the ordinary courts.

It was the intention of the legislature, approved by both employers and employees, to replace the professional judge, trained in Roman law and sitting alone, with a judicial board in which the wingmen were familiar with the facts of industrial life. The new courts were conceived not to apply common law or the few labor acts, but to create new social law by interpreting the broad, mostly oral, individual contracts of employment. Their activities were to be directed at conciliation.

However, industrial and commercial courts were established only at the first level of the ordinary court system. In labor matters they took the place of the lowest ordinary courts *(Amtsgerichte)*, and because of their limited jurisdiction they can be regarded as small claims courts. More important cases, for example, those involving the performance of the peace obligation in collective bargaining agreements or the responsibility for strikes were, as before, decided by the ordinary courts including the Supreme Court *(Reichsgericht)*. In many cases these decisions were unfavorable to the employees and could be attacked as "class justice." This led to the belief that by enlarging the competence of the industrial and commercial courts and thus developing labor courts as a separate branch of the judiciary, class justice could possibly be eliminated.

3. This point of view explains the battle for labor courts from the beginning of the Weimar Republic, and, on the surface, the six long years of bitter fighting were successful. The labor court system, with full jurisdiction over all labor disputes except those over the conclusion of collective bargaining agreements for which conciliation boards were created, was established at three levels: regular labor court *(Arbeitsgericht)*, appellate labor court *(Landesarbeitsgericht)*, and Supreme Labor Court *(Reichsarbeitsgericht)*. But, and this is important, the Supreme Labor Court was in fact one division[3] *(Senat)* of the Supreme Court, and in it the professional judges were in the majority (three judges and two wingmen). Since all decisions of the appellate labor courts could be legally controlled by the Supreme Labor Court, and the lower courts almost always abided by the decisions of that Court in

---

[3] The term *Senat* is used for all judicial bodies in the higher German courts, for example, within the ordinary courts of the *Oberlandesgerichte* and of the former *Reichsgericht,* now the *Bundesgerichtshof.*

spite of the fact that there was no prejudicial system, the structure of the Supreme Labor Court was in fact decisive for the settlement of labor disputes. Its judgments were proof that the professional judges, as members of the Supreme Court, carried on the legal tradition of that Court in all important questions.

The power of the professional judges was reinforced by two other developments: the introduction of statutory conciliation boards, as already mentioned, and the increasing number of statutes regulating labor relations. Since the decisions of the statutory conciliation boards could be declared to become binding collective bargaining agreements by an award of the *Reichs* Labor Minister, a legal distinction was made between disputes over interests, to be decided by the boards, and disputes over rights, to be decided by the courts. And it was this distinction that led to the conviction that the task of the labor courts was the true application of law.

This became increasingly obvious as the Weimar Republic continued to pass labor legislation. During its short existence, the Republic actually created German labor law, although it failed in some important matters as, for instance, in codifying the law on individual contracts of employment or in improving the provisional governmental decree of 1919 on collective bargaining agreements.

In an exhaustive and bitterly critical essay, "The Social Ideal of the Supreme Labor Court," 1931, followed by another classical analysis, "The Changing Function of Labor Law," 1932,[4] Otto Kahn-Freund, who was then chairman of one panel of the Berlin labor court, described the hostile attitude of the Supreme Labor Court towards strikes and the institutions of collective labor law, as well as the court's "fascist" inclination to "peace and order." The essays explained ideologically the mentality of the judges, their admiration of "a petty bourgeois ideal of individual peace," and their failure to understand the political idea of labor law. But these writings, naturally, did not change prevailing attitudes towards labor courts—the time for that was too short.

Two years later the Nazi dictatorship destroyed the whole mighty system of collective labor law; trade unions and employers' associations were prohibited and replaced by the "German Labor Front." The state regulated working conditions through the "Trustees of Labor," and collective labor decrees *(Tarifordnungen)* became the formal substi-

---

[4] Both studies were re-edited (together with some other significant essays on the labor law of the Weimar Republic) and published under the title *Arbeitsrecht und Politik,* Thilo Ramm, ed. (Neuwied: Luchterhand Verlag, 1966).

tutes for collective bargaining agreements. During the twelve years of the Nazi regime, the labor courts regained their former function of developing labor law. They could even interpret the individual contract of employment, because the National Labor Act of 1934* laid down two general obligations: the welfare obligation *(Fürsorgepflicht)* for employers, and the obligation of fidelity *(Treuepflicht)* for employees and sometimes for employers as well. Both obligations could be, and were, used by the courts to develop other, specific obligations for both sides: for example, the obligation to provide paid vacations was derived from the welfare obligation.

4. The memory of the old industrial and commercial courts and the continued confidence in the labor courts during the Weimar Republic, as well as their role during the Nazi regime, explain the somewhat undeserved reputation of the German labor courts of today. But their history is also important with respect to their present legal status. Labor courts were modeled after the ordinary courts; their organization and structure were, and still are, considered to be a modification of the ordinary courts. Therefore, the provisions of the Act of 1877 on the Constitution of Courts—in the language promulgated in 1950—are generally applied to them, and the German Judges Act of 1961† also pertains to labor courts. Furthermore, the LCA requires that the provisions of the Civil Procedure Act of 1877‡ be used to supplement the special rules of labor procedure. This may explain why labor courts are considered special civil courts and labor procedure special civil procedure.

WEST GERMAN LABOR LAW

1. The German labor courts may be called a pillar, perhaps the most important one, of West German labor law. In order to understand these courts, their function and activities, it is necessary briefly to describe the entire German labor law system.[5]

2. On the surface the German labor law system, which does not include the *Beamtenrecht*,[6] may be described as the system of the Weimar Republic—improved and brought back into existence. This char-

---

* *Gesetz zur Ordnung der nationalen Arbeit*, hereafter referred to as NLA.
† *Deutsches Richtergesetz*, hereafter referred to as GJA.
‡ *Zivilprozessordnung*, hereafter referred to as CPA.
[5] This survey cannot and does not represent a complete and detailed report on German labor law. It shall provide the necessary background material only, so that the German labor court and arbitration systems can be understood.
[6] The *Beamtenrecht*, the law concerning public officials, now is almost unani-

acterization is true insofar as the basis of collective labor law was reestablished by the Collective Bargaining Agreements Act of 1949* and the Works Constitution Act of 1953.† Collective bargaining parties now have more power than they had during the Weimar time because compulsory arbitration by the state of new terms of collective bargaining agreements does not exist today. On the other hand, new, important legislation pertaining to individual contracts of employment was passed, for instance, on the protection against dismissals in 1951, and on paid minimum vacations in 1963.

These acts are all federal acts. Indeed, we may say that now the whole West German labor law is federal law. The Federal Republic has made use of the principle of "concurring legislation," provided by the Bonn Basic Law of 1949, in establishing a uniform labor law. However, the constitutions of the states *(Länder)* also contain many labor law provisions with respect to the basic "social rights" of employees, such as the right to a job, the right to a minimum vacation, or the right to strike. Whether these provisions are still in force was, and is, left to the decisions of German scholars and judges. During the time of the "economic miracle" in Germany, attempts were made to ignore or silently disregard the provisions by a liberalistic interpretation of the Bonn Basic Law. But it is possible that during periods of economic recession and under the pressure of international treaties, especially of the European Social Charter of 1964, far-reaching changes may take place. This would legally be possible if the "social clause" of the Bonn Basic Law, stating that the Federal Republic is a social state, were used as a valid general clause.

3. With respect to collective bargaining, the power of the trade unions evidently has considerably increased. The competition for membership during the time before 1933 among the three largest unions—the socialist, Christian, and liberal—did not revive. After 1945 a unified union *(Einheitsgewerkschaft)* was formed; a small surviving splinter group of Christian unionists is of no practical importance. The structure of

---

mously considered to be part of administrative law rather than labor law. There is a tendency to extend this law and to include, in addition to the public officials appointed for life, all public employees, especially public white-collar workers. This found legal expression in the *Personalvertretungsgesetz* of 1955 (Public Personnel Representation Act), under which special works councils were established for the public administration and which assigned control to the administrative courts instead of the labor courts. Therefore, special chambers with wingmen from both sides were established at the administrative courts.

* *Tarifvertragsgesetz,* hereafter referred to as CBAA.
† *Betriebsverfassungsgesetz,* hereafter referred to as WCA.

the unions was also changed entirely in 1945. Prior to 1933 the unions were organized along craft lines; now they are industrial unions affiliated with the Federation of German Trade Unions.‡ Aside from a number of very small unions of public officials *(Beamte)* and public white-collar workers *(Angestellte)*, the one important exception is the German White-Collar Workers Union *(Deutsche Angestelltengewerkschaft)*. The union membership rate varies; on the average it is about 36 percent of the labor force. The economic position of the unions is presently very strong. They have accumulated capital from membership fees that cover strike expenses, but during the time of the "economic miracle" there were practically no strikes. So the unions decided to go into business themselves; one of their best-known enterprises is the *Bank für Gemeinwirtschaft*, one of the largest banks in West Germany.

On the other hand, the position of the unions is now weaker than it was during the Weimar Republic. The unified union is restricted in political activities under the threat of being split up again, and unlike the socialist union, the most powerful before 1933, it had to pay yet another price: it had to give up the Marxist theory of class struggle and of a classless society. Against that ideological background, private employers had been inclined to grant more favorable conditions in collective bargaining in order to prevent a radical change of the social order.

Moreover, the *employers* are now much better organized than the workers—to about 95 percent. Their various industrial organizations are united in a top organization, the Federal Association of German Employers' Organizations *(Bundesvereinigung der Deutschen Arbeitgeberverbände)*.

Aside from the still existing craft guilds, which gained new strength through Nazi legislation, these organizations, which include small and large enterprises, are parties to collective bargaining agreements. Only a few large enterprises, for example, the *Volkswagen Werke*, have special collective bargaining agreements, the enterprise collective bargaining agreements *(Firmentarifverträge)*. The usual collective bargaining agreement is the association collective bargaining agreement *(Verbandstarifvertrag)*.

The collective bargaining agreement *(Tarifvertrag)*, which must be in writing, is binding upon the parties that have concluded it. This is important with respect to the peace obligation, which is considered a necessary part of the agreement even though it is not formally ex-

---

‡ *Deutscher Gewerkschaftsbund,* hereafter referred to as FGTU.

pressed. The peace obligation is a part of the so-called contractual section of the collective bargaining agreement and concerns only the terms of the individual collective bargaining agreement. What is not part of the agreement is not covered by the peace obligation. Thus, for example, a collective bargaining agreement on wages does not prohibit a union from striking for longer vacations or even from engaging in a secondary strike.

The provisions concerning working conditions constitute the so-called normative section of the collective bargaining agreement. These conditions are binding upon the individual employers and employees who are members of the organizations that concluded the agreement. They become legally a part of the individual contract of employment (the so-called immediate and compulsory effect of the "normative part" of the collective bargaining agreement). Any waiver of his rights acquired in this manner by the individual employee is invalid unless the parties to the collective bargaining agreement have consented to it.

The substitution of conditions of the individual contract of employment by those of the collective bargaining agreement enables the individual employee to bring suit in court. The trade union is not authorized to bring suit in its name, as it can under French or Swedish labor law. On the contrary, it is significant in German labor law that the trade unions do not confront the individual employer; he is not considered a party to the collective bargaining agreement if it was concluded by his organization. If he fails to observe the terms of that agreement in his plant, the trade union must submit a complaint to the employers' association, which must exert pressure on its members according to the so-called "performance duty," another part of the contractual section of the collective bargaining agreement. This member relationship, however, falls under the jurisdiction of the ordinary courts.

Collective bargaining agreements apply to nonunion members under two conditions: First, as required by the CBAA, if they contain plant rules or if they change the constitution of the plant, for example, the composition of the works council. These provisions are applicable to all plants owned by employers who are members of the employers' association that concluded the collective bargaining agreement. Second, if they include "joint institutions of the collective bargaining parties," for example, welfare plans, private pension supplements, and wage equalization funds.

The employer may grant the same working conditions to all nonorganized employees in individual contracts of employment, and he always does so in practice. Another legal method of including nonorganized employees and employers in collective bargaining agreements is provided by government decree: the federal Minister of Labor may, after a formal procedure and under certain conditions, extend the terms of a collective bargaining agreement to such employees and employers.

4. The German trade unions have been deprived of much of their influence within the plants by the introduction of the works councils. According to the Weimar constitution of 1919, councils were to be established at three levels for the entire economy: the plant, the district, and the *Reich*. Councils at the district level were never organized, and those at the *Reich* level were only temporarily established and failed to function after a short period of time. Only at the plant level were works councils established and reactivated by the Works Constitution Act of 1953.

The works council is the representation board elected by all employees, but during its three-year term in office it is practically independent of employees' influence. It may take up all questions with the employer and handle grievances of the employees, and it must watch over the application of all statutes and collective bargaining agreements, as well as its own agreements favoring employees that have been concluded with the employer. Agreements between works councils and employers *(Betriebsvereinbarungen)* must be concluded with respect to social matters, such as the beginning of shifts, time and place of payment of wages, etc., but they may voluntarily be concluded for other purposes as well. This distinction is important with respect to the decision of disputes at the plant level by the board of settlement, which acts either as a compulsory or a voluntary arbitration body.

Employer and works council are expected to cooperate with the employers' association as well as with the trade unions. They are prohibited from "endangering labor and peace in the plant," especially from engaging in strikes and lockouts.[7] This means that the works councils must represent the interests of the workers without the strike weapon, and it explains their weak position if they are not backed by the unions. Therefore, everything depends on the strength of the union and the ability of the employer to keep it out of his plant. Indeed, in

---

[7] The German text is quoted literally here in order to give an example of the legislatorial language, which often cannot be translated to reflect the exact meaning: "Arbeitgeber und Betriebsrat haben alles zu unterlassen, was geeignet ist, die Arbeit und den Frieden des Betriebs zu gefährden. Insbesondere dürfen Arbeitgeber und Betriebsrat keine Massnahmen des Arbeitskampfes gegeneinander durchführen. Arbeitskämpfe tariffähiger Parteien werden hierdurch nicht berührt." (Sec. 49, II, WCA.)

small and medium-sized plants the actual influence of the unions is often very slight. The estimate of 30 percent of all enterprises that, according to the statute, should have works councils but have failed to establish them may be correct; probably most of these are small and medium-sized plants. For the remainder, however, it is estimated that the works council members are 90 percent unionized. Thus, there is a good chance of strong union influence in the larger plants.

Works council–employer agreements may cover the same subject as do collective bargaining agreements, thus competing with the latter. In order to prevent a weakening of the unions' position, the WCA provides that works council–employer agreements are "inadmissible" if wages and other conditions of work are "usually" regulated by collective bargaining agreements, except when a collective bargaining agreement permits a supplementary works council–employer agreement. Naturally, this is no solution to the problem because the employer may voluntarily grant all wages and other conditions that he had conceeded in the agreement with the works council, even after the latter was declared null and void.

5. After legislation, collective bargaining agreements, and works councils, the impact of academic writers on German labor law may be regarded as the fourth and last pillar of German labor law. It reflects the traditional influence legal scholarship has had on German law since the era of common law, and in some respects German labor law, scattered as it is in many pieces of legislation enacted over a considerable period of time, resembles common law. Academic writers on labor law have exercised their influence through the courts and through the legislature, but because of their usually apolitical attitude their ties with the legislature, which they had maintained during the Weimar Republic, disintegrated and only those with the courts have remained.

Two examples may serve to illustrate their strong influence:

(a) Under the statute on collective bargaining agreements, unions are capable of concluding collective bargaining agreements. The term *union* is not synonymous with the term *employees' association,* a distinction that reflects certain principles established by the academic writers on labor law to define the independence of a union from the employer so as to exclude "yellow unions." But academic labor lawyers merged this important question with the problem of political and even religious independence by referring to the provisions of a treaty between the Weimar Republic and Poland on Upper Silesia border problems. And they also applied these principles of independence to the employers' associations without considering the substantial differences in equality between them and the unions.

(b) The same insistence by academic writers on labor law upon equality of employees and employers before the law was applied to strikes and lockouts, even though the constitution of many states recognized only the right to strike and ignored the right to lock out. The constitution of Hessen is an exception; it declares lockouts to be illegal. The overwhelming majority of German labor lawyers desire to accord lockouts the same legal recognition as strikes, and to declare the provisions of the constitution of Hessen null and void.

Both these examples may be considered as evidence of the changing attitude of scholars towards the social question, and, even more so, as evidence of the severe damage done to academic labor law by the Nazi regime. Academic labor law still suffers from the death of Sinzheimer and the expulsion of his school of thought, together with all proponents of the idea to establish social justice in law. Academic labor lawyers lost their left wing and with it their ties to the labor movement. Their present thinking reflects authoritarian ideology, which demonstrates that an effective break with the feudal legal philosophy, revived by the Nazi regime, has not occurred.

The settlement of labor disputes must be seen against this background.

LABOR DISPUTES DEFINED

Labor disputes may be classified in two ways: according to the nature of the dispute, and according to the institution by which it is settled.

1. Individual labor disputes may arise between individuals, that is, between a single employer and a single employee. It would seem logical to speak of collective labor disputes as simply belonging to the opposite category, but this term includes different kinds of disputes: first, disputes between parties to a collective bargaining agreement, that is, between a union on the one side and an employers' association, a single employer, or a group of employers on the other; second, disputes arising at the plant level between the employer and the works councils or other representative bodies, or between the employer and a large number of employees.

This definition of labor disputes is derived from the classical source of labor law development—the confrontation of the employer with the employees. However, in a broader definition labor disputes may also be looked upon as including disputes between individual employees and among groups of employees, between employers' and employees' associations and their members, or between the employer and administrative agencies on safety matters, hours of work, etc.

2. Both of these meanings of labor dispute are important for this investigation. Institutions for the settlement of the more narrowly defined labor disputes are the labor courts and arbitration or conciliation boards, established on a voluntary or statutory basis. The more broadly defined labor disputes may sometimes, though not necessarily, also be decided by these specialized courts or boards, but they often fall under the jurisdiction of other courts, such as the administrative or the ordinary courts. For instance, the ordinary courts have jurisdiction over political strikes considered a tort or over questions of membership, because unions and employers' associations have the legal status of voluntary unincorporated and incorporated associations, respectively.

3. In this study labor disputes as such will be discussed, but disputes over new terms of collective bargaining agreements, the so-called disputes over interests, will be excluded. In German legal terminology, a sharp distinction is made between them and disputes over rights.[8] While disputes over interests are settled by strikes and lockouts or by *Schlichtung,* disputes over rights are settled by the labor courts or by the *Schiedsgerichtsbarkeit. Schlichtung* may be accomplished either by conciliation or by arbitration, but it would be called compulsory *Schlichtung (Zwangsschlichtung)* in the latter case. The settlement of disputes over rights may also be accomplished by conciliation if the parties reserve their right to accept the award of a board of settlement as binding, or by arbitration,[9] or these disputes are decided by the labor courts.

---

[8] This distinction was introduced during the Weimar Republic, when special *Schlichtungs* boards were established. Therefore, it was necessary to distinguish between their jurisdiction and that of the labor courts. The distinction made by Jacobi, one of the best labor lawyers of the Weimar Republic, is still significant. In his *Grundlehren des Arbeitsrechts* (1927), pp. 148 ff., he characterized disputes over rights as those to be decided by "legal judgment" according to the legal order, while disputes over interests are to be settled by an adjustment of the voluntary agreement corresponding to the interests of both parties. In case of failure, a legal decision is not possible.

[9] Therefore, *Schlichtung* and *Schiedsgerichtsbarkeit* have not been translated as conciliation and arbitration, respectively, which merely refer to the procedure and its outcome. The study tries to avoid the German terms and use English terminology only.

LABOR COURTS, GRIEVANCE SETTLEMENT IN WEST GERMANY

Not all labor disputes in the broader definition will be investigated in this study. Emphasis will be given to the institutions of settlement—the labor courts and the various arbitration bodies. This may be the easiest approach to explain the settlement of labor disputes in West Germany.

2.
THE LABOR COURTS

STRUCTURE

1. The present German labor court system is patterned on the system of the Weimar Republic. It consists of three levels: at the first are the regular courts *(Arbeitsgerichte);* at the second are the appellate labor courts *(Landesarbeitsgerichte),* which hear appeals on points of fact and points of law; and at the third is the Federal Labor Court *(Bundesarbeitsgericht),* which hears appeals on points of law only. The 113 regular labor courts[1] and the 12 appellate labor courts[2]—one for each of the states with the exception of Nordrhein-Westfalen, which has two—are established by the German states. The Federal Labor Court is a federal institution. However, this distinction is insignificant with respect to the structure and function of the courts, all of which are covered by the LCA so far as the appointment of judges is concerned.

2. The regular labor courts and the appellate labor courts vary in size. Most of the former consist of one or two panels *(Kammern),* whereas the latter have two panels in small states such as Rheinland-Pfalz, Saarland and in city-states such as Bremen, or as many as eight in the

---

[1] Many courts have branches *(Zweigstellen);* for instance, labor courts in the state of Bavaria have ten. The labor courts also hold special sessions at various locations on certain fixed days *(Gerichtstage).* However, there are complaints that employees involved in disputes have to spend too much time traveling in order to reach the courts. (Cf. Hans G. Joachim, "Die Lage der Arbeitsgerichtsbarkeit in der Bundesrepublik," *Jahrbuch des Arbeitsrechts* (1965), vol. 3, at 68.) This problem is important with respect to cost regulations (cf. p. 124).

[2] The seats of the appellate labor courts are at the state capitals, except in the states of Baden-Württemberg and Hessen. The appellate labor courts also have panels in other cities; for example, the court of Baden-Württemberg has 3 panels in Stuttgart, 2 in Mannheim, and 1 in Freiburg.

LABOR COURTS, GRIEVANCE SETTLEMENT IN WEST GERMANY

Ruhr area and in the state of Baden-Württemberg. The Federal Labor Court consists of five divisions *(Senate)*.[3]

TABLE 1
Number and Location of Labor Courts as of January, 1966*

	Appellate Labor Courts		Regular Labor Courts Number of Professional Judges							
		Number of panels	Number of labor courts	1	2	3	4	5	6	7 and over
Baden-Württemberg	1 Tübingen	8	20	12	5	2	–	–	1	–
Bayern	1 München	7	11	–	8	1	1	–	–	1(12)
Berlin	1 Berlin	7	1	–	–	–	–	–	–	1(21)
Bremen	1 Bremen	2	2	–	1	–	–	1	–	–
Hamburg	1 Hamburg	3	1	–	–	–	–	–	–	1(10)
Hessen	1 Frankfurt	6	12	7	2	–	1	–	1	1(8)
Niedersachsen	1 Hannover	5	15	10	3	1	–	1	–	–
Nordrhein-Westfalen	2 Düsseldorf Hamm	8 7	29	12	9	4	2	–	1	1(7)
Rheinland-Pfalz	1 Mainz	2	10	4	6	–	–	–	–	–
Saarland	1 Saarbrücken	2	3	2	–	1	–	–	–	–
Schleswig-Holstein	1 Kiel	3	9	7	1	–	1	–	–	–
Total in Federal Republic	12	–	113	–	–	–	–	–	–	–

*SOURCE: *Handbuch der Justiz*, edited by Deutscher Richterbund, vol. 8 (1966), pp. 218 ff.

---

[3] It began activities in 1954 with two senates composed of 7 professional judges. Since 1960 the present number of senates with 17 professional judges has been established. As in all other German high courts, the judges have "research assistants," who are also professional judges and are proposed for appointment by the states. At the present time there are 9 such assistants (3 in 1956).

3. The composition of all labor courts follows the same pattern: all panels are composed of two laymen[4] and either one or three professional judges. The laymen, or wingmen, are chosen from the employers' and the employees' side. Together with one professional judge they form the panels of the courts at the two lower levels, and with three professional judges, the divisions of the Federal Labor Court. The one exception is the "big division" (*Grosse Senat*) of the Federal Labor Court, a special institution established to provide uniform adjudication of the Court and to develop the law.[5]

4. Professional judges and wingmen have various titles. In the regular labor courts the professional judges are called "labor court counselors" (*Arbeitsgerichtsräte*); in the appellate labor courts the chairmen of the panels are "appellate labor court directors," one of them being the "president of the appellate labor court." The Federal Labor Court has "federal judges," and the chairmen of the senates are presidents of the divisions, one of them being "president of the Federal Labor Court" who is unofficially also called "chief president." The wingmen are called labor judges, appellate labor judges, and federal labor judges, respectively.

5. Professional judges of the labor courts must have the same qualifications as judges of the ordinary courts or of other German courts.[6] The GJA, which applies to all professional judges, requires that the labor court judge, like all other professional judges, must have passed two state examinations in law: the first after studying law for at least three and one-half years at a university, the second after preparatory and uniformly regulated training in courts and administrative agencies, including a two-month period on labor matters.[7] The professional judge is a special public official, who is appointed for life after a probationary period during which he must demonstrate his ability. Normally, a lawyer applies for appointment to the bench after his second state examination. During the first two years on the bench, the judge

---

[4] In exceptional cases there are four, e.g., in cases involving the interpretation of collective agreements. Cf. p. 105.

[5] Cf., on the importance of the "big division," p. 112.

[6] Also, a professor of law with full tenure at a German university who has not passed the two state examinations required for practitioners of law is qualified to hold judicial office (this is a rare exception).

[7] Prior to June 30, 1964, it was possible to appoint persons who had acquired extensive knowledge and experience in labor law as counselors and representatives before the labor courts. This applied mostly to the representatives of the unions, because representatives of the employers' associations are almost always professional lawyers.

can be dismissed without reason. But he can also be dismissed up to the end of the third or fourth year if he is considered to be unqualified to hold office, or if he is refused appointment for life or for a fixed period by the Committee for the Election of Judges *(Richterwahlausschuss)* in those German states in which such a committee was established by the legislature.

Appointment procedures vary in the different states. Usually the candidates are proposed by the Ministry of Labor[8] after consultation with the Minister of Justice, but they also may be appointed by different authorities: for instance, in Hessen by the Minister of Justice; in Baden-Württemberg by the Prime Minister of that state; and in Nordrhein-Westfalen by the Cabinet. In some states, for example, in Hessen, and in the city-states of Berlin, Bremen, and Hamburg, the candidates must previously have been elected by the Committee for the Election of Judges, which usually is composed of representatives of the labor judiciary, the government, and the Parliament. In Hamburg representatives of the unions and employers' associations are included as well.

Prior to election by the committee—in the states that do not follow this procedure, before appointment to the regular labor courts—a special committee must be consulted, established by the state Minister of Labor and consisting of representatives of the unions, the employers' associations, and the labor judiciary. Before electing or appointing judges to the appellate labor courts, the unions and employers' associations must also be consulted. Finally, according to the framework of the federal act on German judges, the "presidential council" of the labor judiciary must furnish a written opinion on the personal and professional qualifications of a candidate who would receive a salary higher than the first step of the pay scale for judges. (The presidential council is composed of one court president and a number of judges, at least half of whom must have been elected by judges of the appellate labor judiciary; the election of the remainder is left to the discretion of the state.) Evidently, this review by the presidential council is designed to prevent "political" appointments by such devices as transferring public officials from administrative authorities to the courts or appointing politicians to important judicial positions. Some states go still further and require that the presidential council must be consulted before any appointment to the bench is made.

---

[8] This term is used as the more meaningful one instead of quoting the statute on labor courts, which stipulates "the highest labor authority of the state." It is always a minister of a state department, although not necessarily of the department of labor.

In actual practice the influence of the labor judiciary on the appointment of new labor judges is very strong. The president of the appellate labor court reviews all applications for appointment, which are submitted either to the state Minister of Labor or directly to him. He recommends or advises against an appointment after a personal consultation with the applicant, basing his suggestion to the Minister of Labor on the professional qualifications of the applicant as shown by the result of the examination and on the latter's knowledge and experience in labor law. This may consist of former work with unions or employers' associations, of employment as work-student, or of completion of an apprenticeship program. In this manner the legal provision of the Labor Courts Act of 1926 has practically been restored, although according to the present language of the LCA the judges need not even possess special knowledge of labor law or of labor matters.

Judges of the Federal Labor Court are appointed as follows: The candidates are proposed by the federal Minister of Labor or by the Committee for the Election of Judges, which is composed of the state Ministers of Labor and an equal number of members elected by the Parliament and chaired by the federal Minister of Labor who does not vote. The committee elects the judges, but the federal Minister of Labor is entitled, after consultation with the federal Minister of Justice, to refuse presentation of the nominee for appointment to the President of the Federal Republic.

Prior to election or appointment, the presidential council of the Federal Labor Court must prepare a written opinion on the personal and professional qualifications of the candidate. Representatives of unions and employers' associations need not be heard, but they are informally consulted by the Minister of Labor or by members of the Parliament.

Contrary to the practice at the appellate labor courts, a number of high officials of the federal Ministry of Labor were appointed judges of the Federal Labor Court. Also, professors of labor law received appointments to that Court but, with the exception of the first president, they did not have full tenure as professors. It may be of interest to note that two of the seventeen judges are women.

The monthly salary scale for judges, varying somewhat in the different states, ranges from about $275 to $1225, residence and dependant allowances not included.

6. Unlike professional judges, the lay or honorary judges serve in individual court sessions in addition to their regular employment or business. The various panels of the labor courts compile separate al-

TABLE 2

Salaries of Professional Judges in the State of Hessen[1]
and at the Federal Labor Court[2]

Salary Step		Basic Salary per Month in dollars (approx.)	Allowances for Residence and Children
A 13	Labor court counselor................	$276 - $485	$47 to ca. $125 6 children
B 2	Appellate labor court director	650	47 to ca. 125
B 3	Appellate labor court vice-president ..	698	72 to ca. 137
B 6	Appellate labor court president.......	849	72 to ca. 137
B 5	Federal judge	$799	$72 to ca. $142
B 7	President of division	898	72 to ca. 142
B 10	Chief president	1,198	72 to ca. 142

[1] According to the statute on salaries of the state of Hessen of October 11, 1965 (GVBL. 1965 I S. 237).

[2] According to the statute on salaries of the Federal Republic of December 12, 1963 (BGBL. I S. 917), as amended on December 23, 1965 (BGBL. I S. 2118).

phabetical lists of employer and employee labor judges. The judges are called to sessions according to their places on the lists; if a judge is unable to attend, the next one on the list will be called. For emergency cases a special list is available of judges who can serve any time.

The labor and appellate labor judges are appointed by the Ministers of Labor of the states from among groups of employers and employees for terms of four years. The federal labor judges are appointed by the federal Minister of Labor. All candidates are proposed by the unions, independent associations of employees having social or occupational objectives (but without power to conclude collective bargaining agreements), employers' associations, and associations of public corporations. The lists may also include members and white-collar workers of the above organizations, and among employers, legal representatives of corporations, managerial employees, and high-ranking civil servants.

As a precondition for appointment, labor judges must be at least twenty-five years old, and appellate labor judges and federal labor judges at least thirty. All applicants must be in possession of their civil rights and must not be restricted by court order in the disposition of their property.

It is desirable that judges of the appellate labor courts and the Federal Labor Court should have served on the bench of the regular labor courts for at least four years. The LCA stipulates that federal labor judges must have "special knowledge and ability in labor law and labor matters," and that "they have been long-time employers or employees in Germany." Refusal to accept office and resignations are permitted under the following conditions: persons who are past the age of sixty-five; who are ill or physically incapacitated; who serve in another honorary capacity; who have served for nine years on any labor court; or who can submit other credible and significant reasons.

It must be pointed out that the right of the Ministers of Labor to *select* the candidates from nomination lists set up by the organizations exists in theory only. The organizations can barely propose the required number of candidates because of widespread reluctance to accept honorary office.

The list of nominees prepared by the Federation of German Trade Unions contains the names of candidates of the various affiliated unions in proportion to the size of their membership. The candidates, usually active unionists who were officials of the unions' youth departments, are proposed by the district heads of the affiliated unions. They have taken training courses in law and are expected to continue participation in these programs while serving on the bench. If they fail to do so, they will not be renominated.

As the composition of the labor judiciary had never been investigated, this author conducted a survey of the regular labor court of Giessen in the state of Hessen, of the appellate labor court of Hessen sitting in Frankfurt, and of the Federal Labor Court. It was found that among 37 labor judges on the employees' side who were proposed by the German White-Collar Workers' Union, 5 were legal agents of unions and 18 were members of works councils. From among 37 labor judges on the employers' side, all proposed by the Association of Hessian Employers, 2 were employees of that Association, 16 were independent businessmen, and 19 were employees with managerial functions.

The only information available for the appellate labor court of Hessen disclosed that from among 162 labor judges, on the employees' side 12 were business agents of unions and 4 were civil servants; on the employers' side 6 were employers and 5 were high-ranking civil servants. Further details could not be obtained.

The investigation at the Federal Labor Court covers the period from the establishment of the Court until August, 1966. Two facts are clearly evident: first, there is a predominance of officials, especially on the unions' side, and of employees with managerial functions on the employers' side; second, all of these labor judges serve for very long terms. Rotation of judges at the Federal Labor Court may be considered the exception rather than the rule.

TABLE 3
Federal Labor Judges*

Number	Position	Term of Office
	Employees	
34	Union officials	9 years average
2	Union officials (retired)	16 years each
2	White-collar workers of public services	8 and 4 years respectively
2	Blue-collar workers of public services	12 and 8 years respectively
1	Official of the Catholic labor movement (not competent to conclude coll. agreements)	4 years
1	Employee of U. S. Armed Forces	4 years
1	Social worker	8 years
1	Chemist (retired)	12 years
1	Attorney	16 years
1	Editor-in-chief (labor gazette of the FGTU)	16 years
1	White-collar worker (employed in plant)	4 years
1	Manual worker (employed in plant)	8 years
	Employers	
16	Officials of employers' associations	11 years
10	Public officials of public services	11½ years
15	Employees with managerial functions	8½ yeasr
4	Self-employed businessmen	13⅓ years
3	Members of boards of directors	13⅓ years

* Composition as of August 1, 1966.
SOURCE: Private investigation (Gerd Metzmaier).

The lay judges are reimbursed for the loss of earnings and for travel and transportation expenses, as set forth in the statute on the compensation of honorary judges of 1957. Compenastion for hours lost from work ranges from 75¢ to $1.25. Employers are also reimbursed for hiring substitutes.

JURISDICTION

1. Since 1890 the jurisdiction of the labor courts has been gradually expanded and seems now to have reached its limits. In order to understand the provisions on jurisdiction of the LCA, one must be aware of the distinction that is made in Germany between individual and collective disputes. However, both these terms are not used in the language of the LCA, and it will be shown that their traditional meaning does not correspond to the provisions of German law, which are much more extensive.

The LCA speaks of the "exclusive jurisdiction" of the labor courts. This term, and its complementary term, the "optional jurisdiction" of the labor courts, merely concerns the relationship between labor courts and the other courts—originally the ordinary courts but now the administrative courts as well. Exclusive jurisdiction does not prevent the intervention of constitutional courts when the constitution or the violation of a constitutional right is involved. Based on the development of labor law out of civil law, the labor courts are generally regarded as "special civil courts."

2. The first category of individual disputes includes the following: private disputes between an employer and an employee arising out of the employment relationship, over the existence or nonexistence of an individual contract of employment, over claims arising out of negotiations of an individual contract of employment,[9] or over obligations that remain after the contract of employment has terminated;[10] or disputes arising out of torts if they are connected with the employment relationship.[11] All of these cases fall under the exclusive jurisdiction of the labor courts. Excluded from this broad jurisdiction are nonfinancial disputes relating to an employee's invention, which must be decided by the patent court. As defined in the statute, the term employee applies to manual workers, white-collar workers, and persons employed for their vocational training, such as apprentices and volunteers. But under the LCA homeworkers and individuals who are economically dependent on another person *(arbeitnehmerähnliche Personen)* also are regarded as employees, while neither civil servants nor persons who are legal representatives of corporations are considered employees. However, persons in the latter group may contractually agree with their employers upon the optional jurisdiction of the labor courts.

A second, entirely different, category of individual legal disputes includes disputes among employees arising out of the employment of work gangs (e.g., over gang piece-rate payment or over the distribution of wages among the members of the gang), or out of torts connected with the employment relationship (e.g., insults because of poor work performance).

---

[9] For example: reimbursement of traveling expenses in connection with employees' interviews, demanded by the employer; expenses in connection with the replacement of letters of recommendation which were lost by the employer.

[10] For example: claims for pensions; claims involving wrongful competition or wrongful revelation of plant secrets.

[11] For example: the dismissed employee inflicts bodily harm on his former employer, seeking vengeance for his dismissal.

3. Collective disputes also include parties to collective bargaining agreements and to works constitutions. The LCA speaks of "private disputes between the parties to a collective bargaining agreement or between them and third parties arising out of collective bargaining agreements, or over their existence or nonexistence; and civil legal disputes between parties competent to conclude a collective bargaining agreement or between them and third parties arising out of torts, if they are actions of industrial dispute or concern the right of self-organization." This long and complicated quotation covers all disputes over the so-called contractual section of the collective bargaining agreement, including the peace obligation; but disputes over the interpretation of the normative section of the collective bargaining agreement are covered as well. The very broad definition of the jurisdiction over torts does not include political strikes, for which the ordinary courts remain competent.[12] The self-organization clause also includes disputes over attempts of either employers' associations or unions to coerce membership.

Furthermore, the LCA sets forth limitations on the legal capacity of an association to conclude collective bargaining agreements. With respect to collective bargaining agreements, the CBAA provides that only a union—and not every employees' association—is permitted to conclude a collective bargaining agreement in order to assure the independence of the organization from the employer. This regulation has now been extended by the LCA to include employers' associations as well.

In deciding these cases, and in legal disputes between parties to a collective bargaining agreement arising out of the collective bargaining agreement or out of the existence or nonexistence of collective bargaining agreements, the panels of the labor courts and appellate labor courts are composed of one professional judge and four wingmen.

The provisions of the LCA concerning the WCA do not speak of disputes over rights, but regulate the jurisdiction of the labor courts according to the case involved. They may be summarized by referring to the authority responsible for deciding the dispute: the panel of the labor court, its chairman, or the president of the appellate labor court. However, the competence of the latter two authorities—with one interesting exception—applies only to disputes over the composition of the board of settlement, which will be discussed later in connection with arbitration procedure. The exception is the decision of the chairman

---

[12] In connection with this disputed question, see Ramm, "Der Begriff Arbeitskampf," *Archiv für zivilistische Praxis* (1961), vol. 160, pp. 336 ff.

of the labor court concerning "disciplinary actions against the employer who continues personnel practices objected to by the court."

Among the various cases are disputes over the existence or nonexistence of a works council–employer agreement and over the rights of the works council. Other disputes involve the requirement, composition, and election of works councils, central works councils, and young workers' representation boards. Into the latter category fall disputes over the dissolution of works councils, the term of office of their members, active and passive voting rights, and eligibility. Finally, the court decides disputes over the election and removal of employees from the supervisory council.

All disputes over problems connected with the WCA and over the legal capacity of employers' and employees' associations are decided in a special procedure *(Beschlussverfahren)*.

4. The jurisdiction of the labor courts has been extended by two additional provisions. The first is designed to avoid a legalistic interpretation of the term "employer"; thus, the legal successor or the legal representative or the autonomous welfare organizations of an enterprise is included in this term. The second is designed to prevent contradictory decisions of other courts in matters legally or economically connected with suits that are pending or simultaneously become pending in a labor court. Therefore, suits brought against employers or employees, parties to a collective bargaining agreement, associations competent to conclude a collective bargaining agreement, or even third parties may also be brought before a labor court. For example, an employer may sue an employee for breach of contract together with the latter's new employer who enticed him to this action. Or, if the wage claims of an employee are guaranteed by the employer's bank and the bank fails to meet its commitment, the employee may sue both employer and bank in the labor court.

5. In contrast to the Labor Courts Act of 1926, the LCA of 1953 does not require separate panels for dealing with disputes of manual workers and those of white-collar workers, but on occasion expert panels will be created for certain professions, trades, or groups of employers. For example, Nordrhein-Westfalen established expert panels in all labor courts for artisans and in two courts for railroad employees; Schleswig-Holstein, in all labor courts for artisans and agricultural workers, in five courts for public employees, and in one court for seamen; Berlin has expert panels for retail and wholesale employees, department store clerks, textile workers, and employees of the public services.

LABOR COURTS, GRIEVANCE SETTLEMENT IN WEST GERMANY

As the result of their historical development, the labor courts, which began as special courts for specific professions, have now become courts for all labor problems. Only criminal and political matters, for example, political strikes, are excluded from their jurisdiction. Moreover, the organization of the labor courts, which does not permit a distinction between manual and white-collar workers, is far more advanced than substantive labor law, which is still based on that distinction.

6. The panels of the appellate labor courts, with the exception of that of Hessen, are established on a geographical basis. The Hessen appellate labor court and the Federal Labor Court have boards for specific occupations.

7. On the average, between 170,000 and 180,000 suits are filed annually in the labor courts; the figure of about 190,000 in 1957 was exceptionally high. The caseload has increased during the last three

TABLE 4

Year	Complaints Submitted to Labor Courts[1]	No. of Employees in Labor Force[2] (including Unemployed)	General Complaints[3] in Regular Proceedings before the Ordinary Courts of First Instance	Total Population[4]
1952		16,440,000	Amtsgericht	50,859,000
1953	170,210	16,591,600	Landgericht	51,350,000
1954	170,400	17,419,400		51,880,000
1955	157,853	18,074,800		52,382,000
1956	159,449	18,785,600		53,008,000
1957	189,992	19,250,700		53,656,000
1958	177,446	19,560,000	886,983	54,292,000
1959	171,198	19,823,500	868,314	54,876,000
1960	160,530	20,488,400	865,866	55,433,000
1961	164,267	20,911,000	847,432	56,175,000
1962	158,566	21,207,000	925,404	56,938,000
1963	164,982	21,489,000	933,555	57,587,000
1964	177,191	21,716,000	934,507	58,266,000
1965	178,287	21,988,000	920,736	59,012,000
1966	182,817	22,031,000	939,360	59,638,000

SOURCE:

[1] Annual reports by H. Rüstig, "Die Gerichte in Arbeitssachen" in *Arbeit und Recht* (vols. 1953 ff).
[2] Annual Statistical Reports of the Federal Republic of Germany, 1952–66, Section: Employment.
[3] Annual Statistical Reports of the Federal Republic of Germany, 1958–66, Section: All Judicial Affairs.
[4] Annual Statistical Reports of the Federal Republic of Germany, 1952–66, Section: Population Growth.

TABLE 5
Complaints Filed[1]
(Excluding *Beschlussverfahren*)

Year	Total Number of Complaints filed in the Federal Republic	Complaints filed by Employees, by Unions, and by Works Councils	Percent	Complaints filed by Employers and their Associations	Percent	Complaints filed by the States	Percent
1953[2]	170,210		97.2		2.8		0.1
1954[2]	170,400		96.1		3.9		0.1
1955[2]	157,853	151,166	95.8		4.2	175	0.1
1956[2]	159,449	150,981	94.7	6,512	5.3	236	0.1
1957	189,992	179,570	94.5	8,232	5.5	206	0.1
1958	177,446	164,558	92.7	10,216	7.2	288	0.1
1959	171,198	159,913	93.4	12,600	6.5	114	0.1
1960	160,530	148,344	92.4	11,171	7.5	136	0.1
1961	164,627	150,981	91.7	12,050	8.2	148	0.1
1962	158,566	143,933	90.8	13,498	9.2	99	0.1
1963	164,982	150,510	91.2	14,534	8.7	102	0.1
1964	177,191	161,974	91.4	14,370	8.5	244	0.1
1965	178,287	162,705	91.2	14,973	8.7	122	0.1
1966	182,817	167,541	91.6	15,460	8.2	250	0.1
				15,026			

[1] SOURCE: Annual reports by H. Rüstig, "Die Gerichte in Arbeitssachen" in *Arbeit und Recht* (vols. 1955–66); *Arbeits- und Sozialstatistische Mitteilungen*, published by the Bundesministerium für Arbeit und Sozialordnung (vols. 1955–67).

[2] Saarland not included.

years, but this increase corresponds vaguely to the overall growth of the labor force and therefore the ratio is relatively constant.

These statistics, which should be compared with suits brought in the ordinary courts and the total number of employees in the labor force, cover a period of economic growth with practically no unemployment. According to general experience, a recession will increase the number of suits before the labor courts, the proportion of suits to the number of employees in the labor force becoming larger.

Nine out of ten suits are filed in the labor courts by employees, unions, or works councils. In 1953 that percentage was higher still—97—but in the meantime complaints of employers and their associations have increased. The proportion of suits filed by the states involving homeworkers has remained constant, but very small, at 0.1 percent.

The number of suits filed by employees in the labor courts *after* termination of the contract of employment is very high. (However, this cannot be statistically proven.) The unions' legal agents have estimated it at 80 percent for their members, and the same or an even higher percentage must be estimated for unorganized employees, according to information supplied by professional judges of the labor courts. This is a result of the employees' fear of repercussions if they go to the labor courts during the life of their employment contracts. The one exception is the public service, wherein claims, as a rule, can be satisfied only by court decisions; the remaining 20 percent of suits brought in labor courts are mainly filed by employees of the public service and of large enterprises. However, the latter hardly ever file suits whose outcome is in doubt during the life of their contracts.

A survey of the main complaints before the labor courts reveals the following: about 50 percent of all cases involve wages, about 20 percent dismissals, about 8 percent vacation time and pay, and another 8 percent credentials and letters of recommendation. The decreasing percentages of disputes over vacation matters may be a consequence of rgulations by the federal statute on vacation; the figures on dismissals become less significant in light of the period of economic growth and full employment.

PROCEDURE

1. As stated in the introductory pages, labor court procedure must be understood as modified civil court procedure; therefore, the provisions of the LCA are supplemented by CPA regulations of 1877. However, since civil procedure was thoroughly reformed in 1921 and 1934, it is now very similar to procedure before the labor courts. This is true

TABLE 6

Distribution of Complaints Involving Major Issues[1]

Year	Compensation	Percent	Vacation Time and Pay	Percent	Termination	Percent	Credentials and Letters of Recommendation	Percent
1953[2]	96,259	52.3	16,716	9.2	41,732	22.9	11,522	6.3
1954[2]	90,913	49.3	17,329	9.4	46,499	25.2	11,382	6.2
1955[3]	89,520	48.8	17,833	9.7	42,312	23.1	13,783	7.5
1956[3]	93,671	48.1	17,467	9.1	42,283	22.1	13,714	7.2
1957	97,413	48.6	17,054	8.5	46,961	23.4	14,066	7.0
1958	112,009	50.8	16,525	7.5	48,683	22.1	14,446	6.5
1959	102,524	49.2	15,429	7.4	46,058	22.1	14,929	7.2
1960	94,566	49.3	15,064	7.9	38,114	19.9	14,440	7.5
1961	98,174	51.2	12,878	6.7	36,816	19.1	13,588	7.1
1962	87,086	47.9	12,100	6.7	38,642	21.3	13,941	7.7
1963	87,917	46.3	13,053	6.9	41,264	21.7	15,561	8.2
1964	101,920	49.8	13,653	6.7	38,781	19.0	15,486	7.6
1965	96,577	49.1	13,540	6.8	36,217	18.4	15,744	7.9
1966	110,756	51.3	14,191	6.5	40,504	18.8	15,931	7.4

[1] SOURCE: Annual reports by H. Rüstig, "Die Gerichte in Arbeitssachen" in *Arbeit und Recht* (vols. 1953 ff.).
[2] Berlin and Saarland not included.
[3] Saarland not included.

especially with respect to the position of the judges who conduct the inquisitory process, the informal discussion without strict rules of evidence, and the broad judicial discretion concerning the value of evidence.

2. Also, the remedies available in the labor courts are like those provided by the ordinary courts. But for both court systems a distinction must be made between the two forms of appeal: appeal on points of law *and* points of fact *(Berufung);* appeal on points of law only, or on the alleged violation of a legal norm *(Revision)*. Appeals on points of law and points of fact may be based on the introduction of new facts and evidence and are decided by the appellate labor courts. Appeals to the Federal Labor Court are restricted to legal questions and generally concern the decisions of the appellate labor courts only. In exceptional cases, a decision of a labor court may be submitted for review on direct appeal to the Federal Labor Court if it involves a collective dispute and the federal Minister of Labor declares an immediate decision of that Court to be necessary, or if an appeal against a similar decision of an appellate labor court would be admitted because of the value in dispute and with consent of the other party. Both forms of appeal are admissible under the statute if the value in dispute is of a certain amount, or, according to the provisions of the LCA, if they are especially admitted by the court in charge of the case.

The appellate labor courts admit appeals if the value in dispute amounts to $75; the Federal Labor Court, if the value in dispute amounts to $1,500.

Leave to appeal may be granted by the labor courts because of the fundamental significance of the case, and the LCA encourages appeal when the court deviates from another judgment involving one of the parties to the dispute that was submitted to it, or if it deviates from a decision of its superior appellate labor court. Another ground for appeal is that the decision concerning a collective bargaining agreement covers more than the jurisdictional district of the court.

Appeals from the decisions of the appellate labor courts may be individually allowed, without stating reasons, by the court. Appeal can be had as a matter of right if the decision of the appellate labor court is based on a deviation from a previous decision of the Federal Labor Court or on a decision of another appellate labor court, or if the legal question at issue has not yet been decided by the Federal Labor Court. Evidently, the legislative aim here is to guarantee uniform adjudication by avoiding contradictory decisions. However, this goal can only partially be achieved because the appellate labor courts have incomplete access to their mutual decisions, most of which are not published, and because only about one-third of the decisions of the Federal Labor Court are published.[13]

The desire to achieve uniformity of adjudication also explains the establishment of the big senate, which is a common feature of German supreme courts, the Federal Constitutional Court excepted. The big senate must render a decision if one division of the Federal Labor Court is inclined to deviate from a previous decision of another division, or in questions of fundamental importance if the division in charge of the case considers the decision of the big senate necessary in order to develop the law and to secure uniform adjudication. During the tenure of the first president of the Federal Labor Court, from 1954 to 1963, the big senate ruled on fourteen cases, all of them involving a question of fundamental importance.[14]

Statistical data provide an interesting background to labor court activities. Only about 4 percent of the cases submitted to the courts are appealed on points of law and points of fact. However, when the number of decisions after litigation is considered, the rate of appeals amounts to more than one-third. About 18 percent of the decisions of the appellate labor courts are appealed; the decreasing percentage and number may be explained by the adjudication of the Federal Labor Court, which decided some disputed questions.

The statistics show that a large percentage of suits is not settled by court decisions after trial. Detailed analyses are given for the regular labor courts in table 8, for the appellate labor courts in table 9, and for the Federal Labor Court in table 10. In these tables compromises are listed as such, but only when they were reached before a labor court.

The very high percentage of compromises before the regular labor courts—30 to 40 percent—results from a special procedure, the conciliation procedure.

3. Originally the conciliation procedure was a special feature of the industrial and commercial courts, distinguishing these courts from the ordinary courts. But the CPA was amended in 1921 and allowed con-

---

[13] The name of the official publication is *Entscheidungen des Bundesarbeitsgerichts*, consisting of 19 volumes to date (1970), published by the de Gruyter Verlag, Berlin. More comprehensive is Hueck-Nipperdey-Dietz, *Nachschlagwerk des Bundesarbeitsgerichts, Arbeitsrechtliche Praxis* (AP), a loose-leaf edition in which a systematic ordering of the decisions, including comments of labor lawyers, has been attempted. Cf. for details my critical comments in "Die Rechtsprechung des Bundesarbeitsgerichts," *Juristenzeitung* (1964), p. 494.

[14] A list of the opinions of these decisions is contained in Ramm. *op. cit.*, p. 494.

TABLE 7
Complaints Submitted to the Labor Courts[1]
(including Berlin)

Year	Total Number of Complaints	Cases Settled by Judgment on the Merits	Cases Appealed	Cases Submitted to Review[3]
1953	170,210[2]	16,901	5,351	—
1954	170,400[2]	17,546	6,846	731
1955	159,449[2]	17,233	6,606	592
1956	157,853[2]	17,120	6,738	625
1957	189,992	17,159	6,422	658
1958	177,446	17,732	6,652	598
1959	171,198	16,965	6,358	598
1960	160,530	16,255	5,930	502
1961	164,627	15,763	5,862	570
1962	158,566	16,344	5,620	515
1963	164,982	17,224	6,527	541
1964	177,191	17,724	6,539	471
1965	178,287	16,423	6,270	542
1966	182,817	17,080	6,062	471

[1] SOURCE: Annual reports by H. Rüstig, "Die Gerichte in Arbeitssachen" in *Arbeit und Recht* (vols. 1953 ff.).

[2] Saarland not included.

[3] The Federal Labor Court began its activities on April 21, 1954.

ciliation before the lowest ordinary courts *(Amtsgerichte)* as well. The two procedures are now more or less alike except that labor conciliation procedure is more detailed and, as explained below, proceedings are considerably longer if conciliation fails.

The LCA sets forth that the first oral plea must be entered before the chairman of the labor court—without the wingmen!—in order to reach an amicable settlement of the dispute. In that session, defined by the statute as *Güteverhandlung*, the chairman discusses with the parties all details of the dispute "under free consideration of all circumstances." In order to elucidate all the facts involved in the dispute, he has wide discretionary power to take immediate steps, questioning under oath excepted. The outcome of that session, especially when a settlement is reached, is noted in the records. If conciliation fails or if one party does not appear before the chairman, the proceedings are continued immediately or within three days before the court, which is now composed of judge and wingmen. In practice, however, usually three months elapse between the conciliation session and litigious proceedings before the courts. In proceedings before the lowest ordinary courts, postponement is not necessary because the professional judge,

TABLE 8

Decisions of Cases Submitted to the Regular Labor Courts[1]

Year	Total No. of Cases Settled	Settled by Compromise	Percent	Settled by Judgment on the Merits	Percent	Settled by Other Judgment[3]	Percent	Settled Otherwise[4]	Percent
1953[2]	168,718	68,134	40.4	16,901	10.0	26,102	15.4	57,581	34.2
1954[2]	168,672	68,639	40.7	17,546	10.4	22,868	13.5	59,619	35.4
1955[2]	154,967	62,782	40.5	17,233	11.1	19,507	12.6	55,445	35.8
1956[2]	161,892	64,289	39.7	17,120	10.6	19,765	12.2	60,718	37.5
1957	170,375	66,526	39.0	17,159	10.1	20,802	12.2	65,888	38.7
1958	189,554	66,056	34.8	17,732	9.4	23,818	12.6	81,948	43.2
1959	177,285	62,571	35.3	16,965	9.6	26,230	14.5	71,519	40.3
1960	161,704	54,509	33.7	16,255	10.1	23,125	14.3	67,815	41.9
1961	165,307	52,642	31.8	15,763	9.5	22,898	13.9	74,004	44.8
1962	156,986	52,741	33.6	16,344	19.4	23,769	15.1	64,132	40.9
1963	160,486	52,761	32.9	17,224	10.7	23,409	14.6	67,092	41.0
1964	174,784	52,609	30.1	17,724	10.1	26,830	15.4	77,621	44.4
1965	167,552	50,694	30.2	16,423	9.8	25,937	15.5	74,498	44.5
1966	185,144	53,784	29.1	17,080	9.2	32,645	17.6	81,635	44.1

[1] SOURCE: Annual reports by H. Rüstig, "Die Gerichte in Arbeitssachen," in *Arbeit und Recht* (vols. 1953–66).

[2] Saarland not included.

[3] "Settled by Other Judgment" includes: *judgment by default* in cases where one party fails to appear in court and the other party petitions for this type of judgment; *judgment on account of acknowledgement* in cases where the defendant acknowledges the justification of the claim against him in proceedings before the labor court; *judgment of abandonment* in cases where the plaintiff abandons the claim. Although accurate figures are not available, judgments by default are by far the most numerous.

[4] This category includes primarily *withdrawal of suits* which most often occurs in cases settled out of court by mandatory conciliation procedures. It also includes cases where the main point at issue was settled after a complaint had been lodged, either because the defendant satisfied the plaintiff's claim or the plaintiff's claim became involved because of other circumstances.

TABLE 9

Decisions of Cases Appealed to the Appellate Labor Courts[1]

Year	Total No. of Cases Settled	Settled by Compromise	Percent	Settled by Judgment on the Merits	Percent	Settled by Other Judgment	Percent	Settled by Award	Percent	Settled Otherwise	Percent
1953[2]	6,560	1,931	29.4	2,409	36.7	125	1.9	—	—	2,095	32.0
1954[2]	6,494	1,675	25.8	2,652	40.8	162	2.5	—	—	2,005	30.9
1955[2]	6,778	2,063	30.4	2,721	40.1	102	1.5	—	—	1,892	28.0
1956[2]	6,648	1,778	26.7	2,836	42.7	99	1.5	433	6.5	1,502	22.6
1957	6,584	1,782	27.1	2,755	41.8	85	1.3	506	7.7	1,456	22.1
1958	6,500	1,742	26.8	2,732	42.0	103	1.6	524	8.1	1,399	21.5
1959	6,661	1,773	26.6	2,825	42.4	85	1.3	492	7.4	1,486	22.3
1960	5,930	1,567	26.4	2,637	44.5	81	1.4	446	7.5	1,199	20.2
1961	5,728	1,481	25.9	2,549	44.5	88	1.5	453	7.9	1,157	20.2
1962	5,799	1,533	26.8	2,599	44.1	60	1.0	466	8.0	1,161	20.1
1963	5,910	1,456	24.6	2,618	44.3	75	1.3	543	9.2	1,218	20.6
1964	6,104	1,534	25.1	2,617	42.9	96	1.6	558	9.1	1,299	21.3
1965	6,405	1,620	25.3	2,807	43.8	114	1.8	559	8.7	1,305	20.4
1966	6,501	1,772	27.3	2,658	40.9	144	2.2	591	9.1	1,336	20.5

[1] SOURCE: Annual reports by H. Rüstig, "Die Gerichte in Arbeitssachen" in *Arbeit und Recht* (vols. 1953–66).
[2] Saarland not included.

TABLE 10

Cases Submitted for Review to the Federal Labor Court[1]

Year	Total No. of Cases Settled	Settled by Compromise	Percent	Settled by Judgment on the Merits	Percent	Settled by Other Judgment	Percent	Settled by Award	Percent	Complaint Withdrawn or Settled Otherwise	Percent
1954[2]	247	4	—	37	—	—	—	111	—	95	—
1955[2]	408	11	2.7	116	28.4	1	0.2	166	40.7	114	28.0
1956[2]	496	24	4.8	190	38.3	2	0.4	116	23.4	104	33.1
1957	642	45	7.0	273	42.5	2	0.3	160	24.9	162	25.3
1958	603	47	7.8	271	44.9	2	0.3	134	22.3	149	24.7
1959	725	148	20.4	291	40.1	5	0.7	115	15.9	166	22.9
1960	710	95	13.4	381	53.7	2	0.3	121	17.0	111	15.6
1961	618	54	8.7	324	52.4	1	0.2	117	19.0	122	19.7
1962	622	54	8.7	272	43.7	1	0.2	118	19.0	177	28.4
1963	560	53	9.5	268	47.8	5	0.9	122	21.8	112	20.0
1964	490	22	4.5	226	46.1	2	0.4	134	27.4	106	21.6
1965	499	46	9.2	237	47.5	—	—	130	26.1	86	17.2
1966	543	109	20.1	230	42.4	—	—	125	23.1	79	14.5

[1] SOURCE: Annual reports by H. Rüstig, "Die Gerichte in Arbeitssachen" in *Arbeit und Recht* (vols. 1955–66).
[2] Saarland not included.

who decides alone, may immediately begin to try the case on its merits.

The duty to try to reach an amicable settlement is not restricted to the first special session before the regular labor court, but must be regarded as one of the characteristic features of the total proceedings before the labor courts and the appellate labor courts. The LCA contains general provisions requiring these courts to attempt "settlement of the legal dispute by compromise during the entire proceedings." This may explain the fact that 25–30 percent of the appeals on points of law and points of fact are still settled by compromise (see table 9), and even 10 percent of the appeals to the Federal Labor Court are settled in this manner (see table 10). However, according to the policy of the Federal Labor Court, these are largely cases that would have been remanded to the appellate labor courts or to another branch of the judiciary for settlement, or that involve legal disputes not of fundamental importance.

The rules on court costs also favor conciliation. If a compromise is reached before the regular labor court or an out-of-court settlement is reported to the court, fees are not charged at that level, even after a trial. The very aim of promoting amicable settlement explains why the termination of a dispute by a judgment of acknowledgement, or a withdrawal of the suit without previous trial at this court, permits exemption from paying court costs. If cases are appealed to the appellate court or to the Federal Labor Court, or if the dispute is terminated by a judgment of default without trial, the fees are reduced to half their ordinary amount. Therefore, not only the officially acknowledged compromises before the labor courts are statistically important. The figures of cases "settled otherwise" (tables 8 to 10) certainly include a very high percentage of out-of-court compromises mostly reached after the conciliation session before the regular labor courts, while out-of-court compromises pending appeal at the appellate labor courts are much less significant.

Some idea of the relationship between compromises reached before the court and those reached out of court may be gained from a statistical compilation of the FGTU that, of course, covers union members only (table 11).

4. Although conciliation has now become a legal duty of the ordinary courts at the first level as well, the *Beschlussverfahren* must still be considered a special feature of the labor courts. The provisions of the LCA are complicated because they distinguish between regular procedure on questions of the works constitutions and three special pro-

TABLE 11

	Labor Courts			Appellate Labor Courts		
Year	Compromise in court	Compromise out-of-court	Disputes settled otherwise	Compromise in court	Compromise out-of-court	Disputes settled otherwise
1950	Compromises: 21,598[1] (incl. social insurance matters)[2]					
1951	Compromises: 23,366[1] (incl. social insurance matters)[2]					
1952	3,661					
1953	3,098					
1954	2,052	2,361[3]				
1955	1,812	2,116				
1956	$1,128,528[4]	$ 453,268				
1957	1,395,178[4]	453,018				
1958	1,776,286[4]	452,552				
1959	750,938	316,114		$50,691	$ 9,043	
1960	704,287	456,995		72,909	3,293	
1961	765,467	341,184		29,652	15,012	
1962	922,704	452,333	$113,289	43,125	7,733	$5,378
1963	879,854	1,054,944	222,411	66,861	5,676	9,839
1964	905,514	534,738	154,758	64,122	8,796	9,375

[1] These figures represent the number of cases.

[2] These figures apply only to the legal-aid activities of local and district boards of the Federation of German Trade Unions.

[3] Figures apply only to the activities of the FGTU's Department of Legal Protection in labor matters.

[4] Figures concern compensations determined by compromise reached in court *and* by court judgment.

cedures: the first relating to disputes over the legal capacity of an employers' or an employees' association to conclude collective bargaining agreements; the second and third relating to disputes on the composition of the boards of settlement in disputes between the employer and the works council and between the employer and the central works council, respectively. The main difference between the special and the regular procedures lies in the various compositions of the courts. The regular labor courts and the appellate labor courts with two additional wingmen—not the Federal Labor Court—rule on the legal capacity to conclude collective bargaining agreements; the chairman of the regular labor court alone rules on the composition of the boards of settlements; and the president of the appellate labor court alone rules on the composition of these boards in disputes between the employer and the central works council.

The order procedure *(Beschlussverfahren)* is not the usual procedure involving two parties; rather, it has the character of an efficient investigation initiated by a petition, which may be filed in all cases by the employer or, as finally decided by the Federal Labor Court, by a union with members in the plant involved. In the proceedings the employer, the employees, and others must be heard, as stipulated by the WCA and supplementary legislation that is expected to be passed in the future. The court has discretion in its decisions, which, however, are controlled by the appellate labor court and the Federal Labor Court.

The number of cases decided by the order procedure is not very large and has been decreasing steadily since 1955, the first year covered by the statistics in table 12. About 85 percent of the cases are submitted by employees, unions, and works councils.

TABLE 12

Year	Cases Decided by Order Procedure (Beschlussverfahren)	Employees	Employers	Supreme Labor Administrative Agency
1953				
1954				
1955[1]	746	629	114	3
1956[1]	409	319	90	–
1957	835	713	122	–
1958	397	341	56	–
1959	588	476	112	–
1960	335	297	38	–
1961	562	491	71	–
1962	383	334	49	–
1963	449	401	48	–
1964	344	300	44	–
1965	507	459	48	–
1966	319	284	33	2

[1] Saarland not included.

5. Generally, the advantages of proceedings before the labor courts are expeditious settlement and lower court costs. This finding is valid when compared with proceedings before the ordinary courts, but not with arbitration, which has a rather modest role in Germany.

The principle of expeditiousness, formally expressed as a procedural axiom, is realized in several ways: there are no court vacations; the periods within which appeals may be lodged are much shorter than at the ordinary courts; the production of new facts before the appellate labor courts is restricted; the appellate labor court may not remand cases to the regular labor court because of procedural errors; and decisions reached in challenges of the impartiality of the judge cannot be appealed. There are also other provisions that simplify and expedite

TABLE 13A

Duration of Proceedings before the Labor Courts

Year	Claims Settled by Judgment[1] Federal Republic	Up to 1 Month	Percent	1 to 3 Months	Percent	3 to 6 Months	Percent	Over 6 Months	Percent
1952									
1953[2]	16,901								
1954[2]	17,546								
1955[2]	17,233	3,677	21.3	8,315	48.3	3,261	18.9	1,980	11.5
1956[2]	17,120	3,474	20.3	8,440	49.3	3,426	20.0	1,780	10.4
1957	17,159	3,011	17.5	8,637	50.3	3,653	21.3	1,858	10.9
1958	17,732	2,792	15.8	8,590	48.4	4,181	23.6	2,169	12.2
1959	16,965	2,468	14.5	7,766	45.8	4,124	24.3	2,607	15.4
1960	16,255	2,691	16.5	7,699	47.4	3,527	21.7	2,338	14.4
1961	15,763	2,572	16.3	7,354	46.7	3,717	23.6	2,120	13.4
1962	16,344	2,385	14.6	7,603	46.5	3,954	24.2	2,402	14.7
1963	17,224	2,202	12.8	8,016	46.5	4,342	25.2	2,664	15.5
1964	17,724	1,907	10.7	7,731	43.6	4,780	27.0	3,306	18.6
1965	16,423	1,881	11.5	7,002	42.6	4,371	26.6	3,169	19.3
1966	17,080	1,928	11.3	7,402	43.3	4,604	27.0	3,146	18.4

[1] SOURCE: Annual reports by H. Rüstig, "Die Gerichte in Arbeitssachen" in *Arbeit und Recht* (vols. 1953–66).
[2] Saarland not included.

TABLE 13B

Duration of Proceedings before the Appellate Labor Courts

Year	Appeals Settled by Judgment[1] Federal Republic	Up to 1 Month	Percent	1 to 3 Months	Percent	3 to 6 Months	Percent	6 to 12 Months	Percent	Over 12 Months	Percent
1952	2,409										
1953[2]	2,652										
1954[2]											
1955[2]	2,721	174	6.4	1,215	44.7	909	33.4	329	12.1	94	3.4
1956[2]	2,836	157	5.5	1,141	40.2	1,016	35.8	413	14.6	109	3.9
1957	2,755	213	7.7	1,099	39.9	984	35.7	362	13.1	97	3.6
1958	2,732	165	6.0	1,318	48.2	863	31.6	302	11.1	84	3.1
1959	2,825	142	5.0	1,313	46.5	911	32.2	344	12.2	115	4.1
1960	2,637	185	7.0	1,285	48.7	734	27.8	326	12.4	107	4.1
1961	2,549	220	8.6	1,158	45.4	732	28.7	331	13.0	108	4.3
1962	2,559	172	6.7	1,147	44.8	744	29.1	357	14.0	139	5.4
1963	2,618	227	8.7	1,162	44.4	747	28.5	319	12.2	163	6.2
1964	2,617	223	8.5	992	37.9	835	31.9	406	15.5	161	6.2
1965	2,807	166	5.9	983	35.0	914	32.6	550	19.6	194	6.9
1966	2,658	153	5.8	1,021	38.4	837	31.5	423	15.9	224	8.4

SOURCE: Annual reports by H. Rüstig, "Die Gerichte in Arbeitssachen" in *Arbeit und Recht* (vols. 1953–66).

[1] Saarland not included.
[2]

TABLE 13C

Duration of Proceedings before the Federal Labor Court

Year	Reviews Settled by Judgment[1] Federal Republic	1 to 3 Months	Percent	3 to 6 Months	Percent	6 to 12 Months	Percent	Over 12 Months	Percent
1954[2]	37								
1955[2]	116	2	1.7	17	14.7	37	31.9	60	51.7
1956[2]	190	3	1.6	10	5.3	42	22.1	135	71.0
1957	273	1	0.4	15	5.5	38	13.9	219	80.2
1958	271	10	3.7	16	5.9	49	18.1	196	72.3
1959	291	9	3.1	9	3.1	24	8.3	249	85.5
1960	381	2	0.5	14	3.7	61	16.0	304	79.8
1961	324	4	1.2	25	7.7	116	35.8	179	55.3
1962	272	3	1.1	20	7.3	152	55.9	97	35.7
1963	268	—		32	11.9	158	59.0	78	29.1
1964	226	1	0.4	36	15.9	150	66.4	39	17.3
1965	237	6	2.5	46	19.4	108	45.6	77	32.5
1966	230	4	1.7	59	25.7	123	53.5	44	19.1

[1] SOURCE: Annual reports by H. Rüstig, "Die Gerichte in Arbeitssachen" in *Arbeit und Recht* (vols. 1953–66).
[2] Saarland not included.

LABOR COURTS, GRIEVANCE SETTLEMENT IN WEST GERMANY

the procedure: decisions are served by the court; all decisions not based upon oral pleas are rendered by the chairman of the court; witnesses and experts give sworn testimony only if this is required for a decision; the value in dispute is determined by the regular labor court without the right of appeal; and court costs are determined, if possible, as part of the decision. But, as the following statistics show, the time from filing a suit to a decision of the court is still relatively long: in 43 percent of the cases submitted to the regular labor courts it was from 1 to 3 months, and in 27 percent from 3 to 6 months; 38 percent of the appeals submitted to the appellate labor courts were decided within 1 to 3 months, and 32 percent within 3 to 6 months; 26 percent of the appeals at the Federal Labor Court were decided within 3 to 6 months, and 54 percent within 6 to 12 months.

Court costs in labor courts are much lower than those in ordinary courts for civil matters; the payment of one fee only is required as compared with the free structure of the ordinary courts, which consists of three amounts. In labor court proceedings the fee is usually increased in proportion to the value in dispute, but again, the increase amounts to considerably less than it would in comparable proceedings before the ordinary courts, as shown in table 14.

This comparison may be illustrated further by the following example: The average value in a dispute decided by the labor court of a town of more than 100,000 residents amounts to $575. Assuming usual proceedings before the courts in which witnesses are heard, court costs at the ordinary courts when this value is in dispute would amount to $50, whereas the fee for labor court proceedings would be $17. In proceedings before the ordinary courts for which an attorney must be retained, an additional $90 is required for his services. Besides lower fees for proceedings before the regular labor courts, fees incurred through appeals are also reduced by 20 percent.

The LCA generally provides that fees are not required for preliminary hearings and that court costs are payable only after termination of the proceedings. By contrast, the ordinary courts require advance payment of fees in order to set a date for a hearing.

According to the general regulations of the CPA, the losing party is responsible for the payment of fees—court costs as well as the fees of the representative of the winning party. The one exception applies to courts at the first level in which the losing party is not required to pay damages to the winning party for time lost in court proceedings, nor the fees of the representative of the winning party.

The provisions of the LCA with respect to court fees are supplemented by those of the CPA. An indigent party unable to pay for

TABLE 14

Comparison of Court Costs in Proceedings before Labor Courts
and Ordinary Courts in Civil Matters
(in dollars)

Value in Dispute	Labor Court	Ordinary Courts in Civil Matters Amts– or Landgericht[1]	Attorney Fees
5	0.25	2.25	3.75
15	0.50	2.25	5.25
25	0.75	2.25	5.25
50	1.50	6.00	12.25
75	2.25	9.00	13.00
100	3.00	12.00	18.75
250	7.50	27.00	41.25
375[1]	11.25	38.25	60.00
400	12.00	40.50	65.00
500	15.00	47.25	78.75
1,000	30.00	68.25	146.25
1,500	45.00	88.50	195.00
2,000	60.00	107.25	221.25
3,000	90.00	133.50	250.00
4,000	120.00	152.25	285.00
4,150	124.50	156.00	292.50
4,175	125.00	159.75	292.50
5,000	125.00	171.00	315.00
6,000	125.00	189.75	339.00
7,000	125.00	208.50	363.00

[1] Calculation of court costs in proceedings before the *Amts–* or *Landgericht* is based on the three-level fee structure (fees for (1) proceedings, (2) examination of evidence, (3) judgment). This structure applies to attorneys' fees as well. *Landgericht* has jurisdiction in disputes involving more than $375; representation by attorney is mandatory.

In addition to court costs, fees are charged for hearing witnesses and experts. Witnesses receive $1.25 per hour on the average for time lost from work, as well as traveling and meal allowances (if less than 6 hours are involved, up to $1.00).

In addition to attorneys' fees, charges are made for secretarial services, mailing and travel expenses, and per diem allowances. Per diem rates for attorneys are $6.25 per hour from 4 to 8 hours, and $12.50 per hour in excess of 8 hours.

procedural costs without endangering his own support and that of his family may apply for exemption from payment under the "poor law"; he will be granted such exemption if the dispute is considered to be "fairly significant and not mischievous."

6. Finally, the special feature of labor court procedure must be mentioned, namely the admission of unions and employers' associations in addition to legal representatives of the parties to a dispute. Unions,

employers' associations, and their top organizations are admitted as parties to a dispute even though they are not legal persons, meaning that the necessary connection between the capacity to be a party before the court and the status of being a legal person under civil law does not exist. This innovation is significant for the unions, which traditionally have not been legal persons since the time of the persecution of the socialist unions from 1878 to 1890. The employers' associations generally acquire the status of legal persons.

All parties to a dispute are authorized to present their case in the labor court to the same extent as in the lowest ordinary court. They may authorize representation by employees of unions, employers' associations, top organizations, as well as indepedent associations of employees having social or occupational objectives.

The much disputed problem in the history of labor courts, whether to admit attorneys before the regular labor courts, has been settled by compromise. Attorneys are admitted if the value in dispute amounts to more than $75, a limitation that is of no practical importance, or "if admission is required in order to protect the rights of the party," and that necessity will always be recognized by the courts if an attorney appears before them. Moreover, an indigent party may have an attorney appointed by the state if the opposing party is represented by counsel.

In proceedings before the appellate labor court, the parties to a dispute must be represented by counsel who has been admitted to the bar of any German court, or by representatives of unions, other employees' associations, employers' associations, etc. In proceedings before the

TABLE 15

Representation of the Parties before the Labor Courts of Hessen

Year	1954	1964
Judgments	1275	1342
Attorneys		
Employers	383 (30%)	526 (39.2%)
Employees	357 (28%)	474 (35.3%)
Union Official or Member of Employers' Association		
Employers	281 (22.1%)	222 (16.5%)
Employees	423 (33.2%)	374 (27.9%)
No Representation		
Employers	611 (47.9%)	594 (44.3%)
Employees	495 (38.8%)	494 (36.8%)

Federal Labor Court, the parties must be represented by attorneys.

General statistics on the representation of the parties before the labor courts are not available. However, the president of the Hessen appellate labor court compiled data for the state of Hessen for the years 1954 and 1964. The following results may come as a surprise: First, the percentage of employers and employees represented by attorneys is about the same. Second, the percentage of representation of both parties by attorneys has increased considerably, while representation by agents (nonlawyers) of the respective associations has decreased—to a larger extent for employers than for employees. The increase in representation by attorneys may be due to the development of "legal aid insurance" policies, which originally covered legal disputes involving automobile accidents but now include legal disputes of almost any kind.

The quality of representation before the labor courts varies for both sides. Large employers' associations hire lawyers who are paid about $400 to $500 per month. Smaller associations and craft guilds employ persons not trained as lawyers; they share the unions' plight or are in a worse position, because their employees usually are not as well trained in law as the legal agents of the unions.

Union employees who appear before the labor courts are called legal aid representatives *(Rechtsschutzsekretäre)*. They are full-time employees of the district or local committees of the FGTU, which are located at the seat of the labor courts. The various unions have their own legal aid representatives at the state level or in some large cities, for example, in Frankfurt/Main. They are active union members who have received training of at least two years at one of the following institutions: the "Academy of Labor," a branch of the Frankfurt University, the "Social Academy" in Dortmund, or the "Academy for Cooperative Societies" in Hamburg; they also may have attended union schools at the federal level. The trainees are instructed by practitioners in law in the principles and procedure of labor law. The three-week courses are followed by an examination. The union member may take a correspondence course in lieu of attending in person.

Any union member, i.e., any person who was an active member for a minimum period of 13 to 26 weeks according to the bylaws of the unions, is eligible for representation in claims against an employer. The union verifies the length of his membership and authorizes the appropriate local or district committee of the FGTU to furnish legal aid. After a discussion with the claimant, the union legal aid representative assesses the chances of winning a suit. This is usually a broad decision; only between 10 and 15 percent of the applications have been refused because of poor chances of success, and in a few cases the member involved then brings suit himself. If the case is lost at the regular labor court, the federal board of the union decides if legal representation at the appellate level of the court system is to be provided.

3.
PRETRIAL SCREENING PROCEDURES ARBITRATION, AND WORKS COURTS

PRETRIAL SCREENING PROCEDURES

1. Pretrial screening procedures are not required in Germany—either by statutes or by collective bargaining agreements. However, the WCA provides for two exceptions that are different in their legal nature.

(a) The WCA provides that the employer must hear from the works council (in plants with more than twenty employees who are entitled to vote) prior to an individual notice of dismissal, and that he must consult with the council prior to mass dismissals.[1] The consultation concerns the kind and number of dismissals required and the "avoidance of hardships"; but details of hearings in individual dismissals are not contained in the Act. This type of hearing evidently is a vestige of the provisions of the Works Councils Act of 1920, which required that the employee to be dismissed was entitled to submit a complaint to the manual workers' council or to the white-collar workers' council. If the council considered the complaint to be justified, it could take up the matter with the employer. If no agreement was reached within one week, the council or the employee was entitled to submit a complaint to the labor court within five days. The hearing provision, however, was not incorporated into the Act on Protection Against Dismissals of 1951.* Therefore, the question as to the legal consequences of not hearing the works council before individual dismissals was, and still is, highly debated.

The Federal Labor Court makes a distinction between dismissals

---

[1] This provision also applies to consultation of the works councils prior to mass hiring (number and job classifications of persons to be hired). However, in the present report this right of codetermination, or the right of the works council to intervene if the employer abuses his hiring prerogative, has not been discussed.

* Hereafter referred to as APD.

when proper notice is given and those without notice—when the employee is fired on the spot. In the first case the employee can be legally dismissed even though the employer does not hear from the works council. But in that event the employer generally forfeits his right to prove that the dismissal was "socially justified," a right provided by the APD when the "reasons with respect to personality or conduct of the employee, or urgent needs of the plant, oppose his continued employment." The employee may appeal to the labor court within a prescribed period for a ruling. The court then decides whether the dismissal was "socially justified," and, if it was not, whether the employee should remain at work or should be paid compensation. The latter determination is made if the court finds that useful cooperation from the employee cannot be expected in the future.

In the second case, when the employee is fired on the spot, the first division of the Federal Labor Court, which has jurisdiction under the Act, does not consider the hearing of the works council to be necessary.

The Federal Labor Court evidently attempted to reach a compromise between the attitudes of the two blocs of academic writers on labor law to the effect that the violation of the hearing provision either made the dismissals illegal or had no legal consequences at all. But it considered the APD as a codification of the entire law on dismissals, which it certainly is not because it does not include dismissals without notice—as the division itself has recognized in its jurisdiction—and it disregards the language of the Act that "the works council *must* be heard."

(b) The WCA lists among the four general functions of the works councils the following: "Watching over the application of all statutes, decrees, collective bargaining agreements, and works council–employer agreements which favor the employee," and "accepting employees' complaints and, if they are justified, seeking to remedy the situation through negotiations with the employer."

The term *complaints* here includes grievances, meaning that the works council has the statutory obligation to enter into negotiations with the employer. Although there are no legal sanctions attached to this duty, continuous violations could lead to a public discussion before the works assembly *(Betriebsversammlung)* or serve as a reason to summon the assembly in extraordinary session. However, the assembly cannot dissolve the works councils. This can only be done upon request of "at least one-fourth of all employees entitled to vote," the employer or the unions having members in the plant, if the labor court finds that "gross negligence of its statutory powers or gross violation of its statutory duties" has occurred.

There have been no studies undertaken to determine how the works council performs its duty to negotiate and whether employees are heard in such proceedings. It must be emphasized that the works council may take up a grievance even without the employee's knowledge or against his will, when it believes that the employer has violated regulations favorable to the employee. General evaluations of the actions of the works councils and their effectiveness are not feasible. Everything depends on their power, exercised through their members, on their confidence in their own legal protection against dismissal, and last, but not least, on the employer's ability to cooperate with the works council.

It must be added that the employer may attempt to exclude union officials, whom he considers third parties, from negotiations. Therefore, negotiations are usually very informal and are often not carried out in works council sessions to which a union official (with consulting vote) must be admitted upon request of one-fourth of the works council's members. Negotiations practically consist of informal discussions between the chairman of the works council and the employer.

2. The informal negotiation activities of the works council are very similar to negotiation conducted by the union legal aid representative before he brings suit in court. He may reach a compromise if he cooperates well with the employer or, in large enterprises, with the personnel director. A compromise is also possible in disputes over small amounts if time that will be lost because of lengthy legal proceedings is expected to be more costly. This is another effect of LCA legislation, which does not provide for reimbursement of such expenses. But this informal method of settlement, often over the telephone, depends on personal contacts that grow in years of cooperation. An idea of the effectiveness of this type of negotiation may be gained by comparing compromises before the labor courts with those reached out of court, as shown in table 11. However, the figures for out-of-court compromises in the table do not distinguish between compromises before and after suit was brought in court and therefore do not permit exact conclusions.

3. It is also feasible that employees in large plants discuss their complaints with the general foreman *(Werkmeister)* or with the head of the personnel department. It has not been investigated how often this is done and how effective this course of action is in reaching a compromise.

4. In order to assess the significance of these screening procedures,

one must remember that about 80 percent of all cases decided by the labor courts are submitted after termination of employment. This implies that in a very large number of these cases the employee had no confidence in the effectiveness of the negotiation procedures described. It cannot be accurately estimated, therefore, if the proportion of suits brought in court would be even higher if prior negotiations with the works councils, especially in disputes that occur while the worker is still employed, had not taken place.

ARBITRATION BETWEEN PARTIES TO COLLECTIVE BARGAINING AGREEMENTS

1. Excluding arbitration in disputes over new terms of collective bargaining agreements, which is not part of the subject under investigation, arbitration can take place at three levels. These may be distinguished according to the parties agreeing to arbitration: parties to the individual contract of employment; parties to the collective bargaining agreement, regardless of whether there is only one employer or an employers' association on the employer's side; the employer and the works council. They may also be distinguished according to the type of contract: the individual contract of employment, the collective bargaining agreement, and the works council–employer agreement. Both sets of distinctions may overlap, though not necessarily in all points, as will be shown in the following pages.

First, arbitration of individual disputes between parties to collective bargaining agreements will be described; then the problems of arbitration in collective disputes will be discussed, which, as far as Germany is concerned, are of much more practical importance. Therefore, the statutory provisions on arbitration are included in this section, but arbitration of disputes between the employer and the works council are discussed separately in the following section, "Arbitration Within the Enterprise."

The complicated provisions of the fourth section of the LCA on "arbitration contract in labor disputes" suggest a hostile attitude towards arbitration with respect to its very limited admissibility and its supervision. The LCA speaks of the exclusion of labor court jurisdiction when expressly stated in arbitration agreements and stipulates that the provisions of the CPA on arbitration procedure cannot be applied to labor matters. Further, the Act sets forth basic rules with respect to arbitration boards, their procedure, and their supervision by the labor courts for arbitration in individual and collective disputes.

However, it is silent on arbitration in disputes between employer and works council or other representative bodies at the plant level.

2. In private disputes arising out of an employment relationship governed by a collective bargaining agreement, the parties to the agreement "can," in the language of the LCA, exclude the jurisdiction of the labor court by the existence of an express arbitration agreement "if the collective bargaining agreement primarily covers stage and film actors, entertainers, or captains and members of ships' crews." These arbitration agreements are binding only on the members of the union and employers' association who concluded the agreement.[2] However, they can be extended to other parties whose working conditions are regulated by the collective bargaining agreement for other reasons if the parties have expressly agreed to arbitration in a written statement, or if they plead before the arbitration board.

Thus, the LCA first of all prohibits all separate arbitration clauses or arbitration clauses in individual contracts of employment if the parties to the collective bargaining agreement are not in charge of arbitration. This regulation is based on the same notion as the provision of the CPA that declares an agreement on arbitration null and void if one of the parties has abused its social or economic "superiority to press the other party into acceptance of the agreement or unfavorable conditions contained therein." German labor law, however, is based upon the assumption that the employer's power predominates, and unions are employed as an instrument to counterbalance this predominance.

But this type of socially guaranteed arbitration is restricted to the very few categories set forth in the LCA, and this restriction is new; it was initiated in 1953. The Labor Courts Act of 1926 had left arbitration in individual disputes to the discretion of the parties to collective bargaining agreements. However, they failed to establish arbitration boards on a larger scale, and even their own attorneys complained of the lengthy procedure, the lack of procedural rules, the necessity of having to go to the labor courts for sworn testimony from witnesses and experts, and of the arbitrator's range of discretion.[3] For these reasons, evidently, the employers' associations and the unions took a stand against arbitration in individual disputes when the draft of the

---

[2] The undisputed immediate effect of the arbitration agreement cannot be theoretically explained. Certainly, it does not belong to the normative part of the collective bargaining agreement as described by the Collective Bargaining Agreements Act.

[3] Cf. Fraenkel, *Betriebsräte und Arbeitsgerichtsgesetz* (1927), pp. 23 f.

LCA of 1953 was debated. Apparently, they were satisfied with the labor courts in view of their performance during the Weimar Republic.

This historical and political review of the attitude towards arbitration, however, does not explain the legal meaning of the statutory limitations on the establishment of arbitration boards and the exclusion of labor court jurisdiction in deciding individual disputes. In looking for legal sanctions against a violation, one may ask whether the limitations imply that arbitration is "inadmissible," in which case suit could be brought to have the arbitration award set aside. But the language of the limitation provision of the LCA does not include the word "admissible"; it merely states that the parties "can" exclude the jurisdiction of labor courts by arbitration. Certainly, the employee cannot exclude that jurisdiction in his individual contract of employment if there is no agreement on arbitration between an employer or an employers' association on the one side and a union on the other. In that case, arbitration is in fact "inadmissable." But if a union secures the balancing of social powers, there is no longer any reason to distinguish between exclusive arbitration in one collective bargaining agreement as against another. Arbitration, then, is always "admissible," and no suit for vacating an award can be based on the statutory distinctions between the various arbitration agreements of the unions.

This finding may be tested with a view to the Bonn Basic Law. The legal possibility of choosing arbitration boards instead of labor courts is part of the freedom of contract, which is, according to prevailing opinion, included in the constitutional "right of free development of the personality." It may be restricted only if it violates the rights of other persons, the constitutional order of which the social state is a part, or the "moral law." The exclusion of individual arbitration agreements may then be justified by the social-state clause, as stated before. But this does not apply to arbitration established by parties to collective bargaining agreements because then the predominant power of the employer is counterbalanced by the union; and this is the same balancing of powers that underlies the legal admissibility of collective bargaining agreements. In the absence of constitutionally permitted limitations, the statutory limitations on union-approved arbitration cannot be interpreted to mean "inadmissibility"; otherwise they would violate the constitution and would therefore be null and void. If the interpretation follows the constitution, then the finding of this investigation will be confirmed. Union-approved arbitration is admissible, and the arbitration invocation must be upheld by the labor courts.

Parties to collective bargaining agreements evidently are not aware of this legal situation and have tried another strategy. Since the LCA speaks only of "exclusive" arbitration agreements, i.e., those that preclude actions in court on the same issue, nonexclusive arbitration seems to be another possibility. Indeed, some agreements provide for nonexclusive arbitration "if both parties to the collective bargaining agreement consider the dispute to be of basic importance," or if they and the individuals concerned approve of arbitration. Apparently, members of such organizations are thought to be well disciplined since it is not expected that they will go to the labor courts. The very interesting question as to the legal significance of nonexclusive arbitration awards with respect to labor courts has as yet not been raised. However, the answer would be purely academic since, according to the conclusions of this study, the problem of nonexclusive arbitration will disappear.

The limitation of arbitration in individual disputes, set forth by the LCA, delineates the economic sectors in which arbitration is still significant. Employers and employees of the theater established a stage arbitration board in their collective bargaining agreement of 1951, excluding the jurisdiction of the labor courts, and the Federal Labor Court interpreted the statutory language of the LCA to the effect that the contract of employment must be determined very broadly from a collective bargaining agreement. Its interpretation also covers contracts of guest performances and other contracts that are not labor contracts and therefore are not regulated by the usual provisions of collective bargaining agreements in this industry. Evidently, the Court intended to prevent overlapping of jurisdiction of arbitration boards and labor courts.

Arbitration for the merchant marine and deep-sea fishing was established by collective bargaining agreements in 1963 and 1966. In this industry nonunion members are always covered by the arbitration procedure, because the arbitration clause is part of the standard contract of employment and the parties to the collective bargaining agreement have a monopoly on all hiring. However, nonmembers suffer a considerable disadvantage: unlike union members they are required to pay fees, sometimes in advance, and they are not entitled to free service under the "poor law" as they were in proceedings before the labor courts. It is doubtful whether these regulations comply with the law.[4] The German social state must guarantee that the poor are not barred from legal decisions of their claims because of procedural costs. The question further arises whether this regulation does not constitute unlawful pressure on the employee to join the union.

---

[4] Monnerjahn, *Das Arbeitsverhältnis in der deutschen Seeschifffahrt*, published by Gustav Fischer Verlag, Stuttgart (1964), pp. 128 ff.

3. Disputes between the parties to collective bargaining agreements arising out of collective bargaining agreements or out of the existence or nonexistence of a collective bargaining agreement may be decided exclusively by arbitration if the parties to the collective bargaining agreement have expressly, but not necessarily in writing, agreed to arbitration. But it must be remembered in this context that the state evidently desires to compete with arbitration by offering the labor courts, composed of four wingmen, to rule on such questions.

A survey of arbitration agreements[5] indicates that most of them are part of collective bargaining agreements, belonging to the contractual, as distinguished from the normative, section of those agreements. Thus, they are considered to become ineffective upon expiration of the collective bargaining agreement. However, the working conditions under the collective bargaining agreement continue in effect as part of the individual contract of employment. The legal interpretation of these conditions, therefore, remains important and should be decided by arbitration.

Another possibility permitted by the statute has not been exhausted by parties to collective bargaining agreements: only 30 percent of the arbitration clauses cover disputes over the existence or nonexistence of collective bargaining agreements.

However, arbitration does not only cover interpretation problems of the so-called normative section of the collective bargaining agreements, but also disputes over the contractual section, which is closely connected with the normative section through the peace obligation and the performance duty.

About 80 percent of the arbitration clauses provide for exclusive arbitration in all future disputes. *Ad hoc* arbitration is rare, and even rarer is the possibility of choice between arbitration and the jurisdiction of labor courts.

The law with respect to arbitration is mixed, containing statutory and contractual elements. The LCA contains the basic regulations on the composition of the arbitration boards, the power of the arbitrator, and the rules of procedure.

The individual arbitrator is unknown in German law. The LCA provides for employer and employee representatives in equal number, who may be joined by an impartial third member. Thus, the statute indirectly prescribes a board.

About half of the 140 arbitration agreements in the survey previously

---

[5] The following information on arbitration agreements is quoted from the unpublished dissertation of my student, Koenigsbauer.

referred to have established arbitration boards with a tripartite structure; the impartial chairman is a member of the board from its inception. About one-fourth of the agreements probably were patterned after the French *conseils de prud'hommes;* the boards are bipartite and only in case of deadlock will an impartial chairman be elected in order to obtain a majority vote for an award. This means that a newly constituted board must try the case again. In routine cases the parties have discretionary power to elect an impartial chairman.

All arbitrators must be of good character and must be eligible to hold public office. They can be disqualified according to the rules established for judges. Motions for disqualification are decided by the labor courts.

The size of the boards varies: about 50 percent have four wingmen, more than 30 percent have six, and the remainder two or eight. Only six arbitration agreements authorize the permanent employment of an impartial chairman; the other agreements require that he must be appointed by the parties for certain periods, usually from 4 to 6 years. If the parties cannot agree on his election, 50 percent of the arbitration agreements require that a neutral authority—usually the president of the Federal Labor Court, the president of an appellate labor court, or a state Labor Minister—appoint a chairman.

Only about 7 percent of the arbitration agreements require that the impartial chairman must be qualified to hold professional judicial office. Actually, most chairmen are professional judges of the civil courts rather than the labor courts, and the parties seem to be satisfied with their performance. Apparently the parties do not want labor lawyers or persons familiar with labor matters to serve on their boards, preferring neutral individuals whom they may trust.

The LCA leaves arbitration procedure to the discretion of the arbitration board except for a few basic regulations: the parties must be given an opportunity to be heard prior to an arbitration award; they may give written authorization to a representative to appear on their behalf; the board may hear witnesses and experts but cannot demand sworn testimony, which can be given only before the labor courts at the request of the boards. But in actual practice this restriction is insignificant with respect to collective disputes, because in these disputes witnesses are not heard by the boards.

According to the LCA, an arbitration award requires a simple majority vote by the members of the board. This is sufficient in 75 percent of the arbitration agreements, but others require a qualified majority or regard the award as a proposal that must be accepted by the parties. The chairman is always entitled to vote. The award must be signed and accompanied by a written opinion unless the parties expressly waive the right to such an opinion.

Attempts to stop proceedings in a labor court on the ground that the issue must be arbitrated will not be successful in the following cases: if the parties failed to nominate an arbitrator in time; if the arbitration board delays procedure; if the board announces that it finds it impossible to make an award. In the first two cases the chairman of the labor court may set the date for a decision.

In general, arbitration procedure is very similar to conciliation procedure; in some cases there is no difference at all. Often the parties combine rules of both procedures in "conciliation [i.e., upon new terms of collective bargaining agreements] and arbitration orders." More than 25 percent of the agreements oblige the board to try to achieve an amicable settlement of the dispute within the procedure; the board must submit offers, even suggest a formal conciliation session. In about 30 percent, formal prearbitration negotiations between the parties are required, called "conciliation sessions" in two agreements employing the language of the LCA with respect to such sessions before the labor court. Moreover, in actual practice the impartial chairman functions as mediator. Although not specifically stated in any arbitration agreement, he negotiates separately with the parties and the wingmen if the case is in deadlock.

The arbitration agreements are silent on the admission of attorneys, with the exception of three that admit them. They merely authorize representation by directors, managerial employees, or other permanent representatives of the parties. This must be interpreted to mean that they do not want the presence of third parties, including attorneys.

Conciliation procedure has also influenced the distribution of expenses. About 70 percent of the agreements stipulate that each party bear half of the procedural costs and the expenses for its legal representative. Only two agreements authorize the arbitration boards to rule on the distribution of costs according to the LCA, namely, that the losing party has to absorb the expenses. The chairman's fee is never set; as in conciliation, it is privately agreed upon. The number of employees involved in the dispute, together with such other factors as the ability of the chairman or the complexity of the case, naturally plays an important role with respect to costs.

In about 80 percent of the agreements arbitration is carried out at one level. In the remainder a second level is established under various names: superior, main, central, or federal arbitration board or office. Sometimes leave to appeal will be denied if the award was made unanimously and the board does not expressly admit the appeal.

4. The LCA provides two possibilities of supervising arbitration by the labor courts. First, an award or a settlement before an arbitration board can be enforced only after the chairman of the labor court has declared it provisionally enforceable. If it is established that suit for vacating the arbitration award has been brought, the final decision is postponed until a judgment is available. This provision applies only to individual disputes, because an arbitration award on the question whether a collective bargaining agreement exists, or how it is to be interpreted, can never be enforced as a declaratory judgment. Such an award has the same legal effect as an agreement upon new terms.

A second possibility of supervising arbitration is by suit for vacating the award. According to the Labor Courts Act of 1926, the labor courts at the first level were authorized to hand down final decisions; today these courts' decisions may be appealed to the appellate labor courts and finally to the Federal Labor Court. Thus, it is theoretically possible that one and the same case will be discussed by five different bodies at five levels—two arbitration boards and three labor courts. But this has not yet happened. Evidently, this peculiar regulation constitutes an effort to reach uniform court decisions on arbitration awards. The LCA of 1953 has extended grounds for vacating an award from "violating strict statutory law" to "violating a *legal* norm," and according to the language of the CBAA, the so-called normative section of the collective bargaining agreement consists of legal norms. Thus, the legal interpretation of a collective bargaining agreement by an arbitration award may be fully supervised by the labor courts.

This is a curious finding indeed, because it completely ignores the fact that very often interpretation consists of establishing terms not covered in the existing agreement, thus creating a new, supplementary agreement in questions of minor importance. In such cases arbitration really means that the parties to a collective bargaining agreement agree in advance to accept the award as a "new" collective bargaining agreement. Therefore, the sharp distinction between legal disputes (over interpretation of an existing agreement) and disputes of interests (over new terms of an agreement) disappears in practice, and from this point of view every effort to reach a compromise between the parties, to achieve conciliation, can be easily understood.

There are two other grounds for setting aside an award: if arbitration was not admissible, or if the award was based on criminal misconduct, such as false testimony, falsified documents, or deliberate miscarriage of justice by the arbitrator.

5. It seems that the provisions of the LCA on arbitration are not sat-

isfactory. In addition to serious legal doubts about the Act's compliance with the constitution, the distinction between individual and collective disputes obviously cannot be observed in practice and must lead to an overlapping of jurisdiction of labor courts and arbitration boards. For instance, if parties to a collective bargaining agreement provide for exclusive arbitration of disputes arising out of the contractual section of their agreement, disputes over the existence or nonexistence of collective bargaining agreements are not covered. Assuming that the language concerning the duration of their agreement is not clear, there are two different grounds for action—one based upon the contractual part of the agreement, the other upon the nonexistence of the agreement. It thus offers free choice between arbitration boards and labor courts and opens the possibility of contradictory decisions.

However, the same situation with the same dangers exists if an individual dispute concerns a term of the collective bargaining agreement that becomes also the subject of an interpretation dispute. For example, if an individual employee demands overtime pay based on unclear terms of the collective bargaining agreement, the LCA requires that his action must be brought before the labor court; it is an individual dispute with his employer since the terms belonging to the normative section of the collective bargaining agreement become immediately and obligatorily part of his individual contract of employment. But the legal problem involved here is the interpretation of the collective bargaining agreement, and the parties to that agreement may have agreed to arbitration. Thus, the same issue will be decided under two different aspects by different agencies.

The LCA does not provide a solution to this problem, and the CAA merely authorizes the "extension of final decisions of the labor courts in disputes between parties to collective bargaining agreements arising out of their agreements, or over the existence or nonexistence of such agreements, to members of the concluding organizations or to third parties." It is curious that a corresponding provision for arbitration awards does not exist, but legal analogy will certainly lead to the same result. Over and above these considerations, however, the factual situation must also be weighed. Although neither labor courts nor arbitration boards which have to decide the collective interpretation dispute are bound by labor court decisions in a dispute over the interpretation of the same term as part of an individual contract of employment, a decision of the Federal Labor Court in this dispute will certainly have some influence on their decisions.

Some parties to collective bargaining agreements have recognized the dangers of contradictory and competing jurisdictions and have attempted to establish a preference for arbitration. About 15 percent of the arbitration agreements provide that parties to the collective bargaining agreement may take over an individual dispute "because of its fundamental importance for the interpretation of the collective bargaining agreement," in order to establish a collective dispute for which arbitration is admissible under the LCA. Other agreements permit the parties to declare an individual dispute to be collective if they have agreed on the jurisdiction of the arbitration board.

ARBITRATION WITHIN THE ENTERPRISE

1. For the "settlement of differences of opinion" between works councils and employer, the WCA authorizes "when necessary" the establishment of a board of settlement *(Einigungsstelle)*. This tripartite board is composed of employer and employee wingmen in equal number and an impartial chairman, who is appointed in case of disagreement by the chairman of the labor court. The board becomes active only if both parties to a dispute apply for or have agreed to its jurisdiction. It decides by simple majority vote after an oral session, but its decision is binding only if the parties have agreed to accepting it in advance, or if they have in fact accepted it.

The board may be replaced by a board established by the collective bargaining agreement *(tarifliche Schlichtungsstelle)* which, as the name implies, settles disputes over interests. The procedure is then altered to the effect that this board may be authorized to issue binding decisions in all disputes upon request of only one of the parties. The reason for this replacement provision evidently was to enable the parties to collective bargaining agreements to maintain and strengthen their influence in the enterprise.

In one significant aspect the function of the voluntary board of settlement has been altered by the WCA. Upon request of only one of the parties, its decisions are binding on the right of codetermination of the works council in social matters, such as beginning and end of daily shifts, breaks, time and location of payment of wages, vacation schedules, participation in vocational training, questions concerning the order of the plant and the workers' conduct in the plant, rules on piece-rate and assembly-line wages, basic wages, and the introduction of a new wage structure. If the works council and the employer cannot agree on such matters, the board of settlement issues binding decisions and establishes a works council–employer settlement, which has the effect of an agreement. It may be disputed whether such decision by the board effectuates or at least confirms the social right of codetermination, or whether it constitutes arbitration on new terms.

2. Disputes over the interpretation of works council–employer agreements, regardless of whether they are concluded on a voluntary or compulsory basis, and disputes over their existence or nonexistence are decided by the labor courts. It is questionable, however, whether they are also subject to arbitration.[6] The LCA is silent on this point; it deals only with arbitration authorized by collective bargaining agreements and prohibits arbitration clauses in individual contracts of employment. The WCA does not contain provisions for compulsory arbitration by the board of settlement in the interpretation of agreements established by itself. But it is another question whether the works council and the employer acknowledge the board of settlement as a voluntary arbitration agency in all disputes, regardless of whether such disputes are over rights or over interests. This problem has been thoroughly discussed, and it has been argued that the board of settlement functions only to establish new terms, i.e., to decide disputes over interests. This opinion is based on the provision of the WCA that permits the replacement of the board of settlement (at the plant level) by the *tarifliche Schlichtungsstelle*, which, as previously mentioned, determines disputes over interests. But this argument overlooks the fact that the WCA also permits submission of disputes to arbitration boards *(Schiedsstellen)* and state agencies only when "a settlement in the plant has not been reached." And the board of settlement must be considered an arbitration board that, as the name implies, may decide disputes over rights as well as disputes over interests. Moreover, the WCA clearly favors cooperation between the employer and the works council and therefore provides for the settlement of all "differences of opinion," which broadly comprises *all* complaints of employees, including grievances. Settlement must be attempted first at the plant level; thereafter, the dispute may be submitted to a board of settlement.

A correct interpretation of the WCA requires that the board of settlement may be used by the employer and the works council to decide all disputes arising out of the works council–employer agreements. However, the parties to the collective bargaining agreement may replace this board with another of their own creation, with the power to decide disputes over rights and over interests.

The range of possibilities offered by the WCA may be illustrated by the following, extreme, example: A *tarifliche Schlichtungsstelle* may be

---

[6] These problems are seriously debated and a prevailing opinion has as yet not been reached.

authorized by the collective bargaining agreement to create a works council–employer agreement in social matters if works council and employer fail to come to terms, and it may be authorized also to issue binding decisions on the interpretation of that agreement. Moreover, an award of the board of settlement or its replacement, which may concern the same legal problem as a collective bargaining agreement, cannot be controlled by the labor court unlike an arbitration award on the agreement, because the works council–employer agreements do not contain "legal norms" like the collective bargaining agreements; the WCA does not provide for this distinction. However, this conclusion may only surprise German labor lawyers who believe in this curious nomenclature.[7]

3. The LCA is silent on the question whether arbitration of individual disputes is permissible at the plant level; as stated before, it only covers arbitration between parties to a collective bargaining agreement and prohibits arbitration between parties to the individual contract of employment. The question arises, therefore, whether arbitration could not be authorized by a works council–employer agreement. The general duty of the works council to watch over the application of regulations favorable to the employees justifies indeed the inclusion of arbitration provisions. It may even be disputed whether such a provision would bind all employees in the same manner as the arbitration provision of a collective bargaining agreement; this notion could be supported by considering the works council the legal agent of the plant's employees. But not only the validity of arbitration at the plant level depends on the resolution of this dispute. It would arise again if parties to the individual contract of employment agree to arbitration, referring to a corresponding works council–employer agreement. The solution, as stated before, rests on the fact that an arbitration agreement must be considered valid if arbitration is socially guaranteed, that is, if the economic power of the employer is counterbalanced. The question then arises if the representation of all employees by the works council, authorized by the WCA, is sufficient to achieve such a counterbalance. However, this question cannot be answered on sociological grounds because the WCA itself provides the answer. It recognizes the works

---

[7] Cf. my articles on the legal norms of the collective bargaining agreements: "Die Parteien des Tarifvertrags. Zur Kritik und Neubegründung der Lehre vom Tarifvertrag," Gustav Fischer Verlag, Stuttgart, 1960; "Der Rechtsnatur des Tarifvertrags," *Juristenzeitung*, 1961; "Der Arbeitskampf und die Gesellschaftsordnung des Grundgesetzes. Beitrag zu einer Verfassungslehre," Gustav Fischer Verlag, Stuttgart, 1965.

council as a substitute of the union because it admits works council–employer agreements instead of collective bargaining agreements as a matter of principle. In view of this consideration and of the overall duty of the works councils to protect the employee, the works council is empowered by statute to counterbalance the economic superiority of the employer. Therefore, it may, together with the employer, authorize the "board of settlement" to arbitrate in individual disputes. This leads to the consequence that, in accordance with the general provisions, this board may also be replaced by the *tarifliche Schlichtungsstelle*, which may function as an arbitration board.

The foregoing conclusion may come as a surprise to those who rely upon the language of the LCA, which limits arbitration to parties to a collective bargaining agreement. They may discover a contradiction between the provisions of the LCA and those of the WCA; but this contradiction really does not exist if the LCA is interpreted according to the Bonn Basic Law.

4. How far this range of legal possibilities is actually employed remains an open question because factual information is not available. But some indications may be obtained by observing another institution that arbitrates individual disputes, the so-called works court.

THE WORKS COURT

1. The works courts *(Betriebsgerichte)* may be established either by collective bargaining agreements or by works council–employer agreements dealing with specific "social matters," that is, "with questions of the order of the plant and the conduct of the employees." Their jurisdiction varies; they may settle cases of unjustified absence from work, drunkenness on the job, violation of fire regulations, damage to property in the plant or theft of plant and fellow employees' property, and of maligning or assaulting fellow employees. Sanctions usually are fines or dismissal.

These private courts, which have been established mainly in the metal industry of Nordrhein-Westfalen, are tripartite boards composed of wingmen from the employer's and the works council's side and an impartial chairman. In some plants the works court issues a decision immediately; in others it does so only if there is disagreement between the employer and the works council in an individual dispute.

2. The question whether the establishment of these courts is lawful or whether it violates the Bonn Basic Law "entrusting the power of ad-

judication to the judges" is seriously disputed.[8] It seems, however, that the essence of this issue is not a question of constitutionality, but rather a difference of opinion concerning arbitration of managerial prerogatives. The fines are contractual penalties, which, according to private law, may be authorized by individual contracts of employment as well as works council–employer agreements. Historically, the employer was entitled to levy fines, but his authority was formerly limited by legislation providing for "rules of order" in the plant and establishing maximum fines which should not violate the honor of the employee nor his good faith. Thirty years later, the Works Councils Act of 1920 required that these plant work rules must be concluded with the works council, and that only the works council together with the employer could levy fines. That regulation was substantially amended by the National Labor Act, which was repealed in 1946. However, the former regulations were not restored.

The absence of statutory provisions may explain the debate over the legality of these privately levied fines. The legal problem turns on the question whether there is a statutory gap, or whether that gap has been closed by including the power of levying fines in the language of the WCA on "questions of the order of the plant and the employees' conduct."

3. Irrespective of these legal problems, the existence of works courts in itself proves that the present system of labor court jurisdiction over individual disputes evidently cannot be considered satisfactory.

---

[8] Cf. Herbst, "Die betrieblichen Ordnungsstrafen," *Betriebsberater* (1965), p. 419; Gaul, "Betriebsjustiz als zulässige Konkurrenz der Rechtspflege," *Der Betrieb* (1965), p. 665; Baur, "Betriebsjustiz," *Juristenzeitung* (1965), p. 163.

The debate began when the Federal Labor Court on May 14, 1964 upheld the dismissal of an employee who had not accepted his employer's proposal of a compromise in a dispute arising out of an insult directed against him (AP No. 5, re Sec. 242 BGB). A complaint against this decision on constitutional grounds was rejected by the Federal Constitutional Court on November 12, 1964 (AP No. 6, re Sec. 242 BGB). The entire debate suffers from the fact that private matters and contractual labor obligations have not been sufficiently separated.

4.
CONCLUSIONS AND REFLECTIONS

THE STRUCTURE OF THE GERMAN LEGAL SYSTEM

1. At first blush, the German system of deciding labor disputes, except those over new terms of collective bargaining agreements, may be characterized from a legal point of view as a labor court system. This certainly is a true picture if it is based on the provisions of the LCA only, which assigns a very dominant role to labor courts and a very modest one to arbitration. But this study shows that the restrictions of that statute lose their significance when its provisions are interpreted correctly, especially in view of the impact of the Bonn Basic Law on the interpretation of the statutes. In this way the natural connection between collective bargaining agreements and their adequate application, namely, arbitration between the parties to the collective bargaining agreement, has been reestablished.

2. Furthermore, this study shows that the German legal system does not merely recognize arbitration between the parties to a collective bargaining agreement. It also permits arbitration at the plant level, and this form of arbitration may compete with arbitration under the collective bargaining agreement. This competition is the counterpart of the competition found in substantive labor law—the competition between collective bargaining agreements and employer–works council agreements, which has not been sufficiently regulated by the WCA. Again, the connection between substantive and procedural law has been reaffirmed.

3. German labor law thus offers two forms of arbitration, arbitration under collective bargaining agreements and under employer–works council agreements. It opens a wide new field to arbitration, wider and more differentiated than in many other systems of labor law. Therefore, the above characterization must be corrected: according to

the legal possibilities, Germany has a mixed labor court–arbitration system.

The labor courts are slightly predominant, however, because they are empowered to supervise the settlement of disputes by arbitration boards established under collective bargaining agreements. They cannot supervise arbitration under employer–works council agreements. This is another inconsistency that stems from the strange position of the WCA in the German labor law system. The works councils, the vestige of the structure of economic councils provided in the constitution of the Weimar Republic, have not been fully integrated into the legal system. Their agreements, which do not distinguish between disputes over rights and disputes over interests, are juridically less developed than agreements of collective bargaining parties.

THE FACTUAL SITUATION

1. It would seem easy to characterize the German system of labor law by referring to the factual situation, but it is difficult to do so because the factual situation must not be confused with its description in the textbooks, which place primary emphasis on labor courts. This attitude can be simply explained by the lack of investigation of the facts in German labor law since the fall of the Empire. German labor lawyers have been kept busy by the legislative machinery, which has introduced a number of complete changes since that time; the activities of arbitration boards, especially at the plant level, are hardly known.

For these reasons the practical significance of arbitration is certainly underestimated. The establishment of works courts may serve as one example that recognized the practical need for arbitration. There also are a number of collective agreements that reserve important decisions of interpretation to arbitration boards; the parties to these agreements employ numerous strategies to circumvent the restriction on arbitration imposed by the LCA in individual disputes. It remains to be seen whether these activities will not lead to a policy whereby all, or at least the important, questions are submitted to arbitration, leaving the disagreeable task of fact-finding and deciding individual disputes to the labor courts.

In view of this situation, the labor courts may still be called the predominant institutions for the settlement of labor disputes. The best proof of this contention is that the unions and the employers' associations waived arbitration of individual disputes when the draft of the LCA of 1953 was debated. Their attitude reflects the lasting myth of labor courts described in the introductory pages, but it may also reflect simply the belief that the wingmen of the labor courts represent the interests of unions and employers' associations, and that both these organizations have a decisive voice in the appointment of the professional labor court judges. From this point of view, the practical distinction between labor courts and arbitration boards seems to disappear, and the organizations may actually consider the labor courts their arbitration boards. The efforts to acquire and maintain this influence upon judicial appointments certainly is the main reason why labor courts fall under the jurisdiction of the Ministers of Labor rather than that of the Ministers of Justice. Therefore, any attempt to transfer the administration of the affairs of labor courts, and of all other special courts, to the Ministry for All Judicial Affairs *(Rechtspflegeministerium)*[1] would meet with stiff opposition from labor organizations, especially from the unions, which still mistrust adjudication of the ordinary courts since the era of manifest class justice.

Finally, the friendly attitude towards labor courts of unions and employers' associations may be explained by their high regard for the conciliation function of these courts, which is still considered to be more effective than the conciliation procedure at the lowest level of the ordinary court system.

We may now pose the question whether the foregoing arguments are justified or not.

THE STRUCTURE OF LABOR COURTS

1. The structure of the labor courts has undergone considerable change since the time when industrial and commercial courts were first established. Originally, the latter courts were conceived to function as conciliation and arbitration bodies in the very sense: a dispute was settled either by a compromise between the parties or by a decision of the courts in an attempt to obtain a reasonable settlement without resort to civil law, which evidently did not adequately cover labor problems. Although the wingmen were the representatives of their respective groups, they were forced to cooperate within the courts; they became "enlightened representatives," able to arrive at

---

[1] The arguments in favor of these proposals are to save court costs and to facilitate transfers from one branch to another. But it also seems true that the judges wish to strengthen their independent position by reducing the influence of the ministries and of political decisions upon appointments to the bench, and to improve their salaries. Cf. on this problem, Müller (currently president of the Federal Labor Court), "Die Ressortierung der Arbeits- und Sozialgerichtsbarkeit," *Recht der Arbeit* (1966), p. 289.

reasonable compromises through the courts' decisions, supported by the chairman who, as said before, was not a professional judge at the industrial courts. Also, the chairmen were often sympathetic to the ideas of the academic socialists *(Kathedersozialisten)*, an influential group consisting largely of university professors who favored an increase in social legislation and especially the growth of unionism.

During the Weimar Republic, a thorough change in the structure of the labor courts took place. The legal recognition of unions and the legislation on collective bargaining agreements provided a statutory framework in place of the purely voluntary relationships that had previously existed. Thus, labor courts became special courts that applied a new law. Moreover, these special courts had their own supreme court, the Supreme Labor Court, in which the decisive influence of the professional judges, who were in the majority, was assured. It was not by accident that the composition of this Court was so strongly debated. Since that time labor law can no longer be considered part of the unsolved "social question"; rather, the remaining problems are merely those of statutory interpretation. As nothing has substantially changed in the intervening years, the concept of deciding labor disputes on a legal basis still predominates; in fact, it is now firmly entrenched.

The uniform application of labor law is guaranteed by the hierarchical structure of the labor courts and the centralization of judicial power in the Federal Labor Court, especially in its big senate. This structure permits the professional judges in the lower courts to play the decisive role of legal expert. They are the only ones who are completely informed of the decisions of the Federal Labor Court, and bcause they are appointed for life they watch over the uninterrupted, uniform adjudication of the court while the wingmen alternate from one session to another. But there are other circumstances that support their strong position: they are the best-informed judges of their panels because they lead the proceedings, prepare the hearings, read all records, and conduct the conciliation sessions alone. Thus, the professional judge has every opportunity to convince the wingmen of the correctness of his opinion, and in this context it is most important to remember that the statute indirectly forces him to do so. The judge must form his opinion prior to the oral session with the wingmen, and he must announce it during the conciliation session in order to achieve a compromise there. Thus prejudiced, he is not likely to change his mind in too many cases later on, probably only after the hearing of witnesses has altered the factual basis of his legal findings; otherwise he would deprive himself of his influence as mediator in future conciliation sessions.

In view of all these factors, the role of the wingmen can no longer be considered important.[2] Their position has lost its former significance, which was one of the characteristic features of the old labor court system. The wingmen now think of themselves as judges rather than as representatives of interest groups; they sometimes even lean over backwards in their efforts to be objective. This is all the more surprising at the Federal Labor Court, most of whose wingmen are officials of unions and employers' associations; but they display the same attitude. It has been reported that *Kampfabstimmungen*[3] over decisions in that Court occur as rarely as in the lower labor courts, i.e., in about 10 percent of all cases. Thus, wingmen now may be described as second-class judges who deal with legal problems, though they are far less knowledgeable in these matters than the professional judges.

This raises the question whether a new justification must be found for the tripartite structure of the labor courts. The professional judges now look upon the wingmen as "experts" in labor matters, generally comparable to "commercial lay judges" who sit in the commercial chambers of the *Landgerichte* and also have some knowledge of labor relations. But it must be asked whether this justification is satisfactory because the professional judge, who is appointed for life, is himself a specialist in labor law. Furthermore, it is doubtful whether the comparison of labor and commercial lay judges is valid; commercial practices are quite uniform in all branches of commerce, whereas labor practices vary with respect to the branch of industry as well as with the size and location of the plant. Thus, we should admit that the present system of labor courts lacks a theoretical explanation. It maintains the tradition, or rather the illusion, of sharing power. At best it may be hoped that the wingmen will keep some basic control over the proceedings of the professional judges in order to prevent a reversion to civil-law thinking. However, this control cannot be very effective because German judges are not allowed to write dissenting opinions. With respect to labor courts, this implies also that unions and employers' associations cannot supervise the activities of their wingmen. They can merely observe the deliberate and continuous bias of the Federal Labor Court directed against themselves and then advise their repre-

---

[2] In this connection it is interesting to note that the presidents of the appellate labor courts proposed at a conference in May, 1960, that the panels of their courts should become divisions, i.e., they should be composed of 3 professional judges and 2 wingmen. Cf. text of the conclusion of the presidents of the appellate labor courts, *Recht der Arbeit* (1961), p. 20.

[3] The term *Kampfabstimmung* refers to cases in which the judges cannot reach consensus. The dissenting judges are unwilling to relinquish their vote, and roll-call voting takes place.

sentatives to resign from the labor court, or refrain from proposing new candidates. Such actions would spell the end of labor courts, but, there is little chance that this will ever happen.

THE ATTITUDE OF LABOR COURTS

1. As stated above, the era of fair compromise in the history of labor courts ended with the statutory regulation of labor relations. As usual, however, traditional thinking has outlasted its factual basis, and labor lawyers therefore have maintained more independence from statutes and contracts than have civil lawyers. This fact may explain why parties to collective bargaining agreements who want decisions based solely on "the law" prefer judges of the ordinary courts to be the impartial chairmen of their arbitration boards. But the distinction between these and judges of the labor courts is merely one of quantity, not of quality. The increasing age of the German Civil Code, the first world war, the German inflation, the world economic crisis of the 1930s, and the break with liberalism that hesitantly began during the Weimar Republic and was carried to the extreme under the National Socialist regime, brought about a decline in the judges' strict adherance to the statutes. German judges no longer consider themselves the "mouth of the statute," but employ the general clauses of the Civil Code to establish a new law of equity, supported by the academic writers. Surely, this development in civil law must have an impact on labor law in which strict adherance to the statutes has declined even more because of the special legal situation. Labor law consists of many scattered statutes enacted at different times, often, and sometimes very poorly, amended. It invites the German lawyer to look for general principles connecting these statutes, and thereby to establish the basis for a labor code. The language of the LCA, stating that the big division should also "develop the law," can be interpreted to mean legislative authorization to do so.

2. The adjudication of the Federal Labor Court must be seen against this background. That Court considers itself independent of statutes as well as of collective bargaining agreements and individual contracts of employment; or, in the words of a German academic writer, the Federal Labor Court is the master of German labor law.[4] A number of quotations from decisions of the Court are cited to illustrate this atti-

---

[4] See Franz Gamillscheg, "Die Grundrechte im Arbeitsrecht," *Archiv für die zivilistische Praxis* (1965), vol. 164, p. 385 (reference on p. 388).

tude. Concerning the interpretation of collective bargaining agreements, the Court says:

> Above all, it is erroneous to believe that, as a rule, it is always clear and unequivocal which decision is correct, and that there can be only one correct decision. Such a belief may apply here and there, especially with respect to property law. However, with respect to criminal and civil law, and therefore also with respect to labor law, this is not so. Which decision, and this is significant, becomes binding upon the parties to a dispute is established only by final judgment, and never in any other way, even though critics may attack that decision as wrong. . . . Terms of the collective bargaining agreement, especially terms concerning piece rates, are never mathematically clear and unambiguous; the one proper decision as to the correct piece rate —if such a decision were indeed possible—can never be read directly from the terms of the collective bargaining agreement. Terms of the collective bargaining agreement are general terms; they must be variously interpreted in the different cases and cannot be applied clearly and unambiguously as a matter of course. The opinion that in interpreting the terms of collective bargaining agreements there is only one correct meaning does not consider that one decision always concerns only one distinct dispute, which must first be subsumed under the terms of the collective bargaining agreement.[5]

Thus, the Federal Labor Court pinpoints the arbitrary element of interpreting collective bargaining agreements. But the question arises whether the parties to collective bargaining agreements had not better interpret their agreements themselves through their own arbitration boards. The less clear or complete the terms of a collective bargaining agreement, the more arbitration is required. Unfortunately, however, the unity of substantive and procedural law is disregarded in Germany. The CBAA, and most of the academic writers, declares that the terms of collective bargaining agreements are "legal norms," and this calls for another method of interpretation than that of contracts, that is, the interpretation that applies to statutes. Yet, the Federal Labor Court employs the same method of interpretation for both statutes and collective bargaining agreements. This seems surprising because in Germany the interpretation of statutes is based on the assumption that all judges will reach the same decision, and this should apply to the legal norms of collective bargaining agreements as well. But the Federal Labor Court employs the opposite approach and transfers the ambiguousness of "legal norms" to the interpretation of the statutes:

> The application of law, mainly in respect of the more general provisions, undetermined legal concepts, or even questions involving judicial discretion, is a volitional decision which is not only cognizant but evaluative, actualiz-

---

[5] Judgment of October 12, 1955, *Entscheidungen des Bundesarbeitsgerichts* (hereafter quoted as *BAG*), vol. 2, p. 165 (reference on p. 174).

ing, integrating, and, in the distinct case, striving for the realization of justice.[6]

How much this element of arbitrariness in adjudication is emphasized by the Court may be illustrated by another decision of the same date, which may be taken as a supplement to the statements quoted above:

> It is not so that only *one* legal decision is absolutely and objectively correct, because even a legal decision can only express what is applicable according to the *conviction* of the court. The decision contains the subjective element of conviction, which, as shown by the contradictory decisions at the various levels of the court system, permits a number of different viewpoints; one conviction is not based solely on logical reasons, but also on an evaluation of the weight and persuasion of these reasons.[7]

The discretion of the Court is far-reaching. It does not only permit deviation from the language of a statute in order to adapt its provisions to changes in economic and social conditions. The Court also accords itself the power to correct the legislator:

> Inasmuch as a provision applies to situations or brings about consequences which were not recognized or included by the legislator, and, although they were recognized or included but not reasonably regulated in this manner, the courts are empowered to develop the law according to their own basic principles and purposes in consideration of the recognized principles of judicial finding of law, unless the requirements of security under the law speak against this. This applies especially to situations where the interests and the actual circumstances regulated by the legislator have been substantially altered, and, therefore, another regulation is also deemed necessary from the point of view of the legislator.[8]

The Federal Labor Court interprets the language of the Bonn Basic Law, stating that the judge is bound to "statute and law," as follows:

> The judge must adhere to the statute to the extent that the statute may be considered as a part of the conceptual entity of law, including its unwritten, basic principles and principles of immanent impact.

Some examples may serve to illustrate the practical consequences of these theories. The Federal Labor Court, rather than the parties to the collective bargaining agreement, felt it had the power to replace an obsolete provision of a collective bargaining agreement with a new one.[9] It changed the language of a provision granting a paid housework day to women working no less than 40 hours a week to 45 hours

---

[6] *Ibid.*

[7] Decision of October 12, 1955, *BAG,* vol. 2, p. 148 (reference on p. 151).

[8] Decision of the Big Division of March 16, 1962, *BAG,* vol. 13, p. 1 (reference on p. 14).

[9] Judgment of October 9, 1956, *BAG,* vol. 3, p. 159 (reference on p. 161).

a week if Saturday is a day not worked.[10] It employed the theory of the impact of constitutional rights upon private law, not to reestablish a liberal interpretation of the individual contract of employment, but to extend its discretionary power by considering these rights as new general provisions. The Court completely changed the law of torts on strikes and lockouts by replacing the old statutory provisions on the deliberate violation of *bona mores*—fully interpreted by the Supreme Labor Court— with a new provision on the "socially inadequate violation of the right of enterprise"; thus, it allowed every opportunity to restrict the freedom of the right to strike.[11]

All decisions of the Federal Labor Court follow the general tendency to restrict the application of collective labor law. This was also the tendency of the Supreme Labor Court, but it is now fully developed. Much more inclusive and aggressive, it covers all significant aspects of labor relations: strikes and lockouts, which are the basis of collective labor law, collective labor agreements, employer–works council agreements, protection of members of the works councils against dismissals, and so forth.

This strange situation has come about in part because of the increasing independence of the judges from the statute and their self-image as lawmakers. But the decisions of the Federal Labor Court also reflect public opinion. They are supported by the general feeling that the unions have acquired too much power after World War II, and that the employers rather than the unions deserve credit for the economic recovery of Germany. Possibly the judges may also feel responsible for maintaining the social order, considering that the development of collective labor law may take a dangerous direction if there is more labor legislation. To be sure, this was, and is, a very significant point. The unions have considerable strength in the federal Parliament: 30 of its 518 members are union officials, and another 45 confess to be union members though that figure actually may be higher. Moreover, the Adenauer government made concessions to organized labor in order to assure economic liberalism and prevent a shift to the left. The unions used the strategy of getting a favorable agreement on one issue or in one sector of the industry and then have it extended by federal legislation. For example, they gained legislation on minimum paid vacations, and on improved wages for manual workers during illness; both reforms were first introduced by collective bargaining agreements. The judges of the Federal Labor Court may have felt that this strategy, or

---

[10] Cf. judgment in footnote 8.
[11] Cf. my review on the jurisdiction of the Federal Labor Court (chap. 2, n. 13), *Juristenzeitung* (1964), pp. 494, 546, 582.

even the competition between the social state and collective bargaining agreements, could endanger the liberal basis of the social order and the economic stability of the nation. They evidently tried to control the labor force by their own interpretation of labor law.

The growth of this tendency could not have occurred had the unions not still suffered from the loss of left-wing German labor lawyers under the National Socialist regime, and had it not been backed by the academic writers. In this context it is significant that the first president of the Federal Labor Court, Hans Carl Nipperdey, was an academic writer. He was a highly reputable professor of labor law at the University of Cologne since the time of the Weimar Republic and well-known as co-author (with professor of labor law, Alfred Hueck) of a textbook on labor law, in addition to being legal adviser to the unions since 1945. This background, as well as his editorship of the only journal specializing in labor law and of a number of commentaries on labor statutes, enabled him to create a new policy of labor law at the very moment when the Federal Labor Court was established.

In view of all these facts, the Federal Labor Court today must be described as a political court, even though its members consider themselves apolitical because they confuse political views with party affiliations.

3. Most of these problems were probably not very important during the economic boom of the postwar years when employers were willing to grant favorable working conditions while making, or even increasing, profits by raising prices, or when strikes and lockouts were rare. Now, however, while the first recession makes itself felt, this time has come to an end. The question therefore arises whether the Federal Labor Court will continue its policy. Persistence in the policy of restriction will meet with the hostility of the unions, which are now beginning to discover the attitude of the Court. On the other hand, the introduction of a new policy—which became possible after Nipperdey's retirement and subsequent appointment of a new president—could endanger the confidence in the stability of the Court's adjudication. Perhaps the Court will gradually change its policy, or perhaps the German Federal Constitutional Court may intervene. The latter has already ruled that the right of self-organization is guaranteed under the constitution as part of the collective bargaining system,[12] and it has made a number of other important decisions on labor matters.[13]

---

[12] Judgment of September 18, 1954, *Entscheidungen des Bundesverfassungsgerichts* (hereafter quoted as *BVerfGE*), vol. 4, p. 96.

LABOR COURTS, GRIEVANCE SETTLEMENT IN WEST GERMANY

Authorized to control the concordance of the interpretation of a statute with the Bonn Basic Law, it is able to supervise the activities of all other high-level courts, including the Federal Labor Court.

STRENGTHS AND WEAKNESSES OF THE GERMAN SYSTEM

1. All conclusions and reflections lead to the question whether a specific national system is efficient in deciding labor disputes, and where its specific dangers lie. The concept of efficiency includes more than the mere working of the system—all systems will more or less work. It may be defined subjectively in terms of the confidence of all persons whom it affects and objectively as covering all labor disputes. Any answer is certainly difficult because a comparison with other systems working under the same conditions is not available. But at least one important criterion of efficiency is supplied by the fact that German employees generally do not go to the labor courts while their contract of employment is still in effect. Evidently, they are afraid of repercussions by the employer. But this state of affairs creates other disadvantages; they are often unable to prove facts related to the dispute because of the lapse in time, or they lose claims based on provisions of collective bargaining agreements because these are valid only during the life of the agreement. Nevertheless, if employees prefer to bring suit after the termination of the employment relationship, it would indicate that proceedings before the labor court, as well as those before any other court, create hostility, making it difficult to continue the employment relationship. It seems that no solution has been found to avoid this dilemma, and that the German system fails to neutralize the labor dispute or to protect the employee against repercussions by the employer. These two shortcomings are not only the fault of the labor courts but of the entire structure of German labor law, which is an unfortunate combination of state intervention, collective bargaining practices, and the system of works councils. In isolation none of these components is strong enough to provide a foundation of labor law, but each of them prevents the other from developing a perfect system. Therefore, neither the state with its labor courts nor the unions or the works councils can guarantee the necessary protection of the employee.

---

[13] Cf. the decisions on the capacity to conclude collective bargaining agreements: on the term "union" in the judgment of May 6, 1954, *BVerfGE*, vol. 18, p. 18; on guilds and guild corporations in the judgment of October 19, 1963, *BVerfGE*, vol. 20, p. 312. The decisions of April 1, 1964, and of November 30, 1965, *BVerfGE*, vol. 17, p. 319, and vol. 19, p. 303, respectively, are also important. They include the representation of unions in the constitutionally guaranteed freedom of union activities.

2. The present situation reveals the predominance of the state—a fact that will not surprise anyone who knows German history. German legal thinking is strongly influenced by the power of the state, rooted in the tradition of the feudal order, enriched by social legislation of the Weimar Republic and the dictatorship of the *Reichs* President in the last years of the Republic, perfected under the National Socialist regime, and finally assured by Adenauer's "chancellor democracy." This legal attitude may explain the attempts to incorporate unions and employers' associations into the structure of the state. The interpretation of the terms of collective bargaining agreements as legal norms is employed to consider unions and employers' associations lawmaking agents of the state, thus performing a function that is otherwise reserved to the state. Also, their participation in proceedings before the labor courts favors the trend to regard them as agents of the state. Therefore, the tripartite structure of the labor courts is indeed essential for the general development of collective labor law, providing a new understanding of labor self-government under the supervision of the state. Politically, as well, all restrictions on collective bargaining or on the freedom to strike require the participation of the parties to collective bargaining agreements. The tripartite structure of the labor courts will therefore be defended to the utmost by the German academic labor lawyers.

3. The German system of settlement of labor disputes is not satisfactory—this is the conclusion of the present study. It is not efficient enough because it endangers the existence of collective labor law, and it violates the supremacy of the Parliament. The lawmaking German judge is in a different position from a judge under a case-law system, because German legal thinking is conceived in terms of codified law. In Germany, judicial decisions always tend to be general, which leads the German judge to compete with the Parliament and allows him to play an un- or even anti-democratic role. Certainly, the Federal Labor Court had ambitions to assume the role of the Parliament, which it considered unable sufficiently to regulate strikes and lockouts.

It is doubtful whether remedies will be found. The more labor law becomes statutory law, the more will the existence of labor courts be accepted as a matter of course. However, the tendency to employ arbitration will perhaps increase—the number of collective bargaining agreements providing for arbitration in collective disputes appears to be growing indeed.[14] A thorough legal examination of the interpreta-

---

[14] Cf. the complaints of the president of an appellate labor court, Hans Gramm, "Gerichte für Arbeitssachen und Schiedsgerichte," *Recht der Arbeit* (1967), pp. 41 ff.

tion of LCA provisions for the arbitration of individual disputes may also lead to arbitration in these cases—assuming that the dissatisfaction with the lengthy procedure and the decisions of the Federal Labor Court grows.

The tripartite structure of the labor courts probably will not be altered. That tradition apparently must be maintained, and its significance would be lost if the courts' decisions reflected strict adherence to the constitution, to statutes, collective bargaining agreements, and employer—works council agreements. The labor courts regard themselves as independent of the law—an attitude that also justifies the tripartite structure of the courts because representatives of the employer and the worker can thereby participate in the making of new labor law. Certainly, this situation is reminiscent of the era when labor courts were first established, but the similarities concern only the form and not the substance. The present labor courts do not overcome the social disparities of private law; rather, they revise social legislation and collective bargaining agreements. As far as the unions are concerned, the original meaning of their participation in labor court proceedings is lost, and we may ask why they should continue to participate. Today, an increase in arbitration with the aid of lawyers trained in observance of the law, even a return to the practice of bringing suit in private courts, would certainly be more to their advantage.

III

THE SETTLEMENT OF EMPLOYMENT GRIEVANCES IN SWEDEN

by Folke Schmidt

Professor of Labor Law
University of Stockholm, Sweden

1.
INTRODUCTION

THE ORGANIZATIONAL STRUCTURE OF THE LABOR MARKET

1. In Sweden local and plant unions were combined in national unions at an early stage. The authority lies with the national union; the branches are considered organs of the national union, though they have some independent functions.

Some of the Swedish national unions represent employees belonging to a particular craft, others those working within a given industry. Gradually the principle of industrial unionism has gained ground. In the building industry, during the last few decades the carpenters and the bricklayers have yielded up their independence and merged into the Building Workers' Union, a union that earlier was predominantly composed of unskilled workers. Some groups, e.g., painters, electricians, and steel-plate workers, are still independent, but many of their own officers consider a merger with the industrial union to be only a matter of time. As in many other countries, the craft unions have their main stronghold in the printing industry. However, the three existing unions, those of the printers, the bookbinders and the lithographers, cooperate and are all affiliated with a special cartel, the Graphic Cartel. The success of the industrial unions is partly to be explained by the fact that the employers organized industry by industry and wanted to have settlements with all their workers in one and the same agreement. The workers found that their bargaining power became strengthened if they were combined in a single union, which would be the sole signatory on the labor side to the prospective agreement.

The unions of manual workers are members of the *Landsorganisation*, generally called LO, a confederation which was founded in 1898. It should be mentioned that the Swedish unions have a very large total membership. It is a fair estimate that, with a few exceptions such as hotels and restaurants and the merchant marine, more than 95 percent of the manual workers belong to unions affiliated with LO.

White-collar workers were relatively late in joining unions. While the manual workers managed to organize before or soon after 1900, unions of white-collar workers did not become a significant factor before the 1930s. These workers formed unions of their own. Partly this was the result of managerial policy. The Swedish Employers' Confederation ordered its members to stipulate that a supervisor—who ordinarily is selected from the rank and file—should not remain a member of his union. Therefore, in order to promote their interests, the supervisors had to form a union of their own, *Sveriges Arbetsledareförbund* (SALF). SALF has members both within the private sector and within the nationalized industries. Partly for other reasons certificated engineers (not university-trained engineers), industrial office workers, and those employed in laboratories, construction departments, etc., chose to have a separate union representing salaried employees in private industry, *Svenska Industritjänstemannaförbundet* (SIF). Salaried employees are not organized to the same extent as manual workers. However, union enrollment is large, probably representing in private industry around 80 percent of all salaried employees below the managerial level.

2. The Swedish Employers' Confederation, *Svenska Arbetsgivareföreningen* (SAF), founded in 1902, has within its own field a position equal to the LO. In 1969 the Confederation had 24,000 member firms. The number of persons employed by its members was 1,220,000.[1] Of these, 804,000 were manual workers. The remaining 416,000 are classified in the Director General's Report as "other employees"; this label is preferred to the name ordinarily used, *tjänsteman*, a word which has a meaning similar to "official" and has a ring of a certain status. The membership of the SAF is divided into a number of sectorial associations, one association for each industry. There is a general division, too, comprising a number of miscellaneous industries. The Swedish Metal Trades Employers' Association *(Sveriges Verkstadsförening)* and the Association of Employers within the Building Industry *(Byggnadsindustriförbundet)* are the most influential ones.

3. During the first decades of this century a uniform pattern of bargaining was established. The employers' association in an industry would meet with the trade unions concerned and enter into a national agreement covering manual workers employed by the member firms of

---

[1] The population of Sweden is 8 million.

the association. This pattern still prevails, although since World War II—with a few intermissions—the bargaining has been split into two rounds. Some specific issues and the question of the amount available for wage increases are decided in a provisional settlement between SAF and LO, whereafter the distribution of the pot and the bargaining over the details are referred to the parties to the national agreements.[2]

It should be emphasized that the national agreement for the industry is a contract for a certain period of time. Indeed, a peace obligation for the term of the agreement is a basic part of the bargain. The agreement continues to be applicable for a fresh term unless notice of termination is given before a certain date, e.g., three months before the date of expiration.

Earlier the usual term was one or two years. In 1966 it was made part of the master agreement between SAF and LO that the national agreements should cover a three-year period (February 1, 1966 to January 31, 1969). The settlement of 1969 covered the years 1969 and 1970.

The union has a means of extending the application of the national agreement; it does so by inviting employers who are not affiliated with the SAF to sign a letter in which they declare their intention to apply the national agreement. Incidentally, such letters are considered collective contracts at law. In a very few cases these adhesion contracts may prescribe additional benefits. Moreover, some kind of union-shop clause is an ordinary part of them. If the employer refuses to sign and the workers strike, their action will prompt the refusal of other workers to replace them. Incidentally, in such circumstances the employer may choose to apply for membership in the SAF, which as a matter of policy is open to all firms of established reputation. If he joins SAF the national agreement for his industry will apply, and as a party to the agreement he will be protected by the peace obligation. There exist, however, a great number of adhesion contracts; they are particularly frequent in the road haulage industry.

A number of specific issues have been settled in agreements between SAF and LO. The first example is provided by the so-called December Compromise of 1906, which dealt with the preservation of the manager's prerogatives. In the same document the employers declared it to be their intention that the right of self-organization should be left inviolate.

---

[2] The national agreement for the metal trades is reproduced in Folke Schmidt, *The Law of Labour Relations in Sweden* (Cambridge, Mass.: Harvard University Press, 1962), pp. 305 ff.

After a general strike in 1909 the relations between the parties of the labor market were tense for some time. A new epoch was introduced with the Basic Agreement of 1938. This agreement provides for a negotiation procedure for grievances in general, and a special procedure for disputes over dismissals and layoffs. It further contains a number of rules intended to prevent injury to neutral third parties during labor conflicts. The Basic Agreement rests upon the assumption that it will be taken as a collective agreement by branch associations of SAF and LO trade unions which are parties to national agreements. The Basic Agreement remains in force indefinitely, subject to six months' notice.[3] At present it has been accepted by all the LO trade unions concerned, with two important exceptions, the Transport Workers' Union (representing teamsters and longshoremen) and the Building Workers' Union.

More recently, some fresh topics have been dealt with in settlements between SAF and LO. The agreements on joint enterprise councils, 1946, amended 1957 and 1964, and the agreement on time and motion studies, 1948, are perhaps the most important ones.

The unions of salaried employees, in their bargaining, focused their attention on such matters as the period of notice, sick pay, and various fringe benefits. The salary of the individual employee was settled individually in each case and was dependent upon what the employer was willing to pay. Consistently the national agreements for salaried employees in private industry and for supervisors, unlike the agreements for manual workers, did not comprise lists of wage rates for different kinds of work. However, in the last few years the employers have accepted the idea of bargaining about wage increases for salaried employees. The initial rate of pay and increases on account of promotion are still a matter of the employer's discretion. In a master agreement between SAF and the respective unions, formulas relating to annual increments are given for the duration of the agreement.

With regard to dismissals there are separate agreements for salaried employees and supervisors, which are counterparts to the Basic Agreement between SAF and LO.

4. As indicated above, there are generally three national agreements for every industry, each for a separate category of employees, namely one agreement between the sectorial association of employers and the LO trade union concerned covering manual workers, another with the

---

[3] The Basic Agreement of 1938 as amended in 1947 is reproduced in Schmidt, *op. cit.*, pp. 263 ff.

SETTLEMENT OF EMPLOYMENT GRIEVANCES IN SWEDEN

Union of Salaried Employees within Industry (SIF) as party to the agreement covering its members, and a third with the Union of Supervisors (SALF). The national agreements for manual workers are individual documents. Consequently considerable divergences may exist, as, for example, between the agreement for the metal trade and the agreement for the building industry. The national agreements for salaried employees are standardized, and they are almost identical throughout industry as a whole. The same is the case with the national agreements signed by the Union of Supervisors.

The national agreements are always made for a specific term. As mentioned before, the latest agreements for the manual workers were for the period 1969–70.

THE COLLECTIVE AGREEMENT AS CONTRACT AT LAW

5. The Swedish scholar, Axel Adlercreutz,[4] has described the introduction of the collective agreement in various countries. The abolition of the old "regulation system" in the middle of the nineteenth century did not imply an immediate break with existing practices. The vacuum was filled by customs and usages originating in the old system. The dominant position of the employer remained. Conditions of work were in fact determined by the employer or—in view of the prevailing liberalist ideology—by the economic laws of supply and demand.

The rise of the collective agreement is intimately bound up with the recognition of the unions and the active part played by the unions in its creation. The attempts to secure a promise from the employer to apply a scale of wages submitted by the union represented the first step. In the beginning the situation was very similar to the old system under which laborers could submit petitions to the masters as to an authority, such as the guild or the bench of magistrates. However, Swedish employers became aware that a union could serve as a guarantor of a strike-free period. Thus, the collective agreement was made a mutual agreement whereby a peace obligation, minimum wages, and overtime pay were parts of the bargain. It became an established practice for the collective agreement to be valid for a definite period, e.g., one or two years.

In the first decade of this century the Swedish collective agreement acquired another characteristic feature—its nationwide scope. As early

---

[4] Adlercreutz, "The Rise and Development of the Collective Agreement," *Scandinavian Studies in Law*, vol. 2 (1958), pp. 11 ff. See also the same author, *Kollektivavtalet. Studier över dess tillkomsthistoria* (Lund, 1954).

as 1910, there were at least fifteen such agreements for different industries or crafts.

6. When, in the case reported in 1915 NJA 233, Swedish courts were called upon to enforce a collective agreement, they had to deal with an established institution. The newspaper *Aftonbladet* had sued the Printers' Union for damages because the union had ordered its members to take part in the general strike of 1909, which according to the plaintiff was a violation of the no-strike clause in the agreement for the printing trade. The union pleaded that the agreement was only a *de facto* peace treaty, which was not enforceable. The Supreme Court explicitly rejected this argument, declaring that the agreement was binding, as a contract at law, and that in case of breach the injured party was entitled to compensation. The action was dismissed, however, the Court finding that the agreement had not been intended to contain a prohibition against sympathetic actions.

When contrasting the willingness of the Swedish Supreme Court to recognize the collective agreements as a contract at law with the situation in Britain and the United States, some principles of Swedish law should be carefully noted. In Sweden there was no legislation corresponding to the British Trade Disputes Act of 1871, 1875, and 1906, which gave the unions immunity against various actions in court. As in the continental European legal systems, the Swedish law of contracts is based upon the doctrine of the mutual agreement as binding by mere consent with no formal requirements; indeed, from the end of the nineteenth century the idea prevailed that the promise was binding as such. The doctrine of consideration has never been part of Swedish law. Further, trade unions and associations of employers are regarded as friendly societies or noneconomic associations which are, in Sweden, legal personalities. Incorporation is not required since there is no statutory law on friendly societies.

However, little use was made of the possibility of bringing an action in a court of justice against a contracting party accused of a breach of a collective agreement. One reason for this was the slowness of the civil courts. The parties could not tolerate the long wait for a final decision while the case was carried through the various levels of appeal. Nor did they believe civil courts capable of adjudicating properly disputes concerning collective agreements. The trade union leaders, with their socialist creed, had additional reasons for abstaining from court actions. They deeply mistrusted the courts, which they looked upon as allies of the employers or as belonging to an autocratic body of public officials. Thus, although collective agreements were in most

SETTLEMENT OF EMPLOYMENT GRIEVANCES IN SWEDEN

cases observed, this was certainly not because of the legal remedies then available.

7. This state of affairs was considered unsatisfactory by those in power. Machinery for the effective enforcement of collective agreements was a necessary supplement to the governmental conciliation service. The principal demand was for a special tribunal competent to adjudicate in cases concerning the interpretation of collective agreements. In 1928 the two fundamental laws governing labor relations in Sweden, the Act on Collective Agreements and the Labor Court Act, were introduced. A quotation from the legislative material indicates the purpose of these enactments: "The rule of law demanded that the solution of disputes concerning collective agreements should not depend upon the respective powers of the belligerent parties." Thus, the idea was to exclude self-help remedies by affirming the binding and enforceable status of collective agreements.[5]

The two Acts of 1928 were carried through by a non-Socialist majority in Parliament against the opposition of the Socialist Party and the trade unions. At the time when the bill was on the floor, the unions had recourse to a general protest strike, and large demonstrations took place outside the House of Parliament. After the Acts had come into operation, however, labor opinion gradually changed. The Social Democratic Party, which came to power with the elections in the fall of 1932, did not take steps to repeal or amend the Acts, and in 1939 the LO explicitly disapproved a private motion in Parliament that the Acts should be repealed.

8. In Germany, a few years earlier, the collective agreement had become a legally recognized institution through an Act of 1920. Some fundamental differences between German and Swedish law must be mentioned against the background of the goals in the minds of the respective legislators. In 1920 Germany was still in a state of revolution. As a part of a general policy aimed at realizing the ideals of democracy, the parties of the labor market were accorded self-government with regard to wages and other conditions of employment.

German law distinguishes between the contractual and the normative part of the collective agreement. The contractual part concerns the relation between the two parties to the agreement, the union and the employer or—more usually—an association of employers. To the contractual part belong not only the provisions regarding the term of

---

[5] A translation into English of the text of the two acts is found in Schmidt, *op. cit.*, pp. 243 ff.

the collective agreement, the period of notice of termination, and possible negotiation procedures, but also the peace obligation. Thus, in German law the peace obligation is a matter concerning the contracting parties exclusively. Provisions on wages and other conditions of employment form the normative part. By virtue of statutory law, they have an immediate impact upon the employment relations of the members since they are obligatory parts of the employment contract.

Swedish (Scandinavian) law presents another solution to the problem of the effect to be given to the collective agreement. Swedish law is based upon a "combination" theory. In the Collective Agreements Act there are no provisions regarding the effect of the agreement upon the parties, since this is taken for granted. SECTION 2 provides that a collective agreement "shall also be binding on members of the association in so far as the trades and sectors of industry specified in the agreement are concerned, whether such members became members of the association before or after the conclusion of the agreement. . . ." As a matter of principle, all parts of the agreement are transferred to and made part of the employment relations. Thus, the peace obligation is incumbent upon individual employers as well as individual union members.

9. In contrast to German law, however, the combined effect of the agreement is never a necessary element (see diagram 1). The parties to the collective agreement are at liberty to decide that a clause of the agreement shall have effect between the parties to the agreement exclusively or create duties incumbent upon them and upon the employer in relation to the union but not in relation to the employees. As a matter of course, clauses concerning the duty to negotiate in case of a dispute or the duty to give notice before resort to economic action or regarding the period of notice of termination of the agreement are provisions which are secondary from the point of view of the individual union members. On the other hand, clauses regarding wages are typically a part of the employment relations, though on some occasions even such clauses have no immediate effect upon the employment relations of the individuals.

It is a salient feature of the National Agreement for the Metal Industry that its clauses concerning piece rates remain on the organizational level. They are wage guarantees which place upon the employer certain obligations in relation to the union. One of these clauses is *Note No. 1*.

Originally, the unions which were parties to the National Agreement for the Metal Industry held that they had a right to open negotiations for higher wages whenever they wanted, and they disputed that they were bound by a peace obligation for the term of the agreement. The union's right to open negotiations at will was abolished in 1923. At the

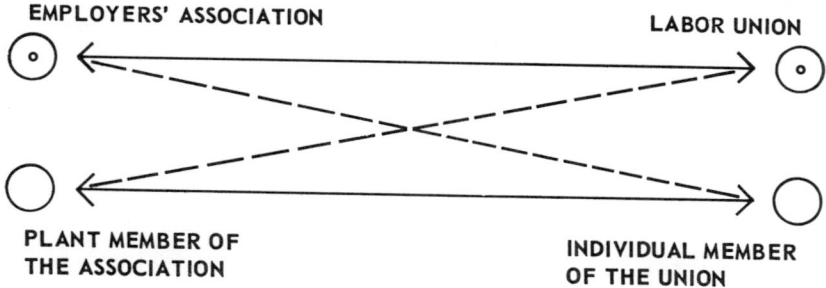

DIAGRAM 1. The combined effect of the collective agreement. Continuous lines indicate contractual relationships instituted by the collective agreement; dotted lines indicate the relation between an association and its member.

same time there was added to the agreement a special wage guarantee, known as *Note No. 1* because of its place. It says: "The parties agree that economic benefits existing in the individual plants when the agreement comes into force cannot be modified during the term of the agreement." On several occasions the parties to the National Agreement have submitted to the labor court disputes with regard to the

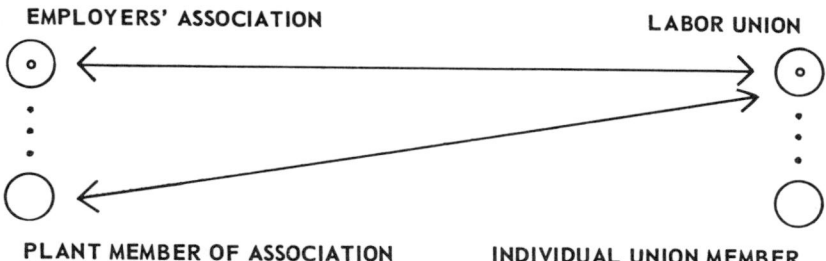

DIAGRAM 2. Clause with effect limited to the organizational level.

bearing of *Note No. 1* (which, incidentally, is still a part of the agreement). In 1934, in its decision No. 181, the court ruled that *Note No. 1* did not embody an obligation in relation to the individual workers but in relation to the union as a party to the agreement. If the union believed that a series of incidents revealed an intention by the employer to depress the income level of the employees at his plant, it was entitled to bring the case to the labor court, possibly with a claim for general damages for breach of the agreement.

Diagram 2 demonstrates the effect of *Note No. 1* as a clause remaining on the organizational level.

THE NOTION OF THE EMPLOYMENT CONTRACT

10. In Sweden, as in continental European law in general, a contract of employment is assumed to exist between the employer and the individual employee. There is no need for express provisions in writing or in any kind of particulars or for a specific oral agreement, and more often than not the creation of an employment relationship is as informal as it is in the United States.

In most cases the employee is hired for an indefinite period. The employment contract remains in force indefinitely, subject to notice of termination and the expiration of the period of notice. In the case of manual workers the ordinary period of notice is two weeks. For salaried employees the period of notice varies, depending upon who gives notice, the employer or the employee, and the length of service. Under the national agreements for salaried employees within industry and for supervisors, the maximum periods are six months in the case of notice given by the employer and three months in the case of notice given by the employee.

When an employer hires a manual worker, he may mention the wage if he offers more than the minimum laid down in the collective agreement. That wages and other terms of employment shall be expressly agreed upon is not a condition of the coming into existence of a contract of employment. Admittedly it is a fiction that certain terms are made part of the individual contract of employment. However, this idea plays an important role in all claims covering individual employees.

According to continental European thinking, the elements of the employment contract are derived from various sources of law:

(a) Statutory provisions are a principal source. However, Sweden has no labor code, and statutory law is mostly aimed at taking care of specific needs. The Paid Vacations Act and the act prohibiting dismissal on account of marriage or pregnancy constitute examples. Like several other statutory provisions, the provisions of these Acts are compulsory and they are read into the contract of employment even where other conditions less favorable to the employee are agreed upon by the employer and his employee.

SETTLEMENT OF EMPLOYMENT GRIEVANCES IN SWEDEN

(b) For all practical purposes the collective agreement is the dominating factor. As indicated before, normally the provisions of the collective agreement are obligatory parts of the employment contract.

(c) In many firms there are works rules laid down by the employer with regard to hours of work, leave of absence, periods of payments, etc. Such rules are often considered as general directives subject to change at the discretion of the employer. Rules regarding pensions or other fringe benefits, however, if laid down in works rules, have been held to constitute vested rights and form part of the employment contract of the individual employee. Works rules as an independent source of the employment conditions are less important today than formerly, because in many sectors the works rules have been embodied in part in the national collective agreement.

(d) Rules agreed to by the employer and the employee themselves form a category of their own. In one case it might be a matter of an addition to the minimum wage provided for in the collective agreement, in another some fringe benefit. I prefer to call these rules the *personal part* of the employment contract.

11. When applying the "combination" theory, the legislators did not intend to transgress the boundaries of the idea of the privity of contracts. According to Sec. 2 of the Collective Agreements Act, the individual plant and the individual employee are bound in their capacity as members of an association which is a party to the collective agreement. In the foregoing section it was assumed that the parties to the employment contract—i.e., the employer and his employee—both had that capacity. When this is not the case the situation is somewhat different.

It should be mentioned that Swedish law is not familiar with the system of authoritative extension (French "extension," German "Allgemeinverbindlicherklärung") of a collective agreement that one meets in French and German law. The application of a collective agreement to an employment contract for other reasons than the prescription in the Collective Agreements Act has to rest upon non-statute law.

We must distinguish between cases when the employer is bound by a collective agreement and other cases. Assume that a nonunion worker is employed at a plant belonging to an association of employers. The collective agreement has various side effects. In several cases the labor court has found that a national agreement for manual workers implies a condition that the employer has a duty to apply the agreement to all workers. The first cases on this matter date from the 1930s—a period of high unemployment. It was in the interest of the union that the employer should not have the possibility of paying nonunion employees less, since he would then be inclined to hire a nonunion man rather than a union member. An implied term not to pay less to nonunion employees lays down a duty in relation to the union. The employer may enter into personal contracts with nonunion employees. Such contracts are valid. However, the union may take action and claim general damages for breach of the collective agreement. Often the difference between the union rate and the actual rate of pay has served as a measure of general damages.

A nonunion person employed by an employer belonging to an association of employers is party to an employment contract with his employer that is not governed by the Collective Agreements Act. In such cases a civil court is always the competent forum with regard to claims between the parties. If an action is brought before the civil court by the employee, e.g., for payment for work performed, or because the employer has withheld part or all of his pay in settlement of an alleged counterclaim, the court will in the absence of a personal contract inquire into the assumptions of the parties. If the court finds that the employer used to apply the terms of the collective agreement to nonunion employees as well, the party who claims that this assumption should not apply will have the burden of proof. In this situation the collective agreement may be described as having effect because of the practice within the plant.

In a case where the employer is not bound by a collective agreement, the national collective agreement of the industry might have effect as constituting customary law. The Swedish Supreme Court found, in a number of cases reported in 1945 NJA 230, that the conditions of the national agreement for salaried employees with regard to periods of notice of dismissal should apply to a plant in the chemical industry. The Court gave as reasons that these conditions were usually applied not only in the chemical industry but also in industry in general. The decision in the case 1963 NJA 331 also relies upon the doctrine of customary law.

THE RIGHT OF SELF-ORGANIZATION

12. The right of self-organization of the manual worker was established already in the years 1900–10, for the fact that an employer enters into bargaining and makes a collective agreement implies the recognition of the contracting union as the agent of its members and a pledge not to discriminate against union members. As already men-

tioned (sec. 3), in the December Compromise of 1906 the SAF explicitly agreed that the right of self-organization should be left inviolate. To the salaried employees in private industry and the supervisors, who began to claim recognition of their unions in the early 1930s, the situation was troublesome. The employers were not enthusiastic about the idea of collective bargaining with these categories and their unions were reluctant to resort to economic action. When the white-collar workers expressed interest in legislation for the protection of the right of self-organization, all political parties took a favorable view, since white-collar workers were not politically oriented in any one direction and therefore represented a large potential group of marginal voters.

It was another matter that the political parties had different conceptions as to what a piece of legislation ought to convey. In non-Socialist quarters it was not held justifiable to enact a statute for the protection of employees against unfair practices of the employer without at the same time protecting those who wanted to remain outside a trade union from pressure to join it. Thus, protection of the right of self-organization ought to be coupled with a right to remain nonorganized. The Social Democrats held that the statute ought to be confined to the right of self-organization. The ordinary rules of the Criminal Code with regard to violence, threats, intimidation, and slander disposed of the other part of the problem. The dissent with regard to the scope of legislative interferences nearly shipwrecked the Bill respecting the Right of Organization and Negotiation, which was introduced in 1936. As a compromise some of the definitions were deleted from the original text, which blurred the meaning of the statute. By an Act of 1940 providing for amendments of the 1936 Act, it was established, however, that the legislators aimed at the protection of the right of self-organization exclusively. By that time the labor court had taken the same position in a number of cases.

13. In theory the Act respecting the Right of Organization and Negotiation, 1936, protects employers against union practices as well as employees against acts of the employer.[6] For practical purposes, it is only the protection of the employees that has had any significance.

The right of organization laid down in the Act is aimed principally at the protection of the individuals as employees. According to SEC. 3, SUBSEC. 3, the right of organization is deemed to be violated if measures are taken by the employer to constrain an employee to refrain from becoming a member of a union or to resign from a union, to refrain

---

[6] The text of the statute is printed in Schmidt, *op. cit.*, pp. 251 ff.

from exercising his rights as a member of a union, or to refrain from working for a union or for the formation of a union, and is likewise considered to be violated if measures are taken by the employer that are calculated to cause prejudice to an employee on the grounds that he is a member of a union, exercises his rights as a union member, or works for a union or for the formation of a union. According to SUB-SEC. 4 of the same section, an infringement by giving notice of termination is null and void. As will be mentioned later, the remedies are reinstatement, compensation for economic loss, and general damages.

The union has no right of organization of its own. It can take no action against measures by an employer which are directed against the union itself. If, however, an act by the employer constitutes a violation of the right of self-organization of one of his employees, the union is entitled to institute an action of its own for damages for "personal injury." It is not required that the employee had a union card; it is sufficient that he was a prospective member.

14. The Act is based upon the philosophy that the right of self-organization of the individual employees is a necessary prerequisite of a right of negotiation. Therefore, the general policy of the Act can be described as the establishing by statute of a right of the union to represent its members as a bargaining agent. Special provisions as to the right to negotiate are contained in Chapter 2 of the Act. It should be mentioned that there is no requirement that a union must have the support of the majority of the employees of an appropriate unit. The Act protects membership of any union. It might be added, however, that the employer's duty to negotiate with the union does not imply more than a duty to meet the union representatives and to take their proposals into consideration. Neither party to a dispute is under obligation to reach a settlement, and a party has fulfilled his statutory duty of negotiation even if he refuses to enter into a collective agreement with the opposite party.

EXISTING BODIES FOR SETTLEMENT OF LABOR DISPUTES

15. The Act on Conciliation in Labor Disputes, 1920, represents the oldest part of existing legislation on labor relations in Sweden. It replaced an Act of 1906. The Swedish conciliation service has functions similar to its American counterpart.

There is a permanent conciliator for each of eight regions. Often conciliators are appointed *ad hoc*. In most cases the conciliator acts alone. In big disputes where important national interests are at stake, the King in Council may appoint a special board, generally consisting of three persons. The conciliators are always neutral. In contrast to France, employers and employees are never members of conciliation boards.

The conciliator is competent to assist the parties in the settlement of any dispute that may threaten industrial peace, and consequently also in the settlement of grievances arising over the application or interpretation of existing collective agreements. But conciliation in such matters is not his principal task. In most cases conciliation concerns the terms of a new agreement.

Negotiations organized by the conciliator are intended to bring about an agreement in accordance with the offers and the proposals presented by the parties in the course of negotiation. The procedure is based entirely upon the personal authority of the conciliator and the desire of the parties to settle their dispute. The conciliator may ask the parties for adjustments and concessions and may put forward proposals. He may communicate tentative drafts for consideration. According to established practice, however, the conciliator is not supposed to make any recommendation of his own unless favorable reactions from both parties are expected. If not, he has to state that negotiations have failed. It is not the task of the conciliator to take into consideration the government's views with regard to the scope for permissible wage increases.

16. There is only one labor court *(Arbetsdomstolen)*, and its jurisdiction comprises the whole kingdom of Sweden. The labor court is a trial court, but its decisions are final and not subject to appeal. Within its sphere of competence the labor court is the exclusive forum for judicial settlements.

Usually the court sits with nine members present. It is composed of

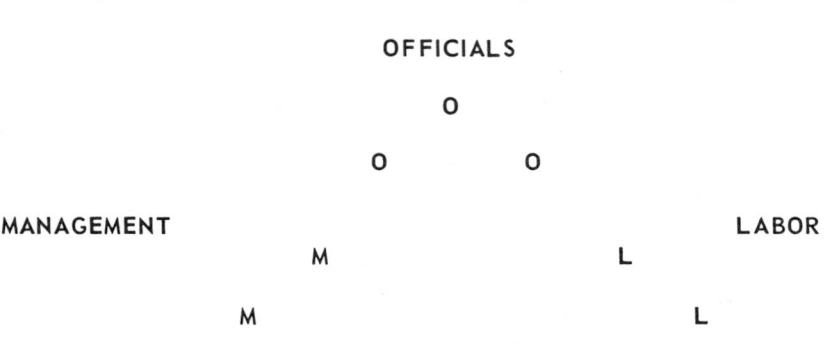

DIAGRAM 3. The composition of the Swedish Labor Court.

three groups—officials, management, and labor—as indicated in diagram 3.

The chairman (according to established practice, a former member of the Supreme Court), the vice-chairman (a career judge), and an impartial labor relations expert form the official element. The two management members are nominated by the Council of Swedish Employers' Associations—a committee formed by the Swedish Employers' Confederation (SAF) and some independent employers' associations; from January 1, 1966, there are alternate members representing the state and the municipalities.[7] The labor element is composed of two union officers nominated by the Swedish Confederation of Trade Unions (LO); there are alternate members representing salaried employees and public officials.

As a matter of principle, all members of the court have equal status and each casts his vote individually. However, the court itself decides its manner of voting and the ordinary rule that the youngest member casts his vote first is not applied.

17. The cases which can be brought to the labor court are narrowly defined in the statute book. These are the main categories:

(a) disputes relating to the validity, contents or interpretation of a collective agreement or relating to breaches of a collective agreement;

(b) actions arising from violations of the peace obligation constituted by a collective agreement;

(c) actions arising from violations of the right of self-organization;

(d) claims based upon statutory provisions prohibiting dismissal on account of military service or on account of marriage or pregnancy, or prohibiting unfair treatment of safety representatives;

(e) claims under the Paid Vacations Act.

With regard to claims under (d) and (e), the labor court is the competent forum only in cases in which the employment contract of the individual concerned is governed by a collective agreement.

According to a rough estimate, category (a) covers about 85 percent of all cases, categories (b) and (c) about 5 percent each, and (d) and (e) together less than 5 percent. Thus, category (a) is definitely the dominating one.

The drafters of the Labor Court Act, 1928, were anxious to avoid

---

[7] On January 1, 1966, the State Officials Act and the Municipal Officials Act came into force. Collective agreements with unions of officials were recognized on matters concerning remuneration and given effect equal to collective agreement within the private sector. The labor court was made the competent forum.

burdening the court with trivial cases that did not need to be handled by experts. It was in the interest of the parties, too, that it should be possible to take such cases to the local civil courts. The labor court should not enforce uncontested wage claims. For this reason in cases belonging to category (a) it was made a prerequisite not only that the action should be based upon a right under a collective agreement, but also that this right should have been disputed by the defendant. Therefore, category (a) may be described as covering "disputes over rights" in a very strict sense of that term.

18. In many industries arbitration was already an established practice before the institution of the labor court in 1928. The state had taken measures to provide the parties with qualified arbitrators. Under the Act on Special Arbitrators in Labor Disputes, 1920, the King in Council appointed persons whom the parties could call upon to serve as single arbitrators or as chairmen of arbitral boards. From 1920 to 1923, there existed a Central Arbitration Board with a tripartite composition similar to that of the labor court. The Board, which had to deal with disputes over the interpretation of collective agreements, assumed jurisdiction when the agreement contained a clause to that effect or the parties had joined in submitting an issue to the Board.

By introducing the Collective Agreements Act, 1928, and by instituting the labor court, the legislators intended to make the collective agreement binding and enforceable as a contract at law with adequate sanctions administered by an expert authority. In the future there would be no need for the state to take special measures for the encouragement of voluntary arbitration. The labor court replaced the Central Arbitration Board.

The vision of the legislators became a reality, in part at least. The parties submitted themselves to the new order and did not try to replace resort to the labor court by resort to arbitration. It may be mentioned that the system of special arbitrators appointed by the King in Council, which was permitted to remain, was used very seldom and became obsolete in a few decades. Gradually arbitration, however, has come to play an important role where specific issues are concerned. Further, in some trades the parties continued to rely upon their earlier systems of special arbitral boards.

The Basic Agreement of December, 1938, between SAF and LO (mentioned in sec. 3) established a joint body, the *Arbetsmarknadsnämnden* (Labor Market Board), with three representatives each of SAF and LO. In cases concerning third party rights in labor disputes the Board had an umpire and acted as an arbitral board.

According to the original text of the Basic Agreement in dismissal cases the Board functioned as a joint council making recommendations to the parties that were not formally binding upon them. In 1964 the Basic Agreement was amended. Dismissals arising out of circumstances affecting an individual worker were distinguished from other cases of dismissals or layoffs. For practical purposes the line of demarcation is drawn between dismissals for personal reasons and dismissals and layoffs on the ground of redundancy. For the adjudication of cases belonging to the former category the Board has an umpire and lays down binding awards.

It may be mentioned in passing that since 1965 the acting president of the labor court, Mr. Justice Hult, has served as the umpire.

In 1965 similar arbitral boards for cases of dismissals were instituted for salaried employees and for supervisors, in accordance with agreements between SAF and SIF and SAF and SALF respectively.

It would not be possible to give a complete review covering all the arrangements that exist in various sectors. The situation within two trades, however, deserves particular attention. The arbitral board for piece rates in the building industry will be the object of a special study. The way in which peace is achieved through arbitration in the Swedish press sector will also be described. Two arbitral boards exist for the press: one for issues of interest, the other for disputes over rights. The former has the power to make the new contract if the parties fail to agree, the latter deals with cases of interpretation of existing agreements.

19. In private litigation, as a matter of principle, the parties have a choice between judicial proceedings and arbitration. An arbitration clause, if entered upon, is binding upon the parties and a court of law must refuse to accept jurisdiction if the defendent invokes the clause. It is binding upon the members of the organizations, too. Some procedural rules are laid down in the Arbitration Act of 1929. An award in compliance with the requirements of the Act is enforceable like a court decision. Within the field of labor relations there are two exceptions to these rules. An agreement to submit to arbitration is not recognized as a bar to judicial proceeding in (a) actions for premature termination of a collective agreement in case of essential breach of the agreement by the defendant, and (b) actions because of a violation of the right of self-organization.

20. It would seem convenient to sum up here the rules concerning which bodies are competent to adjudicate existing grievances. There is a line of demarcation between organized workers, that is, employees

who are members of the union which is the signatory to the collective agreement, and nonorganized workers. As mentioned under sections 7 and 8, the organized worker is made a party to the collective agreement by virtue of the combination theory adopted by the Collective Agreements Act. The term "nonorganized" includes all other employees within the category concerned (manual workers, salaried employees, supervisors). For the present purpose this category also covers those who belong to another union than the one signatory to the agreement. Incidentally, there is a union, with a membership drawn from the building industry especially, which competes with the unions affiliated with LO; it is called the Syndicalist Union because of its heritage from the south-European anarchist-syndicalist labor movement.

The law with regard to the nonorganized worker is simple. An action has to be brought in the civil court of the district. Since the right of self-organization is conferred upon all union members—whatever union they join—and not only upon the members of the signatory union, there is an exception to this rule. Actions respecting violations of the right of self-organization must always be brought in the labor court.

There may be an arbitration clause in the personal contract of employment, in which case the grievance must be settled by arbitration if one of the parties invokes the clause. Such clauses occur in contracts with employees on the managerial level. In other connections they are practically unknown.

It should be added that the number of nonorganized workers in Sweden is small, probably not exceeding 5 percent of all employees.

For organized workers the rules are more complicated. The forum will depend upon whether the labor court, an arbitral board, or the local civil court has jurisdiction. The competence of the arbitral board may rest upon an arbitration clause in the Basic Agreement or any other agreement.

According to specific provisions in the Labor Court Act, the union represents its members in actions before the labor court. In cases where the union refuses to take action, the member is entitled to bring his action before the court himself.

In case of an arbitration clause in the collective agreement, the question arises whether an individual member is entitled to take action and, assuming that he has procedural rights of his own, whether or not he should bring action in the labor court or in the arbitral board concerned. Most likely, the drafters of the 1964 amendments of the Basic Agreement between the SAF and the LO were of the opinion that a member could sue in the labor court. In the case 1967 AD No. 17, the labor court ruled, however, after some statements to that effect by the SAF and the LO, that the member had to take his action to the *Arbetsmarknadsnämnden*. In an agreement of November 23, 1967, the SAF and the LO confirmed this construction of the Basic Agreement.

The following example is taken from the metal industry and refers to manual workers. The Labor Market Board is the forum in cases of arbitrary dismissal, since the parties to the national agreement, i.e., the Swedish Metal Trades Employers' Association and the Swedish Metal Workers' Union, have signed the Basic Agreement as amended in 1964. Only the principal groups of cases are considered.

TABLE 1
Boards Adjudicating Grievances Concerning Organized Workers

Labor Court	(a)	claims based upon a collective agreement, disputed by the defendant
	(b)	claims based upon violation of the right of self-organization
	(c)	claims based upon statutory provisions prohibiting dismissals on account of military service, on account of marriage or pregnancy, or prohibiting unfair treatment of safety representatives, and claims based upon the Paid Vacations Act
	(d)	individual actions of a union member, provided the union has refused to take his case to the labor court
Labor Market Board	(a)	actions for compensation because of dismissals on personal grounds without just cause
	(b)	actions for reconsideration of dismissals or layoffs on the ground of redundancy
Civil Court of the District		uncontested wage claims

THE REMEDIES

21. In civil proceedings damages corresponding to the economic loss constitute the principal remedy. With English and American legal history in mind, it should be noted that Swedish courts have no jurisdiction to issue injunctions for the prevention of injury to persons or damage to property. The choice of legal sanctions was a much-debated issue. The framers of the Collective Agreements Act and the Labor

Court Act, 1928, were anxious to avoid any taint of criminal liability. Basically, they thought that ordinary sanctions of private law should be used in the law of labor relations.

The authors of the 1928 Acts were aware that ordinary rules on damages needed several modifications before being made applicable to breaches of collective agreements. In many cases, the award of damages equivalent to the economic loss cannot always be a sufficient reaction to infringements. Economic loss is negligible or nonexistent in many cases, for example, when an employer is in breach of a duty to post some regulations on the notice board, to have the works rules available in the shop, to issue particulars of the contract of employment, or to keep accounts of overtime work. Compensation is a poor remedy in a case of unjust dismissal, too, if the employee has a new job and does not want to be reinstated. Nevertheless, the dismissal has caused him harm perhaps analogous to pain in case of bodily injury. On the other hand, sometimes it would be inequitable to impose damages corresponding to the injurious effect resulting from an infringement. An unlawful strike lasting a few days might cause losses of such proportion that it would appear unreasonably harsh to order the workers to compensate the loss in full. In the view of the legislators, privileges should be accorded to the workers and their unions by empowering the court to reduce the amount of damages below the actual injury inflicted.

22. The Collective Agreements Act, in SEC. 8, provides for damages to be paid by any employer, employee, or association failing to carry out the obligations imposed by the collective agreement or the Collective Agreements Act. Damages are for loss incurred. The legislative history indicates that the upper limit of damages should be equal to the actual loss. On the other hand, the liability is not limited to cover economic loss only; damage of a moral character is also included. In the words of the statute, "regard shall also be paid to the interest of the persons concerned in the maintenance of the agreement and to other circumstances other than those of a purely financial nature" (SEC. 8,, SUBSEC. 2). Thus, compensation may include both damages for economic loss and for personal injury. It should be noted that damages for personal injury may be awarded to a union, too. Actions for such damages are frequent. Mostly they concern an alleged injury because of the union's interest in the sanctity of the collective agreement.

The labor court has a wide discretion to mitigate by reducing damages below the amount corresponding to the actual loss. Regard must be paid to the degree of culpability of the person who caused the loss, the extent of the loss, and to other circumstances as well. Complete exemption from liability to pay damages may also be granted.

The Acts of 1928 were passed in the face of opposition by the Social Democratic Party and the trade unions. Those in power wanted to do all they could to avoid making the legislation burdensome to individuals. It may be recalled that the Act on Collective Agreements gives a combined effect to the collective agreement. The individual union members are bound to abide by the obligations embodied in the agreement, the peace obligation in particular. In the course of the examination of the bill the Second Standing Committee on Legislation proposed an amendment. A ceiling should be fixed to ensure that the amount of the damages would not exceed what an ordinary worker ought to be capable of paying. Thus, the Act prescribes that an individual employee may not in any case be ordered to pay damages exceeding 200 *kronor* (SEC. 8, SUBSEC. 3). At the time when the Act was introduced, the maximum amount, 200 *kronor*, was almost equal to the monthly earnings of an unskilled worker. It has been left unmodified in spite of the fact that today, because of the depreciation of money and the increase in incomes, 200 *kronor* represents only about two days' pay. It should be added, however, that the right to a 200-kronor ceiling is waivable. In their national agreements the LO unions have agreed upon forfeitures in the case of employees quitting their jobs without notice, which often involve amounts above 200 *kronor*.

23. An unlawful act can give rise also to sanctions other than damages. In disputes concerning wages, overtime supplement, daily allowances for work performed outside the plant, sick pay or other benefits awarded in money, the principal remedy in proceedings before the labor court, as before any other court, is an order to pay the sums that may be due the individual employee.

24. Often there is no need for damages or other payment orders. In a dispute over the true meaning of a clause in the collective agreement, the party is principally interested in an authoritative declaration that the meaning alleged by him is the correct one. If the other party is an association of employers or a national union, he can be almost certain that, once the meaning has been stated, that party will instruct its members to apply the contract correctly. Compensation for possible breaches in times past is an issue of minor importance. Therefore, the declaratory judgment plays an important role in disputes over the meaning of the collective agreements. A great proportion of the decisions of the labor court have the character of a declaratory judgment on one or more disputed issues.

SETTLEMENT OF EMPLOYMENT GRIEVANCES IN SWEDEN

25. In Swedish law of contracts specific performance is a principal remedy, at least in theory; the party non-in-breach may sue the other party in court requesting an order, e.g., that S. shall deliver 100 widgets to B. at a certain place. If the court sustains the action, it may stipulate a fine payable in case of disobedience. Assume that disobedience continues. The court then prescribes a new fine, higher than the original one. Such fines have the character of penalties and are commutable to proportional periods of imprisonment. On this point the Labor Court Act, however, makes an exception. Fines imposed on a person for failure to execute the judgment of the court cannot be converted (SEC. 30). The idea underlying this rule is that no punishment shall be inflicted upon a person who performs an unlawful act in a labor dispute.

The fact that its orders are not sanctioned as strictly as are court orders in general has not made the labor court doubtful of the usefulness of this remedy. The student of the decisions of the court encounters a wide variety of court orders. Sometimes an organization is ordered to refrain from an unlawful economic action, sometimes employees on strike are ordered back to work. In case of a violation of the right of self-organization, an order of reinstatement is always given if reinstatement of the dismissed employee is part of the action.

The labor court may stipulate a fine—which is not commutable—to be paid in case of disobedience, but in most cases no sanction is attached to the order. The court simply takes it for granted that the parties concerned will respect its authority. In a decision, 1970 No. 9, the labor court ruled that a fine cannot be attached to an order stipulating that individual workers go back to work, since the imposition of a fine would not be consistent with the idea that an individual worker shall not have to pay more than damages up to a maximum amount of 200 *kronor* as penalty in case of breach of the peace obligation.

26. As mentioned in sec. 19, actions for uncontested wage claims must always be presented in civil courts. The proceedings are of a summary character. The applicant has to state clearly and completely the basis for his claim and the time of its maturity. A copy of the application is served on the debtor endorsed with a direction to inform the court of his opposition within a specified time. If notice of opposition is not presented, the court declares that the debt has not been contested and may be enforced.[8]

27. Ordinarily, actions of nonorganized workers have to be brought

---

[8] For further details see Ginsburg and Bruzelius, *Civil Procedure in Sweden* (The Hague: M. Nijhoff, 1965), pp. 355 f.

in a civil court.[9] The remedies available are orders for payment of wages or other benefits due the employee and damages corresponding to economic loss.

This is certainly not a satisfactory state of affairs. In the Ester Rannby case, reported in 1960 NJA 63, an action for damages for personal injury and for reinstatement was brought to the Supreme Court in order to test whether a civil court could avail itself of the same remedies as the labor court. Both claims were rejected. The Supreme Court gave in detail the reasons why a civil court should not give an order for reinstatement. The opinion throws light upon the fact that the labor court performs its tasks partly under different conditions from the civil courts.

The Supreme Court conceded that Ester Rannby, who had been employed by Sala municipality as bath attendant, was entitled under her employment contract to tenure. It was not contested that the dismissal was unjustified. (Incidentally, the municipality had already compensated Ester Rannby for her economic loss.) The court first raised the question whether a fine might be attached to an order of reinstatement and concluded that this was not the case. Different rules applied to fines set by a civil court and to fines set by the labor court. In case of disobedience and failure to pay, the fine had to be commuted. Imprisonment, however, should not be used as a sanction in employment relations. Since the court had found that damages for personal injury were not available in the absence of a statutory provision to that effect, there were no sanctions at all attached to a court order for reinstatement. The labor court had a more favorable position than a civil court for another reason, too. It had close connections with the organizations of the labor market and could rely upon their loyal cooperation in carrying out the intentions of the court.

---

[9] Actions based upon the violation of the right of self-organization are to be brought in the labor court, even when plaintiff is not member of a union signatory to a collective agreement (cf. sec. 19).

2.
NEGOTIATIONS AS A MEANS OF SETTLING GRIEVANCES

THE PROCEDURAL FRAMEWORK

1. The law of labor relations in Sweden is based upon the philosophy that grievances arising under a collective agreement are matters of concern to the organizations on both sides, and that the organizations must enter into negotiations for the peaceful settlement of each dispute.

It is instructive to study the history of the first national agreement for the metal industry, which was signed in 1905. After the settlement of an open conflict in 1903, a committee was appointed consisting of one neutral member and representatives of the employers' association and the unions concerned to suggest methods for the peaceful settlement of disputes through negotiation, conciliation, or arbitration. The committee drew up draft rules of procedure and provisions for minimum wages, piece rates, hours of work, and overtime pay. The rules of procedure followed Danish models, but their origin can be traced back to England. Disputes had to be negotiated at different levels. For disputes on interpretation arbitration was suggested as the final step. A party was not permitted to resort to economic action until the procedure was exhausted. After many stages of debate these principles were laid down in the final agreement. It is true that the 1905 national agreement for the metal industry was far more developed than other contemporary agreements. It was important because it came to set the pattern for the future.

2. Practically all existing national agreements contain detailed provisions for a negotiation procedure with regard to grievances that arise under the agreement. As indicated in chapter 1, sec. 3, the majority of the LO unions have signed the Basic Agreement. The procedural rules of the Basic Agreement have served as a model for the procedures that

have been adopted by the parties in other fields of the labor market.

The Negotiation Procedure of the Basic Agreement (Chapter II of the Agreement) is applicable to all kinds of disputes, disputes of interests as well as disputes of rights. The emphasis is, however, on grievances arising under the national agreement. The procedure is not applicable to negotiations on the making and renewal of collective agreements, or to sympathetic actions, or to the collection of uncontested claims for wages, or for other compensation overdue.

According to the procedure, a grievance has to be negotiated first at a local level (local negotiations) and, if the dispute is still unsettled, at the national level (central negotiations). The procedure is strictly formalized. Claims for wages, damages or any other compensation to be paid by the other party must be presented without delay. There is a period of limitation. If the claim has been known to the employer concerned or his association or, on the labor side, to the national union or its local branch for more than four months before it was presented for negotiation, the claimant has forfeited his right to demand negotiations. There is a general limit, too. No claim is permitted if the circumstances upon which the claim is based occurred more than two years previously. Local negotiations are considered closed at the time when the parties have agreed to declare the negotiations to be concluded, or a party has served notice to the other party that he deems the negotiations to be terminated. A request for central negotiations must be made within two months from the date of termination of the local negotiations. Central negotiations have to commence within a prescribed period and may be terminated in the same way as local negotiations. Finally, if a party wants to bring his grievance to court or to an arbitral board, the suit has to be filed within a certain period. Should a party neglect to do so, his right of appeal is forfeited.

In the Basic Agreement there is a special procedure for dismissals and layoffs. There are alternate provisions of similar content in the Agreement on Works Councils. An employer who intends to dismiss or lay off a worker who has been in his employment for at least nine months is obliged to give notice to the local union. This notice must be delivered at least two weeks before the personal notification of discharge or layoff. The national agreement ordinarily provides for two weeks' notice of discharge. Therefore the total period between the notice to the union and the actual discharge will be at least four weeks. The notice to the union has to be served to a representative of the local branch, or, if the Agreement on Works Councils is applicable, to a "notice steward" elected by the workers' representatives on the council.

From the local level the case may be referred to central negotiations. If a settlement is not reached, the national union may bring the case to the *Arbetsmarknadsnämnden* (Labor Market Board). As already mentioned in chapter 1, sec. 18, this board, presided over by an umpire, adjudicates dismissals arising out of circumstances affecting an individual worker. Like arbitral awards generally, the decisions of the board are enforceable. Dismissals "for other reasons" (i.e., redundancy) are dealt with by the board acting as a joint council. If the board arrives at a majority decision, the decision must be communicated to the national associations concerned as a recommendation on how to settle the differences between them.

3. According to the procedure of the Basic Agreement, economic action must not be resorted to because of a dispute (a) by any party before he has fulfilled his duty to negotiate, (b) by any party who has forfeited his right to negotiate, or (c) by anyone without the action having been decided on or approved by the party to the national agreement. The last-mentioned rule makes illegal any unauthorized economic action.

The provision of the procedure extends the minimum required by the Collective Agreements Act. That statute draws a line between disputes covered by a collective agreement and other disputes, the peace obligation being applicable only to the first kind. The procedure, on the other hand, is applicable to all kinds of grievances. First, this implies that peace must prevail even in disputes over matters which are not governed by the agreement; there are, e.g., no provisions with regard to the pay for certain jobs. Second, the statutory obligation is conditioned by the fact that the period of the agreement is still current. The Basic Agreement is independent of the national agreement, and therefore its procedure is also applicable to grievances that arise during possible intermissions between two consecutive national agreements.

4. As explained by the labor court in its decision 1940 No. 77, "the duty to enter into negotiations is obviously not fulfilled by the mere presence of the obligated party at a meeting. He must also contribute to the furtherance of the negotiations by giving a clear account of his attitude and the factual grounds upon which it is based. Thus the duty of negotiation is discharged only if the party enters into serious deliberation with the opposite party on the question at issue."

If the duty to negotiate is not fulfilled, this constitutes a breach of the collective agreement, and in a great number of cases the labor court has held parties showing contumacy in negotiations to be liable to pay damages for injury caused by the infringement upon the other party's interest in the sanctity of the contract. According to SEC. 14 of the Labor Court Act, negotiation must precede legal proceedings. If the defendant puts in a demurrer, the court does not take cognizance of the litigation until negotiations have taken place, unless it appears from the circumstances that the negotiations have encountered obstacles for which the plaintiff is not responsible.

WHO OWNS THE GRIEVANCE?

5. A union as well as an association of employers has the authority, within the bounds of its constitution, to conclude collective agreements. According to SEC. 2 of the Collective Agreements Act, the agreement is binding upon the members of the association. This provision is supplemented by SEC. 13 of the Labor Court Act. The association has a statutory power to represent its members in court. The organization is entitled to sue on their behalf; and the member may not himself sue unless he can prove that the association has refused to take action. In case of a suit against a member, the association has the power to represent its member in the labor court. Because of the interest of the association in claims presented under a collective agreement to which the association is the signatory, it is prescribed that anyone who brings an action against a member—whether an action by an employer against an employee who is a union member or an action by a union against an employer who is a member of an employers' association—has the duty to bring an action against the association, too.

What powers are conferred upon the association? Assume that a union presents a claim that one of its members is entitled to an additional payment of 1,000 *kronor* for a certain job. In the course of the negotiations the employer offers to pay 500 *kronor*. Has the union competence to accept this offer as a settlement without asking the member for his consent?

The labor court had to answer a similar question in the case 1947 No. 13. An employer had made a setoff because of damage negligently caused to his property by some of the employees. The union claimed that the setoff was not justified. After the negotiations had been brought to an end, the union failed to file a suit in the labor court within the time prescribed in the procedural rules of the collective agreement. However, the association of which the employer was a member granted the union a prolongation of the term without obtaining the consent of the employer. The labor court declared that the association was not competent to waive its member's right. "In view of its far-reaching effects upon the members of the association, such competence must be founded upon statutory provision or upon the authorization of the individual member." In its decision 1953 No. 23, which concerned a settlement by a union involving the waiver of claims for overtime pay, the labor court elaborated its opinion in greater detail. The members were not bound by the settlement by the union of their claims for payment in accordance with the collective agreement for work performed.

It is not easy to draw a line between issues in which the union has exclusive competence to decide upon settlements and issues that must be submitted to the member for consent. It is not enough to refer to the formula of vested right, although this gives some idea of where the line is drawn. Indisputably the union is competent to enter into agreements on rules for future employment relations. Within one important field the authority of the union is broader. A decision of the union may influence claims that refer to past times, too.

6. According to established practice, the union decides on behalf of its members in questions concerning the interpretation of the collective agreement. If the parties to the agreement declare that at the time of formation of the contract they intended a clause to have a certain meaning, the members will be bound by their common interpretation. It is not required that the meaning which the parties attach to the agreement shall be consistent with its tenor.

The parties to the agreement must respect certain limits and are not allowed to act arbitrarily. In decision 1953 No. 19, the court defines the limits: "The opinions expressed by the organizations ought, as a matter of principle, to have been adopted by them at the conclusion of the agreement, although this need not always have been explicitly stated. Furthermore, the interpretation must be unequivocal; thus, it must not produce such results that the agreement can be expounded in different senses in two similar situations."

In a recent case, 1967 No. 17, the court seems to have set aside the rule of 1953 No. 19, that an interpretation by the parties should have been adopted by them at the conclusion of the agreement. With regard to obscure clauses, the parties are permitted to come to an agreement, even though the meaning was originally a matter of dispute. In other words, the parties have the power to define the meaning when the issue arises. The facts were as follows: a certain Nancy Winberg had been discharged from her employment at Svenska Philips. The provisions of the Basic Agreement were part of her contract of employment.

The union refused to take her case to the *Arbetsmarknadsnämnden*. Nancy herself filed an application to that board, asking it to try the circumstances of her dismissal and award compensation. From the Negotiation Department of the SAF she received a letter, saying that the technical requirements for consideration by the board were not fulfilled, since the union had not found it possible to support her claim. Later Nancy filed an action in the labor court for reinstatement and for damages compensating economic loss and personal injury. She referred to various grounds. The employer had violated her right to self-organization. Further, there was no just cause for dismissal. The employee was therefore entitled to compensation under the provision in the Basic Agreement. In the labor court the employer invoked the provisions of the Basic Agreement. There arbitration was provided for and the court was not competent to take jurisdiction. Upon the request of the court, SAF and LO as parties to the Basic Agreement made a declaration as to their conception of the meaning of the Agreement; this was opposite to that expressed in the letter to Nancy from the Negotiation Department of the SAF. An individual member was entitled to bring to the *Arbetsmarknadsnämnden*, without the support of his union, the issue whether just grounds existed for his dismissal. The employer's objection was sustained. The court refused to accept jurisdiction on that part of the action which was based upon the provisions of the Basic Agreement.

THE PARTIES ADMINISTERING THE NATIONAL AGREEMENT

7. In the spring of 1967, Dr. Sten Edlund published a study of a selected number of grievances that had been the object of central negotiations under two national collective agreements, namely that for the metal industry and that for the building industry.[1] The national agreements of the metal industry and of the building industry comprise a large sector of private industry. In 1966 the firms affiliated with the Swedish Metal Trades Employers' Association and with the Association of Employers within the building industry employed 213,000 and 81,000 manual workers respectively. These figures should be compared with the total number of manual workers employed by members of the SAF in the same year (863,000). During the course of his study, Dr. Edlund interviewed a large number of persons from other trades

---

[1] Edlund, *Tvisteförhandlingar pa arbetsmarknaden. En rättslig studie av tva riksavtal i tillämpning* (Stockholm, 1967).

SETTLEMENT OF EMPLOYMENT GRIEVANCES IN SWEDEN

who confirmed his observations. My own experience indicates that Edlund gives an accurate idea of actual day-to-day relations between the LO unions and the sectorial associations of the SAF in their administration of the national agreements at the central level.

In the metal industry the number of grievances referred to central negotiations is relatively small. Union officers estimated that about 50,000 grievances arose at the local level each year, but expressed the view that this figure was very uncertain. Out of these, about 150 to 160 grievances reached the national level. In the building industry the situation was somewhat different. The local branches were less successful in settling the grievances by themselves. In 1960, the year from which Edlund collected his case material, the records show that no fewer than 1,600 grievances were referred to central negotiations. Later, the number decreased; in 1965 it was about 1,000.

From his study Edlund excluded grievances over piece rates, a group comprising close to 50 percent of all grievances in the metal industry and about 80 percent of those in the building industry. About 65 grievances from the metal industry and 50 from the building industry were selected for detailed study.

Edlund had access to petitions, to letters exchanged, records and notes in the archives of the organizations on both sides, and the persons who had handled the grievances were interviewed in two rounds. On the basis of this material, he made abstracts of each grievance with the facts at issue, the claims and the arguments of the parties, and the outcome, and added comments with regard to possible motives. These abstracts resemble careful summaries of court decisions with comments.

The grievances are classified in three groups: (a) disputes over failures to observe the rules on local negotiations, (b) disputes because of breach of discipline, and (c) disputes over the application of the agreement. Group (a), to which only three grievances are assigned, may be discarded as being of little significance. The following data concern groups (b) and (c) only.

8. Of the case material, 14 grievances from the metal industry and 15 from the building industry belonged to group (b), viz. disputes because of breach of discipline. In the metal industry unofficial strikes were the main problem; 11 cases concerned such strikes, the other 3, improper behavior towards time-study men. In the building industry only 2 of the 15 cases concerned strikes. Their problem was "runaways" or walkouts. It should be mentioned that in Sweden the contractor hires his worker on a piece-rate basis for the period needed for the

whole construction, with a right for the individual to quit at the end of a piece-rate period. The length of the piece-rate period may be decided by agreement between the contractor and the members of the team. At the time of Edlund's study it corresponded to a phase of the construction work. Thus, for the bricklayers the periods were the work on the outside frame, interior plastering, coverings and floor constructions, exterior works, and supplementary works.

The unofficial strikes in the metal industry had various causes. One main factor was distinguished, namely dissatisfaction with piece rates. This was not unexpected, since the piece rates of the metal industry are objects of continuous bargaining within the individual firm, mostly between the supervisor and the workers concerned. In the majority of cases a considerable number of workers had taken part in the action. Usually peace was restored immediately or after a day or so.

The Swedish Metal Trades Employers' Association follows strictly the principle of not negotiating until the workers are back at work. In nine out of eleven cases the association was the initiator. Often the association had called upon the national union to intervene for the restoration of peace before the request for central negotiations was made.

Reference to central negotiations was used as a sanction. The association considered the incident serious or the circumstances obscure and did not want to have it taken off the records or to leave it to the member firm to clear up the mess alone. It might have happened that the association found the national union was too slow to move and needed a shake-up, but in many cases the central negotiations were directed to the employer, too. The association wanted to demonstrate a strict view with regard to breaches of the peace obligation or to prove that the employer was partly to blame because of his conduct. Further, it was essential to let all have an opportunity to talk in order to relieve the tension that had led to the action and judge what measures should be taken with regard to future relations within the plant.

A review of one of the cases will give some idea of what kind of remedy central negotiations can offer. At a shipbuilding yard—a recent member of the association—the workers had already been on an unofficial strike before the incident concerned. The employer had dismissed B., the president of the union-shop section. He had been reinstated, however. Later B. was laid off because of an alleged shortage of work. Six workers then went on strike. They were dismissed, too. The shipyard company wanted to leave the situation as it was. The association took another view. The workers should go back to work. On the request of the association the dismissals were cancelled. Four of the six workers returned; the others had found new jobs. Central negotiations were requested by the association. The parties agreed upon the following statement: "B. will be rehired, as in the meanwhile one worker had given notice of termination and another was on long leave because of sickness. The national union will call a meeting of the workers next week for the purpose of smoothing out the conflicts between different groups of workers."

Dr. Edlund comments that the association was anxious to teach its new member how to deal with breaches of the peace obligation. It was not willing to make any exception from its policy to demand a return to work. Behind the text of the agreement is concealed a compromise. The employer had been charged with a violation of the right of self-organization, an accusation which the representative of the association did not consider unfounded.

The two cases of unofficial strikes in the building industry are not of special interest and need not be described in detail.

Of the strike cases—thirteen in all—four were taken to the labor court. With some exceptions the workers were found guilty of a breach of the peace obligation and ordered to pay damages to the employer, in most cases the statutory maximum of 200 *kronor*. The figures are too small to admit any conclusion with regard to the proportion between disputes settled out of court and disputes brought to court. The writer of this report can testify that Edlund's case material gives a true picture in that most unofficial strikes do not give rise to court actions.

As indicated before, in the building industry the employers were much disturbed by "runaways" or walkouts. Thirteen of the fifteen cases in category (b) were of that kind. In one case the entire team had left, claiming that the piece-rate period was at an end. The other cases, involving one or more "runaways," arose from dissatisfaction with the earnings on the piecework or from quarrels with the supervisor. Often the contractor was placed in a difficult position because it was hard to find men willing to replace the "runaways." The collective agreement provided that a member of a team who quit without leave of absence forfeited his share of the earnings to the other members of the team. This was a very weak sanction, however, since the total piecework earnings were paid out to the leader of the team, and there was no means of ensuring that the members did not let the "runaway" have his share later on. The prospect that the labor court might order him to pay 200 *kronor* as damages was no deterrent to a man offered a well-paid job by another contractor.

Often the purpose of central negotiations was to achieve the support of the union in an attempt to persuade the man to return to his old job or to throw light upon unfair recruitment of labor by other contractors. It should be mentioned that central negotiations are a prerequisite for court action, a rule which does not apply to actions because of a breach of the peace obligation. Edlund states that the national union was willing to cooperate in undisputed cases, but the union was successful in only 3 of the 10 cases where this was the matter at issue.

In the course of negotiations the parties were able to reach agreement on the settlement of 7 out of 13 grievances. The association took action in 2 cases; 4 cases were left unsettled.

Edlund's study relates to the year 1960. Since then the situation in the building industry has improved and "runaways" are no longer so frequent. The parties are inclined to attribute this mainly to an amendment in 1964 of the forfeiture clause. The share of the "runaway" will be paid to a welfare fund of the industry and not, as before, to the other members of the team.

9. The greater part of Edlund's material—48 cases from the metal industry and 35 from the building industry, a total of 83—concerns disputes over the application of the national agreement. Usually the national union is the initiator; this is explained by the fact that the employer controls the application by his orders about what jobs are to be performed and what wages are to be paid.

In disputes because of a breach of discipline, central negotiations were used as a sanction against acts that in most cases were admittedly illegal. In disputes over the application of the agreement, the initiator takes the position that the agreement was wrongfully applied by the other party. Mostly the case is referred to central negotiations because the employer or his association contests the claim. The dispute may arise out of a difference with regard to facts—the parties holding different views of what actually happened, or out of a difference of opinion as to the meaning of the contract—the parties differing as to what norm is embodied in the contract.

When the parties proceed to central negotiations, there are a number of possibilities as regards the outcome:

(a) The parties may reach an agreement that they both consider to be in accordance with the agreement.

(b) The parties may settle the dispute either by splitting the issue or by one party yielding to the other. Since under both alternatives at least one of the parties has to agree to a solution that he considers inconsistent with the contract, this group of cases has been classified as concessions.

(c) The parties may jointly refer the dispute to a new round of local negotiations.

(d) A party may take action in court.
(e) The dispute may be left as it was, i.e., eventually unsettled.

TABLE 2

The Outcome of Central Negotiations in Disputes over the Application of two National Agreements*
(Dr. Edlund's Study)

	Parties Agree upon the Correct Interpretation (a)	Concessions (b)	Reference to Local Negotiations (c)	Action in Labor Court (d)	Eventually Unsettled (e)
Metal trade	23½	17	5	1	1½
Building trade	7⅔	24	1⅓	–	2

* When a dispute covering a number of workers is settled with respect to some of them but not others, the case appears under different headings with split numbers.

10. Investigation is a regular part of central negotiations. In many of the cases in which the parties agreed upon the correct interpretation (category a), the facts at issue were originally disputed. More important is the observation that there were also many cases in which the parties had different opinions on the meaning of the agreement but later came to an understanding. In those cases the settlement of the dispute had a bearing upon the future relations between the parties, in the same way as precedents laid down by a court.

Category (b) covering concessions is just as large as category (a). Two examples illustrate what deals were made.

In the national agreement of the metal industry there are special rates for skilled workers. At an aircraft factory B. had been employed for eight years in assembling instrument parts and worked with electrical switches. The union presented a claim that B. should be classified as a skilled worker. A declaration by the representative of the association was placed in the records. The employer refused to classify B. as a skilled worker, but to facilitate the settling of the dispute he agreed to pay B. the wage of a skilled worker as from a certain date.

According to the national agreement of the building industry, the employer has to compensate the employee for loss of any personal tools and other auxiliaries necessary for the performance of the job, which by an act of burglary have been lost or destroyed at the workplace in the period between the end of work one day and the beginning of work next day. The bricklayers used to keep their tools in a locked shed. They left them there when they went on vacation on July 14. When they returned on August 4, the tools were missing. In the meantime the shed had been used by other employees and had been left unlocked. The parties agreed that the employer had no duty to pay since there was no act of burglary. However, in view of the circumstances the claim was met.

11. The crucial choice at central negotiations is between the making of concessions effecting a settlement and the resistance to a claim, thus leaving the dispute unsettled or having to be taken to court.

Regard for the individual member was an important factor in the reasoning of the union. The question was not whether or not to adopt a compromise, but rather how far the employer could be pushed and at what point he was willing to give way. The pressure from the members was noticeable in the material from the metal industry in particular. On the employers' side there was less willingness to compromise, especially when a company had once decided to take a firm position. It would be wrong to assume that the representatives of the association should be credited with all the concessions actually made. Sometimes new circumstances had to be taken into consideration, such as, e.g., the interest in avoiding an action in court by the union. A compromise was easier to reach when the parties differed with regard to the facts at issue than when a norm was disputed.

In order to make clear that a dissent on principle still remained, it was an established practice to place in the records a statement that the offer was made to reach a settlement of the actual dispute. This did not prevent the other party from invoking the settlement later. The argument that earlier the parties had settled a similar case in a way favorable to the claimant was frequently relied upon. According to Edlund, however, the argument of existing precedents was more a mode of expression than a factor which brought pressure upon the other party.

The degree of conviction of the validity of one's own view was a relevant factor. If a party was not quite certain that its position would be sustained in court, it was more willing to compromise.

Reasons of equity should be mentioned, too. It would seem that the persons acting at central negotiations were aware that sometimes their own members were guilty of misjudgments, or that the grievance might have its cause in a tacit acceptance of an erroneous application of the agreement. A further factor was a general desire to be generous and to treat the employees fairly.

There are difficulties in stopping a ball that has started to roll. The fact that a grievance has been presented by a union creates expectations among its members which as such bring pressure upon the other party to try to meet. There are values attached to cooperation, quite apart from the desire to get to the end of the negotiations at issue. Dr. Edlund puts his finger on a characteristic feature of Swedish labor relations when he speaks of the professional interests of the actors involved. The representatives on both sides have an ambition to succeed in reaching settlements. There is a philosophy of do-it-yourself at all levels.

12. It remains to show why a party sometimes preferred to leave a dispute unsettled and did not bring an action in the labor court or to submit the case to arbitration. In all the cases in column (e) of table 2, the employer controlled the application. Thus, the choice was in the hands of the union as the initiator. One of the grievances was not considered important enough to be taken to arbitration, which was the alternative in this case. Another grievance concerned a dismissal because of misconduct. The members of the board of the local factory club were in two camps, one of them considering the action of the employer justified. The union took the case to central negotiations without much hope and aware that in any event nothing was to be gained from an action in court. In the rest of the cases under column (e) the probable outcome of litigation in court was also decisive. The employers took a firm stand. They did not expect the union to bring an action because of the risk of defeat.

3.
THE LABOR COURT

GENERAL SURVEY

1. As stated in sec. 16 of chapter 1, there is in Sweden a single labor court with a jurisdiction covering the whole country. It has a tripartite composition with three officials, two employers, and two union officers on the bench, all of equal status. The labor court is a trial court, but its decisions are final and not subject to appeal. Only in exceptional cases—gross miscarriage of justice, new evidence of a decisive character, etc.—may the Supreme Court grant permission for a new trial in a case decided by the labor court.

The provisions on the competence of the labor court are very intricate and a detailed presentation would lead us into a morass of legal technicalities. For our purpose it is sufficient to refer to the broad description in sec. 16, chapter 1. It should be added that the competence of the court at the time of its establishment on January 1, 1929, comprised two categories: (a) disputes relating to the validity, contents, or interpretation of a collective agreement or relating to breaches of a collective agreement, and (b) actions on the ground of violation of the peace obligation constituted by a collective agreement. The jurisdiction of the labor court has been substantially extended by later enactments. Two enactments of 1965, the State Officials Act and the Municipal Officials Act, by which collective agreements with unions of officials were acknowledged as binding at law, represent the last steps.

2. In the period 1929–66 the labor court rendered decisions in 3,359 cases. In an additional 1,200 cases an action was filed but was withdrawn, mostly because the parties were able to reach agreement. From 1950, figures are given in the *Labor Court Reports* with regard to the number of cases that were settled during the course of the preparatory proceedings. With the appointment of a new president, Mr. Justice

SETTLEMENT OF EMPLOYMENT GRIEVANCES IN SWEDEN

Dahlman, the court, as will be mentioned later, partly modified its earlier policy of not acting as conciliator between the disputing parties.

As is demonstrated in diagram 4 and table 3 below, during its first period the court rendered about 150 to 160 decisions each year. Since 1941 there has been a drop, and in the three years 1964–66 the numbers were 31, 36, and 27, respectively.

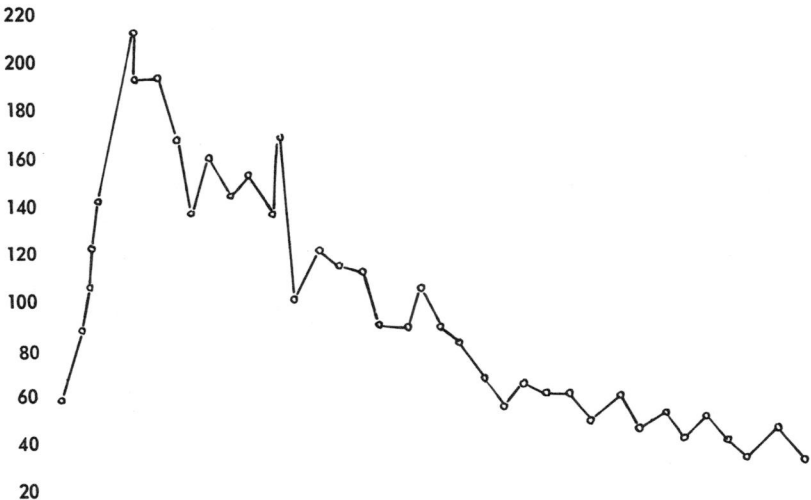

DIAGRAM 4. Cases decided by the Swedish Labor Court, 1929–1966.

This development during a period when the jurisdiction of the court was extended and when the number of organized workers increased is mainly to be attributed to increased efficiency of negotiation procedures of the kind described in chapter 2 above. Other possible explanations will be discussed later on.

3. In labor court suits the organizations that have concluded the collective agreements have a predominant position. Under SEC. 13 of the Labor Court Act, the organization is always competent to sue on behalf of present or former members. If anyone wants to bring an action against a member or a former member of an organization concerning his rights or duties under a collective agreement, the organization which concluded that agreement must also be sued, and the organization can appear as defendant on behalf of the member.

TABLE 3
Cases Decided by the Swedish Labor Court, 1929–66

Year	Number of Decisions	Year	Number of Decisions
1929	65	1948	87
1930	115	1949	77
1931	140	1950	68
1932	204	1951	54
1933	186	1952	41
1934	189	1953	57
1935	154	1954	52
1936	123	1955	44
1937	152	1956	44
1938	134	1957	38
1939	141	1958	43
1940	122	1959	36
1941	157	1960	41
1942	103	1961	36
1943	116	1962	41
1944	106	1963	34
1945	103	1964	31
1946	82	1965	36
1947	82	1966	27

There is no rule that a party must be assisted by a counsel who is an attorney-at-law. On the employer's side the representatives of the association are usually lawyers. In cases of special importance the representative of the association is assisted by an expert from the Legal Department of the SAF. In Sweden the union officials are recruited almost exclusively from the rank and file. Earlier the official of the national union usually presented the case himself; today a lawyer often assists. The LO and some of the big unions have lawyers on their staff as full-time experts.

Unlike the United States, in Swedish law the members of an organization have procedural rights of their own. The member may act as defendant if he prefers to do so, although having the union as his codefendant. With regard to the right to appear as plaintiff, there is a rule intended to prevent individual members from bringing actions before the labor court without first submitting them to their organization. A member is not allowed to sue, unless he can prove that the organization has refused to bring an action on his behalf. Later, special attention will be paid to cases in which individual members have brought actions in court. It should be mentioned in this context, however, that the number is relatively small, not more than about 50 out of a total number of 3,359.

4. The rules of procedure in the Labor Court Act are intended to make possible oral proceedings, concentrated in one hearing. Generally speaking, these rules are identical with those applicable to city courts in civil actions where the parties are allowed to dispose of the object of the dispute by agreement.[1]

Preparatory proceedings are conducted by the president of the labor court. The principal purpose of these proceedings is to prepare the case for the main session. Each party is given the opportunity to amplify or amend his own initial statement of position and to express himself upon the other party's averments and demands. After the issues in dispute have been clarified, the evidence to be presented at the main hearing is outlined.

At the beginning the labor court took the position that it was not the function of the court to conciliate the parties by trying to bring about the compromise. In this respect the Swedish Labor Court differed from the French *conseil de prud'hommes,* in which such conciliation is a special step of the procedure. The court has since somewhat modified its policy. Earlier the preparatory proceedings were exclusively in writing with few exceptions only. From his taking office in 1949, Mr. Justice Dahlman inaugurated the practice of supplementing the exchange of notes with an informal oral hearing. The parties were summoned to the chamber of the president. During the hearing they were not permitted to plead. The questions were always asked through the chair. Information was given with regard to earlier decisions of the court. After the meeting, sometimes the parties were offered the chamber for private negotiations. The court proceeds, however, with great caution and is anxious to avoid situations in which it might appear that the president has committed himself. Mr. Justice Hult, president of the court from 1964, has told the present writer that settlements occur mostly in disputes between unions and unorganized employers. When organizations appear on both sides, the dispute ordinarily concerns a matter of principle, and it seldom happens that an agreement is reached in the course of the preparatory proceedings. The number of cases settled is not very high, roughly about 10 percent of the total number; the figures were 5 of 63 in 1963, 9 of 50 in 1964, and 5 of 48 in 1965.

The labor court has more extensive powers than have ordinary courts

---

[1] The proceedings of civil courts are described in Ginsburg and Bruzelius, *Civil Procedure in Sweden* (The Hague: M. Nijhoff, 1965), pp. 243 ff.

to procure *ex officio* such evidence as it deems necessary. The reason for this is that actions concerning the interpretation of collective agreements are often important for others besides the parties to the action. The character of the action determines to what extent the court is entitled to issue order for the production of evidence on its own accord. Thus, the hearing of witnesses depends upon the initiative of either party, unless such hearing is held to be necessary having regard to the importance of the decision beyond the case at bar (SEC. 21).

According to Chapter 17, SEC. 2, of the Code of Procedure, the civil court must base its decision exclusively upon the findings of the trial. This rule presupposes that, at the trial, the parties repeat the oral and written pleadings presented by them during the preparatory proceedings, insofar as these are relevant to the action. This procedure has been held unsuitable for a court where a party may be represented by a union officer without legal training. The Labor Court Act prescribes that a decision may be based upon other circumstances found in the course of the action apart from those which have appeared at the trial (SEC. 26). Little use has been made of this license, however.

THE LABOR COURT AS A COURT OF JUSTICE

5. As mentioned before, chapter 1, sec. 7, the two fundamental laws governing labor relations in Sweden, the Collective Agreements Act, 1928, and the Labor Court Act, 1928, were introduced so that the rule of law should prevail and that the solution of a dispute should not depend upon the amount of power wielded by the opposing parties. The first president of the labor court, Mr. Justice Lindhagen,[2] consistently took the view that the court should apply strict principles of law. Administration of justice was not a matter of arriving at a compromise, as in conciliation. Incidentally, to the knowledge of the present writer only two decisions of the labor court can be characterized as based upon considerations of equity calling for a compromise solution.[3]

At the time of the establishment of the labor court the law of labor relations was in flux. The time had passed when the individual employee was considered a servant of his master. Several attempts had

---

[2] Lindhagen served as president of the labor court from its establishment on January 1, 1929 until 1946, except for a short period when he was a member of the Supreme Court.

[3] 1931, No. 49; 1934, No. 64. Lindhagen presided over the court in the latter case only. In both cases the employers' representatives dissented in favor of a strict administration of justice.

been made to fill the gap by introducing a statute on the law of contract of employment, but they had failed. Laws on the protection of industrial workers, hours of work, and social insurance represented new elements. The unions had gained in influence. They had become successful insofar as they were recognized as parties to collective agreements regulating wages, hours of work, and overtime pay, but they had made less progress with their demands for a security established by virtue of union membership or for security clauses; the Swedish employers firmly defended their traditional prerogatives.

When the labor court had to answer a question of law, it looked for possible analogies with rules in other fields. It took into consideration opinions expressed in the bills by which the two Acts of 1928 were introduced, as well as earlier draft bills. Already during its first years, the court laid down in its decisions a number of doctrines that are still cornerstones of the edifice of Swedish labor law. The court functioned in the same way as legislators do codifying the law. Its administration of justice had the effect that a legal system in transition was fixed as it was about the year 1928. Since the court has relied upon its own decisions as precedents, there has been little change by way of adjudication once it has expressed its opinion on a disputed point. In their demands for reforms, the unions have had to rely upon collective bargaining or the possibility of bringing about legislative enactments.

The labor court is very strict in its approach to precedents. In 1958, Dr. Lennart Geijer and the present writer published in Swedish a study on the decision-making of the labor court; the title can be translated "Employers and Union Officers on the Bench. A Study of Law Creation in the Labour Market."[4] We made the observation that the labor court was less flexible than the Supreme Court, and we related this phenomenon to the fact that in the former one person, the president, puts his stamp on the products whereas the Swedish Supreme Court is a body of equals, or rather (since the Supreme Court works in three divisions) three bodies of equals which are continuously renewed, old members retiring and new members being appointed. It should be mentioned that Mr. Justice Lindhagen himself was worried over the situation. In a memorandum of 1946 with regard to possible amendments to the procedure of the labor court, he states: "By virtue of its own decisions the Court will as time passes be more strictly bound than before, and the difficulties of adjudicating a case which has

---

[4] Geijer and Schmidt, *Arbetsgivare och fackföreningsledare i domarsäte. En studie i rättsbildningen pa arbetsmarknaden* (Stockholm, 1958).

similarities with an earlier case but has some distinguishing features will increase."

6. In what follows I intend to explain the policy of the labor court on two selected issues, namely (a) what disputes are covered by a collective agreement, and (b) what standards apply to interpretation of collective agreements.

The question what disputes are covered by a collective agreement is often presented with the help of the terms "disputes of rights" and "disputes of interest." It is usually held that, whereas disputes of rights must be submitted to adjudication, a party may resort to economic action in order to achieve a favorable settlement of a dispute of interest. In the view of the present author, these terms do not give an adequate presentation, although they give some idea of how to pinpoint the problems. The critical issue is not that of defining the term "dispute of right," but that of drawing the boundaries of the peace obligation laid down in a collective agreement. The question what disputes are covered by the collective agreement is part of the broader problem of how to draw the borderlines.

According to SEC. 4, SUBSEC. 1, of the Collective Agreements Act, those who are bound by a collective agreement may not, during the period of validity of the agreement, resort to a lockout or strike or any other offensive action in the following situations:

"(1) on account of a dispute respecting the validity, existence, or correct interpretation of the agreement, or on account of a dispute as to whether a particular action constitutes an infringement of the agreement or the provisions of this Act;

"(2) in order to bring about an alteration of the agreement;

"(3) in order to enforce a provision which is to come into operation on the expiration of the agreement; or

"(4) in order to assist others in cases in which these others may not themselves commit offensive actions."

Points (3) and (4) can be disposed of briefly. In point (3) the rule is embodied that under no circumstances is economic warfare permissible in disputes between the parties which have no bearing upon their actual relations. The struggle about the new agreement must not commence until the contractual period of the present agreement has come to an end. Point (4) outlaws certain kinds of sympathetic actions. It is of special significance as an indication that the legislators did not intend to prohibit sympathetic actions in general.

7. In points (1) and (2) the legislators have dealt with the principal issue, defined by the present writer as the question what disputes are

covered by the collective agreement. The provision laid down in point (1) refers to a "dispute respecting the validity . . . of the agreement" and to a "dispute as to whether a particular action constitutes an infringement." Stress must be laid on the word "dispute." According to the basic philosophy of the 1928 Act, each party is obliged to exhaust the negotiation procedure and, in case of failure to reach a settlement on a matter of law, to submit the dispute to a neutral body for adjudication. Offensive actions may not be based on disagreements on the legal situation. It is a duty of all citizens to leave it to a court of justice to state the law of the land and peacefully to perform the duties incumbent upon them according to the true meaning of the contract.

The rule laid down in point (1) that disagreements on the legal situation must not lead to offensive actions is narrow in the sense that it does not totally exclude the use of self-help remedies. The Minister in charge of the Bill on Collective Agreements stated in his exposition that a strike or boycott for collection of wages was not a violation of the peace obligation. This standpoint has also been adopted by the labor court. In the opinion of the court, it is sufficient for the applicability of the peace obligation that the claim is founded upon a right derived from a collective agreement. If the opposite party does not raise any legal objection to the claim—and that is generally the case when the reason for nonpayment of wages overdue is shortage of money—there is no dispute in the proper sense of the word. If the debt is paid, the union is under duty to call off the boycott unless it is lawful on other grounds.[5]

In ordinary contractual relations it is the responsibility of the party who has the duty to perform to decide what measures should be taken in order to comply with his duties. If the other party claims that a delivery was short, the first-mentioned party has to find out for himself whether he should deliver an additional quantity or not. If he decides not to do so, he will be guilty of a breach if the court to which the dispute is submitted finds that the contract prescribed for the delivery of that additional quantity. On the other hand, if the party's judgment of his duty was correct, the action of the other party is dismissed. He was under no duty to deliver as a temporary measure merely for the reason that the issue was under dispute. The Swedish law of collective agreement—in contrast, I submit, to German law and the law of the United States—is designed differently.

The fact that an attacked party raises the objection that the dispute concerns a matter covered by the agreement is sufficient to bring the

---

[5] 1946, No. 24.

peace obligation into application. It is irrelevant that the objection was erroneous, provided that it was raised in good faith. As the labor court put the matter in its decision of 1930, No. 79, the framers of the Act assumed "that it is the natural solution for a dispute concerning a right derived from a collective agreement to be settled by judicial proceedings, and it is consequently immaterial for the application of the prohibition which of the parties has been in the right in the actual controversy." It will also appear from what has been said that the assertion of an erroneous interpretation of the contract is not considered an offensive action, even if the purpose may have been to induce the opposite party to accept that interpretation. If one of the parties holds the opinion that the agreement has ceased to operate, or that the controversial point has not been regulated in the agreement at all, and the oppcsite party contests this opinion, the first-mentioned party has to petition the labor court for a statement that his standpoint is correct. Only after such a statement is he at liberty to resort to offensive action.

In the decision of 1965, No. 6, the labor court had to try a case where the Building Workers' Union had ordered some plumbers who were members of the union and were employed by a subcontractor to refuse to install water and drainage systems as an action to assist the carpenters engaged in a jurisdictional dispute with the main contractor. The case involved many intricate questions of law, and for some reason the objection that the sympathetic action was an infringement of the provisions of the Act was not raised until two weeks after the time when the stoppage had come into effect. The court stated that under these circumstances the union had not resorted to offensive action "on account of a dispute as to whether the action was lawful or not." It would seem as if the court found that the action was not caused by a dispute. The present author is not convinced by this argument. The conclusion is consistent with the basic purpose of the Act, however, since the Act grants the threatened party the power to ward off a proposed attack temporarily. There are reasons for requiring that he shall put his demurrer without delay and not wait until he gets in real trouble.

8. With regard to the provision laid down in point (2) of Sec. 4, Subsec. 1, the critical issue is: Was the matter concerned regulated in the agreement? If that question has to be answered in the affirmative, the offensive action is unlawful as being an attempt to bring about an alteration of the agreement. Often a dispute may arise because one party claims that a clause should be given a broad construction, the

other that it should be construed narrowly. This problem will not be discussed here.

There is another point which is worth special attention. The purpose of an ordinary collective agreement for a trade or for a firm is to regulate the employment relations of the employers and employees bound by the agreement. In a number of decisions the labor court has relied upon the doctrine that certain rules shall be part of the collective agreement even though there are no clauses to that effect in the agreement. The present author has described this doctrine as the method of interpolating certain *naturalia negotii* in the agreement.[6] The Finnish scholar Suviranta[7] expresses the same idea by speaking of "invisible clauses" in collective agreements.

The doctrine of invisible clauses was laid down in the decision of 1933, No. 159. The Metal Workers' Union had ordered a boycott against a shipbuilding company in order to force the company to reinstate certain workers who had been dismissed after a dispute over piece rates. Unlike most other agreements the National Agreement for the Metal Industry, which was in force between the parties, contained no provisions on hiring, dismissals, or layoffs. Nor did the agreement refer in any other way to the manager's prerogatives in respect of dismissals. Therefore, it would seem that the dispute concerned a question which had not been regulated in the agreement. The majority of the labor court, however, took another view. Under general principles of law, a contract of employment which has been concluded for an indefinite period of time may be freely denounced by notices of termination after a certain period. The boycott was intended to deprive the employer of a right under the contract and was consequently in violation of point (2) of SEC. 4, SUBSEC. 1, of the Collective Agreements Act. The court's statement with regard to the general principles of law cannot be disputed. From the fact that a rule is part of the contract of employment of the individual worker, one cannot, however, conclude that this rule must be part of the collective agreement. The court used its discretionary power when it interpolated in the collective agreement a new element, namely the manager's prerogatives with regard to dismissals. In implementation of this doctrine, the union was bound by the peace obligation and was not at liberty to resort to economic action.

The decision of 1964, No. 5, concerned a dispute at the works of the same shipbuilding company which was the defendant in the case

---

[6] Schmidt, *The Law of Labour Relations in Sweden* (Cambridge, Mass.: Harvard University Press, 1962), p. 185.
[7] Suviranta, "Invisible Clauses in Collective Agreements," *Scandinavian Studies in Law*, vol. 9 (1965), pp. 178 ff.

of 1933, No. 159. From 1916 the company had served lunch to its white-collar workers. The charge for this meal had never been changed and was still 40 *öre* (8 cents) in 1963 when the company announced a rise to 1 *krona* 40 *öre*. There was no clause in the agreement reserving the prerogatives for the employer. The union sued for a declaratory judgment that it was not bound by a peace obligation in the dispute over the charge for the meals. The court held, however, that the company was entitled to a manager's prerogatives, including among other things that of deciding on matters of supplying its employees with amenities. The union was therefore not at liberty to resort to economic action.

The doctrine of invisible clauses does not imply that the whole body of law regarding the contract of employment is read into the collective agreement. Assume that a person performs work for another without any previous agreement as to the pay. It is an established principle in Swedish law that in such cases the employee has a claim for pay at the customary rate for the work performed. In its decision of 1947, No. 57, the labor court refused to consider this rule a part of the collective agreement and held that the parties were free to resort to economic action in a dispute over the pay for a job which had not been regulated in the agreement. In its ruling the court could rely upon statements in the *travaux préparatoires*. It was not intended that wages in collective agreement relations should be fixed by the labor court.

9. A central task of the labor court is to render decisions in disputes over the interpretation of collective agreements. The law of contract is based upon assumptions which do not always occur in real life. The ordinary case before a civil court concerns the interpretation of a standard form which the defendant has accepted as an adhesion contract, with little or no knowledge of the duties incumbent upon him. In collective agreement relations the situation is different, and possibly the collective agreement comes closer than any other type of contract to the image in civil-law countries of the true consensual contract. Normally two parties of equal strength bargain for a period of time, starting with draft proposals, continuing with an exchange of numerous offers and counteroffers, and eventually, when their minds have met on disputed points, drawing up a document in which they embody their agreement.

The first president, Mr. Justice Lindhagen, always endeavored to explain the reasoning of the court in clear words. The decisions of the court are still regarded as fine pieces of craftsmanship. In numerous cases principles of interpretation are explicitly referred to. Some of these are part of the Roman-law legacy of all civil-law countries, others are inventions of the court itself.

A collective agreement must be in writing (Collective Agreements Act, SEC. 1). According to the Swedish view, however, formalities required by the law do not imply that the wording of the agreement is given preference over the common intention of the parties. Nor is there any rule corresponding to the parol evidence rule that one is not supposed to look behind the text. On the contrary, it is taken for granted that the bargaining process, like the legislative history of a statutory provision, is a source of information with regard to the purpose of the contract.

It is the history of the disputed clause which is looked into. Since a new national agreement of an industry carries with it, with possible amendments, the provisions of the agreement which was replaced by it, the court may have to investigate events that happened a long time ago. Thus in the case of 1932, No. 105, which concerned the meaning of *Note No. 1* to the National Agreement for the Metal Industry,[8] the court studied the history of certain proposals submitted to the parties by the official conciliator in 1923.

If a common intention of the parties can be ascertained, it is immaterial that the parties have used ambiguous expressions, and also that the wording would seem rather to point to another meaning.[9] It is another matter that the wording of the contract provides a natural starting point. A party that contends that a provision had a meaning different from what is found to appear from the wording has the onus of proving this contention.[10]

In the traditional view interpretation of contracts is only a question of determining the common intention of the parties. If the contentions of the parties concerning the meaning are opposed to each other, the judge decides what was the "true" intention of the parties. One contention is deemed to be true, while the other is held erroneous or not proven. This method is often used by civil courts also in trying cases where an observer must reflect that there was no meeting of minds between the parties on the disputed point. The assumption of a common intention is a fiction hiding a reality of dissent.

The labor court refuses to rely upon fiction and faces the situation as it is when a dispute over the interpretation of the collective agreement is found upon an original dissension of the parties, or upon their

---

[8] Cf. chap. 1, sec. 9.
[9] 1931, No. 109; 1955, No. 15.
[10] See, e.g., 1934, No. 35; 1935, No. 126; 1940, No. 31.

not having foreseen the situation that caused the dispute. According to the traditional view, in the absence of *consensus* there is no contract. For practical reason this conclusion cannot be reached in collective agreement relations. For society it is undesirable that there should be a gap in the contractual provisions, since this will allow the parties to resort to offensive action. Sometimes it would be in flat contradiction to the actual intention of the parties. They have wanted to regulate a question by a certain clause and perhaps even envisaged the possibility of a ruling of the labor court in case of mutual misunderstanding. Indeed, they might have agreed that they were bound by the contract in spite of their not being agreed as to its substance.

In the view of the labor court, principles of interpretation have the character of rules for the negotiation. Certain standards of behavior are applied to the contribution of the parties towards the creation of the contract. The party who has failed to comply has to submit to an interpretation which is favorable to the innocent party.

Earlier I referred to the principle that the wording of the document provides the natural starting point, and that the party who wants to attach another meaning to the text has the burden of proving that his contention was intended by the parties. This rule might be considered a rule regarding negotiations. The parties have a duty to use words in their ordinary meaning.

Several of the rules of interpretation established by the labor court are founded upon the view that a party negotiating a collective agreement is not allowed to confine himself to a passive attitude, but has, on the contrary, a duty to act, in order that the other party shall understand what is intended. This point of view is pertinent in the determination of the responsibility which must be carried by the party who actually drafted the text of the disputed clause. The party who has produced the draft of a clause is not allowed, in a later dispute over its interpretation, to adduce reasons incompatible with its wording.[11] The labor court has also invoked the old principle, found already in the Justinian Code, that the author of a contract must in the event of ambiguity submit to an interpretation of the clause favorable to the other party. The case of 1934, No. 7, concerned a dispute over a clause providing that a certain supplement to wages should be paid for work on the "internal" cleaning of boilers. The employer contended that the supplement should only be paid when the repairer had to perform the work while inside the boiler, whereas the union held that the supplement was also payable for such cleaning of internal parts as

---

[11] 1947, No. 68; 1955, No. 35.

could be done from outside. According to the labor court, it had been incumbent upon the employer in the first place—as it was he who had submitted the draft—to make clear his position, and it was not the duty of the workers to explore by questions whether the employer held an interpretation which was different from theirs.

If a large number of proposals and counterproposals have been exchanged so that it is impossible to ascertain which party actually formulated the clause, various circumstances have to provide the requisite guidance for determining which of them is primarily responsible for the misunderstanding. The court may consider decisive the fact that in the course of negotiations a party withdrew a proposal for an additional clause, without at the same time making it clear that by so doing he did not intend to make a concession to the opposite party, but that the interpretation claimed by him was warranted by the already existing text of the agreement. The principle seems to be that a party who once adopted a certain standpoint has a duty to inform the opposite party if later on he takes up another position.[12]

The system applied as between the parties before the conclusion of the contract is another element of interpretation. The rule for negotiations applicable on this point is that a party who wants to effect a change in existing circumstances has a duty to make this clear. Under a collective agreement for a café all members of the staff were entitled to free meals. The agreement did not mention any exception for Sundays or other public holidays, but earlier, before any collective agreement existed, the practice in the enterprise had been that no lunch was provided on those days, the free meals consisting only of dinner and a coffee snack. In view of this, the labor court found that the clause on free meals did not cover lunch on Sundays and public holidays (1933, No. 58).

It is a common feature of the rules cited above that the interpretation is determined by circumstances attending the conclusion of the contract. Shall facts that have occurred during the subsequent application of the collective agreement be given weight? As repeatedly stated by the labor court, "legal relevance cannot be assigned to the fact that the collective agreement has during a long period of years been applied in a certain way, unless this practice is consistent with the meaning of the agreement."[13] In a number of cases, however, the decision has been in favor of the party contending that the practice is an expression of the meaning of the disputed clause.[14] It may be held that the

[12] 1933, No. 18; 1953, No. 46; 1955, No. 12.
[13] Quotation from the case in 1965, No. 16.
[14] See, e.g., 1930, No. 7; 1933, Nos. 58, 59, and 105; 1939, No. 40.

existence of an established practice constitutes evidence that the contract was originally understood by the parties in the sense in which it was applied. At any rate, an established practice might support the view that an interpretation which accords with the actual application is in itself reasonable and practical. The court may presume that the leaders of a contracting organization ought to inform themselves about any general practice in the workplaces, and, if they find such a practice wrong, declare their position.

The rules of interpretation mentioned before have their limits. Several of them may be invoked in the same case by different parties. One party contends that a clause has a certain meaning according to its wording, the other holds that the text is ambiguous and that the first-mentioned party, as author of the clause, is to blame for any misunderstanding. In such cases the court is confronted with the task of weighing the contentions against one another. It is true that some elements are accorded more importance than others. Thus, strong evidence is needed to move the court to accept an interpretation that is against the clear wording of the contract. Nevertheless, in some situations it must occur that the rules of interpretation give no guidance.

There are other factors, too, which may make it difficult in the individual case to establish the content of the agreement with the help of rules based upon the mechanism of negotiations or upon the application of the contract as established by practice. Perhaps it is hard to find out what actually took place at the negotiations in a case in which the wording of the agreement does not give any definite information, and sufficient time may not yet have elapsed for an established practice to develop. The court might find it inappropriate that the question who is chiefly responsible for producing a misunderstanding should decide the outcome when the disputed clause was framed in great haste during a particularly pressing phase of the negotiations. Nor does the fault principle seem to give sufficient guidance when neither party visualized the situation to which the dispute actually refers. In such cases the court has to try other methods in order to find the answer to the question of the true meaning of the contract.

Occasionally, the labor court has stated the problem as being the task of finding out "what may appear a natural interpretation of the agreement in the light of general considerations." It has then sought guidance in such circumstances as the general principles upon which the contract was based, the practical consequences of different possible applications, the conditions in other trades, or any other facts making one solution appear preferable to another.[15]

---

[15] 1951, No. 44; 1954, Nos. 2, 11, 12; 1955, Nos. 13, 37; 1956, No. 42.

SETTLEMENT OF EMPLOYMENT GRIEVANCES IN SWEDEN

It is not easy to give a generalized answer to the question of the importance assigned by the labor court to the special rules of interpretation as compared with general considerations of the logical or practical solution. To an observer it might seem that about 1950 the labor court became less inclined than before to make pronouncements in magisterial terms on the conduct of a party during the course of the negotiations for the agreement. The reason for this may be that the special rules of negotiation have been so thoroughly impressed upon the parties that it has been held sufficient to state in the judgment how the negotiations have actually been conducted and to follow that description with a bare conclusion on the interpretation, eschewing any moralistic connecting link. It might be explained, too, by differences in the personality of the presidents of the court. Mr. Juctice Dahlman, president in the years 1949–63, had a less dogmatic view of the office of a judge than his predecessors.

DISSENTS BY MEMBERS OF THIS COURT

10. With some simplifications one might contend that there are three creative forces in the law of labor relations, namely the employers' associations, the labor unions, and society. The organizations on both sides constitute two powerful groups, sometimes at war, sometimes cooperating with one another. They make their deals, which they embody in collective agreements. Insofar as a group has political influence, it may try to persuade government and parliament to implement its policies by means of legislative enactments.

Society is a power of its own. Its organs represent other interests besides those of the two parties of the labor market, in particular the interests of the ordinary citizen. Society requires the parties of the labor market to submit to the existing social order. The impetus does not come from the parties of the labor market exclusively. There is a current in the other direction, which is probably more powerful than the currents from the parties of the labor market.

The establishment of the labor court had the effect of confronting the parties of the labor market with the demands of society more effectively than before. The parties of the labor market were deprived of their former sovereign power to govern their own relations. On the other hand, society invited the parties to take part in the administration of justice by nominating representatives to serve on the bench as members of the court.

In Sweden it is an old-established principle that the opinions of

TABLE 4
Decisions of the Labor Court
(Total number, and number of decisions with dissents)

Year	Total Number of Decisions	Decisions with Dissents	
		Number	Percentage of Total Number
1929	65	28	43.1
1930	115	50	43.5
1932	204	58	28.4
1935	154	44	28.6
1938	134	32	23.9
1941	157	31	19.7
1944	106	29	27.4
1947	82	10	12.2
1950	68	11	16.2
1953	57	6	10.5

the members of a court shall be made known to the public. There is public access to the records of the voting and, incidentally, as a matter of principle, to all official documents. Thus a Swedish court is not, like a continental European court, an anonymous body, which in relation to the public appears as if there were no dissents among its members. In our study, "Employers and Union Officers on the Bench," Dr. Lennart Geijer and the present writer focused their attention upon the dissenting opinions of the members of the labor court as a means of finding what were the creative elements within the law of labor relations, the employers, the unions, society. At the same time, we aimed at a deeper insight within one specific area into the general problem of cooperation between the state and the organizations, and between the organizations of the labor market.

The labor court delivered 2,858 decisions during the period 1929–54, a period representing the first 25 years of its existence. Of these, 1,800 were unanimous and 758 were delivered with the dissent of one or more members of the court. As indicated in table 4 below, the proportion of decisions with dissents decreased from over 40 percent in the first few years to about 30 percent in the years 1932–35, and to about 20 percent in the following years. In 1953 the figure was as low as 10.5 percent. This figure is not accidental, for the number of reservations has remained at a low level. In 1963 it was 1 out of 32; in 1964, 2 out of 31; and in 1965, 4 out of 36.

It may be mentioned once more that the labor court regularly sits with seven members: three officials (the president, the vice-president and a neutral expert on labor relations), two employers, and two union representatives. All members except the president serve part time. Have the employers and the union officers judged the cases before them by other standards than those employed by the three official members? Differences may exist that have their explanation in differences in social background and the relations of the employers and the union officers to their ordinary work within the organizations.

Obviously, there are a great number of possible combinations in decisions made by a court of seven members when the bench is not unanimous. One of several members may dissent, and the dissenting members group in various ways. The distribution of the dissenting opinions among social groups is shown in table 5.

TABLE 5

Decisions with Dissents, 1929–1953*
(a total of 758 decisions)

Social Group	Number of Cases with Dissents	
Officials		159
Employers as only dissentients	260	
Employers as dissentients concurring with member(s) of other social group(s)	89	
Employers, total number		349
Union officers as only dissentients	315	
Union officers concurring with member(s) of other social groups	100	
Union officers, total number		416

* Dissents distributed by social groups.

As can be seen, there were dissents by officials in 159, by employers in 349, and by union officers in 416 cases. Compared with the total number of decisions within the same periods (2,858), the figures are as follows: officials dissented in 6 percent, employers in 12 percent, and union officers in 15 percent of all decisions.

11. It is significant that the official members of the court were less frequently in opposition than were the laymen on the bench. In controversial matters the president will usually belong to the majority; one or both of the other official members plus either the employers or the union officers can be expected to concur. During the period 1926–53, the whole official group was only in seven cases in opposition to a majority formed by the two wings. One of the cases, 1936 No. 73, con-

cerned the classification of a job under certain categories in a price list and is of only minor interest. In the remaining six cases—1945 Nos. 35, 36, 77, and 1946 Nos. 41, 59, 64—the factual situation was almost identical. An employer had among his employees members of two competing unions, some belonging to a union affiliated with the LO, others belonging to a "Syndicalist" union. The employer signed an agreement with the LO union containing a union-shop clause. In order to honor his contract the employer ordered a "Syndicalist" employee under threat of dismissal to apply for membership in the LO union. The "Syndicalist" union brought an action against the employer, contending that the latter had violated the right of self-organization. In a majority decision dictated by the four laymen on the bench, the court dismissed that action. The court held that there was no violation of the right of self-organization because the employee was permitted to remain a member of his old union. In a dissenting opinion the three official members concluded that a requirement of membership in a competing union was not compatible with the statutory freedom to organize. It should be mentioned, however, that subsequently the court, by an unanimous decision, 1958 No. 1, overruled its earlier majority decision, thus following the opinion of the official members. I will return to this incident later (sec. 14).

12. It has already been pointed out that the employers and the union officers on the bench were more often in opposition than the official members. It should also be mentioned that the laymen usually acted in groups. Between two-thirds and three-quarters of all their dissents were dissents by two concurring employers or two concurring union officers. In almost every case of lay dissent, the layman voted for an outcome more favorable to his own social group than was the opinion expressed by the majority. Thus, the employers on the bench—when they dissented—cast their votes for a decision favorable to the employer at the bar, the union officers for a decision favoring the litigating union.

It would be a serious mistake to believe, however, that the laymen acted as mere agents of their principals. On several occasions Mr. Justice Lindhagen expressed his appreciation. In his memorandum of 1946,[16] he mentioned that the framers of the two Acts of 1928 had expressed their expectation that the laymen on the bench would not be at war, but "that impartiality would prevail, as one had reason to expect from judicious and experienced persons." This assumption had

---

[16] This memorandum has been referred to before (chap. 3, sec. 5).

been borne out, as was proved by the fact that the court was able to arrive at unanimity in two-thirds of its decisions. The laymen have themselves expressed similar views. Mr. Forslund, a union member of the court in the period 1929–36 (later a Cabinet minister) took part in a debate on the Swedish radio at the 25th anniversary of the court in 1954. As a member of the labor court he had to apply an objective interpretation "in order to come to a judicial conclusion that could be defended." An employer, Mr. Karl Wistrand, who sat on the bench as a substitute member in a great number of cases during the years 1929–33, took part in the same debate. Mr. Wistrand emphasized that "the Court in its first years created precendents at almost every session, and in most cases, where matters of principle were at issue, these principles were laid down in unanimous decisions." It is another matter that in some situations the lay members of the court have been inclined to side with their colleagues at bar.

13. Basically there are three components in the reasoning of a court decision. (1) The court has to state what rules or doctrines of law apply. Generally these are abstract directives addressed to the parties. Thus, Sec. 4 of the Collective Agreements Act prescribes that a person bound by a collective agreement is not allowed to resort to offensive action in certain situations. This part of the reasoning will be called statements of law. (2) Next, the court has to find out what actually occurred. The statement of the factual situation constitutes a second element. (3) Further, the court has to apply the facts to the legal rule, with the practical conclusion which that will lead to. If the action is dismissed, this is the end. (4) If the action is sustained, there is a fourth component, namely the meting out of the sanction.

In some of these elements arbitrariness or use of discretion is involved. Someone may object to this statement. But what are the premises in a statement that a contested fact has occurred? Assume that, as in Sweden, the court has to decide upon matters of fact as well as upon matters of law, and that in trying the fact the court generally has to apply the principle of preponderance. The plaintiff contends that the workers refused to follow an order, the defendant, that they were willing to obey; they were only exploring the piece rate when the supervisor burst in and told them to get out. There are many situations when two contentions seem equally plausible. It is a part of the office of a judge to reach a decision. When, as sometimes happens, two judicious men come to different conclusions, each of them has, the present author submits, made his choice on arbitrary grounds.

The meting out of the sanction is a discretionary process, too. At least this is the case when the law, like the provisions of the Swedish Collective Agreements Act, gives the court power to assess damages for personal injury and to mitigate damages, taking into consideration such circumstances as the defendant's degree of culpability.

Statements of law would seem to have a higher degree of objectivity than the other elements in the reasoning of the court. Often the court quotes its own earlier statements of doctrines of law. But even in cases when a new doctrine is laid down arbitrariness is not permissible. The court has to work upon the assumption that its doctrine in the future will be applied to all factual situations which are basically similar to the situation in the case at bar.

Sometimes discretionary elements are involved within the field of statements of law, too. Not seldom the judge has before him a number of rules which are competing with one another. This may happen when there are two overlapping rules and there is no rule established about which rule shall have priority. Rules of interpretation belong to this category. In a given situation the judge has an option. He may apply the principle that a contract shall be read as its wording indicates, or the principle that the existence of an established practice is evidence of a common intention of the parties that another meaning should be attached to the contract.

Three years were selected at random, 1931, 1941, and 1951, for a detailed study of the dissents. The result is indicated in table 6.

TABLE 6

Dissents in 1931, 1941 and 1951, by Items at Issue*

	Statements on law			
	1.	2.	3.	4.
	Rules of Interpretation	Others	Statements on the Factual Situation	Sanction
Employer wing	12	20	10	5
Union wing	13	29	8	3

* In three cases the dissenting member concurred in the conclusion of the majority, but not in the reasons given. These cases are not included.

As mentioned before, the discretionary element is strong, particularly in items classified as rules of interpretation, statements of the factual situation, and sanction (categories 1, 3, and 4), while a higher degree of objectivity characterizes other statements of law (category 2). Among dissenting opinions from the employer wing, 27 belonged to the former group and 20 to the latter. In the case of the union wing, the figures were 24 and 29.

What do these figures indicate? The employer figure for the group embracing issues of discretion is higher than the union officer figure. Does this imply that the employer wing is more arbitrary in its reasoning? Definitely not. First, one has to bear in mind that the total number of dissents from the employer wing is smaller than that from the union wing. Second, in 85 to 90 percent of all cases an employer appears as defendant since it was the union which brought the action. The employer on the bench, concurring with the majority, will find himself more often than the union officer supporting a decision against the immediate interest of a fellow.

The figures support another theory of some interest. On questions of law there was a wider gap between the union members and the officials than between the employer members and the officials. Were there elements in the officials' interpretation of the existing social order to which the union members were not willing to subscribe?

14. As a part of the study, Dr. Geijer analyzed majority and minority decisions on a number of disputed issues. Employer and union members had in common an inclination to pay more regard to the actual outcome than to the reasoning. In a number of cases the laymen on the bench had judged the evidence differently from the majority or had stretched the possibility of legally defending a desirable outcome in their choice of which principles of interpretation to apply.

It was against this background that one must view the decisions of 1945 and 1946 on the effect of the union-shop clause, in which the employer and union members joined forces against the officials and formed a majority. The SAF had an interest in common with the LO in discouraging membership of "Syndicalist" unions and discharging the employer from the charge of violation of the right of self-organization. As mentioned before, the court by its decision in 1948, No. 1, took a new course, unanimously overruling its earlier decisions. In the meanwhile the Ombudsman had intervened and in a report of 1947 had requested amendments to the statutory right of self-organization. In his opinion the decisions of the labor court were not compatible with the purpose of the Act respecting the Right of Organization and Negotiation. The laymen on the bench gave in and ceased to support a view—incidentally, taken very reluctantly by one of the employer members—which had been declared contrary to the interests of society.

The employers had a nineteenth-century liberalist conception of the manager. They still cherished the vision of the individual entrepreneur, who ought to be protected against the infringements on his freedom in running his business as he wanted. (Incidentally, the SAF in 1904 wrote into its constitution a provision stating that members should ensure that a clause preserving the managerial prerogatives was made part of every collective agreement.) In defending the managerial prerogatives the employers' representatives had an advantage over the union officers on the bench. The common law of Sweden as interpreted by the officials was based upon similar individualistic ideas, as will be demonstrated later with regard to the issue of arbitrary dismissals. The officials took the same view as the employers on some other issues, too. Thus, in disputes over the peace obligation for natural reasons the officials were inclined to hold that the interests of society were best promoted when the parties were not permitted to resort to economic action. Like the employers, therefore, they were inclined to give the agreement a broad interpretation.

15. The union members of the court had other social ideals. Each of the unions affiliated with the LO represented the workers within an industry or a craft. It claimed that its members should be assigned all jobs within its jurisdiction. Any jurisdictional disputes should be settled by the LO as a confederation of all workers' unions. The individual should have security in his employment relations and be protected against arbitrary dismissal. In what follows I shall describe the position taken by the union members of the labor court on two important issues.

The question as to which jobs are covered by a collective agreement has been the principal issue in a great number of cases. In the case 1929, No. 29, in which the labor court laid down the basic principle that still prevails, the factual situation was as follows. The owners of a paper mill planned to repair and rebuild some parts of the plant. Certain employees were ordered to carry out the work. They were paid in accordance with the national agreement for the paper industry. Later the workers came to the conclusion that the agreement did not apply and demanded higher pay. It is probable that an intervention by the Building Workers' Union, claiming the job for its own members, was behind this action. No settlement was reached and the workers went on strike. The labor court found that "an individual employee bound by a collective agreement has a duty with regard to jobs falling within his qualifications to perform, at the agreed payment for the job for which he is hired, all such work that has a natural relation to the production of his employer." The union members of the court, in a dissenting opinion, held that the repairing and rebuilding of the mill should not be considered ordinary maintenance work but as work belonging to the building industry, and that therefore the collective agreement for the paper industry was not applicable.

In the number of cases from the next few years, the union members on the bench followed the same course.[17] In two cases, 1938, No. 90, and 1939, No. 95, they drafted their dissents in blunt language. The work was of such extensive proportions that it was not covered by the agreement. In the case 1941, No. 68, with a factual situation almost identical with that of the case 1929, No. 29, the union members joined the majority. In a unanimous opinion the court held that the production workers of the firm were obliged to perform work on the construction of a new building intended to replace an old workshop. What was the reason for this shift of attitude?

In Sweden a judge who has voted with the minority in one case and meets the same issue in a later case must have special reasons if he dissents again; usually he accepts the earlier decision as a precedent. Did the union members, perhaps, apply this procedure? This would be an erroneous assumption. Within the LO there was dissension with regard to construction work in situations now discussed. If wages were going to be paid according to the agreement for the building industry, the manager might call upon workers from the building trade to do the job. To the workers in an industrial plant, assignment to construction work on their ordinary rate of pay was often preferred to being laid off because of shortages of work. Among the trade unions the view had gained ground that the Building Industry Workers' Union was not entitled to monopolize building work. At its Congress in 1936, the LO adopted a resolution that "the union of each industry ought to enter into collective agreements for such building work as was performed by an employer under his own management and with his own permanent workers, including any building workers permanently on his staff. On the other hand, it was the part of the unions of the building industry to make the agreements for any extensive building enterprises for which workers from the building industry were hired temporarily."

16. No other case has caused so much debate among union people as the case 1932, No. 100. A bus company had dismissed a driver, W., on the ground of an alleged breach of a provision in the work rules that an employee was not permitted to compete with his employer. The union raised a claim for reinstatement with back pay and brought an action in the labor court. W. had not been involved in any prohibited activity. Before the court, the employer—evidently on the instructions of his association—asserted that W. had not been dismissed because of breach of contract. Proper notice of termination had been served,

---

[17] 1930, No. 23; 1933, No. 85; 1934, No. 59; 1922, No. 59.

and the employer was entitled to dismiss a worker at will. In the collective agreement the managerial prerogatives were explicitly preserved in accordance with the policy of the members of the SAF.

The labor court dismissed the action. The court said that in the Swedish statute book there were no provisions with regard to termination of an employment contract entered into for an indefinite period of time. There was no doubt, however, that in Sweden, as in other countries, the general principle prevailed that a contract of employment might be terminated by either party upon notice and that there was no duty to give a reason for such action, whichever party terminated the contract. The provisions in the constitution of the SAF that, in collective agreements entered into by members of that association, a provision should be embodied that the employer had the right to hire and dismiss at will had the effect that the members were not permitted to agree upon a waiver of the general principle but were required to have it confirmed in the agreement.

In their dissenting opinion, the union members of the court explained that they could not share the view of the majority that it was enough in a dismissal case for the employer simply to invoke the provisions in the collective agreements on the right to hire and dismiss at will. According to the practice in many trades, an employee was not dismissed when there was a need for his labor and he was suitable for the job. Furthermore, dismissals were matters of negotiation. This development of the actual application of the employment contract had to be taken into consideration. The action should be sustained.

By the Basic Agreement of 1938, SAF and LO settled a number of disputed issues. As a part of the deal SAF agreed to a procedure for terminations and layoffs. As mentioned before, after local and central negotiations a dismissal case can be taken to the *Arbetsmarknadsnämnden*, a joint board with equal representation of both sides. Under amendments adopted in 1964, the *Arbetsmarknadsnämnden* acts as an arbitral board under the chairmanship of an umpire in trying dismissals on account of some circumstance affecting the worker individually. In the next chapter of this report I shall describe how dismissal cases are administered by the *Arbetsmarknadsnämnden*.

17. In the period from the establishment of the labor court to the present time, the number of disputes in which the court has been called upon to decide has decreased. In 1932 it was 204, and in the next few years after it was between 150 and 200. Now the figures have dropped to 30 to 40 a year. During the same period, the proportion of decisions with dissents to the total number of decisions rendered has

demonstrated a similar trend. There were dissenting opinions in more than 40 percent of the decisions rendered in the years 1929–31, but in the last few years the figure has been about 10 percent.

This development from dissension to unity is to be attributed to a number of factors. The negotiation machinery described in chapter 2 has become more efficient, and there is a growing willingness to make compromises in dealing with obscure claims. On some disputed matters one of the parties of the labor market has yielded to the other party. The cases concerning what tasks an employee has a duty to perform provide an example. The LO reconsidered its earlier policy with regard to the jurisdiction of the Building Workers' Union and took a course more compatible with the views of the officials and the employer members of the court. On other issues the parties have been able to reach an agreement. By the Basic Agreement in 1938, with the amendments adopted in 1964, the parties came to terms with regard to dismissals for personal reasons and on account of redundancy.

The present unity is partly to be attributed to legislative interference, too. In Sweden advocates of reforms are fortunate in that once a law reform is adopted the matter is in most quarters considered as settled. There are few attacks aiming at repeal once a scheme has actually come into effect. As a matter of course, the laymen on the bench feel that in their capacity as judges they are not at liberty to dispute clear directives by the legislators.

Among pieces of legislation during the period now under survey, I should like to mention two enactments of special bearing upon matters of dissent by laymen on the bench. In the case 1935, No. 57, the labor court had to try an alleged act of violation of the right of self-organization. Contrary to most agreements, the collective agreement relevant to the employment contract in the case at bar had no express clause on the right of self-organization. The employer members dissented from a decision of the court to read such a clause into the agreement. With the introduction of the Act respecting the Right of Organization and Negotiation, 1936, they could no longer defend this position.

For some years the question of who should be considered an employee was a disputed issue. Associations representing freeholders in the forest districts who were contractors for the felling and transporting of timber, lessees of petrol stations, and other groups on the borderline between employees and contractors, demanded recognition for bargaining purposes. Individuals belonging to these categories claimed employee status with regard to benefits under social insurance schemes and the Paid Vacations Act. The labor court refused to extend the employee concept to cover new categories, while the Supreme

Court and the administrative authorities were more lenient. In 1945 an act was introduced specially directed at the labor court. To the Right of Organization and Negotiation Act, the Collective Agreements Act, and certain other acts was added a new section. For the purpose of these acts a person is to be regarded as an employee even if no formal employment relations exist, provided he performs work for another person and is dependent in relation to him in the same way as an employee is dependent in relation to his employer.

THE OPTIONS FOR THE INDIVIDUAL WORKER

18. Some general remarks will be made with regard to possible choices available to the individual. The collective agreement controls the employment relation of the individual who is a member of the union signatory to the agreement. A person who wants to avoid being bound must leave the union before the agreement becomes effective, but it is generally accepted that he has to comply with the provisions of the union's constitution. The unions which are affiliated with the LO do not permit members to resign as long as they continue to be employed within the jurisdiction of the union. Other unions have provisions stipulating a period of notice. It is disputed whether a no-resignation clause has full effect; some maintain that a member is always at liberty to resign after a period of notice of reasonable length.

In Sweden membership in a union is looked on as being a matter of course, since the union provides services which might not otherwise be easily available. It is not only that the union takes action upon grievances. If a member has suffered from personal injury, the union will bring an action in a civil court if it considers the employer liable in tort. The union pays benefits to workers who are on strike or subjected to a lockout. It collects the contributions for the unemployment insurance fund, it engages in educational and recreational activities, etc. There is a general feeling that a non-union worker is not so well looked after, even though legal aid from state funds is available to anyone in the lower income brackets.

In the labor court the organization represents its members when taking action. The union will also represent a member in actions brought against him, unless the member enters a defense himself. If the union and the member both happen to appear, it is the member who owns the claim. The union cannot make any concession to the detriment of the member. The member has the right to sue in the labor court if he can prove that the union has refused to take action on his behalf.

SETTLEMENT OF EMPLOYMENT GRIEVANCES IN SWEDEN

19. In 1963 Professor Clyde Summers published a study of individual rights under the collective agreement.[18] Mr. Summers was in Sweden for a considerable time and his findings are based upon first-hand material. He noted 45 cases in which action was taken by an individual union member. This number is rather small, since it represents only 1.5 percent of all actions brought to the court from the employee side.

There has never been any rush of members to bring actions. The largest number in any one year was 6, in 1953, when the total number of decisions rendered was 44. This figure in 1953 is exceptional; there have seldom been more than 1 or 2 cases a year. In one case of 1958 nine members won a notable victory and were awarded considerable sums of money. The union had made a compromise deal with the employer on overtime pay without obtaining proxies from the members. No individual cases were brought to the court in the following years. Summers finds that the small number of individual cases is probably due chiefly to the confidence which the individual has in his organization and his willingness to accept its decisions as fair. Summers tried to discover for what reasons unions had refused to proceed. In 9 of the 45 cases included in his study, the individual's claim appeared as worthless either because of an erroneous interpretation of the agreement or of a version of facts which was not supported by evidence. However, in the majority of cases the claim appeared to be arguable, and often the argument for or against the claim seemed pretty evenly balanced. In 9 of the 45 cases included in the study, the action was sustained. In the case, 1946, No. 31, the union had made a deal with the employer with regard to persons who should be placed on the list for promotion in accordance with certain provisions in the agreement. The court dismissed the objection that the member was bound by this settlement, found that he met the requirements of the collective agreement, and ordered him to be promoted. In the case on overtime pay, 1958, No. 23, referred to before, the union had worked out a compromise solution that gave the individuals only part of their claims. A third case, 1949, No. 91, concerned a member who had been summarily dismissed because of violation of the work rules. The union, after discussing the case with the employer, had agreed that the discharge was justified. The court found that under the circumstances—the employee had acted in good faith—his misconduct did not constitute a reason for dismissal without notice and awarded him pay for the period of notice. In a

---

[18] Summers, "Collective Power and Individual Rights in the Collective Agreement—A Comparison of Swedish and American Law," 72 Yale L.J. (1963), pp. 421 ff.

fourth case, 1956, No. 38, the union had admitted the employer's statement of the facts. In court the member was able to prove that they were not correct.

According to Summers, there may have been some lack of aggressiveness by the unions in protecting the employee's interest. But in none of the cases did it appear that the union's refusal to take the cases to the labor court was due to arbitrariness, favoritism, or vindictiveness.

Summers' study was completed in 1961. The present author knows of one case, 1962, No. 34, which demonstrates that ugly things can happen even in Sweden. In October 1961 an immigrant, K., entered into employment at a candy factory where he did repair jobs. K. had earlier been a union member for long periods. At the time of his employment, however, he was unorganized because he had been an entrepreneur for a period and later had had various odd jobs. The officer of the local branch of the union, Y., asked the company to dismiss K. as a nonunion member. There was no union-shop clause in the collective agreement, and the company refused to take action but suggested to K. that he should join. K. filed an application for membership, which he submitted to the local branch. Y. told him that his application would have to be submitted to the national union. For some reason the union's decision was delayed. Not until February 14, was K. admitted as a member, as from the date of his application, December 18, 1961. In the meanwhile he had been discharged. Before the court the company gave as its reason that K. was not on good terms with the other workers of the plant. Individually and through their representatives they had raised complaints against K. At the time of the dismissal the point had been reached where several workers threatened to give notice unless K. was discharged. Since the company could rest upon its prerogative to dismiss at will, K. had no remedy. The present author, who happened to follow the trial, came to the conclusion that the local officer, Y., had a dislike for K. and had grossly abused his power to influence others.

4.
VARIOUS ARBITRAL BOARDS

1. In labor relations ordinary rules of arbitral procedure apply. As mentioned in chapter 1, sec. 19, the parties may elect to resort to arbitration instead of judicial proceedings and an agreement to arbitrate, if invoked by the defendant, rules out judicial procedure. The award of the arbitrator is binding and can be put into effect after summary proceedings before the chief executory authority.

According to the general view, submission to arbitration is considered an exceptional rather than an ordinary procedure. Whether the number of cases annually decided by arbitrators is less than the number of cases adjudicated by the labor court is hard to say. It is true that *ad hoc* arbitration arrangements are not very frequent, but a great number of arbitral boards have been established for various purposes. It is a normal pattern to have arbitral boards for the adjudication of special types of cases and to submit possible disputes on other matters to the labor court.

There is no survey available on the use of arbitration in labor relations. Under the Basic Agreement—which with some exceptions has been adopted by the organizations within the wide segment of private industry governed by the SAF and the LO—arbitration is provided for in disputes over dismissals and layoffs and in disputes over the provisions in the agreement concerning limitations on strikes, lockouts, and other offensive actions in the interests of public policy and neutral third parties. There are agreements between the SAF and the Union of Salaried Employees within Industry and between the SAF and the Union of Supervisors providing for arbitration in a large number of situations, including disputes over dismissals. In the building industry, arbitration is used in disputes over piece rates while other disputes concerning the application of the collective agreement are referred to the labor court. The metal industry has an arbitral board for disputes regarding the classification of workers as skilled or unskilled. The same industry's board for vocational training has power to arbitrate disputes arising out of the provisions on apprenticeship.

Within the press, arbitration is the paramount procedure. The Swedish Newspaper Employers' Association and the Unions of Typographers, Lithographers and Bookbinders have entered into a Principal Agreement providing for arbitration in all kinds of disputes, disputes over the interpretation of an existing collective agreement as well as over the terms of a new agreement. Thus, an arbitral board is entitled to make the new agreement if the parties fail to reach an agreement through negotiations.

In what follows I shall describe how the *Arbetsmarknadsnämnden* deals with dismissals and layoffs under the Basic Agreement. An account will be given of the Arbitral Board for Piece Rates within the building industry. Some information will be given, too, regarding the arrangement for peace through arbitration in the Swedish press.

THE ARBETSMARKNADSNÄMNDEN

2. As mentioned before (chap. 3, sec. 16), in 1932 AD No. 100, the labor court laid down the rule that the employer has the right to dismiss at will and has no duty to give reasons for his action. With the Basic Agreement of 1938 between the SAF and the LO, a new procedure was introduced with regard to dismissals and layoffs and subsequent reemployment of labor. The prerogatives of management were in part surrendered. Dismissals were made a matter of negotiation on different levels. When entering into negotiations the employer had the duty to state the reasons for his action. Ultimately the case could be submitted to the *Arbetsmarknadsnämnden,* a joint board with equal representation of both sides which was entitled to investigate and to pass a judgment. The passing of a judgment presupposed a decision upheld by a majority. In contrast to ordinary arbitral awards, the judgment of the *Arbetsmarknadsnämnden* did not have the effect of an enforceable decision. The judgment was a nonbinding recommendation which was communicated to the trade federations concerned. It rested entirely upon them to determine the scope and the nature of possible sanctions.

In 1964 the SAF and the LO agreed upon certain amendments to the Basic Agreement. The Basic Agreement, as amended in 1964, distinguishes between dismissals arising out of a worker's individual circumstances and dismissals for other reasons. In broad terms, the line is drawn between dismissals on personal grounds and dismissals and layoffs because of a surplus of manpower, i.e., redundancy. With regard to the former category, important innovations were introduced; with regard to the latter, the earlier rules were left as they were.

3. In cases concerning dismissals on personal grounds, according to the 1964 amendments the *Arbetsmarknadsnämnden* acts as an arbitral board under the chairmanship of an umpire. Thus, its decisions are legally binding upon the parties in the same way as a decision of a court of law. The Board has to consider "whether the employer had material grounds for the giving of notice. If the Board finds that there were no material grounds for giving notice, it may award damages to the worker."

During the course of the negotiations that preceded the 1964 amendments, the fact that the judgments of the *Arbetsmarknadsnämnden* were mere recommendations was not a critical issue. The absence of legal sanctions was not pertinent, since it did not occur that a disputant refused to accept a decision of the *Arbetsmarknadsnämnden* as the final settlement of the dispute. But the unions were not happy with the majority rule applied. They considered that the Board was too parsimonious in meting out compensation. In some cases the union members had felt impelled to vote for a poor compromise in order to avoid the stalemate of a three-to-three vote. By calling upon an umpire they expected to be more successful in taking care of the interests of the individual worker.

The employer experts on the drafting committee proposed the labor court as the competent forum in disputes over dismissals on personal grounds. The union experts held another view, however. They harbored a certain resentment against the labor court because of its earlier decisions in dismissal cases. They feared the use of precedents and wanted more flexible rules to apply during the transition period. Arbitration was to be preferred. To the employers the choice was a matter of minor importance and the LO proposal was therefore accepted.

On another very important matter the employers refused to meet the demands of the LO. In actions concerning a violation of the right of self-organization or of a statutory prohibition against dismissal, the labor court orders the reinstatement of the dismissed worker if this is part of the action. Similarly, reinstatement is ordered when an action is based upon the breach of a clause in the collective agreement, stating that the employer is not entitled to terminate the contract of employment without just cause. As mentioned in chapter 1, sec. 27, in the Ester Rannby case the Swedish Supreme Court followed another course. Reinstatement, it held, should not be used as a remedy in civil court actions.

In the period before 1964, the *Arbetsmarknadsnämnden* used to recommend reinstatement when it found a dismissal to be unjustified. In the negotiations for the 1964 amendments, the employers were strongly opposed to the idea of allowing the Board to order reinstatement in an award which would be binding upon the employer. The SAF considered it a matter of basic policy that an employer should not be forced to provide work for an employee whom he did not want to engage. As a part of the deal the union draftsmen had to accept that, in cases concerning dismissal on personal grounds, damages should be made the sole remedy.

Earlier the decisions of the *Arbetsmarknadsnämnden* were treated as top secret. Now they are always circulated to a considerable number of persons within the organizations concerned, and one of the latest decisions was actually published in the press. The present writer has been given free access to the files and has been able to study all the acts and documents.

4. One might have expected that a considerable number of cases would have come to the Board in the period following the amendments of 1964. But here, as in so many fields, the do-it-yourself spirit prevails. The total number of decisions is very low—until December 31, 1967, only 15. Of these, only 2, both rendered in 1967, are from the period since 1964. It should be added that in 2 cases dating from the period before 1964 the Board was unable to arrive at a decision upheld by a majority. In part the absence of cases in the years 1965 and 1966 was due to a reluctance on both sides to put to the test the new clause concerning dismissals on personal grounds. It is the practice of the two secretaries of the Board—one employer and one union man—to investigate and report as a preliminary step. On some occasions the secretaries were subsequently asked to propose an equitable solution; their recommendations were ultimately accepted by both sides and the case was removed from the list.

What is the meaning of the clause stating that the employer must have "material grounds" for giving notice? Certainly, the drafters of the 1964 amendments had in mind that a dismissal should not be contrary to established standards of good personnel policy. In the decision of May 24, 1967, a dismissal was held to be unjust on such grounds. In June 1966 Mrs. E., a part-time employee at a dress shop, was requested to sign a written promise that during the month of July 1967 she would not take more than two weeks of her annual vacation. The purpose was to ensure adequate staffing of the shop during a difficult month. The Vacation Act provides for annual holidays of four weeks. The period is to be continuous unless otherwise agreed. In Sweden, July is the traditional holiday period. After returning from her 1966 vacation, Mrs. E. was dismissed because she had refused to sign the document. In its decision the Board held that Mrs. E. had been discharged without just cause and awarded her 2,500 *kronor* in damages, a sum probably corresponding to about three months' pay. The Board did not find it necessary to express an opinion as to whether the employer had been entitled to request the employee's signature on the document. The act of dismissal was unjust because the employer had not made it clear to the employee that she had to indicate her attitude towards his proposal before a certain date, nor had he given her an opportunity to reconsider her rejection.

The members of the expert committee that drafted the 1964 amendments made up a list of possible grounds for dismissal. On the list were the worker's refusal to obey an order, failure to produce a valid excuse for absence, breach of the works rules, lack of loyalty, and competing activity. Obviously these are breaches which constitute material grounds for dismissals unless the incidents involved are trivial. Another item on the list was lack of cooperation. In an early decision of the *Arbetsmarknadsnämnden*, lack of cooperation was accepted as a reason why reinstatement was not to be recommended.

The drafters had divergent views on the question when sickness should be considered a sufficient ground for notice of termination. The issue is still unsettled. From decisions of the labor court on similar clauses in collective agreements, one may conclude that a dismissal cannot be justified solely because the employer would find it difficult to get someone to replace the employee during his leave of absence. The situation may be different if the employee is permanently disabled.

5. If an employer is compelled to reduce his labor force, the question which employees are to be laid off as redundant may be submitted to the *Arbetsmarknadsnämnden*. As mentioned before, when trying redundancy cases the Board has no neutral member, and a decision requires a majority vote from a three-plus panel. The judgment of the Board is considered a non-binding recommendation.

In the Basic Agreement certain standards are laid down on the basis of which the Board has to appraise the actions of the employer. Three factors are mentioned, skill and suitability combined, seniority, and duty to support dependants. "Consideration shall be given to the necessity for the employer to be served, so far as possible, by skillful labor suited for the job. Further, when the choice is between workers of equal skill or suitability, the length of service of the individual worker and also any particularly heavy family obligations he must meet shall be borne in mind."

On this point there is little to tell about the decisions of the *Arbetsmarknadsnämnden*. Only a few of them concern dismissals or layoffs because of redundancy, and none is from the period since 1964. A few comments should be made about the text and the actual application of the Basic Agreement in the workshops. The employer has no duty to provide jobs, even if he could do so with profit to himself. The union can dispute only the choice made between its members.

As indicated by the text, skill and suitability combined constitute the principal factor. Economic considerations prevail over social considerations. The actual application is not as rigid, however, as might seem to follow from the wording of the agreement. Great weight is attached to seniority. An employer may apply the principle of seniority for the simple reason that he knows that in that case his action will not be disputed by the union. If preference is given to a worker because of his special qualifications, the employer must be prepared to demonstrate that he had good reasons for his action. It should be added that, owing to the development of social insurance, regard to family commitments is less pertinent today than it was in 1938, when the Basic Agreement came into being.[1]

THE ARBITRAL BOARD FOR PIECE RATES WITHIN THE BUILDING INDUSTRY

6. Arbitration has a long tradition in the Swedish building industry. Arbitral boards existed in the period before the establishment of the labor court. The present system was introduced in 1934. According to the national agreement for the building industry—an agreement which covers about two-thirds of all enterprises within the industry—disputes over piece rates are submitted to the Arbitral Board for Piece Rates, which is a permanent institution. With regard to other disputes the labor court remains the competent forum.[2] It is not possible to state

---

[1] Because of technological changes there has been a rapid turnover of labor in Sweden during the last decades. A system based upon security in employment relations does not give any remedy when a factory is closed down. The LO unions have tried to meet the needs of the individuals by bargaining for severance pay for those who are displaced. Employers belonging to the SAF pay contributions to an insurance fund. Benefits on a modest scale are paid to older workers who at the time of the displacement have been employed by the same employer for more than ten years. Measured by American standards, little has been achieved as yet.

[2] It should be mentioned that the Basic Agreement has not been adopted by the parties in the building industry.

with certainty the reason for this arrangement. Most likely the parties considered it too burdensome to apply the judicial procedure to disputes on piece rates because of their great number. Nor could they be certain that the labor court had the requisite technological knowledge.

By way of background, it is necessary to describe the wage system and the negotiation procedure of the national agreement. The great majority of all jobs in the building industry are carried out on piecework. The parties have established lists of piece rates for all kinds of work which occur regularly. During the term of the national agreement, amendments of existing piece rates are negotiated and prices are agreed upon for jobs for which the remuneration was not settled before. In principle, existing piece rates are to apply. From the worker's point of view, application of the price lists is profitable when he is assigned to a large standardized job; the additional pay then generally exceeds the hourly wage. On the other hand, for repairing, rebuilding, and other odd jobs the return is small and a contractor would have difficulty in finding anyone willing to work at the fixed piece rate. Under the national agreement certain additions are to be awarded in such cases. There is also provision for special arrangements with respect to production on a large scale.

The workers are organized in gangs. Thus, the bricklayers, the carpenters, and the cement workers constitute separate gangs, each with a gang leader. Every two weeks the worker is paid his hourly wage. After a period — ordinarily covering 18 to 22 weeks — the work performed by the gang is measured jointly by two measurers, one of them an officer of the employers' organization and the other a union man. When the measurers have different opinions about which price shall apply or what work has been performed, they make a note with regard to the disputed point. If the local branch of the employers' association upholds an objection by its measurer, it has to present a detailed, written statement within a certain period of time. The disputed amount is withheld and the remainder is paid to the members of the gang as additional remuneration for their piecework.

The negotiation procedure has three steps. After local negotiations the claim, if still unsettled, will be referred to central negotiations. Originally the dispute was thereafter submitted to the Arbitral Board. For a long time there have existed special national price-list committees for bargaining over amendments to the price lists. There is a committee for each of the three groups, bricklayers, carpenters, and cement workers. After 1959 the practice was gradually introduced of referring disputes over piece rates to these committees. Often settlements were reached. In 1966 submission to the price-list committee of the trade was made a compulsory step of the negotiation procedure.

7. In order to give an account of the Arbitral Board for Piece Rates as a working institution, a special study was undertaken[3] as part of the work on this report. A method was applied similar to that used by Dr. Edlund in his study of two national agreements, although the study was less exhaustive and on a smaller scale.[4] Statistical data were collected for the period from 1950. The president and the secretary of the Board and a number of officers from both sides were interviewed. The more recent cases from each trade were selected for special analysis with a view to getting an idea of the methods applied in adjudication. This special study embraced seven disputes over the bricklayers' lists from the years 1963–65, five disputes over the carpenters' lists from 1964–65, and five disputes over the cement workers' lists from 1961–65.

The parties to the national agreement considered the grievance procedure to be exclusively their own concern. It has never been tried whether the union owns the grievance and the individual worker is barred from bringing an action to the Arbitral Board or to the labor court. Nor has it happened that a contractor has taken action without support of his association.

Within this field, one could make the same observation as within other fields, that the number of disputes submitted to adjudication had decreased in the last few years. The practice of referring piece-rate disputes to the national price-list committee of the trade had the effect of reducing the number considerably, as demonstrated by table 7. The figures for 1966 (0) and 1967 (1) indicate that by making submission to the price-list committee of the trade compulsory, the parties had found a way of settling practically all disputes themselves. Nobody, however, suggested the abolition of the Arbitral Board. A prominent representative of the employers told the present author that in his opinion an arbitral board is necessary as the last instance in a grievance procedure for fixed piece rates.

The Arbitral Board is composed of a president, three employers' representatives, and nine union representatives. At the request of the parties to the national agreement, the president has been appointed by the head of the Social Welfare Board, to which the state conciliation service belonged until recently. From 1951 the same person, a pro-

---
[3] The study was carried out by Mr. Per Winnberg, who was engaged as research assistant for a period of time.
[4] Edlund's study is described in chap. 2, secs. 7-11.

TABLE 7
Awards by the Arbitral Board for Piece Rates within the Building Industry

Year*	Number of Awards	Year*	Number of Awards
1950	119	1959	27
1951	54	1960	33
1952	85	1961	34
1953	62	1962	0
1954	74	1963	4
1955	37	1964	13
1956	36	1965	3
1957	36	1966	0
1958	53	1967	1

* The fact that no awards were rendered in 1962 is explained by the circumstance that the price lists were revised in that year. In the course of the bargaining over the new lists the parties settled outstanding disputes.

fessional judge, had served as president. The union representatives constituted three alternating panels, one for each of the three trades. Thus, in a case concerning the carpenters' list, the Board would consist of the president and an equal number of employers and union men from the carpenters' panel.

Only on rare occasions were the members able to reach a unanimous decision. No more than 22 out of a total of 707 decisions in the period 1950–66 were of that character. Usually the employers and the union men on the Board cast their votes first. It was placed in the records that the union men had voted in favor of sustainment of the action, and the employers in favor of dismissal. The president then announced that he intended to render the award of the Board later on. This procedure was sanctioned by the agreement, which provided that in case of an equal division the opinion in which the president concurred or his compromise proposal was the decision of the Board.

The president acted in the same way as the judge of a one-man court. It was an established practice to give reasons for the decision. Some of the awards were very summary, however, as can be seen from the following example: "Since the disputed work cannot be considered as work on a funnel of the kind described in Table 3, point 12 (b), of the list, the suit of the union is dismissed." The wording of the agreement was accorded great weight, as was made clear in awards stating the principal reasons why a certain price on a list was applicable or not. On some occasions the award referred to earlier decisions of the Board as precedents. Sometimes a logical argument was to be found, but only seldom was there a discussion of the purpose or intention of the parties or the suitability of a certain solution.

The persons concerned did not always fully understand why an award had gone in one direction or another and sometimes felt that the decisions looked as if they were the result of a drawing of lots. Here we found one of the reasons why in the last few years the parties had tried to avoid calling upon the services of the Board. In most cases they perferred a settlement through negotiations.

8. Undoubtedly the Arbitral Board for Piece Rates had played a very important role as an instrument for the settlement of disputes. The weight attached to its awards as precedents was significant. The awards were published. On the employers' side reprints of the awards were distributed to the members and to the offices of their measurers. At these offices the awards were filed chronologically. Each office kept an index, too, where relevant awards could be found under the respective heads and numbers of the price lists. The national union had a similar system of informing the offices of their measurers. Yearly conferences were arranged for work-gang leaders.

Indexes were also kept at the headquarters of both sides. From its establishment in 1934 to 1966, the Board had rendered about 3,300 awards. According to information from the employers' organization, 1,223 of these awards were still applicable. The present author found this figure unexpectedly high, considering that the parties held earlier awards to be "overruled" when, during the course of a revision, they had agreed upon a new text of the price list on the disputed point. Thus, at the last general revision which took place in 1962, close to 1,000 awards were discarded as nonapplicable. When seeking an explanation for the fact that such a great number of awards were still in force, we found that there were many related to jobs which nowadays occurred less often than before. It is interesting to note the distribution of the awards between the three trades. Out of 1,223 awards in force, 569 related to the bricklayers' lists, 593 to the carpenters' lists, and only 61 to the cement workers' lists. Bricklayers and carpenters represent trades in which handicraft methods are still applied to some jobs, and they generally speaking have been less influenced by technological changes than the cement workers.

PEACE THROUGH ARBITRATION IN THE SWEDISH PRESS

9. The Swedish Newspaper Employers' Association is party to separate collective agreements with the following unions: the Typographers, the Lithographers, the Bookbinders, the Transport Workers, and

the Journalists. Since 1937 the Association and the three unions of the technical staff have a system whereby all disputes are subjected to arbitration. A Peace Agreement with a procedure of arbitration is in force for a term of its own. The present agreement was entered into in 1969 for the years 1970 to 1979.

It is assumed that the ordinary process of collective agreement will continue, and that the parties will have wages and other conditions of employment regulated by a national agreement of each trade for a more limited period of time. Thus, in 1966 national agreements were entered into with the three unions in accordance with the recommendation of the SAF and the LO for three-year agreements, and in 1969 for the years 1969 to 1970. The Peace Agreement provides for a special procedure. If in the course of negotiations for a new contract there should arise differences of opinion that the parties cannot resolve, in the first round, a nonpartisan chairman experienced in conciliation must be called in. If his attempts at conciliation should fail, an arbitral board must be constituted, which has the power of making an agreement on the disputed points.

In the Peace Agreement certain guideposts are laid down. The parties—as well as the conciliator and the arbitral board—must take into consideration, among other things, the public's justifiable demands for the publication of newspapers, the net price index and its development, the wage situation on the labor market in general and for comparable groups, the productivity (primarily to the extent it is affected by the individual employee) and the justifiable demands of the employees for reasonably good living standards and conditions of employment.

The employers have accepted the idea that they have to give the employees a certain "payment" for sacrificing the right to resort to industrial action. For some years they were given an additional week's vacation, or a reduction of working hours. With the rise of the general conditions of employment by virtue of legislation, the parties had to look for some other kind of additional compensation. Under the present agreements the employees are entitled to a sum in cash in addition to the ordinary pay for vacation periods. At the beginning of his vacation period the employee is paid a lump sum equal to 2.3 percent of his earnings in the previous calendar year. Further, in 1969 a fund was established for the payment of additional benefits to the public unemployment insurance scheme.

The arbitral board has been called upon to make an award on two occasions only. One concerned a wage issue. In 1941 the unions demanded a general raise of 5 percent. The employers would not offer more than 2.3 percent, referring to a joint recommendation of the SAF and the LO that wage increases should not exceed that level. The award was for a compromise.

From a legal point of view, such an award must be distinguished from an award that concerns the interpretation of an existing collective agreement. The award has the character of an agreement made by an agent. Unlike an award concerning interpretation, it cannot be executed.

It may be added that in 1969 a Peace Agreement was entered into with the Journalists Union, similar to that with the technical staff. Attempts have been made to extend the system to the distribution workers as well, but thus far they have not been successful.

5.
AN EVALUATION OF THE SWEDISH SYSTEM

1. The purpose of the two fundamental statutes of 1928, the Collective Agreements Act and the Labor Court Act, was to exclude the use of self-help remedies, to make the collective agreement enforceable as a contract at law, and to provide for adequate sanctions. It cannot be disputed that the legislators achieved these aims.

After a few years the legislation was approved by its once implacable opponents, the Social Democratic Party and organized labor. In 1928 the union leaders believed that the proposed legislation would paralyze the power of the unions. Soon they found that this was a complete misjudgment. It is true that the labor court—on several occasions against the dissenting opinions of union officers on the bench—laid down a broad interpretation of the provisions on the peace obligation embodied in the Act on Collective Agreements; but sympathetic actions still remained permissible in many situations and the Act did not apply to negotiations on the terms of the new agreement after the expiration of the earlier agreement. It should further be noted that unionism spread from manual labor to white-collar workers and professional people. Sweden became a country where in almost every quarter it was taken for granted that an employee should carry a union card.

The fact that the labor court provided the union with means of forcing the employer to live up to his obligations under a collective agreement was another reason why the court soon met with approval in union quarters. Further, the union was granted wide powers to represent its members. A member was not entitled to bring an action in the labor court, unless he could prove that the union had refused to take action on his behalf. In the case of a breach of the collective agreement or of the statutory right of self-organization, the court awarded damages for personal injury, and the plaintiff did not have to bother about proof of economic loss. Here it should be recalled that about 85 to 90 percent of all actions are brought to the labor court by unions.

Of the seven members of the labor court, three are officials, two members represent the employers' organizations, and two represent the unions. It is not possible to estimate the extent to which the laymen on the bench have been able to influence the decisions of the court. Nor is it possible to say exactly what part they have played in an educational process, in the course of which the parties of the labor market have given their consent to a number of basic principles of the law of labor relations, or, if they have not done so, have at any rate reached a state of mind where they consider these principles socially acceptable. Certainly, the high degree of social integration that is a characteristic feature of modern Sweden is partly to be credited to the administration of justice by the labor court.

Sometimes the labor court has demonstrated a power of imagination and trodden new paths. Its standards of interpretation of collective agreements are based upon the idea that those who take part in negotiations are each responsible for their own contribution to the new agreement, and have a duty to disclose facts in order that no misunderstanding shall arise as to the true meaning of a new clause. For a long time now this approach has been accepted by those concerned, and possibly this is one of the reasons why in the last few years the court has not expressly referred to the principle of fault as often as it did before. At present the court is more inclined to give emphasis to the practical consequences of different applications, the conditions in other industries, or other facts making one solution appear preferable to another.

The labor court acts as a court of law. The administration of justice is not, as in conciliation, a matter of arriving at a compromise settlement, but of laying down general principles and relying upon precedents. This legalistic approach has not always been to the liking of the laymen on the bench. During the first decades of the court's jurisdiction the union members, in particular, were often in the minority. In many of their dissenting opinions they expressed social ideas differing from those of the majority. Mr. Wistrand—an employers' representative who at the 25th anniversary of the court was asked to give his assessment of the early years of the court's jurisdiction—was hardly accurate when he said that "in most cases, where matters of principle were at issue, these principles were laid down in unanimous decisions." The common law applied in the court was alien to the actual practices of the workshops. To the union members it was hard to understand, among other things, why in dismissal cases the labor court based its decisions on the managerial prerogative of dismissal at will.

When the SAF and the LO negotiated the 1964 amendements to the Basic Agreement, it was on the initiative of the LO that dismissal cases were taken away from the labor court and referred to arbitration. This is not the only example of judicial procedure being replaced by arbitration. Today there is a general inclination to prefer arbitration when specific issues are concerned. In these circumstances the continuous decline in the number of cases submitted to the labor court would seem alarming. In the period 1931–33 the court rendered about 200 decisions a year, in the period 1964–66, only 27 to 36. In the meanwhile the competence of the court has been extended by several new enactments and the number of organized workers has increased considerably.

In seeking an explanation of this trend, there are many factors to be taken into consideration. The labor court has produced a body of precedents spinning a web over the whole field of labor relations. Many disputes are settled out of court because knowledgeable men are able to forecast what the outcome would be if the dispute were to be submitted to court. The present practice of an oral prehearing before the president has a salutary effect on actions which have their roots more in antagonism than in dissent on legal issues.

The figures concerning the number of decisions annually rendered by the court show a close correlation with those regarding decisions with dissenting opinions. Those circumstances which explain the development from dissension to unity have a bearing upon the question how often disputants have to call upon a court to decide an issue. In some cases a jurisdictional dispute between two unions is the true reason why an action against an employer was brought to the labor court. If the unions are able to reach an agreement with regard to the line of demarcation in accordance with the spirit of the doctrine applied by the labor court, this must have a pacifying effect. Legislative amendments which make clear the meaning of the law on disputed issues also enter into the picture.

The paramount factor is to be looked for in another direction. The negotiation machinery—the system of central negotiations between the parties to the national agreements in particular—is much more efficient today than it was in the 1930s. It is hard to explain why the national organizations in Sweden have been able to reach such a state of maturity that parties seldom go to court because of disputes over facts at issue, and that even questions of law are ordinarily settled by negotiation. It may be highly relevant that the officers on both sides, including the officers of the national unions, remain in office until the age of retirement. The same people meet again and again; they have to find some *modus vivendi*. It is no part of this study to dig deeper into this problem, which would require a description of the whole social context.

Possibly the parties of the labor market consider arbitration the better choice when specific matters are concerned. This does not imply, however, that they are eager to turn to an arbitrator for help. On the contrary, the studies in chapter 4 of the functioning of the *Arbetsmarknadsnämnden* as an arbitral board in dismissal cases and of the Arbitral Board for Piece Rates within the building industry present evidence of a general inclination to prefer settlement by negotiation to any kind of adjudication. The number of cases which has been submitted to the *Arbetsmarknadsnämnden* is very small—there were only two in the period 1964–67. As to the Board for Piece Rates, it is true that at one time it was kept very busy; but now nearly all disputes are settled by negotiation, a great number of them by agreements reached in the price-list committees of the building trades.

2. In his monograph on the administration of the grievance procedures of two national agreements, Dr. Edlund is critical of the methods applied by the labor court.[1] The court was established because those in power did not trust the parties to settle their grievances by peaceful means. The legalistic approach of the labor court was in line with this vote of no confidence. Dr. Edlund doubts the wisdom of the traditional methods. The labor court, in view of its close contacts with real life, should have realized the advantages of the methods applied in extra-judicial administration of justice. If it had done so, it would have contributed to a renewal of judicial reasoning.

Dr. Edlund makes the observation that professional negotiators are generally of the opinon that recourse to court action is a crude, if not primitive, means of resolving disputes.[2] It does not fit into the general pattern that the parties shall cooperate in the administration of their agreements. All those interviewed by Edlund thought that settlement by negotiation was the best method, and that resort to court action should be considered only in cases of emergency. In the perspective of history the jurisdiction of the labor court was to be considered an interlude. The organizations of the labor market, according to Edlund, were reasserting their sovereignty.

---

[1] Edlund, *Tvisteförhandlingar på arbetsmarknaden. En rättslig studie av två riksavtal i tillämpning* (Stockholm, 1967), pp. 342 ff.
[2] Edlund, *op. cit.*, pp. 73 f.

SETTLEMENT OF EMPLOYMENT GRIEVANCES IN SWEDEN

The present author shares these views on the whole, but would make one reservation. As mentioned in chapter 4, sec. 7, a prominent representative of the building industry, with regard to the Arbitral Board for Piece Rates, expressed the view that the Board was necessary as being the last step of a grievance procedure. This statement can be applied generally. Some instance of last resort, a court of law or an arbitral board, is indeed a necessary element in each grievance procedure when the parties are bound by peace obligation and the use of self-help remedies is forbidden to them. This would be so even if, like some of the negotiators of the building industry, they considered submission to this instance to be like drawing lots.

It must be in the interests of society that justice should be administered publicly and not, like arbitration, *in camera*. I shall not develop this argument further; to do so would take us to the field of general jurisprudence. It must, however, be admitted that from the point of view of those concerned there are several drawbacks, among them the loss of prestige suffered by the party whose suit is dismissed and the distress caused to the individuals who will have their doings exposed to view.

Certainly there is nothing wrong in offering the parties the services of a qualified court when, as in Sweden, the parties have the option to provide for private arbitration if they prefer to do so. The fact that the Swedish Labor Court still retains its position as the central body for adjudication is the best possible test of the high quality of its products.

3. The principle of choice applies to another issue, too. The individual member of an organization has individual rights of his own. If the union and the member both happen to appear in the labor court, the union is not allowed to make any concessions to the detriment of its member. A member is permitted to sue by himself if the union refuses to take action on his behalf.

In his study of the cases in which actions had been taken by individual members, Professor Summers comes to the conclusion that, generally speaking, the members had confidence in their organizations and that a member was willing to accept the decision of his organization as fair.[3] In some cases there might have been a lack of aggressiveness in protecting the employee's interest. But in none of them did it appear that the union's refusal to take the cases to the labor court was due to arbitrariness, favoritism, or vindictiveness. The present author

---

[3] Summers' study is described in chap. 3, sec. 19.

would like to supplement Professor Summers' opinion with a comment of his own. It is true that the unions are efficient in protecting their members in disputes with the employer. I have noted, however, that on some occasions union officers are too tame in their defense of the interests of the individual employee when he is involved in a conflict with his fellows and they bring pressure on the employer. The employee may lose his job, though generally, it is true, under less obnoxious circumstances than those in the candy factory case, 1962 AD No. 34.

The present author is critical of the decision of the labor court, 1967 AD No. 17, in which the court refused to accept jurisdiction over an action by a member, and of the consecutive agreement between the SAF and the LO entitling members to take action to the *Arbetsmarknadsnämnden*. From the point of view of safeguards of individual rights, the labor court would have been the preferable forum.

4. It has been mentioned that the representatives of the organizations consider submission to court as a step that should be taken in case of emergency only. It is true that, to them, in some situations arbitration is preferable to judicial proceedings. But both these means of solving disputes are greatly inferior to settlement by negotiation. In these circumstances, the present author submits, there is reason to ask what could be done to improve judicial proceedings. The evils may have to do with the composition of the court, with the formal procedure involving two opposed parties, with the publicity to which the parties are exposed, or with the methods of reasoning upon which the decisions are based. The following comments will concern the last-mentioned aspect, namely the judicial method. Is it appropriate to apply judicial reasoning to disputes arising under collective agreements?

The judicial method of adjudication in private litigations varies from country to country, but in essential respects it is the same everywhere. The judge is supposed to apply an existing rule once the facts at issue have been established. Fundamentally, the method looks back to the past. A retrospective view is natural not only for the reason that adjudication of vested rights means an application of rules that are supposed to exist. Facts have to be proved which relate to the past. Generally, the defendant is held to be in arrears since a claim does not materialize until some time has elapsed. Further, the judge is dependent upon precedents. This is so, whether precedents are considered binding or merely persuasive.

Compared with judicial adjudication, three distinctive features of settlement by negotiation are worth remarking. First, resort to court action in a case where the outcome can reasonably be in doubt is like playing for all or nothing. If the suggested rules are found to apply and the facts at issue are proved, the action will be sustained. On the other hand, the action will be dismissed if the plaintiff fails to convince the court in any of these respects. In negotiations a party may to some extent give the other party the benefit of the doubt and split the claim in a compromise settlement.

Second, there is sometimes a strange contrast between the common law of a country and the actual practices in the workshops. In Sweden, as in many other countries, dismissals have been part of the managerial prerogative. The Swedish experience with regard to dismissal cases brought before the labor court in the 1930s was rather distressing. When the employers, through the Basic Agreement of 1938, accepted the policy of entering into negotiations, the situation improved. In a wide perspective it was a matter of minor importance that until 1964 no legal sanctions were attached, and that an employer could with impunity refuse to follow the advice of the *Arbetsmarknadsnämnden*, a body with equal representation of the SAF and the LO.

Third, the judicial method is retrospective. On the other hand, in negotiations the parties may pay regard not only to possible vested rights, but also to circumstances making one solution preferable in view of situations which may arise in the future.

In this concluding chapter, I have already called attention to the standards of interpretation laid down by the Swedish Labor Court. Basically, the court, with its test of who is to blame for a misunderstanding, applies a fault principle. It has been mentioned, too, that in the last few years the labor court has become more inclined than before to pay regard to the practical consequences of different possible application, to the conditions in other industries, and to other factors making one solution appear preferable to another. With regard to disputes arising under a collective agreement, one would expect to find the germ of a new approach within the field of standards of interpretation. In an article published in 1960,[4] the present author drew a parallel with the law of torts. In disputes over the interpretation of the contract, the all-or-nothing rule should be replaced by a rule of apportioning the damage, which in Sweden, as in many other countries, is the rule applied to contributory negligence in torts. The fact that the court takes into consideration the practical consequences of a solution

---

[4] Schmidt, "Model, Intention, Fault. Three Canons for Interpretation of Contracts," *Scandinavian Studies in Law*, vol. 4 (1960), pp. 177 ff. at 296.

implies regard to the future relations of the parties. Can we expect that the law of labor relations will develop along such lines?

It should be emphasized that in labor disputes the social situation is not comparable to that of business relations. If a merchant brings an action in court against another merchant, the adjudication of the dispute is a one-time incident. Seldom will the same parties resume their relations, making new purchases and sales. To society the breaking down of their relationship will do no great harm, since ordinarily each party will soon find a new party to deal with. Therefore, the ordinary judicial method, with its retrospective approach, does not seem inadequate. Whether traditional judicial methods should be applied within the field of labor relations is another matter. The parties to a collective agreement cannot take the view of the businessman looking for a new party to deal with. They have to continue their relations if they are going to survive. To them the question whether a rule is feasible when applied to situations arising in the future is a matter of great importance. The individual employee is in a position between that of a businessman and that of an organization of the labor market. He may have a great moral interest in the continuation of his employment relationship. Discharge and looking for a new job is, however, an alternative that might be contemplated. The conclusion would seem to be that it would not be so bad to apply traditional judicial methods to individual claims as to apply them to disputes which are of fundamental importance for the relations between parties to collective agreements.

IV

THE SETTLEMENT OF LABOR DISPUTES IN ITALY

by Gino Giugni

*Professor of Labor Law and
Director of Advanced School of
Labor Law, University of Bari, Italy*

1.
INTRODUCTION

THE COLLEGI DEI PROBIVIRI

1. The evaluation of contemporary procedures for the settlement of labor disputes on rights in Italy is possible only if we pay some attention to the developments that have taken place since the end of the nineteenth century. An historical knowledge of the growth of legal institutions is always useful, but in the case of Italy it is essential. As we shall see later in this essay, the past still lives in our intitutions of the present.

In 1893 the first statute on special procedures for the settlement of labor disputes was enacted. And this first step was successful—much more so than subsequent pieces of legislation. The statute provided for the creation of special, tripartite bodies, the *Collegi dei Probiviri*, to be established by royal decree on a local basis and for each branch of industry, but only when deemed necessary. This provision gave the whole system a high degree of elasticity—the network of *Collegi* grew with the economic development of the nation. The *Collegi* were modeled after the French and Belgian *conseils de prud'hommes*. At that time French law had a strong influence on Italian law; in fact, the Italian Civil Code itself was based on the French Civil Code.

The most distinctive feature of the *Collegi* was their composition. The president was appointed by the king from among members of the judiciary (in most cases), or he was chosen from among laymen who had special qualifications. The members, who varied in number, were elected by separate caucuses of workingmen and industrialists. The "jury," the decision-making body of this machinery, always consisted of four members in addition to the president. After 1918, elections were replaced by appointments; the judiciary appointed members from a list which contained twice as many candidates as required, nominated by labor unions and employers' associations.

The *Collegi* had jurisdiction only over disputes involving factory or "manual" workers *(operai)*. For clerical and technical employees special *Commissioni per l'impiego privato* were established in 1923, and for agricultural workers a similar system was introduced in 1917.[1] The *Collegi* functioned generally as conciliation authorities in all kinds of disputes, those over interests included, but action in the latter kind was rarely taken. The *Collegi*'s activities over rights, by contrast, were highly important. They acted through the "jury," and their jurisdiction was limited to claims not exceeding the value of L.200. It must be remembered, however, that this amount was far more than today's limit on claims handled by the *Pretori* (up to L.750,000, almost $1,200) because of the currency values and low incomes of that time.[2]

Procedural rules were also simplified as compared with those laid down for the civil courts, which were based largely on written evidence and written briefs of defense. The parties had to plead either in person or through a family member or a member of their respective "class" (worker or industrialist), but the employer could also be represented by one of his clerical employees. The claim could be presented orally and briefs were prohibited. The decision had to be rendered according to principles of equity, that is, without the observance of *strictum jus*. It could be appealed to a court, but only on grounds of lack of jurisdiction or similar irregularities. An appeal on the merits of the decision would not have been permitted.

According to statistics collected at the time, the number of *Collegi* established and decisions rendered was very high, but it is not necessary to report details here. It is safe to say that this piece of legislation is a rare example of far-sighted state intervention; it is all the more remarkable because it was passed before the industrialization of Italy and at a time when the labor movement was in its very beginning. An important development deserves special attention: At the time when the *Collegi dei Probiviri* operated, there was no statute that covered the contract of employment. The *Collegi*, and the other institutions mentioned above, in fact *created* that law by deciding the cases according to principles of equity. A young lawyer, Enrico Redenti, who was to become one of the most distinguished Italian jurists, was asked by a government agency to prepare a systematic survey of the decisions. His *Massimario della Giurisprudenza dei Probiviri* (A Survey of Probiviri Decisions) was published in 1906 and is considered a basic step in the development of labor law. In the years following, many more

---

[1] Similar institutions were operating in the rice plantations (1907) and in the municipal transportation industry (1923).

[2] See comment in L. Ventura, "Giudice del lavoro, processo del lavoro e crisi della giustizia," in *Rivista giuridica del lavoro* (1964), I, p. 139.

surveys were published in order to provide guidelines for members of the *Collegi* and for the parties to a dispute. They contributed significantly to the establishment of uniform trends in rendering decisions. Thus, the law concerning the contract of employment developed gradually as a combined achievement of case law on the one hand and legal literature, which displayed a high level of scholarship at that time, on the other.

THE MAGISTRATURA DEL LAVORO

2. The *Collegi dei Probiviri* were active until 1928. Two years earlier, the Fascist regime had established the so-called "corporate system." Under that system the unions, but only those loyal to the government, were to be recognized as public agencies. Collective agreements became binding upon all employers and employees in the industry or professional category covered by them. Strikes and lockouts were prohibited, and a special jurisdiction, the *Magistratura del Lavoro*, was appointed within the judiciary to issue binding decisions in collective disputes. Needless to say, the *Collegi dei Probiviri* could no longer persist in this state-dominated system. They were abolished and their jurisdiction was transferred to the ordinary civil courts, although subject to special rules of procedure.

The principles underlying these rules deserve some attention because they were incorporated into the Civil Code in 1942 and extended to all civil matters. At that time civil procedure in Italy was based largely upon written defense and evidence. It was strictly regulated by the "principle of disposition," according to which the parties to a conflict were free to dispose of the matter, which made them masters of the process. The judge had almost no power to direct the proceedings. He was bound to follow the initiative of the parties, and even his powers in the search and evaluation of evidence were restricted. In 1928, and again in 1934, this procedure was revised, but only with respect to labor disputes. The new procedure was considered a testing ground for new principles that were to be extended later to the whole field of civil claims (this was actually done). Among its basic features it provided for partial acceptance of the principles of "orality, immediacy, concentration and free evaluation of evidence," called by leading proceduralists the fundamental items of legislative reform.[3] The powers

---

[3] See M. Cappelletti and J. M. Perrillo, *Civil Procedure in Italy* (The Hague: Martinus Nijoff, 1965), p. 43. This book is an outstanding guide to Italian civil procedure and procedural doctrine. See also M. Cappelletti, J. H. Merryman, and J. M. Perrillo, *The Italian Legal System, an Introduction* (Stanford University Press, 1967), p. 131.

of inquiry of the courts were somewhat enlarged, an attempt at conciliation was made compulsory, and delays between the various steps of the procedure were shortened. Finally, unions and employers' associations were enabled to represent the parties in the proceedings.

The speedy procedure before the *Probiviri* was thus replaced by a new system that was certainly more effective than the one established in the Code of Civil Procedure, but with respect to labor disputes it was a step back towards the restoration of formalism. Also, judgment according to principles of equity was repealed and the courts in deciding labor matters had to abide by the strict rule of law. On the other hand, a statement of policies, the *Carta del Lavoro* (Labor Charter), subsequently implemented through numerous collective agreements with general binding force, filled the gap in statutory regulations on which the *Probiviri* had built their case law.

An important feature, which has persisted until now, was the granting of exclusive appellate jurisdiction to the court of appeals sitting as *Magistratura del Lavoro*. In civil matters the court of appeals exercises its screening power only on judgments reached by courts of the first instance, that is, judgments rendered by a *Tribunale*, which itself reviews decisions of a *Pretore*, a lower-court judge. The exception introduced for labor disputes was based on the alleged expediency of giving appellate power over individual disputes to the same court that had jurisdiction over collective disputes. Moreover, given the alleged importance of the appellate decision from the standpoint of the corporative principle, the public prosecutor was required to render his conclusions on the dispute, another feature that has persisted to the present time. (However, he could not go beyond the scope of the dispute.) Finally, the court of appeals, sitting as *Magistratura del Lavoro* in collective disputes, was specially composed to include laymen (two, vis-à-vis three professional judges) in the adjudicating body. These men were appointed as "experts" from among candidates nominated by unions and employers' associations. They had to have academic degrees or "a special expertise," and this requirement, of course, served to deprive labor of representatives with genuine class links. In individual disputes, two laymen whose qualification requirements were less restrictive could sit beside the professional judges. However, in the absence of a request by either party their appointment was not compulsory and became increasingly less frequent until, as was officially admitted,[4] it was completely discontinued.

---

[4] See Report to the King, *Code of Civil Procedure*, 1940, n. 3.

3. Special attention must be given to arbitration. Prior to 1928, arbitration clauses for the settlement of individual disputes were not infrequently incorporated into collective agreements, primarily when a *Collegio dei Probiviri* had not been established within the territorial or occupational application of the agreement. In this manner, the arbitration procedure supplemented the statutory structure. The Act of 1928, in order to prevent any possible reestablishment of adjudicating bodies other than the judiciary, also provided that any arbitration clause of a collective agreement be declared void. Finally, in the Code of 1942 an extreme position was adopted on this matter: Any agreement of submission to arbitration, even though directly negotiated between the parties to the contract of employment, was declared void. Thus, arbitration disappeared from the scene and the effects of this legislative policy, as we shall see, have partially persisted to the present time.

The need to circumvent the strict rule that all disputes were to be handled by the judiciary was, however, perceived. First of all, the organizations of the two opposing parties acquired by statute an outstanding role as screening agencies. All disputes had to be reported to them before suit could be brought in court, and the two organizations had to attempt conciliation. A suit could be initiated only after failure of conciliation or after the expiration of a fixed period of time from the day the claim was first reported to the organizations. The screening procedure was rather effective; it became so well-rooted in the system that even today the idea of a compulsory attempt at conciliation prior to legal proceedings is embraced by lawyers and policy-makers alike.

From this conciliation role of the unions and employers' associations stemmed what may be considered the most significant attempt to escape the strict logic of the system—to wit, the establishment in 1937 of a special jurisdiction for disputes concerning piece-rate work, the *Collegi tecnici per i cottimi industriali,* which were in many aspects remarkably similar to the *Collegi dei Probiviri* and even more to the arbitration panels. They were composed of representatives of the two opposing organizations in equal number and a chairman who was appointed by the organizations from among the state labor inspectors. A similar structure was established for the *Collegi tecnici per le qualifiche,* which were created two years later as fact-finding bodies in disputes over the recognition of the status of *impiegati* (white-collar workers.) Within the corporate state and its centralized structure, significant trends of a centrifugal nature emerged, which were undoubtedly given impetus by the facts of industrial life. But the piece-rate agencies, which had full power to render decisions and were truly a specialized jurisdiction, were finally suppressed by the Code of 1942.

THE CODE OF CIVIL PROCEDURE OF 1942

Although promulgated under the Fascist regime, the Code of Civil Procedure of 1942 proved to be a piece of legislation with a sound technical basis and very few concessions to the Fascist ideology. A man who contributed much to its sophistication was the distinguished Professor Piero Calamandrei, whose hostility to the regime was rather well-known. He was destined to become one of the "fathers" of the democratic constitution of Italy within a few years. According to Fascist ideology, it would have been desirable to enlarge the powers of the judges in order to make civil procedure truly an instrument of realizing "the will of the state" in adjudication; the pattern, this time, was set by the recent reform of civil procedure in Germany. It was for this reason that the jurists who prepared the Code decided to withdraw some of their original recommendations, but they still desired—although for different reasons—to extend judicial powers in legal proceedings and to restrict the powers of disposition of the parties involved. The main purpose was to establish a quicker, more informal procedure based upon oral pleas and direct contact between the judge and the parties, and to restrict firmly the use of written briefs (principle of orality). Although there were many compromises,[5] the final result of these efforts was a modern, systematic, clear Code, written as an outstanding textbook of civil procedure. However, it did not work.[6] The area of compromise between old and new principles was perhaps too large; it left too much room for conservative forces that were able

---

[5] Cappelletti and Perrillo, *op. cit.*, pp. 41, 44. "The scholars had fought for greater judicial power, but they had hypothesized such power in a free society with an objective judiciary.... In an earlier day, they had fought for judicial discretion; now, they defended the 'principle of legality' as a bulwark against judicial prejudice." See also my review of this volume in the *UCLA Law Review* (1964), vol. 13, p. 482. An interesting document is the speech of Minister of Justice Dino Grandi before the Senate on May 12, 1940. The extension of the judicial power was justified in light of the authoritarian principles of the regime, but as a measure against slowness of procedure as well. At any rate, the Minister warned that the principle of inquisition (independent judicial investigation) had not been fully endorsed; as a matter of fact, it was accepted only to a very limited extent.

[6] See Cappelletti and Perrillo, *op. cit.*, p. 45. "Although the Code proclaimed the principle of orality, it failed to provide the machinery required for it. Neither the court nor the parties were given adequate discovery powers.... The principle of free evaluation of evidence was also proclaimed, but vitiated by the many exceptions carried over from the Code of 1865." More enlarged were, however, the powers of the judge in labor matters. (See chap. 2.)

to counteract the quest for the "new." These influences of conservatism were largely related to the general conditions under which the new Code was implemented.

In the first place, the Code was enacted at the worst possible time—during World War II. In the second place, the criticism of "doctrinairism," voiced by practitioners of law, was certainly justified because the new Code had not brought about the much needed reform of the judiciary.[7] It had considerably extended the task of the judges; they no longer had simply to wait for the parties' briefs and study them; instead, they had to get in touch with the attorneys and pursue the development of the case with them step by step. Also, the workload of the "chancellors," the court clerks who had to prepare written proceedings and keep the records, had increased. But the number of judges and chancellors remained stable for a long time; while litigation increased,[8] court personnel remained inadequate. Therefore, the actual application of the new Code was made possible only by a number of practical steps: hearings became a sheer formality and the written procedure was practically restored; before some big tribunals that handle a large number of claims, even the witnesses were customarily heard by the attorneys of the parties, who then prepared written proceedings and had them signed by the judge. And, of course, the average duration of a law suit increased as the intervals between successive hearings became longer and longer.

Thus, the new Code cannot be called a successful achievement, although few would not acknowledge the good intentions of the legislators. Nobody except a few old-fashioned attorneys wished for a return of the pre-1942 Code, especially after amendments were passed in 1950 to make the new system more flexible.

As was anticipated, the 1942 Code, in a narrow sense, brought about a substantial merger of civil procedure with the special procedure for the settlement of labor disputes. Some basic features of the latter were

---

[7] This need was pointed out by the Minister of Justice in his speech of May 12, 1940. (See n. 5 *supra*.)

[8] This assertion might be misleading. As a matter of fact, total litigation, in spite of the tremendous increase in population and national income, has considerably declined in absolute numbers in sixty years (from 2,315,638 cases annually on the average between 1896 and 1900 to 461,147 annually on the average between July 1, 1964 and June 30, 1965). But the reduction in litigation applies only to the lowest court, the *Conciliatore*, who is a single lay judge with jurisdiction over cases involving a value below L.50,000 ($80). The number of such cases has declined from 1,994,134 to 45,396 over the same period of time. Conversely, suits initiated in courts composed of professional judges (the only ones who have jurisdiction in labor disputes) have increased, albeit slightly, from 321,504 to 415,751. The decline of the ratio of litigation to population is, however, remarkable.

extended to civil procedure, but a few specific rules were laid down, which will be described in chapter 2. What must be said now is that the last vestige of laymen's participation in the adjudicating bodies—at the time restricted to the courts of appeals—had disappeared. It was not carried over into the new Code, and consequently all of the courts were now composed of professional judges only.

2.
LABOR DISPUTES IN CIVIL PROCEDURE

LABOR DISPUTES BEFORE THE CIVIL COURTS

1. The Code of Civil Procedure deals separately with individual and collective disputes. According to the well-known distinction between disputes over rights and those over interests, collective disputes fall into two categories: those over the interpretation of an existing collective agreement (or of a statute), and those over the making of a new one. As we have seen, the submission of disputes over interests to compulsory adjudication was consistent with the principles of the corporate state. But related provisions of the Code, although not explicitly repealed, are no longer considered to be in force because of their apparent contradiction to the principles of free collective bargaining guaranteed in the constitution of 1948. By contrast, a judicial decision of disputes over rights, even though collective, would not violate the principle of the freedom of trade unions. In fact, this is established procedure in many democratic nations and it would appear to be a useful means of settling disputes involving a large number of employers or employees according to a uniform standard. However, under the Italian Code "collective" action could be initiated only by the recognized unions, the only ones existing when the Code was enacted. But since there are no recognized unions in Italy today the whole procedure is inapplicable.[1] As a most significant consequence, the only disputes falling under the jurisdiction of civil courts are individual disputes. Although they may actually concern the interpretation of a collective agreement, the court's decision is binding only for the single case, and the judicial interpretation of a collective agreement, or a statute, may vary from

---

[1] Labor unions and employers' associations have the same *status* of "nonrecognized associations" (ARTS. 36–40 of the Civil Code). They are not legal persons but, according to the provisions just mentioned, may be parties to the proceedings through their presidents or directors; the liability for social obligations is borne by the common fund and by the personal property of the president or director. The

one case to another. In other words, a dispute may, in fact, involve a collectivity of employees or employers, but suit in court can be brought only if it is split up into a definite number of individual claims even though these may be identical. Of course, collective disputes over the interpretation of the terms of a collective agreement, or of a statute, still arise, but in this quality they are unknown to civil procedure.[2]

2. Now we come to individual disputes, which will be discussed extensively. Individual disputes, which fall under the jurisdiction of the civil courts and the special procedure laid down by ARTICLES 429–457 of the Code of Civil Procedure, may concern the following:

(a) Employment relations that are or may be covered by collective agreements. This restriction has lost much of its importance because collective agreements are always possible, except when the employer is the state or a public agency not engaged in an economic activity (see (c)). Even domestic servants, it is generally admitted, may now be covered by collective agreements despite a prohibition in ARTICLE 2068 of the Code of Civil Procedure. However, disputes involving domestic servants usually are considered the major exception.[3]

(b) Labor relations in agriculture, except employment relationships such as sharecropping. Since 1945 most of these disputes have been referred to special sections of the courts, which sit with the participation of laymen.[4]

(c) Employment relations in public agencies, which could be members of employers' associations under the corporative system. This provision has lost its basis because the capacity of membership in an

---

law speaks of "legal subjects" who are not "legal persons," yet are distinct from the members of the organizations. See Ghezzi, *La responsabilità contrattuale delle associazioni sindacali* (Milan: Giuffre, 1963).

ARTICLE 39 of the constitution of 1948 provides for "recognition" of unions and employers' associations as legal persons, but this principle was never implemented by the legislature. See Gino Giugni, "The Legal Status of Collective Bargaining in Italy," in Otto Kahn-Freund, ed., *Labour Relations and the Law* (London: Stevens & Sons, 1965).

[2] Some practical arrangements were worked out for these disputes. See chap. 2, sec. 16.

[3] For an account on this issue, see Pera, "Sulla risoluzione delle controversie individuali di lavoro," in *Rivista trimestrale di diritto e procedura civile*, 1967, p. 205.

[4] For a brief account, see Cappelletti and Perrillo, *Civil Procedure in Italy*, p. 71. It is useful to remember that, with respect to these particular sections, the Constitutional Court ruled the participation of laymen to be constitutional, provided it is guaranteed that the manner of selecting the judges assures their independence from the nominating bodies.

association is no longer legally designated. After long debate, the courts finally agreed to include under this heading public agencies engaged in economic activities if they did not hold a position of legal monopoly. However, in cases in which this position of monopoly was at least questionable, statutory provisions have put these public agencies under coverage of collective agreements and thus have extended to them the jurisdiction of the ordinary courts.[5]

(d) Employees of the state or of public agencies who, by law, are not covered by other jurisdictions. The practical importance of this last provision amounts to almost nothing.

When the jurisdiction of the ordinary courts is excluded, as under items (c) and (d), the disputes are decided by administrative courts which have jurisdiction over public employees *(Consiglio di Stato)*. When a contract of employment does not fall within the range of item (a), the civil court retains jurisdiction but does not follow the special procedure for labor matters. As already stated, this happens in only a very few cases.

STRUCTURE OF THE CIVIL COURTS

3. Because individual labor disputes fall under the jurisdiction of civil courts and, in principle, under the same rules of procedure established for civil matters, a brief account of the essential features of civil procedure appears to be necessary. In this connection, we shall point out significant special rules laid down for labor matters. We shall first describe the structure of the court system and the distribution of jurisdiction among its various branches.

Aside from the Constitutional Court, courts are established at five levels.[6] The *Conciliatore* (conciliator) is a lay judge who sits as the court. (His position may be compared to that of a justice of the peace.) The court's competence is limited to claims not exceeding the value of L. 50,000 ($80). Under Fascism the policy of assigning labor disputes to courts composed of professional judges resulted in the exclusion of such disputes from the jurisdiction of this court; also, its importance has considerably declined over the years.[7]

---

[5] So it is for the National Electricity Board (ENEL, *Ente nazionale per l'energia elettrica,* established in 1962), and for the National Agency for Natural Gas (ENI, *Ente nazionale idrocarburi,* established in 1953). See Pera, *op. cit.,* p. 205, n. 27.

[6] See Cappelletti and Perrillo, *op. cit.,* pp. 69 ff. and pp. 99 ff.

[7] See chap. 1, n. 8. The reasons for this phenomenon are manifold. On the one hand, the decreasing value of the currency has not kept pace with a corresponding increase in the value in disputes assigned to the jurisdiction of the *Conciliatore*.

GINO GIUGNI

The *Pretore* has jurisdiction over claims up to L. 750,000 ($1,200), over possessory and other actions, and, according to a Statute of 1966, over all disputes arising from dismissals. A single professional judge sits as the court. He carries on the entire proceedings according to rules that are somewhat less complicated than those laid down for the higher courts. In labor disputes the role of the *Pretore* is of fundamental importance.

The *Tribunale* is a panel of three professional judges who are competent to decide all other civil cases. It hears appeals from decisions of a *Pretore* except those concerning labor disputes, which can be attacked only in a court of appeals. This questionable exception was established by Fascist legislation for the purpose of concentrating all collective and individual labor disputes in the same court at the second level of the court structure. In large cities a *Tribunale* may be subdivided into sections, one section handling labor disputes more or less exclusively. Judges appointed to such sections may become specialists in labor matters. There are many complaints, however, that the best judges are not assigned to these sections, which, much like in criminal cases, are concerned with factual issues and far removed from the "elegant" legal cases that develop in purely civil claims. A young judge, well-trained in labor law, almost always hopes for assignment to a civil section; thus, the establishment of a permanent body of judges specialized in labor matters is prevented.

The *Corte d'Appello* (Court of Appeals) sits in panels of five judges. Ordinarily it hears cases already decided by a *Tribunale*. In labor disputes its appellate jurisdiction is general, but it, too, has special sections for labor matters. These sections are a vestige of the *Magistratura del Lavoro* (labor courts of the Fascist period); in fact, they are often still called by that name. There are twenty-three *Corti d'Appello* in Italy.

The *Corte di Cassazione* (Supreme Court, in Italy often referred to simply as *Cassazione*), sitting in Rome, reviews questions of law but not of fact or of constitutionality, usually when a decision at the second level is attacked. The most important ground for attack is the "violation of a legal norm." It must be pointed out here that at the present

---

On the other hand, the increase of per capita income brought the value of claims up as well, thereby creating a parallel effect. The numerous minor claims involving property rights have generally declined, and the propensity to litigate, once typical in the country and in villages, has dropped. Today a large proportion of minor disputes concern employment relations, and they lie outside the jurisdiction of this court. Nevertheless, the primary reason for the decline in the number of cases presented to the *Conciliatore* is that persons involved in minor disputes no longer trust the process.

time collective agreements are not considered "legal norms,"[8] but this obstacle is often overcome by appealing on the ground that a norm concerning the interpretation of a contract was erroneously applied (ART. 1362 ff. of the Civil Code). The *Corte di Cassazione* does not have a special section for labor disputes. Although in Italy, as in all other countries of civil law, the precedent is not binding, a decision of the *Corte di Cassazione* very probably will be followed by the lower courts, at least in order to avoid a subsequent possible overruling by the *Cassazione* itself.

The *Constitutional Court* is composed of fifteen judges, a majority of whom are not members of the regular judiciary. It decides on the constitutionality of statutes, but always in relation to an issue raised in the course of proceedings in other courts. If a statute is found to be unconstitutional, it is repealed by the Court itself.

PROCEDURE BEFORE THE TRIBUNALE

4. We shall direct our attention to the procedure before the *Tribunale*. Procedure before the *Pretore* or the *Corte d'Appello* is slightly simpler because of the composition of these courts or the nature of the claims.

Ordinarily a civil suit passes through three stages: introduction, evaluation of evidence, and decision.[9] In the introductory stage, a civil action is initiated by serving the defendant with a citation. The document states the factual and legal bases of the plaintiff's claim and the remedy or remedies prayed for; it also summons the defendant to appear before a *Tribunale*. At that stage, the defendant's plea to the charges is introduced, both parties appear in court, and a magistrate is appointed who will preside over the examination of evidence.

In labor matters, compulsory attempts at conciliation through the "recognized" unions and employers' associations had to be made before suit could be brought in court, but this pretrial procedure was elimi-

---

[8] Collective agreements are not covered by special statutes. They are binding upon the individual employers and employees according to the principle of agency, unions and employers' associations being considered agents and the individual members principals. This construction has often been challenged, but it is accepted by the courts. In 1959–61 the majority of the existing agreements was converted into statutes; therefore, they became binding upon all employers and employees even though they were not members of the organizations. Moreover, a violation of their provisions was subject to attack in *Cassazione*. Agreements concluded afterwards, however, maintained the status of "contracts." For an account of this piece of legislation, see Giugni, *op. cit.*, p. 92.

[9] See Cappelletti and Perrillo, *op. cit.*, p. 145, which was followed almost literally on this page.

nated with the disappearance of the recognized unions. However, the following special rules have remained in force: (a) proceedings before the *Pretore* may be initiated orally, and (b) the parties may appear in person without the assistance of an attorney. Other special rules that are no longer applicable because they refer to "recognized" unions are the following: the possibility of representation by an official of the union or of the employers' association—the representative acting as agent for the party not as substitute for the attorney; the possibility of participation in the proceedings by these unions and employers' associations on behalf of the "category" of employees or employers represented in their status of public law.[10]

There are very few special rules that apply to the introductory stage. Moreover, they are almost never followed in practice and we may say that there is no difference as to how a suit on purely civil or labor matters is introduced.

More relevant differences arise in the second stage—during the examination of evidence.[11] As stated before, Italian civil procedure is governed by the principle of "disposition," which has been somewhat restricted by conferring limited investigative powers upon the examining judge. Of course, the burden of proof lies with the plaintiff, and the decision will be based on alleged facts and evidence. The judge decides on the admissibility of evidence; his discretion is broad, but he must state his reasons. The introduction of evidence through testimony is somewhat more restricted. The judge's powers of investigation consist of his right to extend the area of alleged evidence—e.g., by calling persons to the witness stand who were named in the testimony, by ordering inspection, and, rather important although not frequently used, by ordering the so-called "free" interrogation of the parties (as distinct from the "formal" interrogation requested by one of the parties concerning specific questions and aimed at obtained conclusive admissions). The "free" interrogation is informal; admissions are not conclusive, but the court may draw useful inferences from answers and from the behavior of the parties.

In labor disputes, two very important exceptions are stipulated in the general rules governing evidence: (1) the examining judge can,

---

[10] According to the report to the King by the Minister of Justice (nn. 5, 10), they should have acted as auxiliaries of the court, not as pleaders for the parties. A similar opinion is quoted by Jaeger, "Diritto processuale del lavoro," in *Trattato di diritto del lavoro*, U. Borsi and F. Pergolesi, eds. (Padua: 1960), vol. V, p. 177. (The author can be considered one of the most orthodox commentators on Fascist legislation on the subject.)

[11] See, more extensively, Cappelletti and Perrillo, *op. cit.*, pp. 172 ff.

on his own motion, admit all kinds of evidence on the alleged facts; (2) no restriction is imposed on the admission of testimony as evidence. Of course, the parties still have to submit the facts, but the court is entitled freely to investigate their verity. This is a remarkable deviation from the principle of disposition, although it is infrequently used in practice for reasons to be analyzed later. In addition, the examining judge may suggest that the parties fill in gaps or correct irregularities in briefs and documents—another helpful deviation from procedural formalism (ART. 439). Finally, the free interrogation of the parties should be done whenever possible *(di regola)*.

Attempts at conciliation are not compulsory, but they emerge naturally when the parties are invited to sit down together and informally before the judge. Conciliation plays a very important and vital role in labor disputes, and under statutory law the power of attorney includes the power to agree to a settlement.

5. The case enters the decision stage when it is referred by the judge to the adjudicating panel. The parties have to submit their final briefs, the most important documents which contain a full statement of the facts and reasons in the case. In the hearing that follows, after the examining judge has delivered his report on the case, the parties may argue orally before the panel. Finally, the panel meets and decides the case. The written decision is filed with the clerk of the court within thirty days—a time limit that is only rarely observed. Deliberations are secret and dissenting opinions are not made public. Needless to say, the opinion of the examining judge, who, as a rule, also writes the decision, is very influential if not decisive—one reason why many lawyers question the usefulness of a decision by panel. The judgment is enforceable only if it is not attacked within thirty days; however, the court has the power to order immediate enforcement upon request by one of the parties (ART. 282)—a request that is often made in labor disputes. Of course, in proceedings before a *Pretore*, who is a single judge sitting as the court, the distinction between the second and third stage is less marked and the rules governing decision by panel obviously cannot be applied.

In its decision the court also rules on the payment of expenses. Usually, the losing party has to bear the burden of the other party's expenses, including the attorney's fee, but the court has some discretionary power in this matter. It may deviate from this rule because of various circumstances (ART. 92), and may decide that each party bear its own expenses, a practice often followed in labor disputes when the worker's claim was rejected.

In labor disputes, the hearing before the panel must take place within twenty days from the conclusion of the second stage, the evaluation of evidence. Although the Code intended to expedite proceedings before the court, this time limit is seldom observed because of the heavy caseload of the examining judge. In disputes over piece rates, the time limit is ten days and the decision must be made public at the end of the hearing. In labor disputes, the court may not rule that the losing party pay the attorneys' fees. Furthermore, since 1958 labor suits in which the value is less than L. 1,000,000 ($1,600) are exempt from tax burdens (sealed documents and registration fee), while those over larger amounts enjoy a 50 percent exemption (Law of March 2, 1958, No. 319). The amount of the attorney's fee, as determined by statute, is lower in labor disputes than in civil suits (Law of June 13, 1942, No. 794). Free legal aid may be provided for a party who supplies evidence of being in a "state of pauperism" (Royal Decree of December 30, 1923, No. 3282), and whose claim in all probability will be upheld. Recourse to this form of assistance is rare, however. This is discussed more extensively in sec. 18 *infra*.

6. After ruling out arbitration and the quasi-arbitral procedure established in 1938 for disputes over piece rates, the authors of the Code felt they had to make a few concessions with respect to special procedures in disputes over technical matters. Thus, when a dispute is of "a prevailingly technical nature," the parties can appeal to the court to have the ruling assigned to a "technical expert" or to a panel composed of lay experts from both parties, presided over by an impartial chairman. The decision is rendered according to principles of equity, to wit, without the observance of *strictum jus*. Moreover, in disputes over piece rates "technical" fact-finding may be entrusted to a labor inspector,[12] whose opinion is conclusive in ascertaining and technically evaluating the facts. These two procedures were intended to provide a useful adjustment of the doctrine of unity in jurisdiction to the practical needs of life. But they need not be discussed further because they are never implemented. Once a dispute is referred to a court, neither the parties nor the court are willing to resort to arbitration. Moreover, suits over piece rates, as we shall see, are almost never filed in court.

The procedure before the *Corte d'Appello* is patterned on that before the *Tribunale*. If new facts are presented, the examining judge has to go through the second stage of the case, the evaluation of evidence. But in most cases he will examine the formal propriety of the appeal,

---

[12] See chap. 3, sec. 1.

make an attempt at conciliation, and set a date for the hearing. Unlike decisions at the first level, the judgment of the *Corte d'Appello* is always enforceable; enforcement can be suspended only on application of the parties after attack in *Cassazione*. The one relevant special rule for labor disputes—another vestige of the former system—provides that the public prosecutor must deliver his conclusions at the hearing (ART. 70). In the corporate state this rule was based upon the assumption that an individual dispute, at least when appealed, was relevant to the public interest.

No special rule is established for review in *Cassazione* of decisions on labor disputes, which are handled by the civil sections of that court. Upon finding that an error has been committed in rules governing jurisdiction, procedure, or substantive relationships, the court reverses the existing decision, determines the legal provisions that should have been applied, and remands the case to a lower court for a new judgment. Upon appeal by one of the parties, the *Cassazione* may also suspend the enforcement of a judgment if serious and irreparable harm would result from it. The public prosecutor takes part in this procedure.[13]

OPERATION OF CIVIL PROCEDURE

7. General statistics on civil disputes reflect an irregular movement so far as the number of suits on the docket is concerned:

Year	Suits on the Docket (first level of court structure)
1960	495,585
1961	459,296
1962	439,673
1963	465,403
1964	475,992

Considering that Italy experienced a recession during 1963 and 1964, we may assume that there is a tendency of increasing litigation in periods of economic stagnation. This would seem natural because in such times a great number of breaches of contract, bankruptcies, and layoffs occur. By contrast, however, the number of terminated proceedings has constantly decreased, from 477,909 in 1960 to 401,492 in 1964. The decisions—at the first level and in the appellate courts—have also decreased, from 220,282 to 187,058. Finally, the number of proceedings

---

[13] For a detailed account, see Cappelletti and Perrillo, *op. cit.*, pp. 270 ff.

pending has regularly gone up, from 594,006 in 1960 to 797,375 in 1964. There is only one explanation: When the courts are overloaded the average duration of each proceeding becomes longer, and, at the same rate of judicial efficiency, fewer proceedings can be completed. Unfortunately, the available data include all civil suits, but the trend described is certainly evident with respect to labor disputes although the number of decisions rendered each year seems to be more stable here—nearly 20,000 (20,076 in 1963, including appeals). However, this figure exceeds the number of decisions rendered in 1956, which was 15,825.

The number of labor disputes (excluding those involving social security matters) decided in 1963 by courts at the first level was 16,528, compared with a total of 135,743 civil judgments. The ratio of 12 percent shows the rather high proportion of litigation in labor disputes, surpassed only by the categories of "contracts of sale" and "torts."

8. Some data collected locally for the purpose of this research are more significant. Such data are not always homogeneous and are often based on estimates. Also, statistics at local levels are scarce,[14] and the inquiry had to be carried out mainly through interviews with members of the judiciary. We shall give some account of the organization of the courts and of the number and quality of cases heard by them, classified according to various criteria.

In the Tribunal of Milan, the economic capital of Italy, labor disputes are heard by a specialized section to which ten judges are assigned. Because of the large caseload, the section is divided into two panels so that a case may be heard either by one panel presided over by the president of the section himself or by another panel presided over by the dean of the section. Hearings before a panel take place once a week. Most steps in the proceeding are taken by the examining judges, who hear cases three times a week. In this Tribunal (less often in other tribunals; the judiciary in Milan is among the best organized), the examining judges are also specialized since it is the practice to assign to each of them cases relating to the same industry or professional branch.

Also in Milan three *Pretori,* who are single judges sitting as the court, are assigned to labor disputes. Hearings take place three days a week. The *Corte d'Appello* has a special section for labor matters, a vestige of the *Magistratura del Lavoro.* However, only three judges

---

[14] In 1954 a thorough survey was conducted of a sample of 488 suits brought in the districts of Milan, Turin, and Naples. Although somewhat outdated, it is still of interest because a similar survey has never been attempted. See *Commissione parlamentare d'inchiesta sulle condizioni dei lavoratori,* vol. IX, *Le controversie individuali di lavoro (Camera dei deputati,* 1958), pp. 178-212.

are permanently assigned to labor cases while almost ten rotate among the various other sections. Thus, paradoxically, in the institution that has a permanent, special section for labor matters, there is less specialization in the performance of the task. On the other hand, in the appellate stage presumably less judicial specialization is required since the delicate task of examining evidence usually has already been performed by the lower court.

Now, if we consider the Tribunal of Bari, an important city in southern Italy with some industrial plants and a large university, we find that it has no special section for labor matters. But labor claims are always assigned to the same section—composed of five judges—which *de facto* becomes a "special" section. Here, too, the distribution of claims among the examining judges is made according to the criterion of homogeneity. Hearings before examining judges and before the panel take place once a week. Five *Pretori* are usually, but not exclusively, assigned to labor disputes. The court of appeals has a labor section with six magistrates, but only 60 to 70 percent of the cases involve labor disputes because the section also handles civil matters. On the whole, we find that the idea of specialization has been carried farther in Milan than in Bari.

With respect to the number of proceedings, we find that the *Pretori* of Milan in just one year—1966—handled 3,000 claims. Assuming that there are three *Pretori* handling labor claims, the average caseload for each of them was 1,000. In the *Tribunale* we find the following number of claims per year.

```
1963:  2942
1964:  3803
1965:  4191
1966:  4733
```

Litigation is thus increasing at a quick pace. The average caseload for each examining judge was 430 claims in 1966. In the *Corte d'Appello* the claims have increased at an even faster pace, from 341 in 1963 to 617 in 1966. However, the average load for each examining judge in 1966 was a reasonable 41. As was already pointed out, when a decision is appealed, new examination of the evidence often is not required so that the procedure is much faster.

Again, the situation in Milan is far better than that in Bari where the average caseload of each judge of the *Tribunale* ranges from 700 to 800 claims. In the first half of 1967, the *Pretori* had 182 claims on the docket but handed down only 40 decisions. Unfortunately, more specific data on the number of labor disputes were not available. We know, however, that litigation increased before the *Tribunale* and decreased before the *Pretori* because of the gradual but constant rise in the value of claims—a trend that was stopped in 1966 by extending the jurisdiction of the latter court from disputes over L. 250,000 to L. 750,000 (almost $1,200). The distribution of disputes *decided* by the *Tribunale* and by the *Pretori* is as follows:

	1961	1962	1963	1965	1966
Tribunale	56	104	98	143	197
Pretori	41	53	35	16	11

Although claims decided are only a fraction of those on the docket, their distribution over the years is plausible proof of the trend described.

In Rome, where the labor section handles over 30 percent of all civil suits,[15] an examining judge will have records for 35 to 40 cases on his bench at each hearing. This finding is most significant, for it reveals *prima facie* the poor conditions under which Italian judges have to work. On the one hand, the inevitable consequences are slow proceedings. On the other, it has become impossible to implement the special rules of procedure aimed at granting the examining judge a leading position in the proceedings because it would require more time for discussions with the parties and for study of the merits in each case.

Let us recall that in 1963 slightly more than 16,000 labor disputes were *decided* in civil courts throughout the country (courts of the first instance). Assuming that it takes about two years to reach a decision, we may go back to 1960 and find that at the end of that year nearly 22,000 disputes had been reported to the labor office that had *not* been settled.[16] Since a high proportion of cases brought before a court, as we shall see, are settled either by conciliation or are withdrawn, the total number of cases submitted to the civil courts would have been much larger than the total number of claims reported to labor offices that are not settled and can only be decided in court. This leads to the conclusions that, besides the application of voluntary settlement procedures on which general statistics are not available, the courts are involved in a remarkable amount of litigation, including a large number of disputes that are not reported to conciliation agencies.

9. We now come to the central issue—the time required to complete

---

[15] See Chiucchiarello, *Crisi della giustizia del lavoro nel quadro della crisi generale della giustizia - Il procedimento*, IV Convegno Nazionale dei Comitati di Azione per la Giustizia, Bologna, April 28–May 1, 1967, p. 49.

[16] The labor office conducts attempts at settlement, but disputes are reported to the office on a voluntary basis. (See chapter 3 for more extensive treatment.)

proceedings. The national average of time in litigation,[17] as estimated for 1961, came to 15 months before the *Pretori,* 2 years before the *Tribunali,* and only a little less for cases in appeal; there was a definite trend of increasing time in litigation over the years. In 1956, 38.98 percent of the claims were settled in less than 6 months, but only 25.45 percent were settled in 1963. The highest percentage, 45.72, lies within the range of 6 months to 2 years.[18] Labor disputes and cases involving property claims were found to require slightly more time for settlement than is shown by the national average.[19]

Here again, local samples of time in litigation are more representative of the actual situation, as shown by data collected for the courts in Milan and in Bari.[20] In the Tribunal of Milan the distribution of claims according to the time in litigation, from serving of the citation to rendering of the decision, is as follows (from a sample of 542 claims decided between 1963 and 1966):

up to 1 year	8 percent
1–3 years	65 percent
3–4½ years	25 percent
more than 4½ years	42 percent

(a maximum of 7½ years is on record)

---

[17] See M. Cappelletti, J. H. Merryman, and J. M. Perrillo, *The Italian Legal System, an Introduction* (Stanford University Press, 1967), p. 126, who refer to d'Agata, *Elementi di statistica giudiziaria,* 1963, p. 231.

[18] See C. Castellano, C. Pace, G. Palomba, *L'efficienza della giustizia italiana e i suoi effetti economico-sociali,* Bari, 1968, p. 23.

[19] *Ibid.,* p. 30.

[20] The survey mentioned in n. 14 *supra* yielded the following findings concerning the average duration of labor disputes:

in courts of the first instance	670 days (*Pretori* 474 days)
	(*Tribunali* 702 days)
in courts of appeals	338 days
time elapsed between the two courts	92 days
total	1100 days

This very accurate survey unfortunately was never repeated, and its findings (1954) are now somewhat outdated. It must also be pointed out that areas are included where the time in litigation probably is the longest because of the heavy caseloads; the national average would have been lower.

With respect to the disposition of the claims, the time in litigation was the following:

for claims completely upheld	908 days
for claims partially upheld	1153 days
for claims rejected	1177 days

The conclusions are obvious: The figure obtained for claims upheld indicates that these claims are often less complicated, require less evidence, or do not present difficult legal problems (e.g., a suit for back pay).

Estimates of time in litigation before the Tribunal of Bari show the following:

> 1–2 years   25 percent
> 2–3 years   50 percent
> more than 3 years   25 percent
> (a maximum of 9 years is on record)

In the other courts of these cities the time in litigation is shorter; before the *Pretori* of Milan the average time is almost 13 months, while in the *Corte d'Appello* of Bari 50 percent of the claims are decided within 5 to 6 months. Before the tribunals of both cities the bulk of the cases requires about 2 years in litigation at the first instance.

After the decision is rendered, it usually takes 2 months (sometimes 3 or more) before the judgment is recorded. Because the case must be appealed within 30 days from receipt of the recorded judgment, and assuming that the appeal takes only 6 months, it follows that a claim may be almost 3 years in litigation, including time in appeal. If the judgment of the courts of the first instance is not made enforceable, which is within the courts' discretion, the claimant will have to wait that much longer to get satisfaction. Furthermore, even though the court has ruled the judgment enforceable, it can still be attacked in *Cassazione* where proceedings in civil matters, including labor disputes, last approximately 2 years.

Justice rendered too late is equivalent to justice denied—a well-known truth that may be applied to the present situation in Italy. Labor disputes much more so than civil disputes require a quick decision. The claimant, who is almost always a worker, cannot afford to wait. But also the nature of the claim is often such that a delayed examination of the case may become extremely difficult, for instance, when it is impossible to collect evidence on the spot because the organization of the shop has changed and the court must rely on witnesses, namely on second-hand knowledge of the facts. Besides, as we shall see later, a claim is almost always initiated after the expiration of the employment relationship. All of these circumstances result from, and contribute to, the fact that the lapse of time between the occurrence of the events in the dispute and the decision is extremely long.

The reasons for this lengthy procedure are not peculiar to labor matters. One factor is the small number of judges and clerks, at least in the courts with the heaviest caseloads (proceedings in small courts in the countryside are often much faster). But this is not the only reason, perhaps not even the most important one. The reasonable efficiency of the *Pretori*, at least when compared to that of the *Tribunali*, shows that simpler proceedings before a single judge may be much more effective. The fact of the matter is that the existing procedure allows the parties, particularly the defendant, too many opportunities to delay a decision. The "blight of postponements" is one of the main reasons for lengthy proceedings.

Attorneys fight bitterly over the briefs, but they get along very well when requesting the examining judge to postpone the hearings. They start at the very outset: The defendant is technically required to appear in court and announce his defense 5 days before a date is set for the first hearing, but he *may*, and he almost always does, appear on the day of the hearing so that the plaintiff will need additional time to read the brief of the defense. Consequently a new date for a hearing must be set. As far as the examining judge is concerned, he may welcome an opportunity to have his heavy caseload of the day reduced. The same manipulation happens at subsequent steps. It is "fair" to please an attorney colleague whose brief is not ready and who begs for a postponement; some day the other attorney will be in the same position and will have to ask for a postponement himself. The judges, at least the best of them, will try to expedite proceedings; but overburdened as they are they won't press too hard. Only if they grant a reasonable number of postponements will they be able to study the records prepared for each hearing. And in light of the large number of cases on the docket, the next hearing will be set 2 or 3 months ahead or even longer.[21] The same happens when a hearing before the panel has to be set. Prior to that hearing, the parties have to prepare their final briefs, which is by far the most important aspect of the entire proceedings—much more important than the arguments before the panel, which are often a sheer formality. They will need time because final briefs are usually very long. In its turn, the panel is overburdened with cases as much as is the examining judge, and the date for a hearing will be set as late as possible. The 30-day requirement between completion of examination of the evidence and the hearing, established for labor disputes, is never observed. In light of all these circumstances, it is easy to understand the lengthiness of the proceedings.

10. The frequency of attacks on judgments is a subject closely related to the one discussed above. The rate of decisions of appeals on labor claims seems to be rather stable, although in the long run the trend points to an increase: 2,391 in 1956, 3,420 in 1960, and 3,548 in 1963.

---

[21] According to Art. 81 on "Rules of Implementation of the Code of Civil Procedure," a statute attached to the Code, the time between two hearings should never exceed 15 days. However, in practice this rule is routinely disregarded.

Data on averages for Milan, 1963 to 1966, show the following:

> attacks on decisions of the *Pretori*—40 to 60 percent per year;
> attacks on decisions of the *Tribunali*—30 to 35 percent per year;
> attacks in *Cassazione* on decisions of the *Corte d'Appello*—50 percent.

The higher percentage of attacks on *Pretori* decisions is probably due to two factors: the decisions are less accurate, and the time in litigation is more "normal," that is, the losing party at the time the decision is rendered is still psychologically strongly involved in the case and less prepared to give up. If this is true, it could be inferred that the number of attacks on *Tribunali* decisions is rather low, although it corresponds to the national average (which was 30 percent in 1960).[22] On the other hand, we find that when a dispute becomes lodged in appeal, in one out of two cases it will probably be referred to *Cassazione*, although the national average of attacks in *Cassazione* was much lower in 1960—17 percent.

11. The distribution of claims according to the initiating party shows that in the Tribunal of Milan, out of the sample mentioned above, only 4 percent are lodged by employers, and 5 percent by employees during the life of their contract. Concerning the latter point, which is rather surprising, it must be added that almost all of these claims are lodged jointly by groups of employees either in one suit or in a number of suits filed more or less simultaneously. Data for the courts of Bari confirm this finding, which points to a well-known situation: Actions brought by individual employees during the life of their contract of employment are extremely rare, perhaps between 1 and 2 percent, even in cities such as Milan which has many job opportunities and a sophisticated working class.

The distribution of claims according to economic sectors reveals the interesting fact that inclination to litigation does not correspond to the *ratio* of employment among these sectors. In Milan, out of the sample of 542 claims, 40 percent originated in industry, 40 percent in commerce, and 5 percent were lodged by domestic laborers. Since employment in industry is higher than in commerce, litigation in the courts is supposedly higher in commerce because it offers less stable employment and poorer working conditions (largely in the small shops). Correspondingly, litigation is comparatively lower in industry, a more unionized sector of the economy where many disputes are

---

[22] See Cappelletti and Perrillo, *Civil Procedure in Italy*, p. 256.

settled through union channels. The two explanations are not conflicting.

The distribution is very difficult in Bari, but it validates, to some extent, the above hypothesis: 60 percent of the claims originate in industry, 30 percent in commerce, and 10 percent in agriculture. The less efficient the unions, the higher the litigation in industry. The percentage of claims originating in agriculture is here extremely low and mostly involves disputes over sharecropping. But this lower rate of litigation in court must be expected from a labor force composed largely of day laborers.

12. The distribution of claims in the Tribunal of Milan according to category of workers shows the following: 40 percent were filed by factory workers, 40 percent by clerical and technical workers, 5 percent by foremen, 10 percent by executives, and 5 percent by others. The white-collar workers predominate, even though they are fewer in number employed. This higher inclination to litigation is not surprising for categories of workers who have more social status, but it must also be remembered that they are less organized and use union channels to a lesser extent.[23]

Finally, another analysis may be made involving the nature of the claims. In Milan the largest number of claims concern the following issues:

a) declaration that the employment relationship was based on a contract of employment instead of a contract of (indepedent) services;

b) declaration of the *qualifica*, to wit, the classification of the job, clerical, skilled, etc., which determines wages and working conditions;

c) declaration of the indefinite duration of a labor contract which seems to contain a date of termination (the first alternative being more advantageous to the employee);

d) determination of the minimum wage as guaranteed by ARTICLE 36 of the constitution;[24]

---

[23] In the survey mentioned in n. 14 *supra*, the claims were filed by the following categories of employees: 7 percent by executives, 30 percent by white-collar workers, 7 percent by foremen, and 56 percent by manual workers.

[24] "All workers have the right to remuneration proportionate to the quantity and quality of their work, and in any case sufficient to provide a free and dignified existence for themselves and their families." This provision has been interpreted to mean that if the parties to a contract of employment agreed upon a wage that is apparently too low, the judge may declare that part of the contract void and determine the fair wage himself as though wages had not previously been established. (ART. 2099, Code of Civil Procedure.) The evaluation of "fairness" is usually based on comparisons of wage rates set by collective agreements, even though the latter are not binding in the specific case.

GINO GIUGNI

   e) equality of compensation for male and female workers;
   f) cause of discharge;
   g) severance pay;
   h) determination of the coverage of collective agreements, and many others.

It is significant to note that none of these grounds for disputes except the last relates to labor–management relations; only before a *Pretore* are a few claims lodged involving the legality of a strike or a lockout. Usually they are submitted by individual workers who have been disciplined for participation in an allegedly illegal strike, or who have been deprived of their wages during a lockout. The value in dispute is low in these claims, although they are important as a matter of principle; therefore they are taken before a *Pretore*.

In the courts of Bari, grounds for litigation more narrowly concern the following issues: classifications of the job; wages; overtime; notice of discharge; paid vacations; others. In a less developed economy the predominant type of litigation tends to be based on ambiguous grounds, for example, the classification of the job is not obvious, overtime is requested but not recorded, and wages are kept far below the average level determined by collective agreements—but the employee is not organized.[25] Evidently, it is a difficult task to take evidence and decide these claims.

We call attention to the fact that litigation over piece rates or incentive payment was not mentioned, though these nevertheless are a perennial source of collective disputes. Since such claims arise mostly during the employment relationship and the value in dispute is low, they are never brought to court and are rarely settled outside of union–management channels.

RULES OF CIVIL PROCEDURE

13. It is no exaggeration that the rules laid down for labor disputes are rarely observed in practice. A brief survey will validate this assumption. As pointed out before, some of these rules are considered repealed or not applicable because they concern "recognized" unions and employers' association. But even rules that could be observed often are not applied, so that the "special" procedure for labor disputes has

---

[25] If the employer is not organized—even proving that he is organized is sometimes difficult—the plaintiff applies for the implementation of ARTICLE 36 of the constitution. (See n. 24 *supra*.)

SETTLEMENT OF LABOR DISPUTES IN ITALY

become an almost theoretical concept. The more important "special" rules are the following:

(a) Personal appearance, without representation by an attorney, before a *Pretore*. Almost never have the parties made use of this possibility. If a plaintiff attempted to appear before the *Pretori* of Milan without counsel, he would not be allowed to present his claim and would be requested to name an attorney.

(b) Initial pleas before a *Pretore*, allowed under the Code, are never entered.

(c) Application of the rule concerning the free examination of evidence, by far the most important rule, extends the powers of the examining judge far beyond the principle of free disposition of the parties. According to general opinion, not even this rule has been implemented. During the examination of evidence, judges are never fully apprised of the merits of the case because they restrict themselves to directing the activities of the parties. In this passive position, the judges have only an approximate idea of what evidence to admit, and they cannot take any initiative. It is generally true, however, that in a few cases the extended power to admit evidence is used, though moderately. For example, witnesses not named by the parties are called to testify, or the wording of questions framed by the parties is changed and completed by the examining judge. Therefore, this special regulation on the examination of evidence *might* be implemented if judges had more time to study the merits of the case, and further, if the thinking of judges and attorneys did not adhere so tenaciously to the traditional principle of free disposition of the parties. In the final analysis, this attitude results from their traditional inclination to ignore the exceptions to this principle provided by the Code itself. Undoubtedly, this is a result of merging civil and labor disputes into the same pattern of procedure, and under these conditions exceptions permitted by the statute are surrendered to the preponderant force of the principle.

(d) The special provisions of "arbitration by experts" and fact-finding in piece-rate disputes by the labor inspector were never implemented by the courts. Also, the "technical expert," who is to be appointed by the examining judge to assess the technical aspects of the dispute, is rarely called. Excepting disputes over workmen's compensation or over disability, which often call for an evaluation of the degree of incapacitation of the claimant worker, judges feel that the "expert" is a useless burden, especially in light of the questionable regulation requiring that when an expert has been appointed and has reported to the tribunal, another expert must be appointed and must report to the court of appeals even though the conclusions of the first expert have not been challenged by the parties.[26]

(e) Finally, there is the important rule allowing the court to order the personal appearance of the parties at any stage of the proceedings either for informal interrogation or in attempting conciliation, or, most likely, for both. In the language of the Code, this should be done *de regola* (ART. 440). However, the court "very rarely"[27] orders such personal appearances, even though they could provide the examining judge with additional information of the case as well as with an opportunity to attempt conciliation.

14. An attempt at conciliation in court is not strictly compulsory. When the Code was enacted compulsory conciliation was stipulated for the "recognized unions," and there was reason to require the parties to undergo another compulsory attempt at conciliation before the court. Therefore, this point falls under the general provisions of ART. 185 of the Code of Civil Procedure, according to which such an attempt should be performed by the examining judge in all civil cases when the nature of the dispute makes it expedient. Labor disputes are generally considered to be of this nature, meaning that attempts at conciliation are to be performed as a necessary step of the proceedings. In order to facilitate settlement, the Code provides in ART. 436 that in labor disputes the power of attorney implies the power to agree to a settlement. However, in order to obtain relief from any responsibility, attorneys will often request the parties to sign the agreement or to provide them with special power of attorney. As proof of the great importance attached to judicial settlement, it should be noted that a court order certifying that conciliation has taken place, once signed by the parties or by their attorneys, is enforceable against the defendant, usually the employer, and that conciliation before the court cannot be attacked under the general principle providing that the worker cannot waive his rights. That principle, established by ART. 2113 of the Civil Code, sets forth that any waiver or compromise can be attacked within three months from its occurrence, or from the date of expiration of the contract of employment, if the waiver or compromise occurred during the life of the contract. (The underlying idea is that a com-

---

[26] There is general consensus against this rule. See Pera, "Sulla risoluzione delle controversie individuali di lavoro," in *Rivista trimestrale di diritto e procedura civile*, 1967, p. 211. The same may be said for the rule requiring the intervention of the public prosecutor when the case is appealed (ART. 70), a regulation that cannot be avoided but is considered to be a useless burden. See again Pera, *op. cit.*, p. 209.

[27] Thus, Pera, *op. cit.*, p. 216.

promise most often was brought about by the waiving of rights in some form.)

Therefore, conciliation before the judge is rather frequent although other possibilities for settlement are available to the parties before bringing suit in court, such as compromise through union channels or through the labor office which will be discussed below. However, the following data show that conciliation is not as frequent as it could be.

Out of a sample of 1713 disputes handled by the *Tribunale* of Milan from 1963 to 1966, 31 percent were settled by judgments and 15 percent by conciliation; but 54 percent of the suits were withdrawn. The number of conciliations decreased from 108 in 1963 to 38 in 1966, while the rate of withdrawals remained stable. About 25 percent of the disputes before the *Pretori* were settled by conciliation. In the *Corte d'Appello* conciliation occurs very seldom.

In the *Tribunale* of Bari, only an estimated 20 percent of the suits were withdrawn and, according to interviews of the judges of that court, conciliation is less frequent as well. By contrast, in proceedings before the *Pretori* the inclination to conciliate seems to be higher although withdrawals still predominate. During the first semester of the court in 1967, 182 new suits were filed, but 201 were cancelled in the meantime through conciliation or withdrawal, and only 40 cases were decided.

The percentage of withdrawals is significant but cannot easily be interpreted. According to general opinion, in the majority of suits cancelled because of inactivity of the parties—the usual form of withdrawal of which the courts are rarely officially notified—agreement probably was reached between them. Why do they prefer an out-of-court settlement? Why don't they formalize a settlement through conciliation before the judge, which would have the advantages described above? On the one hand, the parties may wish to avoid paying taxes by settling out of court; on the other, they need not seek enforcement of the agreement by court action if, as so often happens, the employer complies with its terms immediately after it was reached.

Of course, conciliation procedures followed by the judges are not uniform. There is general complaint that the judge does not have sufficient time to study the issue, to press the parties to reach agreement, or even to call for personal appearances. Most often, therefore, he merely invites their attorneys to appear in court, often at the parties' own request. When he plays a more active role he maintains his impartiality and never reveals his attitudes to the parties. This is standard practice in some courts, for example, in the Tribunal of Milan.

The attitude of the attorneys is another important variable. They usually favor conciliation, but there are some who prefer to go through the entire proceedings in order to raise their earnings; they may then become a serious obstacle to quick settlement of the dispute.

A number of the judges interviewed estimated, perhaps with some exaggeration, that as many as 70 percent of the disputes could be settled before the courts if the conditions were different. As a matter of fact, this figure is almost correct if the claims abandoned were to be included—the latter being a phenomenon whose real nature is a matter of unverifiable assumptions.

In conciliations the court should make sure that the worker does not accept an unfavorable settlement because of pressing economic need. But in actual practice little is left of that function of the court, and we may well assume that a large number of settlements in- and out-of-court are accepted by the worker because he cannot, or does not want to, wait from two to three years longer for a judgment, even if his claim is well-founded. It is true that he is assisted by counsel in the conciliation sessions, but the latter often encourage the worker to agree to a settlement because of the time and effort involved in pursuing a case through the courts.

15. The nature of the decisions, of course, does not follow a uniform pattern. The national average is nearly 3 to 1 in favor of the plaintiff in the courts of the first instance; it is 1 to 1 in appellate courts (where the plaintiff may be the employer if he lost in the first instance). In the courts of the first instance of Bari, the ratio of judgments favorable to the plaintiff (almost always the worker) to those favorable to the defendant reveals a striking difference between the two courts. In the *Tribunali* the number of claims rejected fluctuates between 20 and 40 percent, while before the *Pretori* it is as low as 2 to 6 percent. It is difficult to interpret this finding; one reason may be the fact that *Pretori* are generally younger and more sympathetic toward workers. But it must also be taken into consideration that many well-founded claims are abandoned by the worker in *Tribunale* because of the lengthy procedure, and a reasonable compromise in- or out-of-court is preferred. On the other hand, the fact that a claim was upheld does not tell anything about the relationship between the size of the claim and the judgment. A suit often contains many claims, and each of these may be "padded" by the plaintiff, ostensibly for the purpose of establishing a higher basis for a compromise. In its decision, even if it is favorable to the plaintiff, the court almost always reduces the value in dispute by a large amount. Sometimes most of the claim will be rejected and only enough will be granted to charge the defendant with

the burden of court costs, a settlement that the courts benevolently try to achieve whenever possible.

It may be expected that civil courts are more legalistic and conservative in their attitude than specialized courts, but this is only partially true. A survey of the decisions of the last twenty years would prove that labor law has advanced considerably because of court decisions and is at times even blamed for being too liberal in its interpretation of the statutes. However, there is a deep cleavage between lower and higher courts, among the latter especially the *Corte di Cassazione*. Although there is unquestionable evidence of that Court's conservative attitude in many criminal cases, in labor disputes the Court appears to be merely more cautious than the lower courts, and it cannot be said that it is firmly committed to a conservative stand. Rather, Italian courts may be characterized in terms of the German labor courts of the Weimar Republic,[28] namely, they tend to favor the individual worker rather than to enlarge the legal framework of collection action. For example, fairly extensive interpretations in matters of the right to strike[29] were handed down by the Constitutional Court, not by the *Corte di Cassazione* whose judgments were much more restrictive.

Judgments rendered by *Pretori* on the same subject matter are generally more favorable to unions or to collective actions than are decisions of a *Tribunale* or a *Corte d'Appello*. But even these courts, while upholding some restrictions on the right to strike, try to avoid too serious consequences. Workers indicted for sit-down strikes or city traffic policemen indicted for allegedly leaving their posts were released, because the action, although illegal, had been committed without intention, namely in the *bona fide* conviction that it was lawful. The principle laid down in these cases was restrictive, but the judgment was benevolent to the individual worker involved in the action.

Consistent with this attitude is the trend that if a conflict involves an individual and a collective interest, the judge will almost always sup-

---

[28] See Otto Kahn-Freund, "Das soziale Ideal des Reichsarbeitsgerichts" in *Arbeitsrecht und Politik,* Thilo Ramm, ed. (Luchterhand, 1966). No research of this kind was ever made in Italy in any of the branches of civil law.

[29] The only existing provision is Article 40 of the constitution ("The right to strike shall be exercised within the limits of the laws regulating it."). Since no "law" was enacted, the right to strike is unrestricted unless its exercise clashes with public interests guaranteed by criminal sanctions. In the absence of a statutory regulation, the task of finding the limits of a "lawful" strike was eventually assigned to the courts, whose judgments have often been conflicting. See Gino Giugni, "The Right to Strike and to Lock-Out under Italian Law," in *Labour Relations and the Law,* Otto Kahn-Freund, ed. (London: Stevens & Sons, 1965), p. 211. More recently, see Ghezzi, "Diritto di sciopero e attivitá creatrice dei suoi interpreti," in *Rivista trimestrale di diritto e procedura civile,* 1967, n. 4.

port the former. This happens in many cases, for example, when an individual worker claims that a collective agreement is void because it violated statutory regulations by stretching their interpretation for the purpose of winning the case. In such cases the court almost never considers the need for stability in collective bargaining and will often upset an agreement in order to uphold the interests of the individual worker. The same attitude explains the prompt stripping of nonrecognized unions of all privileges granted to the recognized unions, even in civil procedure. And the same reasoning may explain why settlement of labor disputes through union channels is considered to be attackable, unlike conciliation before a court, if a waiver or a compromise had been agreed upon.

Thus, the general attitude of the courts is somewhat paternalistic, and while it is not management-oriented it is not constructive with respect to developing the law of labor–management relations. However, the responsibility does not lie solely with the courts; as was pointed out, the present system recognizes only the individual dispute and ignores collective disputes. Therefore, even union attorneys who represent only individual workers pay no attention to the stability of collective relations and not infrequently initiate action to void collective agreements.

"COLLECTIVE" DISPUTES BEFORE THE CIVIL COURTS

16. Although a collective dispute cannot be submitted to the courts as such, disputes involving a large number of workers do exist and are brought about by two types of action, the "pilot" and the "mass" action. Quite often these disputes are initiated by the legal department of a union, and not infrequently it is the legal department itself that "invents" the claim and induces a sufficient number of workers to sign a complaint and bring suit.

A pilot action may simply consist of a single claim, pursued in the hope of obtaining a favorable judgment or of inducing an employer to change a practice or accept a reasonable compromise. Sometimes a pilot action may be initiated as a mass action by filing numerous claims, but attorneys and judges agree to process only one of them and freeze the remainder through subsequent postponements of hearings. Mass action occurs when identical claims are joined into one suit or when they are submitted to the courts as separate suits. Attorneys prefer the second alternative, because if suits are successful they can charge the losing party fees for each of them. In such cases the courts often have the power to order the parties to join their suits, but they rarely do so—perhaps to avoid dissatisfaction among the attorneys.[30]

The following figures may convey an idea of the importance of this practice in a large city like Milan, where unions and their lawyers are remarkably efficient. It is estimated that about 50 mass actions are filed each year before the *Pretori*, initiated by 20 to 80 claimants for each action. Mass actions are less frequently submitted to the *Tribunali*, perhaps because the value in dispute for each claimant is often low. The total number of plaintiffs over the last five years ranged from 50 to 2,200. In most cases action was initiated by employees of the city's public utilities who have job security. In Bari such actions occur less often, although they are certainly not unknown. On the other hand, a larger number of suits were brought against social security agencies, for example, a case was lodged against such an agency by 2,300 workers.

This technique, which was invented by the attorneys, has met the practical need of solving the dilemma of collective disputes. Although it is certainly not the best solution, it became the only one possible once collective disputes were eliminated from civil procedure. The possibility of filing a collective dispute would be a more economical solution, however. In fact, some authors[31] argue that a union could sue an employers' association or a single employer to obtain a declaratory judgment on the interpretation of a statute or of a collective agreement. But even if this were possible, a judgment would not bind the individual workers who are not parties to the dispute, and who could therefore raise the same issue in another suit. It is perhaps for this reason that actions to obtain declaratory judgments are practically unknown. A serious problem, moreover, may arise when an interpretation question is settled by uniform decisions on a mass action by one court, and the same claim is taken to different courts by various groups of workers, resulting in conflicting and contradictory decisions.

THE ROLE OF UNIONS BEFORE THE CIVIL COURTS

17. Once barred from representing the claimant and from intervening in the proceedings, unions and employers' associations no longer play an official role before the courts, although the examining judge is still

---

[30] Besides, the joining of claims would frequently not be possible because, though based on identical issues, they involve different values in dispute.
[31] See Ghezzi, *La responsabilità contrattuale delle associazioni sindacali* (Milan: 1963), p. 279.

entitled to obtain written information from them that becomes part of the record. However, this loss of power is not considered very significant; the organizations rarely made use of these prerogatives. In individual disputes the unions can still furnish the worker with considerable support through their lawyers, who may be either on the staff of their legal departments or, more often, are professionals who regularly serve one or more unions. It is an almost universal practice not to charge the worker any fee for counsel if the claim is rejected, and to charge that fee to the employer if he loses the case. This practice works well because a union's attorney will always derive reasonable earnings from the large number of cases he handles. Union support is available practically to all workers, members as well as nonmembers. Insofar as nonmembers are concerned, disputes offer a good chance of inducing them to join the union. Of course, they will have to pay dues, but these are very low in Italy and are sometimes paid out of monies received through court action.

Legal assistance is also a source of revenue for the unions, which retain a small percentage of settlements obtained by judgment or by compromise. Moreover, the unions perform an important service in calculating the amount of the worker's claim. Although many claims are "padded" on the basis of unverifiable factual circumstances, they are technically admissible and the judges acknowledge their usefulness.

Thus, the unofficial role of the unions in individual disputes is not negligible, and it is indeed doubtful if they could do more by representing the claimant or by intervening in the proceedings.[32] In this author's opinion, representation of the parties, primarily the worker, would still be important, especially in cases involving questions of principle when the value in dispute is small and the claimant has no desire or interest to continue the proceedings. Intervention at the side of the parties would probably be less useful, because the organizations would almost always duplicate the arguments and conclusions of the individual parties concerned.

COURT COSTS

18. Court costs are generally lower for labor disputes as compared with civil disputes. The usual requirement that all briefs, proceedings, and judgments must be written on special paper to which a seal must be affixed subject to a tax *(carta da bollo)* does not apply, nor is a registra-

---

[32] Jaeger, "Diritto processuale del lavoro," in *Trattato di diritto del lavoro,* Borsi and Pergolesi, eds. (Padua: 1960), p. 180.

tion tax charged on the judgment or conciliation proceedings if the claims do not exceed L.1,000,000 ($1,600). Fifty percent of that tax is charged if the value in dispute exceeds that amount. In the *Tribunali* the claimant worker has to pay from $3 to $6 in advance for judicial fees and services, and from $10 to $20 if the claim exceeds L.1,000,000 ($1,600).[33] Initial costs of cases before the *Pretori* are, of course, lower —not more than $3.

It is difficult to estimate the total cost involved in a claim, but a recent survey found that expenses vary with the amounts in dispute, as shown in table 1.[34]

TABLE 1

Court	Amount of Claim	Nature of Claim	Expenses in Percent of Claim
Pretore	Claims up to $162	Labor matters*	139.8
		general average	170.6
Pretore	Claims above $162	Labor matters	41.3
		general average	60.9
Tribunale	Claims up to $1,600	Labor matters	37.4
		general average	51.5
Tribunale	Claims above $1,600	Labor matters	18.04
		general average	8.44
Corte d'Appello	Claims up to $1,600	Labor matters	64.5
		general average	70.3
Corte d'Appello	Claims above $1,600	Labor matters	1.1
		general average	2.2

* Including Social Security Claims

SOURCE: C. Castellano, C. Pace, G. Palomba, *L'efficienza della giustizia italiana e i suoi effetti economico-sociali*, Bari, 1968.

It appears that costs of a suit involving a small claim are extraordinarily high, amounting to 2½ times as much as the amount of the claim. In addition, as the author of the above survey points out,[35] costs were figured on a sample of judicial decisions and the attorneys' fees assessed by the judges are very often far below the actual amounts of these fees. Finally, the estimated figures show that labor disputes are only slightly less costly than other civil disputes (by a few percentage points), and that in one case they seem to be even more costly.

Of course, the costs are to be paid by the employer if he loses the case, but not necessarily. In cases involving a large amount in dispute

---
[33] Castellano, Pace, Palomba, *op. cit.*, p. 59.
[34] *Ibid.*, pp. 62 ff.
[35] *Op. cit.*, p. 60.

the actual fee of the worker's attorney will be charged to the employer and the worker has to pay the difference between it and the cost assessed by the court. On the other hand, if the worker loses the case his attorney charges a rather low fee, or perhaps no fee at all if his services were provided by a union. Also, according to civil procedure the court may rule that only a fraction of the attorney's fees have to be paid by the worker.

The worker also may have the possibility of applying for legal aid (Royal Decree of December 30, 1923, SECTION 3282). He files an application with a special committee of judges and attorneys, showing that he is unable to bear the expense of litigation and, in addition, that his position is legally tenable *(fumus boni iuris)*. For such applications representation by counsel is required. If the applicant does not name an attorney willing to represent him, the committee will assign a member of the bar to his case. The attorney's fees are payable by the opposing party, but only in case of success. He will not receive remuneration in case of defeat, but the worker will be charged with the fee of the employer's attorney. Resort to legal aid is rare in labor disputes; the procedure is lengthy and the worker seldom meets the qualifications of being "poor" as prescribed by law. But if he does, he may still receive more efficient support from a union, which practically provides the same benefits, as was pointed out above.

3.

VOLUNTARY SETTLEMENT OF LABOR DISPUTES BY STATE AGENCIES

1. At the local level the Ministry of Labor acts through two agencies: the *Ispettorati del Lavoro* (offices of labor inspectors) and the *Uffici del Lavoro e della Massima Occupazione* (offices of manpower and employment). These agencies have offices at the regional and the "provincial" level (the region being a larger territorial unit than the province), which are referred to in the text as labor inspectors and labor offices.

THE LABOR INSPECTOR

The position of labor inspector was established in 1906. An inspector's main duty involves checking that employers observe statutory regulations concerning employment contracts and social security matters if this is their responsibility under threat of criminal sanctions. The inspectors have wide powers of control. If they find a violation of statutory regulations, they may issue an order requiring compliance within a short period of time; if the violation persists, they may report it to the attorney general for prosecution on criminal charges; if the violation is serious, they may immediately report it to the attorney general without issuing an order of compliance. However, their powers are restricted to statutory rules that concern responsibilities covered by criminal sanctions. For example, they cannot act on behalf of a worker who was requested to work more hours per week than agreed upon with his employer, but less than the maximum of the 48 hours prescribed by law. The labor inspectors control the observance of terms of collective agreements only insofar as such agreements have become law,[1] according to the Act of 1959 that established the criminal liability of the employer. Violations usually concern social in-

---

[1] See n. 8, chap. 2.

surance matters, safety standards, rules for the placement of workers by state placement bureaus, employment records, hours of work, and weekly days off.

Labor inspectors do not formally promote conciliation, and it would be misleading to say that they actually deal with labor disputes. Of course, a violation may be reported by a party in the form of a claim against another party,[2] but a violation, by definition, excludes conciliation—a concept that is based on negotiations between the parties. In the areas controlled by the labor inspectors, the parties cannot negotiate over rights; these are matters of public interest, where compromise cannot be reached and full compliance with the law must be assured. Of course, these principles become somewhat diluted in actual practice. Before issuing an order of compliance or reporting a violation to the attorney general's office, the inspector tries to persuade the party to discontinue the violation, at least when it was not intentional or too serious. On the other hand, complaints on matters that do not directly concern him are frequently reported to the labor inspector, for example, a claim against an employer for insufficient compensation not covered in a collective agreement binding on him. The inspector then often attempts to persuade the employer to observe the standard rules on compensation, and he has a good chance of success because employers, for obvious reasons, wish to keep good relations with labor inspectors. In this capacity the labor inspectors play a rather important role in getting employers not bound by collective agreements to observe them voluntarily; thus they may informally promote conciliation.

The role of the labor inspectors, then, is very significant, but more so with respect to removing causes for disputes than to promoting a settlement in the proper meaning of the word. Their activities will not be further described in this study, but the inspectors will again briefly be mentioned in a later section in connection with voluntary settlement procedures, which provide for their appointment as chairmen of conciliation, fact-finding, or arbitration panels. However, they volunteer to serve on these bodies quite apart from their official function as labor inspectors.

THE LABOR OFFICE

2. The role of the labor office in the settlement of labor disputes is

---

[2] In 1964, 36.6 percent of the violations were reported by workers, 43 percent by social security agencies, 13.5 percent by unions or legal aid agencies run by unions, 6.3 percent by labor offices, and 13.4 percent by others (*Ministero del Lavoro, Relazione annuale sull' attivitá dell' Ispettorato del Lavoro*, 1966, p. 39). Only 5 percent were rejected as being groundless.

defined by statute. Labor offices were first established by order of the Allied Military Government after the corporative system was discontinued and some of the functions previously carried out by the recognized unions and employers' associations had to be assigned to a public agency. Established in haste, charged with varied functions, and staffed with randomly selected personnel, the labor offices have not acquired the fair reputation generally accorded the labor inspectors. The offices are established at the regional and provincial level. Their most important duties involve the placement of workers and manpower policies. In addition, the statute states only that they are also charged with the task of attempting to settle labor disputes.[3] The lack of more precise statutory rules of procedure has been filled by administrative practice. Conciliation attempts by the labor offices are not compulsory because the law is silent on that point, nor does it prescribe a time limit for submitting a dispute to conciliation. In 1966, the act on dismissals[4] contained a specific provision, setting forth that the dismissed worker, prior to filing suit, *may* report to the labor office within sixty days. If conciliation is not reached, the parties may submit the dispute to arbitration or, of course, initiate a suit.

"Labor disputes," of course, may be either individual or collective in nature. With respect to the latter, it suffices to say that only conciliation will be attempted; the official assigned to the dispute is not entitled to make formal recommendations. Some disputes are frequently handled for conciliation by authorities other than the labor office. For example, more significant disputes are often submitted to the *Prefetto*,[5] the highest ranking representative of government in the provinces, while disputes of national importance are handled by the Minister of Labor, acting by himself or through his officials. There is no definite pattern of procedure for collective disputes and jurisdictions are frequently overlapping. Within the jurisdiction of the labor offices, collective disputes are often submitted to the regional directors and individual disputes to the branch offices of the province.

Although collective disputes may concern either questions of rights or those of interests, they are handled in the same manner. A dispute over rights taken to a labor office becomes a dispute over interests because it is settled by negotiation rather than by adjudication. Settlement of a dispute over rights may often involve a compromise and sometimes a waiver, but it is still an open question whether such a

---

[3] Presidential Decree of March 19, 1955, n. 20.
[4] Law of July 14, 1966, n. 604.
[5] See Robert Fried, *The Italian Prefect* (Yale University Press, 1963).

settlement can be attacked. By and large, the legal validity of a settlement is more vulnerable if it was not reached with the assistance of a labor office. In the case of individual disputes, the courts reject attacks on settlements negotiated through the labor offices, but judgments with respect to collective disputes do not exist.[6] It goes without saying that the "collective" dispute will have to be split up into individual claims if settlement cannot be reached and suit must be brought in court.

For the reasons outlined above, a conflict over rights will be processed and recorded merely as a collective dispute. Moreover, the subject of negotiation often includes new terms of a collective agreement, as well as the implementation of terms already agreed upon. Therefore, it is not possible to quote any specific data on the frequency of this kind of dispute. The labor offices are often approached in matters relating to mass dismissals, allegedly unlawful strikes, and sit-downs, or new terms of local agreements when negotiations are particularly difficult. But in industries or in locations where unions and employers are more powerful or have more experience in negotiation—largely in the industrial areas of northern Italy—they try to avoid state conciliation and settle the dispute on their own. By contrast, in the agricultural areas of southern Italy the *Prefetto* often intervenes when long strikes occur or when the operation of public services is threatened, and especially when a collective action erupts into violence and riots. But, as stated above, there is no distinct pattern of procedure and much is left to local and personal variables and practices.

In national disputes, e.g., in negotiations of nationwide collective agreements, the parties call upon the Ministry of Labor considerably more often than they consult the labor offices for local matters. A national dispute requires a higher degree of political responsibility of the parties, and conciliation by the Ministry of Labor, who also has political rather than bureaucratic responsibility, proves to be more effective. On the other hand, it may restrict the freedom of the parties for this very reason; the Minister or one of his representatives is not a "neutral" conciliator like, perhaps, the "bureaucratic" labor officer. But the propensity of the unions to resort deliberately to this type of conciliation seems to be decreasing; perhaps it was so frequently used in the past because the unions had weak bargaining power and were always trying to obtain support from the state in order to achieve an agreement. The current trend shows an increase in their bargaining power, and state support is no longer necessary and

---

[6] See sec. 3 *infra*.

may, in fact, be dangerous. For example, it has been the practice of state conciliators to request unions to call off strikes during conciliation sessions, an unwritten rule that the unions had to observe as a precondition for conciliation, but that, of course, they never endorsed and are less and less willing to accept in individual disputes. However, mediation by the Minister of Labor, on his own motion, still is very frequent when the dispute may affect a public interest.

CONCILIATION BEFORE THE LABOR OFFICE

3. Conciliation techniques, both in collective and individual disputes, vary according to local situations and the personal attitudes of the officials assigned to the case. Moreover, the labor offices are overloaded with cases and individual disputes are often disposed of in a single session; sometimes the parties are simply invited to meet in another room and settle their differences. When the labor officer has an opportunity to play a more active role, he may exert most pressure. Since he does not have to render a decision, he may consider it expedient to disclose his opinion of the issue in dispute; he may often be inclined to support the worker's claim because he is not a judge but an official of an administrative agency established to protect the workers' rights. In statistical records, the amount of money "recovered" by workers with his help is pointed out with considerable pride as a major achievement.[7] And when the parties seem willing to arrive at a settlement that would practically constitute a waiver of the worker's rights, he may sometimes try to prevent the latter's acceptance. It was for this reason that the courts, after a period of uncertainty, decided that a waiver or a compromise countersigned by a labor officer cannot be attacked. ARTICLE 2113 of the Code of Civil Procedure sets forth an exception to the general rule of nonwaiverability. If a settlement is reached before a court or before the "recognized" unions and employers' associations, it cannot be attacked. It was deemed acceptable, however, to read the present 'labor offices' in place of 'recognized associations' into the statute because the former were specifically established to replace the latter.[8] On the other hand, the possibility of vacating a settlement reached through union grievance procedures without the participation of public agencies remains an open question. This problem will be discussed in a later section.

---

[7] See sec. 7 *infra*.
[8] See *Cassazione*, Sept. 14, 1956, n. 3211 and others.

4. A date for the conciliation session is set by the labor officer, usually at the request of one of the parties. In collective disputes he may invite the parties on his own initiative, but he will more often urge either the union, the employers' association, or the individual employer to file a formal request. In individual disputes he always acts on the initiative of one of the parties.

Attendance at conciliation sessions scheduled by the labor office is not compulsory and there are complaints that employers, especially owners of small enterprises, do not appear. Although this now happens less often, the demand to apply sanctions against the party failing to appear seems reasonable.[9] A request for conciliation is filed by the individual worker or employer, almost always by the former who is assisted by a lawyer or a union representative. Conciliations through union grievance procedures or achieved before the labor office cannot clearly be separated. The claimant worker is often taken to the labor office by the union itself, either as an additional step to the grievance procedure established in collective agreements or in its place. The latter occurs largely in the less developed areas of the country, where the unions' formal procedures often are not efficient. Moreover, after having reached a private settlement, the parties may submit it to the labor office to have it signed and thus rendered immune to attack. Such requests are often made by employers, who fear subsequent actions aimed at vacating the agreement on the ground that it contained a waiver or a compromise. As a result, conciliation activities through union grievance procedures and labor offices are partially overlapping.

5. The activities of the labor offices are accurately recorded and statistics are published, enabling us to present a rather thorough account of their functions as well as to isolate some points that may serve as a basis for significant tentative generalizations.

Concerning the number of claims, the figure of recorded disputes in the prewar period, when compulsory attempts at conciliation were carried out by the recognized associations of the two parties, was considerably higher than the present figure of conciliation before the labor offices.[10] This is easily explained. Since the reporting of disputes to labor offices is not compulsory, the parties have the alternatives of bringing suit in court or using the unions' grievance procedures for

---

[9] The 1966 act on dismissals failed to establish enforceable sanctions. However, it set forth that the court, in determining the amount of money payable to the worker in lieu of reinstatement (which is not compulsory), will consider the "behavior of the parties," which may include refusal of the employer to appear before the labor office.

[10] See B. Rossi-Ragazzi, *Le controversie individuali di lavoro*, 1940.

TABLE 2

Individual Disputes Reported to Labor Offices Each Year, 1950–1965

Sectors	1950	1955	1958	1960	1961	1962	1963	1964	1965
Agriculture	24,295	13,372	8,499	7,162	6,274	5,256	4,695	4,615	4,426
Industry	36,536	34,365	28,606	28,879	26,311	24,856	23,976	26,057	24,675
Commerce	9,557	9,916	10,701	10,457	9,692	9,721	8,872	9,252	8,933
Banking and Insurance	223	125	105	177	161	144	107	161	169
Others	2,257	3,618	3,966	4,916	5,408	4,813	5,323	5,836	6,362
Total	72,868	61,396	51,877	51,591	47,846	44,790	42,973	45,921	44,565

SOURCES: R. Purpura: "I conflitti di lavoro in Italia," in *Rassegna del lavoro*, vol. IV, n. 10, October 1958, p. 1693.

F. Volpe: "La conciliazione delle controversie individuali di lavoro," in *Rassegna del lavoro*, vol. XIII, n. 5, May 1966, p. 7.

voluntary settlement. As was stated before, the number of suits taken to the courts exceeds the claims submitted to the labor offices. Therefore, the latter cover only a portion, though a significant one, of dispute settlement in labor matters.

TABLE 3

Percentage of Disputes According to Sectors of the Economy

Sectors	1940	1951	1955	1960	1965
Agriculture	20	20	22.0	14	10
Industry	70	60	56.5	56	55.4
Commerce	6	10	16.1	20	20
Others	4	10	5.4	10	14.6
Total	100	100	100.0	100	100.0

SOURCES: B. Rossi-Ragazzi "Le controversie individuali del lavoro," 1940; G. Stagnitta: "Nuovi dati sulla litigiosità nel rapporto di lavoro," in *Rassegna di statistiche del lavoro*, May-June 1959, p. 122.

The number of claims has been decreasing, although there was a slight increase in 1963 and 1964 because of an economic recession. It must also be taken into consideration that the statistics cover the years of postwar recovery—years of economic adjustment, of social and political unrest, and of splits in the labor movement. Moreover, there was a large backlog of claims from the war years that was gradually finding its way to settlement. But the decrease is so remarkable and constant that it must be explained by other reasons, and the distribution of claims according to economic sectors offers a basis for an hypothesis.

Claims originating in agriculture have decreased by 80 percent in 15 years, certainly a by-product of falling employment in that sector. However, employment in general has increased, particularly in industry and in the services. But claims originating in industry show a declining tendency as well, and there are two possible explanations: First, the workers who improved their working conditions by migrating from the agricultural, depressed South into the industrial, expanding North have had fewer claims to report. Second, the more efficient grievance procedures of the unions have taken over a considerable portion of pre-court and out-of-court litigation. The decrease of cases involving the application of collective agreements or payment of wages owed (see table 10 *infra*, p. 298) confirms that the change that occurred in the structure of the labor force, together with an improvement in management practices, has contributed to the decline in claims. On the other hand, the increase of disputes in the "Others" category, originating in such areas as professional establishments (medical offices, law firms, etc.), pharmacies, private educational institutions, domestic labor and laundries, confirms the latter hypothesis because these areas show a very low degree of unionization. Likewise, some statistics of the Labor Office of Bari indicate a decline in disputes reported to labor offices after 1963—from 1054 in 1963 to 642 in 1965—together with a sharp increase in cases settled through the unions' grievance procedures—from 62 in 1963 to 211 in 1965 and even more in 1964. Thus, our conclusions do not seem arbitrary.

TABLE 4

Regional Distribution of Disputes for the Years 1955, 1960, 1965

Regions	1955	1960	1965
Piemonte	3,321	186	94
Val d'Aosta		3,755	4,081
Lombardia	8,114	9,314	8,851
Trentino Alto Adige	1,766	364	1,370
Veneto	3,380	3,216	2,796
Friuli Venezia Giulia	399	1,122	1,337
Liguria	2,907	3,230	2,864
Emilia Romagna	2,956	3,446	3,119
Toscana	2,551	2,536	2,441
Umbria	622	1,136	871
Marche	2,701	1,706	1,364
Lazio	2,360	4,438	5,363
Abruzzo Molise	3,704	2,443	1,759
Campania	3,645	3,881	3,534
Puglie	7,468	3,612	2,530
Basilicata		1,097	651
Calabria	3,848	2,248	1,398
Sicilia	9,088	7,848	5,218
Sardegna	1,545	1,670	492
Total	61,396	57,308	50,133

6. The distribution of disputes according to geographical regions supports the conclusions presented in section 5. Table 4 shows a definite trend towards fewer disputes in regions with a high ratio of agricultural labor, all of which experienced a decline in employment accompanied by considerable migration of workers to industrial regions. This trend is especially evident in the islands and in southern and lower-central Italy, in Calabria, Puglie, Basilicata, and Abruzzo Molise. The region of Campania, where Naples is located, is an exception; but it must be remembered that Naples is a highly industrialized city whose workers traditionally have been strongly inclined to litigation. Industrial regions such as Piedmont and Lombardy show a trend toward increasing litigation. In Lazio the same tendency is largely

the result of the huge migration of workers to the nation's capital, where they are mostly employed in the service industry and the building trades and where their employment is often precarious. Many factors, therefore, affect the amount of litigation, but the change in the composition of the labor force from agricultural to industrial employment appears to be the most significant.

TABLE 5

Regional Distribution of Disputes Reported to Labor Offices in 1965

Regions	Agri-culture	Industry	Com-merce	Insur-ance	Others	Total
Piemonte	358	2,518	721	8	416	4,081
Valle d'Aosta	4	61	22	–	7	94
Lombardia	708	5,564	1,173	25	1,381	8,851
Trentino Alto Adige	96	555	533	2	184	1,370
Veneto	182	1,552	684	9	369	2,796
Friuli Venezia Giulia	12	596	539	3	187	1,337
Liguria	52	1,672	750	8	382	2,864
Emilia Romagna	691	1,492	542	20	358	3,119
Toscana	266	1,196	536	18	435	2,441
Umbria	237	410	88	–	136	871
Marche	397	629	193	5	140	1,364
Lazio	228	2,968	1,505	23	639	5,363
Abruzzi Molise	192	1,140	241	2	178	1,759
Campania	74	2,368	672	11	409	3,534
Puglie	388	1,337	484	2	319	2,530
Basilicata	127	355	25	29	115	651
Calabria	316	602	198	4	278	1,398
Sicilia	622	2,575	1,070	23	928	5,218
Sardegna	87	219	92	3	91	492
Total	5,043	27,815	10,068	185	7,022	50,133

The ratio of claims to employees in the labor force according to regions and economic sectors is shown in table 6. Although the net percentage for agricultural employment included in column 3 of that table is not available, agricultural regions rank higher in litigation than industrial ones. But it is interesting to note that claims originating in industry are proportionately much higher in southern Italy than in the northern regions, while the percentage of disputes originating in commerce is by and large uniform except for local variations clustered primarily in smaller regions and in such large ones as Lazio, Sicily, and Liguria. It may thus be concluded that litigation in less developed areas occurs more often, even in industry, because of less favorable working conditions and a higher proportion of "weak" industries such as the building trades. Other deviations from the general average per-

TABLE 6
Ratio of Claims to Labor Force, 1965*

Regions	Industry	Commerce	Other
Piemonte	3.16	3.27	4.42
Val d'Aosta	3.59	3.60	3.00
Lombardia	3.24	2.58	6.51
Trentino Alto Adige	6.83	10.27	9.79
Veneto	3.20	3.46	4.33
Friuli Venezia Giulia	4.22	8.12	4.86
Liguria	7.60	6.14	4.22
Emilia Romagna	3.12	2.71	3.79
Toscana	2.70	3.07	4.68
Umbria	6.23	3.00	8.81
Marche	11.2	3.61	5.43
Lazio	10.48	7.58	5.84
Abruzzo Molise	13.45	4.38	7.79
Campania	8.51	3.95	4.16
Puglie	8.02	4.26	5.78
Basilicata	14.01	1.73	20.00
Calabria	8.12	3.44	9.43
Sicilia	12.81	7.01	10.69
Sardegna	3.01	1.71	3.95
Total	4.72	3.72	5.78

* $\dfrac{\text{Claims}}{\text{Labor Force}} \times 1000$

centages may be easily explained. For example, the high frequency of litigation in Liguria, both in industry and commerce, is a result of local economic hardships.

7. The statistical records indicate that the service of the labor offices in the settlement of individual disputes apparently is rather efficient. The ratio of disputes examined to those reported is about 89 percent per year. Table 7 shows that the percentage of settlements has increased over the years except in 1965. However, since the ratio of concilia-

TABLE 7
Percentage of Disputes Settled to Disputes Examined by Labor Offices

1950	1955	1958	1960	1961	1962	1963	1964	1965
33.83	34.8	36.8	38.9	41.4	42.2	42.6	42.0	38.6

SOURCES: G. Perotti, "L'attività conciliativa nelle controversie di lavoro," in *Rassegna del lavoro*, vol. 1, n. 4, June 1955, p. 714.

F. Volpe, "La conciliazione delle controversie individuali di lavoro," in *Rassegna del lavoro*, vol. XII, n. 5, May 1966, p. 16.

TABLE 8

Disputes Examined by Labor Offices According to Their Outcome

Sectors	1950	1955	1958	1960	1961	1962	1963	1964	1965
Settled	24,803	21,583	19,335	19,770	20,061	19,047	18,126	19,469	18,881
Not settled	34,849	29,824	21,804	22,742	20,325	17,553	15,993	16,417	16,529
Withdrawn	11,699	9,785	10,491	7,439	7,213	7,789	7,597	9,324	8,479
Transferred to other offices	1,976	738	841	914	833	772	827	1,059	1,115
Total	73,327	61,930	52,471	50,865	48,432	45,161	42,543	46,269	45,004

SOURCES: G. Perotti: "L' attività conciliativa nelle controversie di lavoro," in *Rassegna del lavoro*, vol. 1, n. 4, June 1955, p. 714. F. Volpe: "La conciliazione delle controversie individuali di lavoro," in *Rassegna del lavoro*, vol. XIII, n. 5, May 1966, p. 7.

tion in agriculture appears to be lower, the accompanying decline of disputes in that sector may be the reason for the increase in settlements, rather than the improved efficiency of the labor offices. Table 8 indicates that withdrawals of claims also are increasing somewhat, but it is not known how many private settlements are included in these percentages. There is a considerable increase in cases transferred to other offices. This category includes a variety of disputes, and its growth may be the result of improved administration accompanied by a more accurate demarcation of jurisdictions, i.e., many cases may have been turned over to the labor inspectors when criminal liabilities were involved.

The percentage of settlements is high, but probably not as high as it could be. If estimates of the possibilities of conciliation in court are correct, even more claims should have been settled before the labor offices. However, since data of actions after failure of conciliation are not available, what actually occurs remains an assumption. To be sure, a significant number of complaints "not settled" are later dropped because of insufficient grounds, and, in a way, these may be considered settlements as well. Formal conciliation always implies some concession to the worker, but many a case taken to the labor office is not based on serious complaints. It is also true that many well-founded claims not settled there will not be submitted to the courts because the claimant worker does not want to engage in lengthy and risky proceedings. However, this is not the fault of the conciliation agency, but rather that of judicial procedure.

On the other hand, the quality of the settlements appears to be satisfactory. The ratio of sums claimed to amounts awarded to the worker—although changing over the years—is around 75 percent reaching 78 percent in 1965. Considering that claims are often "padded," this figure is undoubtedly significant, meaning that when settlement is reached it is probably a good one. And this, of course, is an indication of the efficiency of the conciliation function of the labor office.

8. The percentage of claims reported after termination of the employment relationship is very high, practically as high as that quoted for suits brought in court. The trend is constant, and when there is a decline it is probably a result of claims involving large numbers of workers. During the employment relationship, the risk of suing an employer is less when there are numerous claimants. The higher figure of disputes of this kind in agriculture may be explained in this manner; in that sector group claims are submitted frequently.

This finding becomes even more significant if compared with percent-

TABLE 9

Disputes Reported After Termination of Employment
(in Percent)

Sectors	1955 (first 6 mos.)	1956 (first 6 mos.)	1957 (first 6 mos.)	1963 (first 6 mos.)	1964 (first 6 mos.)	1965 (first 6 mos.)
Agriculture	81.6	79.5	83.6	84	87	84
Industry	96.3	93	97	95	94	94
Commerce	98.1	95.6	97.7	97	97	96
Banking and Insurance	97.1	95.5	89.7	94	92	85
Others	97.4	97.6	98	97	95	94
Total	93.4	94.4	94.7	94	94	94

SOURCES: G. Stagnitta: "La distribuzione regionale delle controversie di lavoro," in *Rassegna del lavoro*, February–March 1959, p. 211.

ages of the prewar period when conciliation was carried out by unions and employers' associations. For the years 1937 to 1940, an average of 83 percent of claims was reported after termination of the employment relationship. Although there were more agricultural disputes in that time because of higher employment in that sector, the unions' grievance procedures proved to be more effective in overcoming inhibitions to file claims against the employer during the employment relationship. The enactment of a statute on dismissals in 1966 perhaps will have some impact, but it is not yet possible to evaluate the results. However, since the act does not provide for compulsory reinstatement, it

TABLE 10

The Nature of Disputes Reported to Labor Offices*

	1956	1965	1956 Percent	1965 Percent
Recognition of wages set by collective agreements	29,531	18,879	18.21	15.25
Notice of discharge and severance pay	25,116	21,571	15.49	17.42
Paid holidays	21,314	16,719	13.14	13.50
Paid vacations	15,873	14,690	9.79	11.96
Overtime and night work	14,511	10,334	8.95	8.35
Payment of wages due	13,670	9,086	8.43	7.34
Family allowances and social insurances	9,071	5,419	5.59	4.38
Weekly days off	6,941	7,111	4.28	5.74
Others	26,119	20,007	16.12	16.06

* The apparent discrepancy with tables showing the number of reported disputes is explained by the fact that a dispute may contain a number of claims.

TABLE 11

The Nature of Disputes Reported to Labor Offices and their Distribution According to Sectors of the Economy, 1965

	Agriculture	Industry	Commerce	Banking and Insurance	Others	Total
Recognition of wages set by collective agreements	1,965	11,500	3,602	84	1,728	18,879
Notice of discharge and severance pay	1,269	12,418	4,271	69	3,544	21,571
Paid holidays	1,128	8,055	4,279	49	3,208	16,719
Paid vacations	981	7,415	3,516	34	2,744	14,690
Overtime and night work	1,067	5,577	2,616	31	1,043	10,334
Payment of wages due	886	4,986	1,835	13	1,366	9,086
Family allowances and social insurances	192	3,715	958	6	548	5,419
Weekly days off	868	2,975	1,821	27	1,420	7,111
Others	3,439	10,511	3,825	102	2,130	20,007
Total	11,795	67,152	26,723	415	17,731	123,816

will possibly not be decisive in overcoming the fear of discharge. Furthermore, we are convinced that that reason, although important, is not the only one, the main one being rather the embarrassing situation into which an employee actually is drawn when he is a party to a claim, which at least potentially introduces a lengthy civil suit against his employer.

9. The nature of the claims is given in tables 10 and 11. Disputes over the application of collective agreements, wages due, and family allowances show a decreasing tendency (nearly −3, −1, −1, respectively), but the first category still maintains a leading position in agriculture. All of these claims are somehow typical of an underdeveloped economy. An increase in disputes in the categories "Notice of discharge and severance pay" as well as "Paid vacations" is a result of more stable employment, but the fact that "Notice of discharge" precedes "Paid vacations" is also a result of the overwhelming majority of claims reported after termination of the employment relationship, a phenomenon that presumably brings about restriction in the amount of claims not related to rights engendered by the termination of employment itself. The increase in disputes over "Weekly days off" is caused simply by a controversial interpretation of statutory regulations on this subject, which has been raised frequently in recent years.

4.

CONTRACTUAL SETTLEMENT OF LABOR DISPUTES UNDER COLLECTIVE AGREEMENTS

1. A large portion of labor disputes is covered by voluntary settlement procedures and machinery, established by collective agreements. Unfortunately, overall statistics are not available, but some data are quoted in connection with the individual procedures.

TYPES OF SETTLEMENT PROCEDURES

Voluntary procedures may take a variety of forms. A brief survey is followed by a discussion of the most important legal problems raised by these procedures; then, a more detailed analysis of their practical application is presented. The main types of settlement procedures established by contractual agreement are the following:

(a) Three-step conciliation procedures consisting of (1) submission of claims to the foreman; (2) meeting of representatives of management and the works council;[1] and (3) attempt at conciliation by repre-

---

[1] Works councils—*Commissioni interne di fabbrica*—were first established in 1943. They are governed by collective agreements, the most important of which is the agreement of April 18, 1966, covering the entire industry. The major tasks of the works councils are: (a) to present claims to the employer and attempt to settle them; (b) to render nonbinding opinions on plant rules and implementation of contractual provisions on hours of work, vacations, etc.; (c) to participate in the administration of social welfare institutions (cafeterias, health services, etc.).

Work councils are elected by all workers on tickets that are most often, but not necessarily, presented by unions. Salaried employees vote in a separate caucus. Members of the councils are protected by contractual provisions against unjust dismissals and plant-to-plant transfers. At the present time, labor unions are engaged in restricting the tasks of the works councils and taking over a part of them. The 1966 agreement reaffirmed strongly that works councils are not entitled to conclude collective agreements (as had happened rather frequently in the 1950s). On works councils, see Neufeld, *Italy: School for Awakening Countries* (Ithaca, New York: Cornell University Press, 1961), pp. 450 ff.

sentatives of the union and the employers' association. This procedure is usually established by nationwide agreements. It may be varied somewhat with respect to the type of dispute, e.g., the first step may be omitted in collective disputes, but the pattern is more or less standardized. In some agreements this procedure is mandatory before suit can be brought in court; in case of noncompliance the claimant worker forfeits his right to sue the employer.

(b) Bipartite committees composed of representatives of the unions and employers' associations in equal number. They are also established by nationwide agreements, largely in the public utilities. Their jurisdiction is usually restricted to "the interpretation of the agreement" and to collective disputes, that is, they cannot decide the case itself but furnish only a general interpretation. Their joint decision becomes a part of the agreement.

(c) Joint committees composed of representatives of the unions and management (or employers' associations) for the settlement of disputes over job evaluations. They are established by companywide agreements and act upon the motion of an individual worker or a group of workers. However, a decision changing the classification of a job is binding upon all workers in that category, irrespective of whether they have filed a claim.

(d) Joint fact-finding committees for disputes over incentive pay or job classifications. These committees were first established in 1966 in the metal-mechanical industry by nationwide agreements. They submit reports on the facts involved in the dispute to the union and the employers' association, which subsequently attempt a settlement of the dispute. Some agreements require that the committees prepare recommendations which, if unanimous, become binding unless the dispute is pursued soon thereafter.

(e) Arbitration panels composed of wingmen appointed by the unions and employers' association and headed by an impartial chairman, who is nominated with their consent. Although this arbitration procedure is not often used, it has been employed for almost twenty years in disputes over individual dismissals (as distinct from collective or redundancy dismissals).

2. All of these contractual procedures are available to union members only or, according to some agreements, to workers "who assign specific powers to a union."[2] If the procedure is set forth in a multiemployer

---

[2] Of course, the union, in turn, may refuse assistance to the nonorganized worker; but in in light of the pluralistic composition of the Italian labor force, the worker would appeal to a rival union.

agreement, the employers, too, must be members of their respective organizations. A union member who files a claim against a nonorganized employer will have to call upon the labor office or go directly to the courts.

A serious legal issue was raised in connection with the application of the Act of 1959 (the Law of July 14, 1959, No. 741). Under the Act, the Parliament empowered the government to enact statutes on fair working conditions for the various branches of industry. The provisions of each of these decrees had to be identical to the terms of the collective agreements in effect at the time. When the government made use of these powers, it incorporated all provisions of each collective agreement into its decrees—without discrimination. Thus, contractual procedures and machineries were transformed into statutory rules, but at that point the following legal issues were raised:

First of all, the Act of 1959 empowered the government to enact decrees on *wages and working conditions.* The question arose whether procedural provisions, as well as all kinds of institutional or contractual clauses,[3] such as the peace obligation, dues check-off, works councils, and contractually established social security measures, etc., were to be included in that category. The answer, repeatedly handed down in opinions of the Constitutional Court on specific issues, was in the negative. The government had gone beyond the powers granted by Parliament and the procedural provisions were thus gradually repealed.[4] Another consideration concerned a more important legal aspect. If these procedural provisions were to be transformed into statutory rules, they would be enforceable for nonorganized employees and employers as well, and thus constitute a violation of the principle of freedom of association for the following reasons: (1) an employer would be bound by a settlement reached by an association of which he is not a member; and (2) the union or the employers' association

---

[3] We recall here a common distinction in continental Europe: contractual provisions establish obligations for the parties to the collective agreement; normative provisions establish working conditions. The latter affect the individual contract of employment. See Otto Kahn-Freund, Introduction to *Labour Relations and the Law* (London: Stevens & Sons, 1965), pp. 1 ff. Procedural provisions are mixed insofar as they bind individual employers and employees, but their implementation requires the performance of duties by unions and employers' associations.

[4] Note that the Constitutional Court can act only upon the motion of a court, which, during ordinary proceedings and usually upon request of one of the parties, raises the issue of constitutionality in the case under consideration. The issue was raised on the ground that the government had gone beyond the limits of the powers granted by the Parliament (ARTICLE 76 of the constitution). Of course, not all enacted decrees were repealed, only those which had become controversial in the course of ordinary proceedings. Therefore, many decrees remain in force but are subject to repeal if controversial issues are raised.

would have to process claims raised by nonorganized employees or employers. Therefore, the Constitutional Court repealed all decrees submitted for review on the grounds of unconstitutionality.[5] Of course, these procedural rules remain in force as contractual provisions insofar as they bind members of the respective organizations only; but they were repealed as statutory rules, which affected their extended application.

Another legal issue was raised with respect to the validity of provisions barring the worker from bringing suit in court if contractual procedures had not been previously exhausted. Under the corporative system (ARTS. 430–432 of the Code of Civil Procedure), the court was required to reject a claim if conciliation through the unions' grievance procedures had not been attempted. At the present time, many a decision stipulates that a "private" collective agreement cannot embrace the same principle, which can be established only as a statutory rule.[6] It is now recognized that a party who does not observe this principle is liable for damages,[7] but the court cannot reject the claim. Actually, the awarding of damages is a poor remedy because it is difficult, if not impossible, to assess the damages suffered by an employer if the opposing party decides to ignore the contractual procedure for settlement. The only application consists of not charging court costs to the defendant in case of settlement, on the assumption that court action could have been avoided if the plaintiff had observed his obligation to attempt conciliation. But even in light of this conclusion, it appears that the actual effectiveness of these provisions has been considerably eroded by the decisions of the courts.

Another, more significant, threat to settlements reached through union grievance procedures is their vulnerability to attack under ARTICLE 2113 of the Code of Civil Procedure. As was pointed out before, it spells out the rule governing the vacating of a compromise, but it states an exception if the compromise was reached before a court or through union–employers' association procedures. The question arises whether nonrecognized associations are also covered by this rule. A literal interpretation of the provision would yield a negative answer,

---

[5] Among the most important decisions are the following: *Corte Costituzionale*, July 13, 1963, n. 129; July 26, 1965, n. 56; March 9, 1967, n. 26.

[6] *Cassazione*, July 17, 1956, n. 2763; *Cassazione*, April 9, 1960, n. 809; *Cassazione*, March 7, 1960, n. 422 (*Sezioni Unite*, Joint Sections, which meet to decide over very controversial issues).

[7] *Cassazione*, May 10, 1961, n. 1116; *Cassazione*, December 7, 1961, n. 2793; *Cassazione*, May 10, 1963, n. 1145.

and this conclusion appears to prevail.[8] The courts view nonrecognized unions with distrust, and there is also fear that, lacking regulations concerning their representativeness, a settlement could be reached between an employer and a company union or a "phony" union. In spite of these legal reservations, however, this type of settlement procedure continues in use and the ratio of attacks to settlements seems to be extremely low. It proves that contractual procedures, even though their legal framework is a fragile one, may still be preferred because they rely upon relations of goodwill that are somehow considered to be more important than the legal framework itself.

THE LEGAL POSITION OF ARBITRATION

3. The legal position of arbitration is a matter of considerable question. ARTICLES 806 and 808 of the Code, as stated before, prohibit arbitration and submission agreements in labor disputes. The prohibition was not repealed, and the opinion that it is no longer in force after the dissolution of the corporative system is shared by a mere minority. This prohibition was prompted by political considerations of the Fascist regime, which could not allow any evasion of state jurisdiction in labor disputes. But there was another reason, namely, that submission to arbitration, like a compromise, was deemed a disposition of unwaiverable rights. By avoiding adjudication of the state and by granting the power of deciding a dispute to a private party, the worker would implicitly accept a private settlement that might not be in his favor and might even deprive him of vested rights. This interpretation of the statute is still accepted by many, perhaps the majority, of the lawyers.

However, the practice of arbitration has been little affected by these conclusions and has received considerable support from the courts themselves. The so-called formal arbitration is as enforceable as a court's judgment after the award has been filed with a *Pretore,* who examines its compliance with formal regulations. But this is not the only possible type of arbitration. In commercial relations, it has been common practice for many decades to resort to the so-called informal arbitration in order to avoid the legal complications attached to the formal procedure, and to escape tax obligations.

Informal arbitration is often described as a "blank" agreement to compromise between two parties who appoint a third party to supply

---

[8] See Corte d'Appello Napoli, October 13, 1959; Corte d'Appello Roma, January 22, 1959 and mainly *Cassazione,* July 6, 1957 n. 2667; Corte d'Appello Brescia, November 27, 1964.

the terms. In its simplest form, it consists of a signed, blank sheet of paper that is then given to the arbitrator for completion. This legal device was upheld by the courts as having the same force as an agreement—not as a judgment. In case of subsequent noncompliance, the aggrieved party would have to bring suit in court in order to obtain a judgment. Such a compromise can be attacked in the same manner as a contract, that is, for reasons of violence, fraud, illegality, etc.

Arbitration hearings in cases of dismissal were first conducted in 1947. (See also chapter 5 for a more detailed account.) Until that time, except for a few postwar decrees that temporarily prohibited discharges, the power of the employer to dismiss a worker had been virtually unrestricted. Dismissals without notice could occur for disciplinary reasons, and with notice for other reasons; investigations were permitted only in the former. In 1947, a collective agreement covering the whole industrial sector established arbitration boards to investigate the reasons for all dismissals. The courts ruled that this was "informal" arbitration, and since the prohibition under the Code applied only to formal arbitration, the informal procedure was considered to be valid.[9] As a matter of fact, a legal construction defining this type of arbitration as a blank agreement to compromise in a dispute could have fallen under the general rule prohibiting the waiver of rights (ART. 2113 of the Civil Code), but this construction was rejected on the ground that the worker did not have a statutory right to protection against dismissals, at least against discharge with notice. However, that reasoning could not be applied to arbitration in discharges without notice for disciplinary reasons, which are governed by law (ART. 2119 of the Civil Code) yet subject to arbitration by the collective agreements mentioned above.[10] But the assumption itself is weak because the construction of informal arbitration as a blank agreement to compromise has been challenged by lawyers.[11] At any rate, we may conclude that

---

[9] The landmark decision that paved the way for a large number of similar judgments was: *Corte di Cassazione,* June 28, 1952, n. 1894. As a matter of fact, collective agreements never made it clear whether the parties meant formal or informal arbitration. The generous interpretation as informal arbitration was prompted in part by the implicit intention to avoid the serious consequences that prohibiting of this type of arbitration would have on collective labor relations.

[10] Only a few judgments, however, vacated awards on this ground, among them, *Cassazione,* June 18, 1955, n. 1896, and *Corte d'Appello,* Messina, October 30, 1965.

[11] On the ground that it does not cover the cases in which an arbitrator upholds or rejects a claim instead of compromising between the claims of the two parties, as, for example, in arbitration on dismissals. The most consistent opinion holds that informal arbitration is an agreement to interpret a contract through a third party, not to compromise between opposing claims. For a full account, see M. Grandi, *L'arbitrato irrituale nel diritto del lavoro,* Milan, 1963.

arbitration in labor disputes, although practiced, is still based on very uncertain legal provisions.

With respect to dismissals, the statute of 1966 finally provided explicitly that collective agreements, presumably with their procedural provisions, remain in force in these matters and that even individual parties not covered by these agreements are entitled to submit their cases to an "informal" arbitrator. In fact, after the enactment of this statute the practice of arbitration continued, although a claim against unjust dismissals with notice may now be filed in court.

4. Arbitration on dismissals raised many legal issues, the most important of which involved (a) the legal remedy available to the worker when the employers' association had not complied with the obligation to appoint, jointly with the union, a panel or arbitrators, and (b) the effect of a strike called before or during the proceedings protesting the discharge of a worker.

The courts did not render uniform decisions on the first issue; although the workers' claims were upheld in all of them, they were conflicting as to the remedies. In some cases,[12] the court appointed an arbitrator upon request of the worker, applying a rule connected with *formal* arbitration when a party to a submission agreement fails to cooperate in the appointment of an arbitrator. But this rule concerns formal arbitration, and it is doubtful whether it can be applied to *informal* arbitration as well. Other decisions allow for a second possibility, namely, that the court itself act as the arbitration board and render a judgment.[13] Most decisions, however, provide merely for the possibility that the worker is entitled to recover damages.[14] But what kind of damages? In order to properly assess damages, the court had to decide whether or not the dismissal was based on just cause. If unjustified, damages would have been equivalent to the lump sum the worker would have recovered through arbitration, in view of the fact that reinstatement is not compulsory.[15] If justified, the worker, although defeated, might not be required to pay the other party's court costs. In practice, the second and third possibilities lead to the same conclusions: The court has to inquire into the merit of the dismissal, either by acting as the board of arbitration or as a preliminary step to the assessment of damages.

---

[12] *Cassazione,* July 29, 1958, n. 2748.
[13] *Cassazione,* May 16, 1962, n. 1049.
[14] *Cassazione,* April 1961, n. 872, followed by most lower courts.
[15] A worker dismissed without just cause can be reinstated or receive a sum determined by the arbitration board from 5 to 12 months' wages (5 to 8, before 1965), and up to 14 months if he has more than 20 years seniority.

Strikes before or during the proceedings occurred frequently, most often at the beginning. Under such circumstances, employers' associations would refuse to pursue the contractual procedure and would sometimes discipline workers for participating in an allegedly illegal strike. The assumption is that the agreement on dismissals contains a no-strike pledge, although not clearly spelled out, and that the employers' associations have the right to refuse observance of the agreement when it has been violated.

A more intriguing situation arises when an unofficial strike occurs, or when a strike is called by a union other than the one to which the dismissed worker assigned the claim.[16] The writers on labor law are divided on this issue. Some share the opinion that irrespective of who initiates the strike, it is incompatible with contractual procedure and inhibits its operations; consequently the worker forfeits his substantive rights[17] under the collective agreement. But all conclusions on this issue had to be revised after the enactment of the statute on dismissals in 1966, because the statute no longer permits loss of statutory rights for actions of the parties other than those of the individual worker.

CONCILIATION PROCEDURES

5. Conciliation procedures are established by almost all nationwide collective agreements and follow a more or less standardized pattern. In the agreements of the very important metal-mechanical industry (steel and engineering),[18] which have established precedents for some matters, the procedure is very simple. The worker complains first to his foreman and then to the works council; there are no regulations as to the form of the complaint. If the works council cannot reach a settlement, the worker may report the grievance to a union that will

---

[16] Or when the dismissed worker does not take part in the collective action: See *Cassazione,* April 29, 1959, n. 1285.

[17] The 1965 agreement for industry (see chap. 4, section 1) made it explicit that the "peaceful solution" of the dispute is a "condition" for the implementation of the agreement itself. This provision, however, is still ambiguous and does not necessarily imply the solution backed by these authors.

[18] Since 1962, two nationwide collective agreements have been in force in the metal-mechanical industry, one for privately owned plants (employing almost 1,200,000 workers), and the other for government-owned companies (employing almost 250,000 workers mainly in steel, shipbuilding, and automobile manufacture). The present agreements became effective as of the date of signature, December 15, 1966, and November 15, 1966. They expire after three years. For a full account of the bargaining structure of this industry, see Gino Giugni, "Recent Developments in Collective Bargaining in Italy," in *International Labour Review,* vol. 71 (1964) p. 309, partially reprinted in Northrup, *Compulsory Arbitration and Government Intervention in Labor Disputes,* Labor Policy Association, Inc., 1966, pp. 389-392.

request a meeting with the employers' association.[19] Collective disputes are settled by the organizations at the provincial level, and in case of failure, at the national level. The 1966 agreement of the metal-mechanical companies, which are owned by the government, contains a provision forbidding any strike action in collective disputes during the life of the agreement until conciliation at the national level has been attempted, or until a term of twenty-five days has expired. With respect to collective disputes, in some sectors of the industry, for example, in textiles, a sharp distinction is made between claims involving the "interpretation" of the agreement, which are handled by the organizations at the national level, and claims involving its "application," which are handled at the provincial level. Of course, this distinction is often ignored in practice because the different concepts "interpretation" and "application" frequently overlap in a specific issue.

At any rate, the trend points toward the development of more detailed grievance procedures, as shown in a large number of the agreements concluded after 1960. In the textile and chemical industries,[20] the grievance procedure at the shop level consists of four steps: (1) the grievant orally informs the foreman of his complaint; (2) the foreman must either uphold or reject it within 1 week; (3) the worker may resubmit his claim to the works council within 10 days from step 2; (4) the claim must be discussed by the worker, assisted by members of the works council, and representatives of management within 20 days from step 3. It is interesting that the works council can also act on its own motion if the claim involves several workers or "a collective interest." In general practice such actions occur frequently, but specific provisions, as those just described, are an exception.

If the dispute cannot be settled at the shop level, the grievant may report his claim to a union. Except for recent examples that will be discussed shortly, this step was seldom regulated by detailed provisions. An interesting case is that of a local (provincial) agreement of the building industry in the provinces of Naples and Caserta.[21] It established a formal procedure for the settlement of disputes by setting the term for the first meeting between representatives of the union and employers' association (15 days), by limiting postponements to two,

---

[19] In case of failure, conciliation at the national level may be provided for; see collective agreements for the oil industry of July 7, 1967, art. 58.

[20] Collective agreement of June 5, 1964 for the (private) chemical industry, general section, art. 18; collective agreement of November 5, 1964 for the textile industry, general section, art. 15.

[21] Provincial collective agreement of October 2, 1959, implementing the national agreement of July 14, 1959.

by determining the items to be covered in the hearing, and by providing that attorneys can be admitted only if explicitly invited by either the union or the employers' association. The last provision is a rare exception indeed. The screening procedure at the shop level is usually ruled compulsory before the case can be submitted to a union. But the building trades are an exception; because the companies are usually small and employment is unstable, grievance procedures at the shop level cannot operate effectively. In commerce, according to a collective agreement that covers all of that sector,[22] the proceedings of conciliation sessions have to be filed with the labor office, and if settlement has not been reached that office will make another attempt—an interesting fusion of private and public conciliation procedure. Also in commerce, another agreement provides for a voluntary check-off in favor of the conciliation service, this provision being the only one of its kind.[23]

Many recent agreements have incorporated the formal conciliation procedure by establishing a board composed of union and employer representatives who are authorized to attempt the settlement of disputes. Since 1964 joint bodies have been established at the provincial level in the chemical and textile industries (in commerce they have been in existence since 1958[24]). They are composed of representatives of all unions and management in equal number.[25] The boards act on the motion of the union to which the worker or the works council has assigned the claim. The claim has to be filed within 10 days from completion of the shop-level procedure. The boards are appointed on an *ad hoc* basis and render their opinion within 20 days; if it is not unanimous, it may be attacked within 30 days by appeal to the organizations at the national level, who will make a further attempt to conciliate. Until the entire procedure is exhausted, the parties can neither bring suit in court nor call a strike.

In the banking sector the aggrieved employee may appeal directly to a joint committee after the shop-level procedure is exhausted.[26] The committee meets either in Rome or in Milan and has to conduct a con-

---

[22] Collective agreement of October 29, 1962, arts. 2 and 3.
[23] Collective agreement of November 3, 1962.
[24] Collective agreement of June 28, 1958, art. 120.
[25] It must be emphasized that in the traditional settlement procedure only one union intervened in each case. Under the recent regulations, all unions are represented in the joint committee so that a union representative participates in proceedings concerning members of a rival union. This does not lead to discrimination but promotes the accomplishment of uniform policies.
[26] Collective agreement of August 27, 1966 for clerical employees in banking, art. 103.

ciliation hearing within 30 days. If signed by the parties to the dispute, the settlement is final and binding. This is set forth in a number of agreements, but, as stated before, an appeal in court on the grounds that rights cannot be waived still has a good chance of being upheld. Other examples of joint panels are found largely in more recent agreements. Special boards established for certain types of disputes are described in another section of this chapter.

INTERPRETATION BOARDS

6. Disputes over the interpretation of the terms of the agreement, or, more broadly, collective disputes, are now often referred to special, joint boards. According to these regulations, a dispute over "interpretation" is in fact a collective dispute. It may arise out of an individual case, but once the parties argue about the interpretation of the rule applying to the case, any settlement will consist of general terms and will be binding on all workers affected by the "interpreted" rule. In the agreements of the banking sector, a dispute is considered collective and is referred to a board of interpretation if it "appears to concern a common and general interest."[27]

In the telephone industry a board of interpretation has existed for many years.[28] It is composed of union and employer representatives in equal number, including representatives of all unions that are parties to the agreement, and it meets within 60 days from the time the request is submitted either by a union or the employers' association. If deemed expedient, the board may appoint a neutral president, in which case the final settlement truly may be an award rather than a negotiated solution. Although it has existed for many years, this board meets very seldom, perhaps once every 2 or 3 years, and proceedings are usually lengthy before agreement is reached.

In the banking sector the interpretation board consists of eight union and eight employer representatives. The board is established on a permanent basis for the duration of the collective agreement, and its members must be selected from among the negotiators of the agreement. It meets within 30 days from receipt of a claim, which is submitted by registered letter to one of the organizations represented on the board. The chairmanship rotates between employer and union representatives and the employers' association provides clerical assist-

---

[27] Art. 104 of the agreement quoted in n. 26 *supra*.
[28] See now collective agreement of July 23, 1965, art. 50.

ance. If the decision is unanimous, it becomes part of the collective agreement and is binding in the same manner as the agreement.

Other, similar joint bodies usually have a simpler structure. In the oil and chemical industries,[29] collective disputes over the interpretation and application of the agreements are referred to a committee composed of six representatives of each of the parties to the agreement, who must decide the issue within 2 months. If the parties agree to the decision, it has the same effect as a new agreement but cannot be applied retroactively.

FACT-FINDING BOARDS

7. Special, joint, fact-finding boards have been established in large number during the last two years for individual disputes. The first board was stipulated in the collective agreement of 1966 for the metal-mechanical companies owned by the government. The privately owned companies in that industry followed this example very soon, and other branches of the economy now have also established fact-finding boards. The creation of these boards, to which union stewards are appointed from among workers in the plant, is considered a concession to union demands for a more representative role at the plant level that was worked out after difficult negotiations.

Fact-finding boards were not, however, an innovation in bargaining practices. Toward the end of the "corporative" era, joint committees chaired by labor inspectors were frequently established for the purpose of examining the evidence in disputes over proper job classification, usually of white-collar workers, in terms of the job performed. After examination of the evidence these committees had to prepare a report, which—according to SECTION 96, Implementation Rules of the Civil Code—would have prevented a court from admitting new evidence in case of a subsequent suit. The committees were also authorized to conduct conciliation hearings and to issue recommendations.

After the collapse of the Fascist regime, many collective agreements continued to establish fact-finding boards. In some agreements a two-step procedure was provided with possibility of appeal to a national board.[30] The courts ruled, however, that since the unions were no longer "recognized," the prohibition against new evidence was no

---

[29] In the chemical industry, supplement 3 of the agreement; in the oil industry, art. 58, n. III of the agreement.

[30] In the building trades, by collective agreement of November 14, 1947, art. 52.

longer in force.³¹ Perhaps for this reason or, more likely, because these institutions were merely inherited by the new unions as a vestige of corporative practice, they did not function effectively and only reasonably well in the textile industry.

The same conclusion may be drawn for similar boards established by some agreements for disputes over piece rates.³² It must be pointed out that all of these boards were established at the provincial level; they did not conduct meetings within the plants, and members usually were officials of the provincial branches of the respective organizations. Therefore, particularly in disputes over piece rates, they lacked specific technical knowledge as well as proper links to life inside the plant.

The concept that underlies these newly established boards is rather different; they are more closely patterned on the boards for the settlement of disputes over job evaluations, which were set up by a number of company agreements to be discussed later. They were created, as was mentioned above, in order to give the union a direct voice in disputes at the shop level. Their complicated structure and procedure reflect the difficult compromise worked out in hard bargaining with employers' associations.

In the privately owned plants of the metal-mechanical industry,³³ joint boards have to be established in all plants with more than 350 employees. They are required to conduct fact-finding investigations into questions of job classifications, incentive wages, and special allowances for hazardous jobs. Each board is composed of one to five representatives of the unions, appointed by them from among workers in the plant, and an equal number of representatives of management. The unions represented on the board are those that have cast more than 5 percent of the votes in work-council elections. The board is established on a permanent basis and members are appointed for terms of two years. However, each union can appoint additional members, who will then alternate according to the subject in dispute; for example, white-collar representatives deal with disputes involving the qualifications of white-collar workers, etc.

Because of the unwillingness of employers to accept union representation in the handling of grievances at the shop level, a compromise

---

³¹ See *Cassazione* (Joint Sections), June 26, 1954, n. 2208.
³² See, for example, collective agreement of December 6, 1950 for the textile industry, art. 16.
³³ See n. 18, *supra*. The agreement for government-owned companies, which was signed first, is rather similar. The most important difference is that no provision was included for representation of unions other than those which were parties to the agreement, and that they are represented even though they have no representatives on the works councils.

solution was worked out setting forth that the provincial branches of the organizations submit the dispute to the board as a new step in the already established conciliation procedure (see sec. 5 in this chapter). At this stage of the grievance procedure—which implies completion of the first two steps, foreman and works councils—the union representing the worker's claim submits a request to the employers' association to call a meeting of the board. The employers' association forwards the request to the employer involved within 5 days. The board conducts its investigation within 10 days and reports to the respective organizations. If its conclusions are unanimous and the dispute is not resumed by the organizations within 10 days, the settlement is final and binding.[34] In order to allow the board to accomplish its objective, the employer "will do whatever is necessary." Agreements for government-owned companies provide the use of a room for conciliation hearings on the company's premises for this purpose.

As was pointed out before, this procedure is somewhat unwieldy, and it is doubtful whether it will always be carried out faithfully. Of course, the unions may try to take claims directly to the board and ignore, or reduce to sheer formality, the intermediate steps. A simplified procedure may be adopted in future negotiations, but for the time being the present solution is the only one possible in light of the rigid attitude of the organizations—the unions claiming the right of representation at the shop level, and the employers unwilling to concede it.

Similar boards have now been established in other branches of the industry. In the textile industry,[35] the boards are set up on an *ad hoc* basis and their activities are restricted to answering specific questions framed by the organizations. Their jurisdiction is extended to disputes over the number and type of equipment each worker is required to operate. In dealing with such disputes, the boards have replaced an unsuccessful arbitration procedure of previous years, as well as the joint board chaired by the labor inspector in disputes over piece rates. In the building trades,[36] the board has jurisdiction in disputes involving job classifications and piece rates, but it is established at the provincial level for the reasons stated above.[37] The board is permanent and has to conduct its investigations within 10 days of the filing of the claim. On the basis of its recommendations, the employers' association

---

[34] The latter provision is contained in the agreement for government-owned companies (art. 5, general section).

[35] Collective agreement of June 23, 1967.

[36] Collective agreement for building trades (manual workers) of November 25, 1966, art. 55.

[37] See sec. 4, *supra*.

and the union attempt to settle the dispute. In the food industry,[38] the board handles disputes concerned with job classifications and piece rates.

Thus, fact-finding boards are gradually being established in most branches of the industry that have followed the example of negotiations in the metal-mechanical sector during the past few years. It is too early to evaluate their effectiveness. It may happen, as was the case in other instances, that the tendency to follow examples established in other branches of the industry where conditions are different may bring about some disappointment.

ARBITRATION IN JOB CLASSIFICATION DISPUTES

8. In addition to its extensive use in cases of dismissals, arbitration is increasingly provided for other types of disputes, for example, disputes over job qualifications for categories of workers. Unlike the agreements on dismissals, the provisions covering these disputes usually do not contain a submission clause, but merely set forth that the parties may resort to arbitration and establish some rules for the appointment of arbitration panels. In the food industry, resort to arbitration is possible if conciliation attempts through union channels fail.[39] In the telephone industry,[40] a temporary arbitration procedure was established for disputes over the new, uniform classification of jobs after the five telephone companies had merged into one operating company. If the specially constituted, joint committee deadlocks in a dispute, a neutral chairman will be appointed to render the decision. However, the worker can still bring suit in court.

In the chemical and oil industries,[41] again in disputes over job classifications, it is left to the unions to promote arbitration. If a request for arbitration is submitted, a panel will be established composed of one representative of each of the parties involved, appointed by their respective organizations and presided over by an impartial chairman. The chairman is appointed by the two organizations; if they are unable to agree on his nomination, a name is drawn from a list of

---

[38] Collective agreement for bakery and confectionary workers of October 20, 1966; collective agreement for cheese industry, November 11, 1966.

[39] Agreements n. 38 *supra;* collective agreement for noodle workers of May 11, 1967.

[40] Award on new job classifications, rendered by the Undersecretary of Labor, July 30, 1966, sec. 13.

[41] Collective agreement for oil industry, art. 58; collective agreement for chemical industry, art. 3 of the general section.

twelve persons who should previously have been agreed upon. These rules follow the pattern established for arbitration in cases of dismissal; but note that whereas the joint boards of investigation (above, section 6) include representatives of *all* unions that are parties to the agreement, the arbitration panels include only *one* representative of the union to which the worker has assigned his claim.[42] The panel meets within 10 days; if evidence has to be examined, the hearing may be postponed for no longer than 15 days. The award, however, is not binding; each party may appeal to the unions or employers' association at the national level, which will then meet and try to settle the dispute. It seems obvious that if a settlement cannot be reached, suit may be brought in court.

These examples of recent agreements[43] show that distrust of arbitration has not disappeared; while the idea is gaining ground, the implementation of the procedure is approached with extreme caution and the actual operation is not frequent. Preoccupation with the legal effectiveness of awards may account for this attitude, but, as will be discussed in the Conclusions, not every union has endorsed the principle of arbitration.

9. Official records of the voluntary settlement procedures just described are not available and information as to their working is both scant and difficult to collect. Moreover, in a general evaluation of their effectiveness the settlement of disputes at the plant level should not be overlooked. But here again, we face the same difficulties of collecting information. In large and medium-size enterprises the works councils are firmly established. And once established, they eventually become active bodies for the handling of grievances, in fact, the most important ones for claims of workers whose contracts of employment have not expired.

Resort to subsequent steps, such as attempted conciliation through unions and employers' associations, is increasing as well. In the province of Bari, the number of disputes handled by the two largest unions[44] rose from 112 in 1961 to 311 in 1965, corresponding roughly to 1/6 and 1/2, respectively, of the claims reported in the same years

---

[42] In the oil industry, if there is more than one claim handled by more than one union, the panel will be enlarged to include representatives of all the unions involved.

[43] In the textile industry, an arbitration procedure of the type described in this section has been followed since 1950 (collective agreement of December 6, 1950).

[44] Namely CISL and CGIL, the two general confederations that organize probably more than 80 percent of all union members. See Horowitz, *The Italian Labor Movement* (Harvard University Press, 1963).

SETTLEMENT OF LABOR DISPUTES IN ITALY

to the labor office. Although the latter appears to be by far the more effective agency, it must be remembered that many claims are processed through both channels, that is, claims are reported to the labor office after previous attempts at settlement have failed.

This last point is supported by some data collected in the province of Milan. In industry, only an average of 25 percent of the claims reported to a union (CISL) is settled by voluntary procedures. Eighty percent of the disputes not adjusted in this manner are settled by the labor office. In commerce, of 50 percent of the claims adjusted prior to court action after having been reported to the same union, 40 percent are settled by the labor office. In many cases the labor officer plays merely a formal role; by his endorsement he renders the settlement immune from attack. But it may be inferred that the two procedures are closely linked to each other, and that the labor office often supports the union's actions.[45]

---

[45] See sec. 5 of this chapter, where mention is made of the agreement for commerce in which this link is openly recognized.

5.
VOLUNTARY SETTLEMENT PROCEDURES IN OPERATION

1. In this chapter we will discuss a number of voluntary dispute settlement procedures that deserve special attention because of their remarkable success or their significant role in labor relations at the plant level: arbitration in dismissals provided since 1947, and joint boards for job evaluation claims at the steel company *Italsider* and at the chemical company ANIC.

ARBITRATION IN DISMISSALS

Arbitration in dismissals in industry was established by an agreement of April 29, 1965, which was, however, preceded by two other agreements, one of August 7, 1947, and the other of October 18, 1950. Almost all data concerning the working of the arbitration procedure are based on the latter agreement. Therefore, it will be discussed in some detail and the main differences between it and the agreement now in force will specifically be pointed out.[1]

In plants employing more than 35 workers—smaller plants are not covered by the agreement—a worker dismissed either for disciplinary reasons ("just cause") or for ordinary reasons (dismissal with notice) may request a union to attempt a settlement with the employers' association at the provincial level. The request must be filed within 3 days (now extended to 5 days) from the announcement of the dismissal, and the union must contact the employers' association and attempt conciliation within 4 days (now extended to 5 days). If attempts at settlement fail, the worker may file another request for arbitration

---

[1] Economic sectors other than industry may come under the application of different agreements. For example, in banking the national agreement of August 27, 1964 (for *funzionari*, or officials) provides for the establishment of a national board. The procedure is very similar to the one enforced in industry, described above.

within 10 days (now 20 days) from the date of dismissal. Rather often, the request for arbitration was presented immediately, circumventing the attempt at conciliation.

The arbitration panel is composed of one representative of each of the parties to the dispute, appointed by the union and the employers' association, and presided over by a chairman elected by a panel of twelve persons who have previously been agreed upon. However, quite frequently he is appointed directly by the two organizations, either on a permanent basis or, more often, as an *ad hoc* arbitrator.

The panel must determine whether the dismissal is based on a credible reason according to "equity" *(secundum conscientiam)* rather than according to law; until recently there were no legal provisions restricting the power of the employer to discharge a worker, the giving of notice excepted. If a dismissal is held "unjustified," the employer is invited either to reinstate the worker with recognition of his previous seniority (but not with back pay)[2] or to pay a special indemnity to be assessed on the basis of 5 to 8 months' wages. Under the pressure of unions for more effective remedies, this procedure was slightly altered in the agreement of 1965. An award must now stipulate reinstatement, and unless it is carried out within 3 days, the panel meets again to grant the indemnity, now based on 5 to 12 months' wages (14 months for employees with more than 20 years seniority). The burden of proof lies with the employer. The decision must be rendered within 10 days; according to the 1965 agreement, the term now runs from the day of the first hearing (the attempt at conciliation), and it may be postponed for another 15 days if it becomes necessary to take evidence.

If the worker was dismissed without notice for disciplinary reasons, the procedure is the same, but the employer is allowed to request that it be suspended. The dispute will then be referred to the national confederations for an attempt at settlement. If it fails, the worker may sue the employer. and if the court rules that no grounds existed for a disciplinary dismissal, arbitration proceedings will be resumed in order to ascertain if there was at least proper cause for dismissal with notice. If the employer is again defeated at that stage, he must either reinstate the worker or pay double indemnity. This curious procedure for disciplinary dismissals is based on the assumption that the claims could already have been submitted to the courts for screening under statu-

---

[2] A recent decision of an appellate court stated, however, that if the worker is reinstated, he may sue the employer for damages and claim back pay. See *Corte d'Appello di Milano*, July 11, 1967, in *Revista giuridica del lavoro*, 1967, II, 477. This decision will probably cause a hot debate.

tory law, and that the parties to the agreement did not dare completely to ignore the public judicial system. However, the 1965 agreement includes a statement of policy urging employers' associations to waive the right to suspend the proceedings whenever possible.

Members of works councils enjoy special protection, now ruled by the national agreement of April 18, 1966 for the industrial sector. A dismissal has to be authorized by the union and the employers' association. If authorization is not granted, the dismissed employee may present his claim to an arbitration board. The procedure is like the one described above, except that if intentional discrimination can be proved the dismissal is set aside and the employer no longer has a choice between reinstatement and paying the indemnity. If the award stipulates reinstatement but the worker is not allowed to perform his job, he will receive either damages or, according to a more plausible opinion, payment of his wages although work was not performed.

2. The application of the 1950 agreement over the past fifteen years has recently been analyzed in a survey based both on national and local sources.[3] The total number of claims filed is rather high, although it is far below the number of probable dismissals during that period. Their geographical distribution is uneven. The number of claims is high in provinces with large cities and drops considerably in those without major urban areas. It is true that the latter are largely agricultural, mainly located in southern Italy, and that the agreement does not cover that sector of the economy. Also, industrial plants are mostly small in these provinces and the agreement does not cover establishments with fewer than 35 employees. But it was found in some provinces[4] that employers' associations would frequently reject claims without implementing the arbitration procedure, while the unions, on their part, would not take countermeasures or would not encourage the dismissed workers to file claims. Inefficient leadership, a scarcity of full-time officials, and a lack of interest in individual disputes as compared with collective disputes (which supposedly are of more political value to the unions) are the main factors that bring about this attitude of poor involvement of the unions, but the situation is gradually changing.

The frequency pattern of claims over the years shows a constant drop up to 1960 (from 1,616 in 1951 to 1,026 in 1960); then it rises to

---

[3] Gruppo di ricerca C.N.R. sulla formazione extralegislativa del diritto del lavoro, *I licenziamenti nell' industria italiana*, (1950–1964) Bologna, 1968. See also Veneto, in *Rivista trimestrale di diritto e procedura civile*, 1965, pp. 1761-1776.

[4] *I licenziamenti nell' industria italiana, op. cit.*, p. 71.

2,367 in 1964, and falls again to 1,776 in 1965. Considering that there was a recession in 1964 preceded by years of economic growth, it becomes clear that the pattern is rather independent of economic fluctuations. Of course, economic expansion is helpful to unions in their organization efforts, but its effects are not immediately cancelled out by a subsequent recession. Thus, the general economic situation is influential, but only as far as its impact upon the power of the trade unions is concerned. Furthermore, there is no reverse correlation between higher employment and the number of claims protesting dismissals. On the contrary, the latter increased during the period of economic boom.

The figures reported above concern dismissals with notice only. The pattern of claims protesting disciplinary or "just cause" dismissals shows a significant, constant rise, from 188 in 1951 to 983 in 1964. This sharp rise cannot be explained by itself; rather, the explanation lies in the improved implementation of the contractual procedure over the years.

An important finding concerns the size of the plants involved in the claims. The information is partial but significant. In the province of Genoa only 7 percent of the cases heard in fifteen years concerned plants with more than 1,000 workers, while 58 percent originated in plants with 36 to 100 workers. On the one hand, a dismissal in a large plant is probably based on more plausible grounds because decisions always go through a more formal internal procedure. On the other, large companies often pay dismissed workers a supplementary indemnity in order to prevent a claim from being raised.

With respect to the outcome of the proceedings, there is an overwhelming prevalence of conciliation. Awards in cases of dismissals with notice now amount to no more than 4 percent (21 percent in 1951),[5] but local variations are significant—the number of awards is higher in provinces that do not have large cities. Since these provinces also report fewer claims, it can probably be said that the fewer the cases, the more decisions are rendered. The largest number of awards is reported by the province of Genoa (13.6 percent from 1951 to 1964), the only province of those investigated[6] with a permanent board. Turin and Venice, both highly industrialized provinces, show a record of awards being granted in 3 percent or less of the cases. Bari, a province in southern Italy and only partially industrialized, ranks low with 2.5 percent. The higher number of awards in Naples, 7.5 percent, is ex-

---

[5] These data concern dismissals with notice and refer to such dismissals hereafter unless specific distinctions are made.
[6] A sample of 14 out of 92, including a wide variety of local situations.

ceptional among provinces with large cities and *ad hoc* boards.[7]

Conciliation may take place either before the board or prior to the formal meeting of the board. Almost everywhere conciliations are more frequent prior to the formal board meeting, at the step which may be considered a screening procedure (e.g., in the province of Turin the ratio is 55.4 to 10.1 of the total number of claims). Genoa proves to be an exception, probably because of the operation of a permanent board; here the ratio is reversed, 14.2 to 20.4.

According to national statistics, around 10 percent of the claims are withdrawn, but local data show almost twice that amount. However, the number of withdrawals is less than withdrawals of suits in court, and this is significant evidence of the efficiency of this contractual procedure. There is a striking difference between national and local data on claims rejected by the employers' associations. According to national sources, they follow an irregular pattern but never go above 10 percent; in 1964 they amounted merely to 1 percent. According to local sources they amounted to approximately 30 percent in the provinces investigated. This difference is probably a result of varying mechanics of tabulation, e.g., claims rejected by the employers' association and claims abandoned are often lumped together in local statistics.[8]

The employers' associations may reject claims for various alleged reasons: the terms of the collective agreement have expired; the employer is not organized or has fewer than 35 employees; or the worker is not entitled to file a claim (because he is an apprentice, or he is over sixty-five years of age, etc.). Of course, this practice of refusing to implement the procedure instead of allowing the board to decide the matter is sometimes questionable. It is certainly questionable when the very reason of refusal becomes a matter of dispute, for example, when the agreement is not enforced with respect to apprentices or older workers. Sometimes the claims are rejected on the merits, that is, the claim is assumed to be groundless. This violation of the agreement occurs not infrequently in small areas where there is not much industry. When the unions were not watching over the implementation of the agreement, the employers' associations sometimes made every effort to arrive at the same negative result.

3. What are the results of implementing the procedure? Reinstate-

---

[7] Naples is a special case in every respect; see chap. 3, sec. 6.

[8] *I licenziamenti nell' industria italiana, op. cit.*, p. 73. This author assumes that the heading "abandon" also means "rejection," but there is no satisfactory evidence of the assumption.

ment after an award was rendered almost never occurred. But interestingly enough, there are instances of reinstatement through conciliation: about 7 percent in cases of dismissals with notice prior to hearings before the panel, about 4 percent in disciplinary dismissals, and 1 to 2 percent after hearings before the panel. It may be said that to the extent that the proceedings are carried out, the probabilities of reinstatement become less. Suspension of the procedure requested by the employer in disciplinary dismissals is not as frequent as might be expected; about 20 percent of the claims in 1963 is the highest number reported. At any rate, this is probably a further incentive to conciliation. The number of awards upholding the workers' claims in disciplinary dismissals is very low, and it may be inferred that an employer will submit to arbitration when his hopes for success are high. Otherwise he will request suspension of the proceedings and leave the opposing party the only choice of a drawn-out suit in the courts.

Concerning the contents of the awards, we find that arbitrators behave much like the average judge, but then most often they were judges or attorneys or are retired judges, and less often professors of labor law. There are almost no leading decisions. When matters of principle are involved, for example, issues touching on the right to strike or the right to organize, the arbitrators seemed to display a rather conservative attitude. When a worker challenges a discharge based on his alleged low rate of performance, he often loses the case because of supporting evidence introduced by a foreman or a supervisor on behalf of the employer. An employer generally is required to prove dismissal for lack of work, but if proof of any kind is submitted the discharge is assumed to be "justified." In general, we found that when a fact was proven, the arbitrators usually were not very critical in the evaluation of that fact. When a point of law was in question, they followed the prevailing orientation of the courts, although they were not required to do so because their awards cannot be attacked.[9] Therefore, arbitration was more a determination of the facts underlying the dismissal than a judgment of its reasonableness. This lack of critical attitude was also caused by the poor circulation of the awards; they are rarely published and made accessible to the public at large.

The arbitration procedure is simple but not uniform. Sometimes there is only one hearing without examination of evidence; this is the practice in the provinces of Turin, Milan, and Naples. Sometimes the arbitrator does not even furnish a written opinion; this is done, for

---

[9] See U. Romagnoli, in *I licenziamenti, op. cit.*, p. 27.

example, in Naples.¹⁰ Under such circumstances the entire proceedings may take only from 1 to 2 months. In other areas, for example, in Genoa, Venice, and in the province of Emilia, the procedure includes the formal examination of evidence, an opinion is rendered, and the proceedings may take from 2 to 6 months or even 1 year. It is worth noting that according to the 1950 agreement hearings before the panel were to last no longer than 10 days, and the entire proceedings no longer than 20 days.

In general, the arbitration experience points to certain inconsistencies. Arbitration of dismissals, or, rather, the conciliation–arbitration procedure, was effective in the large cities of northern Italy, where labor unions and employers' associations are more sophisticated and have developed attitudes of cooperation. A comparison between results of conciliation attempts and arbitration hearings, with few exceptions, shows that conciliation is more successful. On the one hand, the case law laid down by arbitrators is not a significant contribution to the development of labor law. On the other, the speedy and informal procedure made a quick settlement of the dispute possible. Moreover, at least in some instances the implementation of this procedure contributed to the process of change in unionism from an "ideological" stage to a more pragmatic attitude. Arbitration of dismissals paved the way for the settlement of disputes through industrial autonomy, which was fairly new in the history of industrial relations in Italy. While it has not been fully successful, it may lead to interesting developments in the future.¹¹

JOINT BOARDS FOR JOB CLASSIFICATION DISPUTES

4. The joint boards for disputes over job classifications were established at the steel company *Italsider* in 1962 (company agreement of January 15, 1962) and charged with the evaluation of jobs under a point-rating system. In each of the eleven plants of this government-owned company, the three main industrial unions that are signatories to the agreement appoint their stewards, who are called "experts," from among the employees. A grievance is initially referred to such an expert, who is chosen by the worker, within six days from its occurrence. It is the steward's responsibility to determine with management the matters in controversy. Thereafter the claim is examined by a joint board composed of 3 members of management and 1 each of the three

---

¹⁰ Now compulsory, according to the 1965 agreement.
¹¹ See Conclusions, sec. 2.

unions. If the board renders a unanimous decision as to the proper classification of the job, it is final and binding on all workers employed in that classification, whether or not they have filed a claim. If no agreement is reached, the claim is referred to the unions at the provincial level, which then take it up with representatives of management. The final step consists of a meeting between union members at the national level representing the worker and members of the central management of the company. The *Italsider* agreement was the first agreement signed by a large Italian company that granted union representatives a role *inside* the plant, bypassing the works councils. The company itself provided special training in job evaluation for the plant "experts."

Between 1962 and December, 1966, 7,000 cases were processed in the manner described above; 6,300 were filed by manual workers.[12] Eighty percent of the claims were settled by the joint boards, and only 58 went through the final step of the procedure. It is significant to note that a settlement was always reached, even though there was no arbitration provision in the agreement. The third step—union and management representatives at the provincial level—proved to be the least effective because the parties usually would be represented by the same people who sat at the joint boards in the second step.

As for the outcome of claims, the average request concerned the following: manual workers requested an improvement of 3.1 job classes (out of 24 job categories or "classes"), and clerical and technical workers, 2.1 job classes (out of 16 job categories or "classes"). The average concession agreed upon was 1 job "class" for manual workers and 0.4 for the other employees. Thus, the workers obtained a substantial improvement in the ranking of their jobs through this system of dealing with disputes.

Another advantage of the procedure is the quick settlement of disputes. The ratio of claims settled to claims filed in one year is now 80 percent, and it has been increasing over the years. However, it must be pointed out that for almost 3 years it was common practice to submit *almost all* jobs to a joint review once the high inclination of employees to file claims had been established. That review was planned and conducted in an orderly fashion, department by department and job area by job area. At that stage, the procedure was implemented as a process of joint determination of job classification rather than as a process of handling grievances. But once this almost general review was accom-

---

[12] All data were kindly made available to us by the company.

plished, it began to work properly and specific grievances were settled upon request of the individual worker.

5. In the three plants of the chemical company *ANIC,* which is owned by the government through E.N.I. public holdings,[13] joint boards for the settlement of disputes arising out of job classifications under a point-rating system were established by agreement in 1964 (agreement of March 27, 1964). The procedure requires that a claim must be filed with the forman. If the claim is rejected or after 10 days have elapsed, the worker reports to a union, which calls for a meeting of the joint board. The boards are composed of representatives of the three main industrial unions that are signatories to the agreement, appointed from among the employees, and an even number of representatives of the employers' associations.[14] The latter are appointed from among members of management of the plant, and one of these also serves as chairman of the board. Moreover, each union is entitled to invite to the meeting an "expert" who is not an employee of the plant. He should be a true expert in contrast to the language in the *Italsider* agreement described above, in which that word was somewhat improperly used.

Decisions of the joint board must be unanimous, with labor and management each having one vote. The examination of the claim begins within 30 days after it was filed. If the claim is deadlocked before the board, the union may refer it to a board at the national level within 15 days. The national board sits in Rome and is composed of national representatives of the unions and employers' associations. The rules governing the procedure are the same as those for the local boards, so that a deadlock may also occur at the highest level.

Some special rules were established for the protection of committeemen. They receive wages for the time spent in attendance of the meetings, and discharge or disciplinary actions cannot be carried out before the union is heard by management.

Recently, this system of handling grievances was extended to the oil and natural gas companies owned by the same public-holding corporation. The right of the worker to bring suit in court in order to receive

---

[13] *Ente nazionale idrocarburi,* a government agency active in the oil and hydrocarbon industry and in the transformation of these raw materials. Like the other big public-holding concern *(Istituto per le Ricostruzioni industriali)* to which *Italsider* belongs, E.N.I. operates through specialized joint-stock companies owned by it.

[14] *Associazione sindacale per le aziende petrolchimiche e collegate a partecipazione statale* (A.S.A.P.). It organizes the companies under E.N.I. control. Unlike the companies that join a separate organization, workers here are organized by the same unions that organize privately owned companies. This applies as well to the other large public-holding concern (I.R.I.).

SETTLEMENT OF LABOR DISPUTES IN ITALY

the proper classification for his job is openly recognized under these agreements and need not be discussed. However, there is one important restriction: Once the contractual procedure has been put into operation, the claim must be processed through each step provided for before suit can be brought in court. Moreover, no direct action can take place until the contractual procedure is exhausted.

The activities of the joint boards over two and one-half years cover a significant number of claims:[15] From the beginning of July, 1966, 2,500 claims filed by about 25 percent of the employees have been examined by the local boards, the highest percentage—60 percent—originating in a plant in Ravenna in northern Italy that has a well-organized and militant labor force. There were 2,070 claims decided, a very high proportion. Forty-five percent were rejected by management representatives, 30 percent (a considerable proportion) unanimously, and 25 percent were upheld.

During the same period the national board handled 766 claims, 80 percent of which were settled. Forty-six percent were rejected by the employers' association, 40 percent unanimously, and only 14 percent were upheld. It should be noted that the lower figure of claims upheld is offset by the increase in claims rejected unanimously, meaning that management or the employers' associations were not rigid in their attitude. Also, there was a decline over the years in claims rejected by the employers' association only. That development accompanied the end of the early phase in the operation of the procedure, which was characterized by a pronounced inclination to file claims for whatever reasons. It is interesting to note that in a plant in Valbasento in southern Italy the percentage of claims unanimously rejected—49—is much above the national average. There is not much rivalry among the unions in that plant and the CISL local, which plays a dominant role in the handling of claims, became able to act as a screening agency, an achievement that is almost impossible if the distribution of membership in the various unions is more even and the rivalry increased. Moreover, it was found that the ratio of claims upheld to claims filed is uniform among the various unions, meaning that the opposing party did not discriminate in favor of a particular union.

The total number of classifications revised under this procedure is lower than at *Italsider*. At that company, the grievance procedure had been used for a general revision of job classifications and had, in turn,

---

[15] I am indebted for these data as well as their critical evaluation to Dr. Francesco Porcari, Advanced School for Labor Law and Social Security, University of Bari, 1967 (unpublished dissertation).

inflated the claims. At *ANIC*, 6 to 7 percent of the workers were granted a revision of their job classification and, according to the company, that percentage corresponds to the predictable margin of error in the implementation of a job-evaluation plan. If this assumption is correct, it may be inferred that the grievance procedure has not become a channel of communicating needs for improvement to management, but rather a tool for the correction of technical mistakes.

6.
CONCLUSIONS

1. There are many complaints about the inefficiency of civil procedure in labor disputes, yet almost nothing has been done since the reform of 1942 (which, from the author's point of view, was more a counterreform) to alleviate its present major shortcomings.

Resort to voluntary systems of settlement, in turn, was not a matter of choice, but rather a practical day-to-day arrangement that undoubtedly worked more satisfactorily than the court system. But it did not, and could not, replace the latter. In this context it must be emphasized that a voluntary system does not guarantee protection to workers who are not union members,[1] and these are presently in the majority. Besides, the principle that all workers have a right to minimum standards of wages and working conditions is deeply rooted in Italian tradition. The concept of legal enactment[2] or of legislative action was embraced at a time when organized labor was much more influential in the political arena than in industry, and a pattern of state intervention for minimum standards was established and became firmly entrenched. Moreover, collective agreements are legally binding, and at times they may be binding on nonunion members as well. It would be consistent with this legal framework, therefore, if an efficient public system for the settlement of labor disputes were available to all workers.

On the other hand, many people doubt that labor unions will ever be able efficiently to replace state systems with voluntary systems. Al-

---

[1] As we have seen (p. 302) procedures of this kind are frequently available to nonmembers who file the claim through the union. Very often, however, when they demand support, they also join the union. This is a useful device to increase union membership.

[2] Sidney and Beatrice Webb, *Industrial Democracy*, 2d ed. (London: Longmans, Green, 1911), chap. IV.

though this skeptical opinion is far from universal,[3] it is true that the substitution of industry autonomy for state machineries would imply a lengthy process. Therefore, a commitment to this solution, in a realistic appraisal of the problem, should not mean that state systems should be left the way they are.

Unfortunately, neither the government nor the Parliament has thus far made serious efforts in that direction. A number of bills were introduced by representatives of both the government and opposition parties, but they were never debated. Some of them were designed to support voluntary machineries,[4] others, to reform specific points, for example, attempt at conciliation or the entire special procedure for the settlement of labor disputes.[5] In 1959, the government began work on a bill revising the Code of Civil Procedure, but not much attention was paid to labor disputes. The main change would have been, more or less, a provision for compulsory attempt at conciliation before the labor office.

In 1965, unions and employers' associations were questioned by the Ministry of Justice on eight points concerning the settlement of labor disputes. These were part of a large questionnaire on the Code of Civil Procedure that was sent to judicial bodies, bar associations, and law faculties. No action was taken by the government after the questionnaires were returned. However, in the spring of 1967, before Parliament adjourned, the bills mentioned above excepting those on voluntary settlement machineries were joined into Bill No. 2848. That bill was passed by the Chamber of Deputies, but the Senate, the other branch of the Parliament, had adjourned before it could start a debate. Therefore, according to Italian parliamentary practice the bill was shelved; but in October, 1968, the government, presided over by Gio-

---

[3] See, e.g., the opinion of two distinguished scholars: Pera, *op. cit.*, pp. 222 ff.; Cessari, "Trattazione extragiudiziale delle controversie di lavoro," in *Rivista giuridica del lavoro*, 1966, I, p. 446. See also Giugni, "Controversie di lavoro: la composizione stragiudiziale," in *Comitati di azione per la giustizia*, IV Convegno Nazionale, Bologna, April 28 to May 1, 1967, *Proceedings*, pp. 181 ff.

[4] In the 1963–68 Parliament: bill of May 14, 1964, introduced by the Honorable Butté (a leader of ACLI, the powerful association of Catholic workers which is not a union) and others; bill of June 6, 1964, introduced by the Honorable Storti (the General Secretary of CISL) and others.

[5] In the 1963–68 Parliament: bill of December 12, 1963, introduced by the Honorable Zoboli and others; bill of March 3, 1964, introducted by the Honorable Amatucci and others; bill of April 9, 1964, introduced by the Honorable De Florio and others.

All bills mentioned in this and the previous footnote are published by Istituto di Scienze sociali, *Per una riforma della giustizia del lavoro*, Genova, 1965, pp. 105 ff.

SETTLEMENT OF LABOR DISPUTES IN ITALY

vanni Leone, introduced a new bill that included the text of the one just mentioned (Bill n.524/C, October 14, 1968).

The bill is very interesting. It follows strictly the pattern of the present Code, merely improving a few provisions here and there. It is clear at the outset that the bill does not offer much improvement overall, and for that reason it is representative. The bill is an expression of what the politicians of almost all major parties feel should and could be done. Looking for the largest basis of consensus, possibly unanimity, the authors of the bill allowed for changes that should gain the widest support. The result is a bill that falls far short of facing the issue properly, let alone of solving it.

2. The main points of the government's bill are the following (page numbers in which this essay deals with the subject matter are indicated in parentheses):

1. All disputes arising out of a contract of employment may be brought before a civil court and shall be governed by the special procedure set forth in the amended Code (p. 258).

2. The plaintiff, before bringing suit in court, may request an attempt at conciliation either through a voluntary procedure or through a state conciliation board. This step is not compulsory, that is, it may be bypassed by bringing action directly in a court. The conciliation board —this proposal already was contained in a bill on voluntary procedures[6] —is composed of four members appointed by labor unions and four by employers' associations, presided over by an official of the labor office. For regular meetings the participation of at least one representative of each side is required. The worker may be assisted in his case by his union or by counsel. The importance of this amendment must not be overestimated. It is merely a variation of the present conciliation procedure before the labor office, in which unions and employers' associations already cooperate rather frequently with the representative of the government. More significant is the amendment that a settlement agreement, concluded either before the conciliation board or through a voluntary machinery, is rendered enforceable by an order of a *Pretore*.

3. The provision enabling unions and employers' association to bring action in court on behalf of the individual parties is repealed. The reader is reminded that this rule (pp. 274 f.) was never applied. Also, the intervention of unions in the individual case is no longer provided for.

---

[6] The bill introduced by the Honorable Storti, n. 4 *supra*.

4. The power of the attorney to settle the dispute, implied in the powers of attorney, is repealed (p. 276).

5. Shorter terms are established for appearance in court.

6. Personal appearance and attempt at conciliation before the examining judge are made compulsory (p. 276) at the first hearing and may be repeated at any time, even during the appeal.

7. Amounts due not questioned by the defendant may be ordered by the examining judge to be paid immediately.

8. When the examining judge feels that sufficient evidence about a part of the claim was submitted, he may, upon request of one of the parties, report to the panel. The panel, in turn, may order the immediate payment of a sum of money to the claimant, but such an order may be revoked by the final judgment.

This latter provision may be useful. However, it would require that the examining judge could evaluate evidence *before* the end of the proof-taking stage, which he can rarely do because of his heavy caseload. The new provision, therefore, merely skirts the main issue instead of getting at the heart of it. It may result in new complications of an already complicated procedure.

9. All decisions may be ordered enforceable even though appealed (p. 263).

10. No appeal can be lodged against decisions involving a claim of less than L.100,000 ($165).

11. The exclusive jurisdiction of the court of appeals over decisions on appeal from the courts of the first instance is rescinded. The intervention of the public prosecutor in cases on appeal is no longer required.

By and large, the bill incorporated suggestions made by members of the bar association,[7] and by judges, attorneys, and professors of law at a convention in 1967.[8] These suggestions are widely supported by practitioners of law. It must be pointed out, however, that even at that convention much more attention was given to union participation in the courtroom, to the establishment of special, lower courts, and to the specialization of judges than is reflected in the bill.

The bill eliminates a number of meaningless obstructions from the new procedure (e.g., item 11 above). It increases opportunities for conciliation (items 2 and 6), and it will be more helpful to the plaintiff worker (items 7, 8 and 9). But even if approved, it will not lead

---

[7] IX Convegno Nazionale, Venice, September 27-29, 1967, Resolution No. 2.

[8] Comitati di azione per la giustizia, IV Convegno Nazionale, mentioned in n. 3, *supra*.

to a faster, more specialized procedure. Moreover, the unions are almost ignored in the bill; the idea of a "democratic" administration of justice carried out through the participation of social groups is not reflected—the approach is one of typical individualism.

3. Voluntary machineries for the settlement of labor disputes are at the center of angry debate. Unions and employers' associations are divided in evaluating their effectiveness, having taken positions that do not always coincide with organizational lines.

(a) Recommendations for conciliation procedures are generally accepted and supported. Employers' associations, however, demand that settlements be rendered immune to attack (p. 304). Opinions differ on the point whether resort to a voluntary procedure should be made compulsory, at least for union members, before suit can be brought in court. But there seems to be some consensus that that decision should be left to the claimant party. However, a number of collective agreements have already incorporated the compulsory principle, even though its legality is questioned (p. 310).

(b) The newly created joint committees for piece rates and job classifications (pp. 312 and 313) are strongly supported by the unions, largely because their establishment implies recognition of union stewards at the shop level.

(c) The most heatedly debated issue is arbitration. Following is a summary of the conflicting opinions:

The Confederation CISL strongly supports arbitration, which is consistent with its belief in industrial autonomy. This belief is almost an ideology—CISL even opposed the 1966 act on dismissals on the ground that it infringed on the area of collective bargaining. While the UIL does not have an official position on this matter, the CGIL is on the whole overwhelmingly against arbitration. A distinction must be made between pragmatic and ideological reasons for this opposition, however.

Pragmatic reasons concern the difficulties of operating arbitration procedures effectively when unions are financially poor, officials too few and not trained for the job, and impartial chairmen "rare birds." These reasons are not without foundation; objections[9] would follow the argument of the chicken and the egg—one cannot sit back and wait until conditions are optimal because more frequent use of arbitration would affect these conditions themselves. It would result in

---

[9] See Giugni, address of reply at the convention of Comitati di azione per la giustizia, *Proceedings, op. cit.,* pp. 473 ff.

better training of union officials through experience, it would provide a larger selection of chairmen, and so forth.

But the "ideological" reasons for the opposition are perhaps predominant. First, the Communist wing of CGIL mistrusts means of achieving social peace, such as arbitration. However, this attitude might be overcome if it could be agreed that arbitration be provided for individual disputes over rights only, never for disputes over interests or for collective disputes over rights. Second, many Communist labor leaders feel instinctively that the difficult job of filling the statutory gap in terms of industrial autonomy would not pay as many political returns as would denouncing the failure of governments which did not carry out the revision of the Code. Finally, opposition to arbitration is often cited in defense of the statutory principle of unwaiverability of rights, on the formalistic assumption that submission to arbitration constitutes a waiver (p. 305).[10] This argument is hardly tenable on legal grounds, but it masks the more substantial opposition of the type discussed above.

Even judges and members of the bar have not shown a favorable reaction towards arbitration. Perhaps this is an expression of subconscious self-defense against what might be considered usurpation of institutional roles by industrial autonomy. But it is also caused by the lack of knowledge of industrial relations practices on the part of lawyers and judges, and by the lack of emphasis in labor law on industrial relations as taught in Italian universities. At any rate, we recognize again the predominance of cultural forms which grow out of a strong belief in individualism. The theory of unwaiverability is based upon the consideration of the worker as an individual, not as a member of a group. Arbitration is looked upon as a means of escape from the judiciary and the statutory law administered by it, rather than as a natural development of collective decision-making.

4. Special courts, and implicitly labor courts, are prohibited by ARTICLE 102 of the constitution. This law was enacted after the Fascist regime had abused the concept of special courts by creating a number of them in order to bar the independent judiciary from their jurisdictions. It can hardly be said that this constitutional principle meets with the needs of modern society, which, it would seem, require specialization; but nobody has gone so far as to think of a possible amendment to the constitution.

The constitutional provision, however, does not bar specialization

---

[10] See address of A. Forni, vice-secretary of CGIL, at the above-mentioned convention, *Proceedings, op. cit.,* p. 317.

within the system of general jurisdiction of the ordinary courts. As a matter of fact, it clearly authorizes "specialized sections of the ordinary courts for specific subjects," in which "qualified citizens not drawn from the judiciary may participate." Thus, it was suggested that special sections for labor disputes be established, to be composed of wingmen and of professional judges, or even of citizens appointed for that purpose from outside the ranks of the professional judiciary (but subject to the rules concerning the latter, as, for example, the *conciliatore* for minor disputes.)[11] These would be courts of the first instance, subject to screening by the higher courts; wingmen would, of course, be appointed by the unions and employers' associations. Proposals of this kind, however, have not met with much support. The majority desires merely an improvement in the existing machinery, and its opinion will prevail until experience shows that the ordinary civil courts, even with improved procedure, are not the best possible decision-making agencies in labor disputes, particularly not in a country in which collective bargaining—a nonstatutory source of law—has achieved a primary role.

A number of people, largely followers of CISL, believe that voluntary bodies and machineries are definitely to be preferred. In the author's opinion, the two possibilities—special sections for labor disputes and voluntary machineries—should not be considered conflicting. Both may coexist. As was pointed out, voluntary machineries, especially at present, may be efficient in some branches of the industry only, or in some geographic regions, or for specific matters in dispute. Wherever voluntary machinery does not effectively operate, however, the state should provide for procedures of its own. Unorganized workers and sectors of the industry in which labor unions have not acquired an effective role should not be left by the state without proper and specialized means for the settlement of labor disputes. Meant here are disputes over rights only; disputes over interests, of course, should be left to free negotiations between the parties. There is no doubt about this, except perhaps among a dwindling number of individuals who remember with nostalgia the corporative system.

5. We may now summarize the two basic concepts that obstruct far-reaching but necessary changes in the present system of dealing with labor disputes in Italy.

The first concept centers on the wrong identification of labor disputes with civil disputes—an identification that brought about the

---

[11] See Ventura, *Il superamento della crisi nella prospettiva di riforma delle strutture giudziarie*, report to the above-mentioned convention, *Proceedings, op. cit.*, p. 31; Ventura, reply, *ibid.*, p. 463.

submission of labor disputes to the jurisdiction of the ordinary courts with very little variation in procedure. It is currently believed that labor disputes are not merely civil disputes because of "technical" points of fact that are often involved (for example, claims over piece rates or job classifications). Although this assumption is far from erroneous, it is not the main point of differentiation between the two types of disputes, nor is "technicality" peculiar to labor disputes only (e.g., it is a typical ingredient of many commercial disputes). But two distinctive features are peculiar to labor disputes, namely, the irreversibility of the situation, and the inequality of economic power between the parties.

Irreversibility characterizes the matter in dispute. Back wages to be paid after a decision is rendered, a discharge to be set aside when the worker is employed elsewhere, the right to promotion to be acknowledged when the contract of employment has expired, a piece rate to be proven when the shop organization has changed—all these actions do not grant remedies but merely palliatives. Late compensation in money is not a remedy for an unjustified discharge or a rejected promotion. New remedies will have to be found, remedies that are as yet almost unknown to civil law and to civil procedure.[12] But above all, the proceedings in these matters have to be expedited; the worker should have an opportunity to bring action immediately when he believes his rights have been violated. Needless to say, the tendency to postpone a claim until the contract of employment has expired (pp. 297 ff.) embraces the opposite of what the situation should be.

The inequality of economic power implies that the worker cannot hold out as long as the employer. Lengthy proceedings do no damage to an enterprise; on the contrary, its lawyers will draw them out as much as possible. But the worker must have immediate satisfaction to take care of his basic needs. Oddly, the inequality of economic power is presented as the very basic assumption of labor law, but few people understand that the same assumption applies to labor process as well. It demands that proceedings should be as speedy as possible, but it also lends perspective to the primary importance of unionism, by means of which the strength of a group overcomes the weakness of an individual.

The second concept standing in the way of change, then, is an individualistic approach that prevails in the law and dominates common

---

[12] The injunction is almost unknown in continental Europe. See Alexander H. Pekelis, "Legal Techniques and Political Ideologies," 41 *Michigan Law Review*, 665-692 (1943). See also my review of Cappalletti and Perillo, *Civil Procedure in Italy*, in 13 *UCLA Law Review*, 482 (1966).

thought. Even voluntary systems for the settlement of labor disputes are based on the principle that the individual worker owns the grievance, and that the union merely performs a service in his behalf.

However, the facts contradict the principle; quite often these systems are used to obtain union objectives, for example, when the unions themselves induce the workers to file claims that merely *seem* to be individual claims (p. 280). Thus, in spite of the legal form of the dispute, group interests tend to prevail over individual interests, or at least they give the latter a more general content. This trend should be encouraged, although specific solutions to labor problems should not ignore the basic interests of the individuals and subject them to a dictatorship of the "collectivity." It is widely recognized that collective action is the means that enables the individual to overcome his economic weakness; the principle stands for both, the making of rules (collective agreements) and their implementation. Thus, it is probably true that a worker can be expected to pursue his legitimate interests while employed only insofar as he is backed by group solidarity. And here we wish to restate our conclusion: Justice cannot be achieved without a real balance of power between the parties to a dispute. A radically revised system operated by the government would, therefore, be most welcome, but it would never eliminate the necessity of voluntary machineries.[13]

---

[13] For a more specific comparison between state-operated and voluntary systems, see the symposium on *Dispute Settlement Procedures in Five Western European Countries* (University of California Los Angeles, Institute of Industrial Relations, 1969), and specifically Giugni, *The Public and Private Ordering of Dispute-Settlement Procedures.*

INDEX

Action syndicale, 44, 44n8
Adhesion contracts, 163
Agricultural workers, 17–18, 106, 250, 258
ANIC (chemical company), 326–328
Appeals: of civil court decisions, 43, 260–261, 264–265, 271–272; of arbitration awards, 65–66, 137; proposed reforms, 74, 332
—of labor court decisions: France, 19–20, 19n, 32, 32n26, 33, 39; Germany, 85–86, 96, 111–112; Sweden, 175; Italy, 250, 251–252
Arbetsmarknadsnamnden. See Labor Market Board
Arbitration: compulsory, 12, 49, 69, 69n, 70n64+65, 69–71; history, 46n14 +15, 177–178, 185, 253; legal status, 305–308
—relation to other procedures: France, 9, 12, 13, 49, 56, 56n36, 76–77; Germany, 94, 138, 139–140; Sweden, 178, 179, 190, 227–228, 241–242, 244; Italy, 287, 302
—workings of: France, 59–71; Germany, 227–238, 241–242; Sweden, 131–143; Italy, 302, 315–316, 318–324, 333–334
—evaluation: France, 68–71, 75, 76–77; Germany, 145–147, 156–157; Sweden, 241–242; Italy, 316, 318–324, 333–334
—special purpose boards: Germany, 140–143; Sweden, 178, 187, 222, 227–238; Italy, 264, 275, 315–316, 318–324
Artisans, 106

Banking, 310–312
Basic Agreement of 1938, 164, 177– 178, 179, 185–187, 222, 223, 227–232, 241, 245
Building industry, 161, 162, 178, 190–197, 206, 227, 232–236, 310

Cadrés, 38–39
Calamandrei, Piero, 254
Chemical industry, 309, 310, 315, 326–328
Civil Code, French, 3, 10, 34, 66
Civil Code, German, 85
Civil Code, Italian. See Code of Civil Procedure of 1942
Civil courts. See Courts, civil
Clerical workers, 250
Code of Civil Procedure of 1942, 251–259 *passim,* 275–276, 289, 304–305, 306, 312, 329–333
Collective agreements: as source of labor law, 3–6, 279–280, 303–304; negotiation, 4, 105, 162–164, 185–188; application beyond parties, 5–6, 89–91, 129, 171–172, 178–180, 303–304, 329; kinds of disputes, 8–9, 41–42, 52, 57, 89–91, 93, 118, 204–208; legislation affecting, 88, 105, 204–208, 285–286, 303–304; history, 162–168 *passim,* 173, 178, 185, 251, 253; compared with arbitration award, 67–68, 138; legal view, 156, 168, 261, 261n8, 279–80, 329; adhesion contracts, 163; invisible clauses, 207–208
—settlement procedures: France, 8, 13, 45–50, 52, 57, 61–63; Germany, 105, 118, 131–143, 145, 146, 150–153; Sweden, 176–185, 188–198, 204–213, 225–228, 239, 240; Italy, 253, 257–258, 285–286, 288, 301–302, 304–305, 307, 308n17+18,

INDEX

Collective disputes: jurisdiction, 43–45, 83, 103, 105, 252; 308–317, 318–328
—concept of: France, 9–12, 28, 41–46, 72, 75, 75n, 78, 80; Germany, 93, 139; Italy, 257–258, 280–281
—settlement procedures: France, 44–46, 55, 68–71, 75–80; Germany, 83, 103, 105; Italy, 279–280, 287–289, 290, 309, 311–312

Company procedures. *See* Workplace procedures

Conciliation: history, 46n14+15, 185, 252–253, 261–262; voluntary, 47–50, 75, 185, 308–311, 316–318, 322, 323; evaluation, 54, 75, 76, 253, 263, 268, 316–317, 324, 329–333 *passim*
—statutory: France, 26, 28–30, 32–33, 47–54; Germany, 85, 86, 112–113, 117; Sweden, 174–175; Italy, 252–253, 276–278, 287, 289–300
—working of: France, 26, 28–30, 32–33, 47–54; Germany, 94, 137, 147, 148; Sweden, 174–175; Italy, 263, 265, 268, 276–278, 287, 289–300, 322–323

Concurring legislation, 88
Constitution of 1948, 257
Constitution of 1958, 4, 7
Construction. *See* Building industry
Contract law, 3–6, 166, 208–211, 305–306
Contract of employment (individual): history, 3–6, 72, 84–85, 150–153, 202–203, 250–251; legal view, 6, 41, 84–85, 142, 150–153, 170–171, 250–251; settlement of disputes, 10, 38, 67, 104, 131–134, 142, 176, 285; relative to collective agreements, 72, 90–91, 170–171; legislation on, 88, 202–203, 285; provisions of, 90–91, 170–171, 207–208
Courts, civil: history, 166, 250–252, 254–256
—jurisdiction: France, 9, 13, 19–20, 39–40, 43–45; Germany, 94, 105; Sweden, 172, 177, 179, 180, 183–184; Italy, 251–252, 257–261, 335–336
—evaluation: France, 68, 75; Sweden, 183–184; Italy, 329–336
—relative to other settlement procedures: France, 68; Germany, 87, 109, 111; Sweden, 184, 201–202; Italy, 250, 282–284, 304–305
—workings of: Germany, 109, 111; Sweden, 184, 201–202, 224; Italy, 259–284, 292, 304

Courts, labor: history, 3, 15–16, 83–87, 147–150, 173, 249–252
—relative to other settlement procedures: France, 13, 33–36, 43, 43n4, 77–79; Germany, 94, 119–120, 124, 128–129, 131–134, 137–140; Sweden, 177, 244–246; Italy, 334–335
—jurisdiction: France, 15–19, 37–38; Germany, 94, 103–107, 131–133, 137, 139–142; Sweden, 176–178, 179–180, 184, 198, 204–208, 232; Italy, 249–250
—evaluation: France, 18–20, 25, 35–36, 73–74, 77–80; Germany, 87, 144, 156–157; Sweden, 239–246
—workings of: France, 9, 16–40, 43, 43n4; Germany, 83, 96–103, 107–127, 144–155; Sweden, 169–171, 175–176, 180–184, 188–190, 198–204, 208–226, 240

Department store clerks, 106
Dismissals: remedies, 34–36, 181, 184; legislation, 88, 170; collective agreements concerning, 164, 302, 306–308, 320
—settlements of disputes arising from: France, 4–8; Germany, 128–129; Sweden, 174, 176–178, 184, 186, 187, 221–222, 226–232; Italy, 260, 287–288, 290n9, 298, 318–324
Domestic workers, 17, 258

Edlund, Sten, study by, 190–197, 242
Employers' associations: history, 4, 86, 252–253
—rights and obligations: France, 4, 23, 44; Germany, 90, 99, 100, 101; Sweden, 162–164, 188–190; Italy, 252, 303–304, 307, 309–310, 311–312, 318–319, 320, 326–328
—and courts: France, 23, 27–28, 44; Germany, 99, 100, 101, 124–127, 146–147, 149–150; Sweden, 176, 213–224; Italy, 252
—legal status: Germany, 89–90, 92–93, 105, 124–125, 156; Sweden, 162, 166; Italy, 257n, 262, 289, 331
—and collective agreements: Germany, 90, 105; Sweden, 162–164, 168–170; Italy, 301–302, 303–304, 307, 309–310, 311–312, 316–320, 322, 326–328, 333

INDEX

Enforcement: contract of employment, 6; conciliation, 29, 53–54; arbitration, 65, 65n54+56, 67–68, 138, 178, 187, 228–229, 245, 305–306; collective agreements, 167, 177; court orders, 183, 263, 265
Entertainment field, 132, 134
Evaluation: court procedures, 12, 18–25 *passim*, 30, 35–36, 39–40, 73–74, 75, 144, 154–155, 254–256; voluntary procedures, 12, 54, 53–59, 68–71, 130–131, 138–140, 316–317, 324
—nation's entire labor settlement system: France, 13–14, 72–80; Germany, 145–146, 155–156; Sweden, 239–246; Italy, 329–337

Fascist regime (Italy), 251–256, 259, 260, 305, 312, 334
Food industry, 315

Hotel workers, 162

Individual disputes: distinguished from collective disputes, 9–12, 42, 72, 80, 93, 139, 257–259; jurisdiction, 26, 38, 83, 103–104, 131–134, 142–143, 144, 257–259, 287–300, 312–315; evaluation of settlement procedures, 72–73, 74n4, 144, 279–280; history, 252–253
Interests, disputes over: distinguished from disputes over rights, 8–11, 45, 72, 76, 78, 94, 94n8, 138, 204–208, 287–288; jurisdiction, 49, 57, 86, 140, 250, 257
Italsider (steel company), 324–326

Job classification boards, 324–328
Journalism, 38, 178, 228, 236–238

Kahn-Freund, Otto, 86

Labor courts. *See* Courts, labor
Labor inspector (Italy), 264, 285–286
Labor Market Board, 177–178, 180, 187, 189–190, 222, 228–232
Labor office (Italy), 285–300, 316–317
Labor unions: history, 4–5, 86, 88–89, 148, 165–167, 172–174, 252–253, 298; character, structure, etc., 4–5, 5n, 13, 88–89, 153–154, 161–162, 203, 224, 239; and individual disputes, 11, 73, 224–226, 243–244; legal status, 92–93, 105, 124–127, 156, 165–167, 176, 257, 257n, 262
—in non-judicial settlement procedures: France, 8, 13, 45, 70n65, 71, 75; Germany, 91–92, 130, 132–133; Sweden, 162–164, 165–167, 168–170, 178–180, 190–197; Italy, 253, 272–273, 288–289, 292–293, 298, 301–328, 331–334, 336–337
—and courts: France, 23–24, 26–28, 44, 44n9, 74; Germany, 90, 99–102, 124–127, 146–147, 149–150, 154; Sweden, 166, 167, 176, 178–180, 181, 199–201, 213–226, 239–240; Italy, 252, 272–273, 280–282, 289, 304–305, 331–334
—rights and obligations: Germany, 90, 99–102, 105, 154; Sweden, 164, 168–170, 172–174, 176, 179, 188–190; Italy, 252, 303–304, 331
Lawyers, 27, 125–127, 136, 137, 200, 271, 275, 277–278, 280–281
Legislation: and unions, 8, 166, 173–174, 179
—labor, general: France, 3–4, 13–14, 41n, 41–42; Germany, 87–88, 140–144, 150; Sweden, 166, 170, 180–183, 188, 239; Italy, 254–259, 260, 264, 285–286, 287, 298, 330–333
—history: France, 3–5, 15–16, 46n14; Germany, 86–87, 148; Sweden, 166; Italy, 249–250, 253, 254–256
—and collective agreements: Germany, 105, 131–136, 138–139; Sweden, 167–168, 179, 204–208; Italy, 253, 303–304
—on nonjudicial settlement procedures: conciliation, 47–50, 112–113, 117, 174; mediation, 54–55, 55n23, 57; arbitration, 60–61, 61n, 64–65, 131–136, 138–140, 145, 177–178, 253, 305–308; other, 8, 46n14, 117–119, 128–130, 142–143, 185–188, 287
—on labor courts: France, 15–16; Germany, 83, 87, 100–106, 109, 111, 120, 124, 138, 145, 151–153; Sweden, 176, 179, 198, 201, 202, 223–224
Lindhagen (labor court justice), 202, 202n2+3, 203, 208, 216
Lockout, 48, 49, 49n22, 93, 153, 204–208, 224, 227, 251

Managers, 38–39, 38n2, 162, 164–165, 173
Manual workers, 17, 104, 106, 107,

341

INDEX

161–162, 164–165, 172–173, 249–250
Maritime disputes, 37–38, 106, 132, 134, 162
Mass action, 280–281
Mediation, 54–59, 55n33, 58n40, 75, 76
Metal industry: Sweden, 162, 168–170, 180, 185, 190–197, 207, 227–228; Italy, 308n18, 308–309, 312, 313–314

Nazi period, 83, 86–87, 93, 150, 154–156
Negotiation: of terms of employment, 3–6, 210–213, 223, 240, 241–242; in settling disputes, 129–130, 174, 185–197, 242, 244–246, 287–289
Nipperdey, Hans Carl, 154
Nonunion workers: Germany, 90–91, 134; Sweden, 171–172, 179, 183–184, 226; Italy, 282, 302–303, 329, 329n1

Oil industry, 312, 315, 326–328
Order procedure, 117–119

Peace obligation: Germany, 89–91; Sweden, 163, 165–166, 168, 176, 187, 198, 204–208, 237–238; Italy, 308, 309
Pilot actions, 280–281
Printing, 161
Public employees, 17n5, 88n6, 104, 106, 258–259

Railroad employees, 106
Restaurant workers, 162
Redenti, Enrico, 250
Remedies: France, 27, 34–36, 66, 66n60, 67–68, 74, 74n2; Germany, 111; Sweden, 172, 174, 180–184, 229–230; Italy, 307, 319, 319n, 320, 336
Retail workers, 106

Rights, disputes concerning
—distinguished from disputes over interests: France, 8–11, 45, 72, 76; Germany, 94, 94n8, 138; Sweden, 204–208; Italy, 287–288
—settlement procedures: France, 33, 43, 57, 57n39, 76–80; Germany, 86, 94, 94n8, 138; Italy, 250, 257

Salaried employees (Swedish concept), 162, 164–165, 173
State, role in labor disputes, 8, 13–14, 50, 53n31, 156, 175–176, 258–259, 285–300
Steel, 324–326. See also Metal industry
Strike: right to strike, 4, 45n11, 70, 70n65, 71, 93, 153, 204–208, 251, 279, 279n29; relative to settlement procedures, 48, 49, 49n22, 91, 165–166, 191–193, 227, 288, 289, 307–309; employer's remedies, 181; union benefits to workers, 224
Summers, Clyde, study by, 225–226
Supervisors. See Managers

Telephone industry, 311, 315
Textile workers, 106, 309, 310, 314
Torts, labor, 104, 104n11, 105, 153, 224, 245

Unions. See Labor unions
Union shop, 163, 216, 219

Weimar Republic, 85–86, 87–88, 89, 91, 94n8, 96, 133, 148, 150, 156
White-collar workers: France, 17, 38n2 +3, 39n4; Germany, 89, 104, 106, 107; Sweden, 162, 173; Italy, 253
Workplace procedures: France, 6, 8, 13, 51, 72–73; Germany, 91–92, 106, 118, 128–131, 140–146, 153, 155; Sweden, 171, 186; Italy, 301–302, 308, 309–310, 312–315, 316, 318–324